CAUSING PSYCHIATRIC AND EMOTIONAL HARM

Though mental harm can be profoundly disabling, the law imposes strict limits on who can recover damages for it. In the absence of physical injury, compensation is not normally available for negligently caused mental suffering, however severe, unless it constitutes a 'recognisable psychiatric illness'. Claimants whose mental trauma stems from injury caused to someone else are subject to arbitrary restrictive liability rules that dispense with established legal principles and cannot be reconciled with scientific advances. The book traces the history of civil liability for mental harm up to the present day. It is argued that the reluctance to provide redress reflects an enduring suspicion of intangible injury and undue fear of proliferating claims. The scale and legal ramifications of the Hillsborough disaster; the emergence of claims arising from work-related stress, and other new categories of claims based mainly on prior relationships between the parties, have all added to a 'floodgates fear' that has intensified due to popular perceptions of a 'compensation culture'.

The book contrasts the limited scope for liability under English law with developments in several other jurisdictions. It is argued that statutory reform is needed to achieve greater legal coherence, and to provide a remedy that tracks the relative gravity of harm without being exclusively confined to psychiatric disorders. A new legal framework is offered, with a liability threshold of moderately severe mental or emotional harm. To allay concerns about proliferating claims, modifications to the compensatory regime for personal injury generally are proposed.

Causing Psychiatric and Emotional Harm

Reshaping the Boundaries of Legal Liability

Harvey Teff

OXFORD AND PORTLAND, OREGON
2009

Published in North America (US and Canada) by
Hart Publishing
c/o International Specialized Book Services
920 NE 58th Avenue, Suite 300
Portland, OR 97213-3786
USA
Tel: +1 503 287 3093 or toll-free: (1) 800 944 6190
Fax: +1 503 280 8832
E-mail: orders@isbs.com
Website: http://www.isbs.com

© Harvey Teff 2009

Harvey Teff has asserted his right under the Copyright, Designs and Patents Act 1988,
to be identified as the author of this work.

All rights reserved. No part of this publication may be reproduced, stored in a retrieval system, or transmitted, in any form or by any means, without the prior permission of Hart Publishing, or as expressly permitted by law or under the terms agreed with the appropriate reprographic rights organisation. Enquiries concerning reproduction which may not be covered by the above should be addressed to Hart Publishing at the address below.

Hart Publishing Ltd, 16C Worcester Place, OX1 2JW
Telephone: +44 (0)1865 517530 Fax: +44 (0)1865 510710
E-mail: mail@hartpub.co.uk
Website: http://www.hartpub.co.uk

British Library Cataloguing in Publication Data
Data Available

ISBN: 978-1-84113-216-7

Typeset by Hope Services, Abingdon
Printed and bound in Great Britain by
CPI Antony Rowe Ltd, Chippenham

For Shlomit

ACKNOWLEDGEMENTS

I am particularly indebted to Bob Sullivan for reading the entire text and making many valuable suggestions. It is a pleasure to record my gratitude to my wife, Shlomit, for her invaluable insight and encouragement throughout, and to Helen Teff for her skilled assistance, especially in the final stages of preparing the manuscript. Finally, of course, my thanks are also due to the publishers.

CONTENTS

Acknowledgements	vii
Table of Cases	xiii
Table of Statutes	xxi

1: Psychiatric Harm, Emotional Suffering and Legal Redress	1
Categorising Personal Harm	1
Introduction	1
Mental and Emotional Harm	4
Some Problems of Classification	5
Medical	5
Legal	7
Underlying Hostility: Disparaging Intangible Harm and its Redress	10
Mind and Body	10
The Stigmatisation of Mental Illness	12
The 'Blame and Claim' Culture	18
Embracing Liability for Mental and Emotional Harm	20
Some Modern Statutory Developments	20
The Special Case of Psychiatric Illness Caused by Stress at Work	22
The Scope for Liability at Common Law	26
Mental Distress resulting from Breach of Contract	26
Damages in Tort for Mental Distress	28
Some Criminal Law Comparisons	31
Caveat and Conclusion	33
2: The Development of Redress for Emotional Harm and Nervous Shock	37
'Harm' at Common Law	37
Minimum Actionable Harm at Common Law	37
Early Legal Views on Intangible Harm	40
The Victorian Era and 'Railway Spine'	41
Development of Liability for 'Mental And Nervous Shock': The 'First Hundred Years'	43
Recoverable Harm: a 'recognisable psychiatric illness'	52

An Overview of the Period	54
Conclusion	56

3: Contemporary Provision for 'Accident-Based' Psychiatric Illness — 59

McLoughlin v O'Brian: Policy or Principle?	59
The 1990s: From *Alcock* to *Page* to *White*—'Thus Far and No Further'?	65
Alcock v Chief Constable of South Yorkshire Police	66
Alcock on Appeal	67
Proximity of Relationship	68
The 'Immediate' Aftermath	69
The Mode of Communication	69
Sudden and Gradual Assaults on the Nervous System	70
Page v Smith and *White v Chief Constable Of South Yorkshire*: The 'Patchwork Quilt' Embedded	74
Primary/Secondary/Both/Neither?	75
The Mixed Messages of *Page v Smith*	77
Confused Legal Doctrine	77
The Unfulfilled Promise of 'Law Marching with Medicine'	82
Hillsborough Revisited	83
A Misconceived Public Relations Exercise in the Name of Distributive Justice?	91
White v Chief Constable of South Yorkshire: Weary Resignation?	93

4: Liability for Psychiatric Harm 'Beyond the Mainstream' — 97

Introduction	97
Negligent Provision of Services	99
Communicating Bad News	103
Negligent Communication of Information	103
Fear for the Future	109
Medical Negligence: The Declining Significance of the 'Sudden Shock' of a 'Horrifying Event'	113
Introduction	113
Lord Ackner's Conception of Shock	115
The Event	115
Suddenness	116
Horror Violently Agitating the Mind	117
Claims resulting from Medical Negligence	117
Negligence Causing Psychological Detriment	122
The Doctrinal Basis for Exceptions to the Special Rule Structure	125

'Assumption of Responsibility'	126
A Reversion to First Principles	128
An Australian Exemplar: *Tame v New South Wales; Annetts v Australian Stations Pty Ltd*	130
Legislative Developments	135
Conclusions	137

5: Policy Concerns — 141

Some Common Policy Justifications for Special Controls — 141

Diagnostic Uncertainty	143
Litigation and Rehabilitation	145
Liability Disproportionate to Culpability	148
The Potential for Proliferating Claims	149
The Potency of the 'Floodgates Fear'	149
Disincentives to Claiming	151
The Claims-handling Process	153
The Frequency of Claims	155
Personal Injury Claims in General	155
The Incidence of Claims for Psychiatric Harm	158
The Impact of Employees' Claims for Stress-Induced Psychiatric Illness	161
Conclusion on the Floodgates Fear as regards Psychiatric Harm	165
Broader Policy Considerations	166
Chilling Effects: The 'Perils' of a Risk-Averse Society	166
Risk Aversion and Mental Harm	169

6: A Proposal For Reform — 171

A New Test for Remediable Suffering — 171

The Substantive Basis of Liability	171
The Case for a Monetary Threshold	177
Is a Monetary Threshold a Step Too Far?	179
Conclusion	183

The Proposed Framework in Outline — 185
Remaining Barriers to Reform — 186

A Legally Undervalued Core Value	186
Lingering Doubts Specific to the English Law Context	188
Concluding Remarks	189

Bibliography	191
Index	201

TABLE OF CASES

A v Essex County Council [2004] 1 WLR 1881 (CA) 100, 101
AB v Leeds Teaching Hospital NHS Trust & Cardiff and Vale NHS Trust [2005] Lloyd's Rep Med 1..98
AB v South West Water Services Ltd [1993] QB 507 (CA) 29
AB v Tameside & Glossop Health Authority [1997] 8 Med LR 91 (CA) 105
Adams v Bracknell Forest Borough Council [2005] 1 AC 76 ....98, 123, 124
Addis v Gramophone Ltd [1909] AC 488..25, 26
Agar v Hyde (2000) 201 CLR 552 138
Alcock v Chief Constable of South Yorkshire Police [1992] 1 AC 310; [1991] 3 WLR 1057 (CA); [1991] 2 WLR 814, 843..........3, 66–72, 100, 149, 186
Al-Kandari v JR Brown & Co [1988] QB 665 (CA) 101
Allin v City & Hackney Health Authority [1996] 7 Med LR 167 ....97, 106
Anderson v Smith (1990) 101 FLR 34 (Australia)...131
Anderson v Wilson (1999) 175 DLR (4th) 409 173
Anderton v Clwyd County Council, sub nom *Phelps v Hillingdon London Borough Council*..122
Andrews v Secretary of State for Health (1998) 54 BMLR 111 109
Annetts v Australian Stations Pty Ltd [2002] 211 CLR 317 ....8, 22, 25, 88, 108, 123, 130, 131–5, 138–9, 141, 174
Anns v Merton London Borough Council [1978] AC 728.....................................60
Archibald v Braverman 79 Cal Rptr 723 (1969)...60
Armsworth v South-Eastern Railway Co (1847) 11 Jur (NP) 758..........................42
Arrowsmith v Beeston (unreported, CA, June 1998) 147, 172
Aston v Imperial Chemical Industries Group (unreported, 21 May 1992) 109
Attia v British Gas plc [1988] QB 304 (CA) 64, 69, 125, 160
Bagley v North Herts Health Authority (1986) 136 NLJ 1014.................................21
Baker v TE Hopkins & Son Ltd [1959] 1 WLR 966 (CA)..................................51, 93
Barber v Somerset County Council [2004] UKHL 13; [2004] ICR 457 ....111, 162
Barnard v Santam Bpk 1999 (1) SA 202 (South Africa)....................................8, 161
Barrett v Enfield London Borough Council [2001] 2 AC 550 98
Beecham v Hughes (1988) 52 DLR (4th) 625 72
Bell v Great Northern Railway Co of Ireland (1890) 26 LR Ir 428....................43, 44
Benson v Lee [1972] VR 879..60, 62, 115
Bester v Commercial Union Versekeringsmaatskappy van SA Bpk 1973 (1) SA 769..161
Blake v Midland Railway Co (1852) 18 QB 93; 21 LJQB 233............................39, 42
Bliss v South East Thames Regional Health Authority [1987] ICR 700 27

Blue Circle Industries Plc v Ministry of Defence [1999] Ch 289 39
Boardman v Sanderson [1964] 1 WLR 1317 (CA) 51, 52, 55, 60, 67
Bourhill v Young [1943] AC 92; 1941 SC 395 ....16, 48, 50, 51,
55, 67, 78, 79, 82, 186
Brewster [1998] 1 Cr App R 220 32
Brice v Brown [1984] 1 All ER 997 ....77, 78, 79, 144
Brown v Mount Barker Soldiers' Hospital Inc [1934] SASR 128 104
Bryan v Phillips New Zealand Ltd ([1995] 1 NZLR 632 174
Burstow [1998] AC 147 32
Burton v Pinkerton (1867) LR 2 Ex 340 26
Byrne v Great Southern and Western Railway Co (unreported,
  Irish CA, Feb 1884) 43
Calascione v Dixon (1991) 19 BMLR 97 7
Campbell v Animal Quarantine Station 632 P 2d 1066 (Haw 1981) 161
Campbell v North Lanarkshire Council [1999] ScotCS 163 [42] 82
Campbelltown City Council v Mackay (1989) 15 NSWLR 501 ....8, 131
Caparo Industries plc v Dickman [1990] 2 AC 605 ....56, 65, 92, 110
Carmarthenshire County Council v Lewis [1955] AC 549; [1953]
  2 All ER 1403 (CA) 49, 93
Carty v Croydon London Borough Council [2005] EWCA Civ 19 98
Cassell & Co Ltd v Broome [1972] AC 1027 41
CBS Songs Ltd v Amstrad Consumer Electronics plc [1988] AC 1013 ....65, 149
Chadwick v British Railways Board [1967] 1 WLR 912 ....23, 51, 60, 89, 114
Chan-Fook [1994] 1 WLR 689 32
Chief Constable of West Yorkshire v Schofield [1998] 43 BMLR 28 (CA) 117
Christopher Jones [1981] Crim LR 119 39
Clay v AJ Crump & Sons Ltd (1964) 1 QB 533 (CA) 103
Coates v Government Insurance Office of New South Wales (1995)
  36 NSWLR 1 ....131, 174
Consolidated Rail Corporation v Gottshall 512 US 532 (1994) 175
Coppin v Braithwaite (1844) 8 Jur 875 26
Corr v IBC Vehicles Ltd [2008] UKHL 13 79
Coultas v Victorian Railways Commissioners (1886) 12 VLR 895 130
Cox v Fleming (1995) 15 BCLR (3d) 201; (1993) 13 CCLT (2d)
  305 173
Cox v Philips Industries Ltd [1976] 1 WLR 638 (CA) 27
Coyle or Brown v John Watson Ltd [1915] AC 1 ....16, 46
*Creutzfeldt-Jacob Disease Litigation Group B Plaintiffs v Medical
  Research Council* [2000] Lloyd's Law Rep Med 161 ....81, 99, 102, 109, 110
Daw v Intel Corp (UK) Ltd [2007] EWCA Civ 70 163
Diesen v Samson 1971 SLT 49 26
Dillon v Legg (1968) 29 ALR 3d 1316 ....61, 160
Donoghue v Stevenson (1932) AC 562 ....47, 54, 55, 73, 125, 133, 138
Donovan [1934] 2 KB 498 (CCA) 39

Table of Cases

Dooley v Cammell Laird & Co Ltd (1951) 1 Lloyd's List Law
Reports 271 ....51, 76, 93
Dulieu v White & Sons [1901] 2 KB 669..................................44, 45, 46, 50, 52, 54, 82
Duwyn v Kaprielian (1978) 94 DLR (3rd) 424 174
Dziokonski v Babineau 380 NE 2d 1295 (Mass 1978)..60
Farley v Skinner [2002] 2 AC 732 ....27, 28
Farrell v Avon Health Authority [2001] Lloyd's Rep
Med 458 ....22, 97, 104, 106, 107 127
Farrell v Merton, Sutton and Wandsworth Health Authority
(2000) 57 BMLR 158...99, 119, 127
Fenn v City of Peterborough (1976) 73 DLR (3d) 177..60
Froggatt v Chesterfield and North Derbyshire Royal Hospital
NHS Trust [2002] All ER (D) 218..116, 119
Frost v Chief Constable of South Yorkshire [1997] 3 WLR 1194 (CA)......25, 77, 117
Furniss v Fitchett [1958] NZLR 396 104
G (A Minor) v Bromley London Borough Council, sub nom Phelps v
Hillingdon London Borough Council 122
Galli-Atkinson v Seghal [2003] Lloyd's Rep Med 285 (CA)...........98, 105, 116, 120
Galt v British Railways Board (1983) 133 NLJ 870 76
Garrett v Camden London Borough Council [2001] EWCA Civ 395 ....91, 162
Gifford v Strang Patrick Stevedoring Pty Ltd (2003) 214 CLR 269 ....133, 135
Gillies v Lynch 2002 SLT 1420 21
Glasgow Corporation v Muir [1943] AC 448..49
Government Insurance Office v Best (1993) Aust Torts Rep 81-210 174
Graham v MacMillan (2003) 10 BCLR (4th) 397...174
Graham Barclay Oysters Pty Ltd v Ryan (2003) 211 CLR 540.....................137, 138
Greenberg v Stanley A2d 588 (NJ 1958) 2
Grieves v FT Everard & Sons [2007] UKHL 39 ....1, 14, 39, 81, 111, 112, 113
Griffiths v R & H Green & Silley Weir Ltd (1948) 81 Lloyd's L Rep 378................16
Groom v Crocker [1939] 1 KB 194...26
Grotts v Zahner 989 P 2d 415 (Nev 1999)...61
Guay v Sun Publishing Co [1953] 4 DLR 577 104
GW Atkins Ltd v Scott (1991) 7 Const LR 215...28
Haley v London Electricity Board [1965] AC 778..49
Hambrook v Stokes Bros [1925] 1 KB 141 (CA) 45, 46, 47, 50, 51, 55, 56
Hamlin v Great Northern Railway Co (1856) 1 H & N 408 26
Harriton v Stephens (2006) 226 CLR 52...179
Hartman v South Essex Mental Health and Community Care
NHS Trust [2005] ICR 782..127, 162
Hatton v Sutherland [2002] EWCA Civ 76 ....22, 24, 91, 111, 127, 129, 162
Heaven v Pender [1883] 11 QBD 503 (CA) 54
Hedley Byrne & Co Ltd v Heller & Partners Ltd [1964] AC 465 55
Hegarty v EE Caledonia Ltd [1997] 2 Lloyd's Rep 259 23
Heil v Rankin [2001] QB 272 (CA) 180, 181

Henderson v Canadian Atlantic Railway Co (1898) 25 OAR 437 44
Henderson v Merrett Syndicates Ltd [1995] 2 AC 145....................................103, 127
Hevican v Ruane [1991] 3 All ER 65...64, 160
Hill v Chief Constable of West Yorkshire Police [1989] AC 53 125
Hill v Van Erp (1997) 188 CLR 159 73
Hinz v Berry [1970] 2 QB 40 (CA) 2, 8, 26, 52, 53, 55, 56, 67, 131, 143
Hobbs v London & South Western Railway Co (1875) 10 QB 111 26
Hodgson v Trapp [1989] AC 807 183
Hogan v City of Regina [1924] 2 WWR 307..46
Home Office v Butchart [2006] 1 WLR 1155 (CA) 129
Home Office v Dorset Yacht Co Ltd [1970] AC 1004..49, 55
Hughes v Lord Advocate [1963] AC 837 55
Hunter v British Coal Corp. [1999] QB 140 ....77, 94
Ireland [1998] AC 147..32
Jackson v Horizon Holidays Ltd [1975] 1 WLR 1468 (CA)....................................26
Jaensch v Coffey (1984) 155 CLR 549 ....23, 72, 74, 114, 117, 131
James v Woodall Duckham Construction Co Ltd [1969] 1 WLR 903 (CA)..........146
Jarvis v Hampshire County Council, sub nom Phelps v Hillingdon
    London Borough Council..122
Jarvis v Swan Tours (1973) QB 233 (CA) 26
John v MGN Ltd [1997] QB 586 (CA)..28
Johnson v Gore Wood & Co (a firm) [2002] 2 AC 1...27
Johnson v Ruark Obstetrics and Gynecology Associates PA 395 SE 2d
    85 (NC 1990)...175
Johnson v Unisys Ltd [2003] 1 AC 518 ....25, 26
Johnstone v Bloomsbury Health Authority [1992] 1 QB 333..........................24, 164
Justus v Atchison 565 P 2d 122 (Cal 1977)...161
Keating v London Borough of Bromley, sub nom X (minors) v
    Bedfordshire County Council...123
Kemp v Sober (1851) 61 ER 200...42
King v Phillips [1953] 1 QB 429 (CA) 50, 51, 52, 55, 67, 78, 79
Knightley v Johns [1982] 1 WLR 349...84
Koehler v Cerebos (Australia) Ltd (2005) 79 ALJR 845.................................136, 163
Koufos v C Czarnikow Ltd (The Heron II) [1969] 1 AC 350..................................49
Kralj v McGrath [1986] 1 All ER 54...29
Kuddus v Chief Constable of Leicestershire [2002] 2 AC 122 29
L (A Child) v Reading Borough Council [2001] 1 WLR 1575 (CA).....................129
Leach v Chief Constable of Gloucestershire Constabulary [1999]
    1 WLR 1421 (CA) 22, 81, 97
Leong v Takasaki (1974) 520 P 2d 758 (Haw) 6
Livingstone v Rawyards (1880) 5 App Cas 25...148, 180
Lynch v Knight (1861) 9 HL Cas 577..42
McDermott v Ramadanovic Estate (1988) 27 BCLR (2d) 451, 172
McFarlane v E E Caledonia Ltd [1994] 2 All ER 1 (CA).......................................90

Table of Cases

McFarlane v Tayside Health Board [2000] 2 AC 59..92
McLoughlin v Jones [2002] 2 WLR 1279 (CA)...........................22, 97, 99, 101, 102,
103, 105, 116, 129, 163
McLoughlin v O'Brian [1983] 1 AC 410; [1981] QB 599
(CA)..10, 15, 16, 23, 47, 57, 59-64, 86, 87, 100, 112,
114, 115, 119, 131, 141, 144, 145, 148, 149, 159, 160, 186
Mahmud v Bank of Credit and Commerce International [1998] AC 20.................25
Majrowski v Guy's and St Thomas's NHS Trust [2007] 1 AC 224........................10
Malcolm v Broadhurst [1970] 3 All ER 508..77, 78
Marshall v Lionel Enterprises Inc (1971) 25 DLR (3rd) 141 60
Mason v Westside Cemeteries Ltd (1996) 135 DLR (4th) 361 173
*Melville v Home Office, sub nom Hartman v South Essex Mental
Health and Community Care NHS Trust*..163
Merrett v Babb [2001] 3 WLR 1 (CA) 137
Molien v Kaiser Foundation Hospitals 616 P 2d 813 (Cal 1980) 175
Morris v Ford Motor Co Ltd [1973] QB 792 (CA) 54
Morris v KLM Royal Dutch Airlines [2002] QB 100 (CA).......................................11
Mount Isa Mines Ltd v Pusey (1970) 125 CLR 383 ....6, 55, 88, 104, 131
Mustapha v Culligan of Canada Ltd 2008 SCC 27..174, 186
Nettleship v Weston [1971] 2 QB 691 (CA)..54
*New Brunswick (Minister of Health and Community Services) v
G (J)* [1999] 3 SCR 46 173
New South Wales v Seedsman (2000) 217 ALR 583 164
Nicholls v Rushton (1992) *The Times*, 19 June 123
North Eastern Railway Co v Wanless [1874] LR 7 HL 12.......................................54
North Glamorgan NHS Trust v Walters [2003] Lloyd's Rep Med 49
(CA) 22, 25, 70, 94, 114, 115, 116, 119
Ogwo v Taylor [1988] AC 431 ....84, 93
Osman v United Kingdom (1998) 29 EHRR 245 100
*Overseas Tankship (UK) Ltd v Miller Steamship Co Pty (The Wagon
Mound (No 2))* [1967] 1 AC 617, PC..49
*Overseas Tankship (UK) Ltd v Morts Dock and Engineering Co Ltd
(The Wagon Mound (No 1))* [1961] AC 388, PC 46, 52, 78, 79
Owens v Liverpool Corporation [1939] 1 KB 394 (CA)..52
Page v Smith [1996] AC 155; [1994] 4 All ER 522
(CA) 2, 7, 74, 75, 76, 77–83, 102, 149, 172
Page v Smith (No 2) [1996] 1 WLR 855 78
Perre v Apand Pty Ltd (1999) 198 CLR 180 138
Petch v Customs and Excise Commissioners [1993] ICR 789 ....24, 91
Phelps v Hillingdon London Borough Council [2001] 2 AC 619 ....16, 98, 122–4
Polemis and Furness, Withy & Co, Re [1921] 3 KB 560 (CA) 46
Public Service Employee Relations Act (Alberta), *Re* (1987) 1 SCR 313 26
Pyrenees Shire Council v Day (1998) 192 CLR 330..138
R v Deputy Governor of Parkhurst Prison, Ex parte Hague [1992] 1 AC 58.........127

xviii   *Table of Cases*

Rabideau v City of Racine 627 NW 2d 795 (Wis 2001) 61
Ravenscroft v Rederiaktiebolaget Transatlantic [1992] 2 All ER 470;
    [1991] 3 All ER 73 .... 64, 160
Rees v Darlington Memorial Hospital NHS Trust [2004] 1 AC 309 92
Reeves v Commissioner of Police of the Metropolis [2000] 1 AC 360 138
Reilly and Reilly v Merseyside Regional Health Authority [1995]
    6 Med LR 246 (CA) 1
Rhodes v Canadian National Railway (1990) 75 DLR (4th) 248 ..... 53, 73, 114, 173
Robertson v Forth Road Bridge Joint Board, 1995 SCLR 466 91
Robinson v Post Office [1974] 1 WLR 1176 (CA) 55
Robinson v St Helens Metropolitan Borough Council [2002]
    EWCA Civ 1099 .... 98, 124
Rookes v Barnard [1964] AC 1129 41
Rothwell v Chemical & Insulating Co Ltd [2006] EWCA Civ 27 113
Rowling v Takaro Properties [1988] AC 473 66
Ruxley Electronics and Construction Ltd v Forsyth [1996] AC 344 27
Salter v UB Frozen and Chilled Foods Ltd 2003 SLT 1011 101
Schneider v Eisovitch [1960] 2 QB 430 77
Simpson v Imperial Chemical Industries Ltd 1983 SLT 601 144
Sion v Hampstead Health Authority [1994] 5 Med LR 170 (CA) 23, 97, 116, 118
Sloane v Southern California Rail Co 44 P 320 (Cal 1896) 44
Smith v Johnson & Co (1897) DC (unreported) 55
Stephen v Riverside Health Authority [1990] 1 Med LR 261 39
Storm v Geeves [1965] Tas SR 252 .... 53, 131
Sullivan v Moody (2001) 207 CLR 562 137
Swain v Waverley Municipal Council (2005) 79 ALJR 565 136
Swinney v Chief Constable of Northumbria [1997] QB 464 (CA) 99, 125, 129
T (A Minor) v Surrey County Council (1994) 4 All ER 577 103
Tame v New South Wales [2002] 211 CLR 317 .... 8, 22, 25, 95, 123,
                                                                                    130, 131–5, 138–9, 141, 174, 186
Tan v East London and City Health Authority [1999] Lloyd's
    Rep Med 389 .... 114, 116, 118
Taylor v Somerset Health Authority (1993) 4 Med LR 34 117
Taylorson v Shieldness Produce Ltd [1994] PIQR P329 (CA) 116
Thing v La Chusa 771 P 2d 814 (Cal 1989) 61, 161, 175
Thompson v Commissioner of Police for the Metropolis [1998] QB 498 (CA) 29
Tomlinson v Congleton Borough Council [2004] 1 AC 46 .... 138, 167–8
Tredget and Tredget v Bexley Health Authority [1994]
    5 Med LR 178 .... 25, 116, 118
Turbyfield v Great Western Railway Co (1937) 54 TLR 221 67
van Soest v Residual Health Management Unit [2000]
    1 NZLR 179 .... 2, 9, 53, 104, 143, 172
Vanek v Great Atlantic & Pacific Co of Canada (1999) 180 DLR (4th) 748 173
Vellino v Chief Constable of Greater Manchester [2002] 1 WLR 218 151

Table of Cases

Vernon v Bosley (No 1) [1997] 1 All ER 577 ....7, 144, 148, 172
Vernon v Bosley (No 2) [1999] QB 18 (CA)..148
Victorian Railways Commissioners v Coultas (1888) 13 App Cas
    222 (PC) 18, 44, 130, 146
W v Essex County Council [2001] 2 AC 592; [1998] 3 WLR 534
    (CA) 22, 95, 97, 99–101, 103, 126, 135
Wagon Mound, The (No 1) [1961] AC 388 PC, *sub nom Overseas
    Tankship (UK) Ltd v Morts Dock and Engineering Co Ltd*
Wagon Mound, The (No 2) [1967] 1 AC 617, PC, *sub nom Overseas
    Tankship (UK) Ltd v Miller Steamship Co Pty*
Wagner v International Railway Co 133 NE 437 (NY 1921) 93
Wainwright v Home Office [2004] 2 AC 406..45
Walker v Northumberland County Council [1995] 1 All ER 737......................24, 90
Wallace v United Grain Growers Ltd (1997) 152 DLR (4th) 1 26
Walters v North Glamorgan NHS Trust [2002] Lloyd's Rep Med 227...................97
Ward v Leeds Teaching Hospitals NHS Trust [2004] Lloyd's Rep
    Med 530..117, 120–1
Warren v King [1964] 1 WLR 1 180
Watts v Morrow [1991] 1 WLR 1421..26, 27
West (H) & Son Ltd v Shephard [1964] AC 326.. 43
White v Chief Constable of South Yorkshire Police [1999] 2 AC
    455 ....3, 16, 79, 80–81, 100, 141–3, 181
White v Jones [1995] 2 AC 207 103
Whitmore v Euroways Express Coaches Ltd, The Times, 4 May 1984 53
Wieland v Cyril Lord Carpets Ltd [1969] 3 All ER 1006 103
Wilkinson v Downton [1897] 2 QB 57...45
Williams v Natural Life Health Foods Ltd [1998] 1 WLR 830 (HL) 103
Wilsons & Clyde Coal Co v English [1938] AC 57..24
Wong v Parkside Health NHS Trust [2003] 3 All ER 932 (CA)...............................45
Wyong Shire Council v Shirt (1980) 146 CLR 40 136
X (Minors) v Bedfordshire County Council [1995] 2 AC 633............92, 99, 122, 127
Yates v South Kirkby Collieries Ltd [1910] 2 KB 538 (CA) 55
Young v Charles Church (Southern) Ltd (1997) 39 BMLR 146 ....23, 80
*Younger (Katie) v Dorset & Somerset Strategic Health Authority
    and South East London Strategic Health Authority* [2006] LS
    Law Medical 489 124

TABLE OF STATUTES

Access to Justice Act 1999..153
Administration of Justice Act, 1982
    s 1 (1)(b)..28
    s 3..21
Charter of Rights and Freedoms (Canada)
    s 7..173
Civil Liability Act 2002 (New South Wales)..182
    s 16 (1)...136
    s 30...136
Civil Liability Amendment (Personal Responsibility) Act 2002 (New South Wales)
    s 32...136
Compensation Act 2006
    s 1...168
    Part II...153
Consumer Protection Act 1987..142
Courts and Legal Services Act 1990
    s 58...153
Criminal Injuries Compensation Act 1995 182
Damages (Scotland) Act 1976
    s 1(4)..21
Disability Discrimination Act 1995 9
    s 8(4)..21
Employers' Liability Act 1880 42
Employment Rights Act 1996..24
Fatal Accidents Act 1976..2
    s 1A (as amended by the Administration of Justice Act 1982, s 3) 21
Health and Safety at Work Act 1974...24
Nuclear Installations Act 1965 142
Offences against the Person Act, 1861
    s 20...31
    s 47...31
Personal Injuries (Liability and Damages) Act 2003 (Northern Territories).....182
Protection from Harassment Act, 1997 9
    s 1(1)...10
    s 1(A)..10
    s 1(2)...10

s 3(2) 10, 21
s 4(1) 10
s 7(2) 10, 21
Public Service Employee Relations Act (Alberta) (1987) 1 SCR 313, 368 26
Race Relations Act 1976 9
   s 57(4) 21
Sex Discrimination Act 1975 9
   s 66(4) 21
Social Security (Recovery of Benefits) Act 1997, s 23 (1) 156
Wrongs Act 1958 (Victoria) as amended by the Wrongs and Other Acts
   (Public Liability Insurance Reform) Act 2002 (Victoria) 182

1

Psychiatric Harm, Emotional Suffering and Legal Redress

[T]o the sufferer, what is the difference between physical pain and emotional pain? Indeed the former may be easier to bear, especially with modern analgesics, than the latter.[1]

Categorising Personal Harm

Introduction

SOME YEARS AGO, an elderly couple were trapped for over an hour in a negligently maintained hospital lift. The fear, panic and discomfort which they suffered resulted in chest pains, sleeplessness, nightmares, claustrophobia and vomiting, and caused them psychological disturbance over a two month period. This combination of reactions was described by the Court of Appeal as 'normal emotion in the face of a most unpleasant experience',[2] for which it was the 'sound policy of the law' not to provide compensation. One evening, in 2001, a guest at a dinner party in Bath fell through the seat of a new glass chair. The hostess and other guests helped to free her and she went to the bathroom to attend to a graze. A little shaken and embarrassed, but otherwise unhurt, she returned and was found another chair. Not long afterwards, she left. In due course, her solicitors sent a letter to the hostess, claiming damages for personal injury, on the basis that she had been 'negligent under the Occupiers' Liability Act for providing defective seating'. If proved, such a claim would attract compensation, and the hostess agreed to pay £200 by way of settlement out of court.[3]

What counts as harm for the purposes of legal redress is highly instructive. It tells us much about social and judicial perceptions, illustrating how, and sometimes how slowly, they change. In particular, the law has always taken physical

---

[1] *McDermott v Ramadanovic Estate* (1988) 27 BCLR (2nd) 45, 53, *per* Southin J.
[2] *Reilly and Reilly v Merseyside Regional Health Authority* [1995] 6 Med LR 246, 249, *per* Mann LJ.
[3] *The Times*, 19 May 2001. A court, however, might deem a particular cut or scratch too trivial to constitute physical injury in law: *Grieves v FT Everard & Sons* [2007] UKHL 39 [47] and [73], *per* Lord Hope and Lord Scott, respectively.

injury much more seriously than mental harm and emotional distress. Whereas, in principle, a minor cut entitles you to damages, the negligent infliction of 'purely' emotional harm, such as shock, anxiety or stress, normally does not.[4] This is so even if the disturbance or suffering is 'plainly out of the range of normal human experience',[5] unless it amounts to a 'recognisable psychiatric illness'.[6]

Yet damages *are* recoverable in negligence, even for minor emotional harm, if it results from *physical* injury.[7] What are we to make of this? Does the physical injury somehow legitimate a claim which, standing alone, might be thought of as trivial, imagined or perhaps simulated? In his classic work on *Damages*, the American scholar McCormick observed that '[t]he various forms of mental suffering are as numberless as the capacities of the human soul for torturing itself'.[8] Is the precondition of a physical source simply a crude limiting device, a convenient means of discouraging the development of a 'compensation culture' and the proliferation of claims? Where there is no tangible physical injury, not only is proof of a 'recognisable psychiatric illness' essential, but it is much easier for claimants to succeed if they were exposed to physical danger. From its inception to the present day, the applicable and unduly intricate English law has largely centred on the claimant's proximity to a particular, physical event. A typical example would be the motorist or passenger traumatised but otherwise unharmed in a crash caused by someone else's negligent driving. Such claimants are now legally classified as 'primary victims',[9] and their physical imperilment entitles them to recover for psychiatric harm, even when such harm was not itself foreseeable. For them, it suffices that some form of 'personal' injury was foreseeable as a result of the negligent conduct.[10] By contrast, people not exposed to physical danger, who foreseeably suffer psychiatric harm from seeing or experiencing the negligent injury or endangerment of others, receive much less favourable treatment. Labelled 'secondary victims', they can recover damages only if they satisfy an array of restrictive criteria, also based on notions of proximity. Foremost among these are close proximity to the accident (or its aftermath) in time and space; experience of the event or its immediate aftermath through their own unaided senses, and proximity of relationship, namely, close ties of love and affection with an immediate accident victim. In addition, their illness must normally have been *shock*-induced, that is,

---

[4] There are certain statutory exceptions to this principle, eg, under the Protection from Harassment Act 1997, and in cases of bereavement: Fatal Accidents Act 1976. See below 9–10 and 21, respectively.

[5] *van Soest v Residual Health Management Unit* [2000] 1 NZLR 179, 206, *per* Thomas J (diss) (New Zealand).

[6] *Hinz v Berry* [1970] 2 QB 40, 42, *per* Lord Denning MR.

[7] Cf 'where the defendant's negligence occasions some personal physical injury to the plaintiff, no matter how slight, the plaintiff may recover for fright, shock, and mental anguish': *Greenberg v Stanley*, 1958, 51 NJ Super 90, 143 A 2d 588, 597.

[8] See CT McCormick, *Handbook on the Law of Damages* (St Paul, Minn, West Publishing Co, 1935) 316.

[9] *Page v Smith* [1996] AC 155, 184, *per* Lord Lloyd.

[10] *Ibid*, 187.

caused by a 'sudden assault on the nervous system'[11] and not, as is often true of depressive states, for example, by the cumulative impact of events.

Consider the mass disaster, in 1989, when a televised FA Cup semi-final was held at the Hillsborough football ground, in Sheffield. Due to serious overcrowding on the terraces at one end of the ground, 96 spectators died, most from asphyxiation, and hundreds were physically injured. What happened at Hillsborough 'also scarred many others for life by emotional harm.'[12] The *physically* injured, and the *physically* imperilled were, as 'primary' victims, entitled to damages for psychiatric harm, on proof that negligent crowd control by the Chief Constable had caused them reasonably foreseeable personal injury. This standard negligence test did not, however, cover equally traumatised relatives present elsewhere in the stadium, or watching the events unfold on TV, or identifying bodies in a makeshift mortuary at the ground. Nor did it avail traumatised on-duty police officers assisting at the scene.[13]

However readily foreseeable their psychiatric condition, none of the physically unendangered claimants met all the special proximity requirements for 'secondary' victims, as laid down by the House of Lords in *Alcock v Chief Constable of South Yorkshire Police*.[14] Relatives and friends at the ground failed because they did not present special evidence of close ties of love and affection, perhaps unsurprisingly, since the need for this invidious evidence had not been made explicit in the pre-*Alcock* case law. Though such close ties were presumed to exist (subject to rebuttal) in the case of parents, children, and spouses,[15] the claimants in these categories whose cases were considered by the House of Lords had not been present at the ground. Their perception of what had happened by means other than actual sight or hearing was not equated with direct experience through unaided senses. Even the live TV coverage, because it did not depict the suffering of identifiable individuals, was deemed incapable of inducing a 'sudden assault on the nervous system' as distinct from 'feelings of the deepest anxiety and distress.'[16] Identification of a victim at the mortuary some eight or nine hours after the disaster was considered to be beyond the 'immediate' aftermath. As for the on-duty police,[17] once they were designated 'secondary' victims,[18] they were doomed to fail for lack of close ties with the immediate victims.

Although the Hillsborough disaster was exceptional in its scale, the legal reasoning in the ensuing litigation was far from untypical. For too long, the law on liability for harm caused by mental trauma has been tarnished by artificial restrictions which

---

[11] *Alcock v Chief Constable of South Yorkshire Police* [1992] 1 AC 310, 398, *per* Lord Keith. Cf 'the sudden appreciation by sight or sound of a horrifying event, which violently agitates the mind': 401, *per* Lord Ackner. It is unclear to what extent, if at all, this requirement applies to 'primary victims'. Plainly, it does not apply where the psychiatric illness arises from occupational stress. See below 23.
[12] *White v Chief Constable of South Yorkshire Police* [1999] 2 AC 455, 491, *per* Lord Steyn.
[13] Ibid.
[14] *Alcock*, above n 11.
[15] And possibly fiancé(e)s: *Alcock, above n 11*, 397, *per* Lord Keith.
[16] *Alcock*, above n 11, 398 and 405, *per* Lord Keith and Lord Ackner, respectively.
[17] *White*, above n 12.
[18] Ibid.

confound legal principle, defy logic and are at odds with medical understanding. This is especially true of 'secondary' claims, where arbitrary distinctions have been a source of endless confusion, attributing disproportionate causal significance to circumstantial details. Even before *Alcock* reached the House of Lords, it had produced four different judicial views on the proper test for proximity of relationship, as well as mental gymnastics of questionable medical validity on the difference between the effects of direct vision, watching live and recorded TV and listening to live radio. From a medical standpoint, the claimants' emotional characteristics, the intensity of their traumatic experience and the intensity of their relationship with an immediate victim would have been the key predictors of psychiatric illness.[19] Hair-splitting over whether live TV constitutes 'direct perception', or how many hours there are in an 'aftermath', seems quite divorced from the causal realities of psychiatric harm. Nowhere in the House of Lords judgment in *Alcock* is there an explicit reference to the medical determinants of psychiatric illness.

It is easy to understand why the law is much preoccupied with physical injury and its threat. Without cogent justification, a tangible, visible invasion of the body evokes a deep-rooted sense of affront and commands universal condemnation. It has a resonance and immediacy which we do not instinctively associate with the infliction of mental suffering. In addition, its victims routinely attract sympathy. Untainted by the social stigma and suspicions which have surrounded mental disturbance over many centuries, they do not normally experience negative or hostile reactions or feel a comparable urge to conceal their condition. Nor, generally speaking, do their injuries provoke the same degree of diagnostic controversy. It is also significant that the scope for negligently causing physical injury is highly circumscribed by the constraints of time, place and mode of infliction. By contrast, negligent conduct may induce mental harm in all manner of ways and in more diverse circumstances. The spectre of proliferating claims and 'virtually limitless liability' should the controls be abandoned has always weighed heavily in the case law, and it remains a distinctive feature of the leading House of Lords decisions.[20] The courts, then, are still disposed to grant pride of place to redress for physical injury, despite the fact that harm to the psyche often has a more devastating impact on people's lives. Whether, or to what extent, this stance can be justified by the reasons advanced is another matter.[21]

Mental and Emotional Harm

Although 'personal harm', as generally understood, extends well beyond bodily injury, no single term fully captures the sheer range of suffering which is not manifestly physical. As well as psychiatric illness or disorder, and other kinds of

---

[19] See below 5–8.
[20] Alcock, above n 11, 417, *per* Lord Oliver. Cf *Page*, above n 9, 189, *per* Lord Lloyd, and *White*, above n 12, 494, *per* Lord Steyn.
[21] See below Ch 5.

mental distress or disturbance, harm to the person more broadly construed would include the sense of affront and indignity associated with deprivation of liberty, injury to reputation, interference with privacy, discriminatory practices and various other ways in which personal equilibrium and wellbeing can be diminished.[22] Plainly, these latter forms of harm can cause serious distress, for which damages may be available, increasingly through statutory developments.[23] Insofar as the relevant statutes acknowledge the appropriateness of such damages, they have a bearing on our general theme, though they have a broader and more fundamental concern with human dignity and, in some contexts, with social cohesion. Our main aim is to focus more directly on liability for the negligent infliction of mental and emotional harm. How, as a matter of relativities, should it be accommodated in the law's general structure for redressing personal injury?

To say that our field of inquiry is legal redress for 'mental and emotional harm' immediately raises formidable and unresolved difficulties of appropriate terminology. For example, the expression 'emotional harm', as well as being imprecise, has the drawback that, in ordinary speech, 'emotion' tends to be equated with impulsive and excitable responses.[24] However, emotional reactions can be suffered to such a degree that a serious psychiatric disorder ensues. Even when not a prelude to psychiatric illness, emotional disturbance can prove seriously disabling, sometimes more so than certain 'recognised psychiatric illnesses'. It is therefore a useful concept to indicate the broad range of 'non-physical' suffering for which legal remedies either are, or could be, available. It is of interest, in this connection, that in many United States jurisdictions the term 'emotional distress' is used to cover both minor reactions and major damage to the psyche. Medicine, too, does not speak with one voice on these terminological issues. To that extent, 'emotional harm' might be said to have the virtue of *not* laying claim to linguistic precision, in a field where scientific controversy and conflicting views on diagnostic categories are not uncommon. At all events, a broad distinction can be made between psychological states, involving emotional responses such as 'distress, anxiety, sadness, grief or disappointment', and a psychiatric illness or disorder with a medically recognised pathology.[25]

Some Problems of Classification

Medical

Emotional reactions to traumatic stimuli are often more nuanced than the effects of physical injury. To an extent not always open to the law, medicine can allow for

---

[22] See J Feinberg, *Harm to Others* (New York, Oxford University Press, 1984) ch 1. Damage to property and economic loss are beyond the scope of this book.
[23] See below 20–21.
[24] See P Handford, *Mullany and Handford's Tort Liability for Psychiatric Damage* (Sydney, Lawbook Co, 2nd edn, 2006) [3.50].
[25] See, eg, I Freckleton, 'New Directions in Compensability for Psychiatric Injuries', *Psychiatry, Psychology and Law*, vol 9; 2002: 271, 274.

levels of uncertainty and gradation when categorising a patient's mental condition. A basic distinction can nevertheless be drawn between 'primary' and 'secondary' reactions to trauma. Primary reactions are immediate, automatic and instinctive. They are transient, subjective sensations, such as fear, anger, or shock, which have various physiological repercussions that affect the nervous system. Though very common, such symptoms are normally offset by a defence mechanism which allows the sufferer to cope. In a small minority of cases, however, longer-lasting secondary reactions develop, often in the form of traumatic neuroses.[26] A person's emotional makeup is a key predictor of such consequences, but there will be other significant variables, such as the intensity of the stimulus, the degree of preparedness for it and, crucially when injury to another is the trigger, the intensity of the relationship between the individuals concerned.

The main neurotic reactions to trauma are now commonly divided into 'post traumatic stress disorder' (PTSD) and certain other conditions, such as depressive illnesses, adjustment disorders and anxiety disorders.[27] All of these conditions can be induced by shock, but PTSD is distinctive in that the diagnosis *depends* on exposure to an external and severely traumatic event, outside the range of normal human experience. PTSD is also characterised by 're-experiencing' the traumatising event and by the emergence of persistent 'avoidance' and 'arousal' symptoms. It is widely acknowledged within psychiatry that the boundaries of mental disorder are not exact, and this very brief outline does not purport to convey either the extent of doctrinal dispute or the intricacies of diagnostic overlap and multiple diagnoses. Although there is no definitive classificatory system of mental disorders, the most widely accepted works of this kind are those of the American Psychiatric Association (DSM-1V) and the World Health Organisation (ICD-10). As works of reference which set out diagnostic criteria, these manuals constitute a valuable resource for the psychiatric profession. In the context of litigation, their criteria also routinely feature in the written opinions and evidence of expert witnesses.[28]

Plainly, however, DSM-1V and ICD-10 are not designed to satisfy legal criteria for remediable harm. There is no universal agreement within psychiatry on what constitutes a 'recognisable psychiatric illness'; nor, if there were, is it obvious that

---

[26] DJ Leibson, 'Recovery of Damages for Emotional Distress Caused by Physical Injury to Another' (1976–77) 15 *Journal of Family Law* 163, 201ff; M Gelder *et al*, *Oxford Textbook of Psychiatry* (Oxford, Oxford University Press, 3rd edn, 1996) ch 6, esp at 137–8. Cf 'It is, however, today a known medical fact that severe emotional distress can be the starting point of a lasting disorder of mind or body, some form of psychoneurosis or a psychosomatic illness': *Mount Isa Mines Ltd v Pusey* (1970) 125 CLR 383, 394, per Windeyer J. And see *Leong v Takasaki* (1974) 520 P 2d 758 (Hawaii).

[27] Gelder, *et al, ibid*, 137 ff; Law Commission No 249, *Liability for Psychiatric Illness* (London, HMSO, 1998), Section B: The Medical Background, 38–54.

[28] American Psychiatric Association, *Diagnostic and Statistical Manual of Mental Disorders* (Washington DC, American Psychiatric Association, 4th edn, TR 2000) and World Health Organisation, *International Classification of Diseases and Related Health Problems* (Geneva, World Health Organisation, 10th Revision, vol 1, 1993). For an instructive account of psychiatric assessment and its application in the forensic context, see N Eastman, 'Case Study: Psychiatric Injury', *Medical Negligence Update* Conference Paper (London, IBC Legal Studies and Services Ltd, 1996).

it should be the legal recovery threshold for negligently inflicted 'pure' mental harm. There is no reason why one should expect the particular classificatory system in a medical treatise to be totally congruent with the requirements of a liability regime that are inevitably shaped by the development of legal doctrine, as influenced by notions of culpability and various social and economic considerations. In the court setting, then, DSM-1V and ICD-10 serve as valuable guidance to be considered in the light of other relevant factors, which include clinical judgment. Such works cannot be dispositive of legal decisions, and some medical experts maintain that their categories 'do not reflect the complexities of the psychological impact of trauma',[29] given that conditions not 'officially' classified may prove more disabling, depending on the particular facts.[30] For example, several conditions not included in DSM-1V and ICD-10, such as chronic fatigue syndrome (CFS) and pathological grief disorder (PGD) have been deemed 'recognisable psychiatric illnesses' by the English courts.[31] Nonetheless, the influence of these diagnostic systems in the legal context is undeniable, as is apparent from how soon PTSD became a prominent basis of claims once they had accepted it as a distinct diagnostic category. What remains unfortunate is the extent to which certain legal criteria of liability fly in the face of generally accepted scientific understanding.

Legal

If medical opinions differ on how to define and label particular mental conditions, so, too, the law is far from uniform in classifying and providing remedies (or sanctions) for mental and emotional harm. To begin with, the various branches of our legal system have developed in different ways and do not pursue identical aims. In very general terms, the scope for liability is influenced by such diverse considerations as changing social values, the historical development and conceptual foundations of particular torts, the ambit of certain contractual obligations, and the differing objectives of civil and criminal law.[32] It is also apparent that, within the same branch or category of law, comparable legal systems have adopted divergent rules and terminology for mental harm, an obvious case in point being the blanket coverage of the term 'emotional distress' in US jurisdictions.

It is instructive, in this context, to consider the chequered history of the term 'nervous shock'. In England, the quest for clarity was notoriously obstructed by the longstanding use of this confusing and unscientific expression, which unhelpfully elides the distinction between the cause and nature of the condition

---

[29] L Com Rep No 249, above n 27, para 3.29.
[30] See Scottish Law Commission, *Discussion Paper on Damages for Psychiatric Injury* (Edinburgh, The Stationery Office, 2002) No 120, para 2.8.
[31] Eg, *Page v Smith* [1996] AC 155 (CFS); *Vernon v Bosley (No 1)* [1997] 1 All ER 577 (PGD) and *Calascione v Dixon* (1991) 19 BMLR 97 (PGD).
[32] See P Cane, *Responsibility in Law and Morality* (Oxford, Hart Publishing, 2002) 49–51 and 214–16.

described.[33] First appearing in the medical literature in the 1870s,[34] it was soon to become a familiar legal term for mental illness caused by shock. Despite being discarded in medicine by the 1930s, for most of the twentieth century 'nervous shock' dominated judicial discourse on what is now legally defined as a 'recognisable psychiatric illness'.[35] Lingering on to this day in the occasional judgment, references to 'nervous shock' serve as a graphic reminder of the law's eagerness to confine liability to injury caused by sudden sensory perception. To psychiatrists, the legal prerequisite of shock, an acute emotional reaction, is an irrational limitation. It is often not a good predictor of later psychiatric illness, notably so for depression,[36] whereas other atypical responses may be, especially when prolonged and severe.[37] Continued use by the courts of the 'nervous shock' label did, however, perpetuate, and seemingly legitimate, the lay image of instant, momentary fright as a common source of mental harm.

Yet English law's recasting of 'nervous shock' as a 'recognisable psychiatric illness' is not free from difficulty either. As a criterion of liability, it, too, allows a restrictive and contested label to trump the actual severity of the claimant's condition. We can be too easily beguiled by the label and lose sight of what should be our main concern—whether the disturbance, suffering and dysfunction experienced by the claimant merit compensation.[38] As the Scottish Law Commission has noted, psychiatrists can often agree about the extent of a claimant's disability even when they disagree about the diagnostic label to attach to it.[39] For this reason, the Commission had initially favoured the term 'significantly disabling psychiatric injury'; though, as Case has pointed out, the term 'harm' seems preferable to 'injury', since a focus on 'injury' might tempt judges to confine liability to swiftly inflicted harm, undermining the Commission's intention that the 'shock' require-

---

[33] Cf 'It is highly artificial to imprison the legal cause of action for psychiatric injury in an outmoded scientific view about the nature of its origins.' *Campbelltown City Council v Mackay* (1989) 15 NSWLR 501, 503, *per* Kirby P.

[34] H Godefroi, 'On Compensation for Railway Injuries', *Papers Read before the Juridical Society: 1863–70*, vol 3, 689, 690–1; JE Erichsen, *On the Concussion of the Spine, Nervous Shock and Other Obscure Injuries of the Nervous System* (New York, William Wood and Co, 1875), cited in D Mendelson, *The Interfaces of Medicine and Law* (Aldershot, Dartmouth Publishing Co, 1998) 48.

[35] *Hinz v Berry*, above n 6.

[36] PTSD, on the other hand, by its very nature, is almost bound to satisfy English law's general insistence that a claimant's psychiatric illness must have been *shock*-induced.

[37] Eg, chronic stressors, as in cases of occupational stress, may have more far-reaching psychological consequences than acute ones. Cf '[t]he common law, however, seems to unduly emphasise the severity of initial emotional response while de-emphasising the severity of the stressor itself. It is the latter which in fact causes later psychiatric illness . . . not the emotional response of the plaintiff at the time of impact': C Tennant, 'Liability for Psychiatric Injury: an Evidence-based Approach' (2002) 76 *Australian Law Journal* 73, 74. It is noteworthy that whereas some Commonwealth jurisdictions have rejected the 'sudden impact' test, eg, *Barnard v Santam Bpk* 1999 (1) SA 202 (South Africa); *Tame v New South Wales; Annetts v Australian Stations Pty Ltd* [2002] 211 CLR 317, English law has, for the most part, retained it, despite growing judicial and academic criticism. Cf Law Com No 249 (1998), above n 27, para 5.33. And see below Ch 4, 113–21.

[38] See D Butler, 'Identifying the compensable damage in "nervous shock" cases' (1997) 5 *Torts Law Journal* 67. And see further below Ch 6.

[39] See Scottish Law Commmission, *Discussion Paper*, above n 30, para 2.8.

ment for secondary claimants should be discarded. In the event, it opted for the expression 'medically recognised mental disorder'.[40] We will argue that it is neither desirable nor necessary for a 'recognisable *psychiatric* illness' to constitute the threshold. It is not desirable precisely because there can be severe emotional harm without it. It would not appear to be necessary, because, contrary to conventional wisdom, it is reasonable to suppose that trivial emotional harm, like its physical counterpart, would very rarely be the subject of litigation.[41] If this supposition is correct, there is no need for a threshold at all. Should one nonetheless be deemed necessary on precautionary grounds or for pragmatic reasons, a more flexible and inclusive criterion than proven psychiatric illness would be preferable, such as 'moderately severe mental or emotional harm'.[42] Such a threshold would resemble the requirement, in the tort of nuisance, of a 'substantial and unreasonable' interference with a claimant's land or use and enjoyment of land. If we have the right not to be unduly disturbed in our enjoyment of land, are we not also entitled to be free from undue, culpable disruption of our wellbeing as such?

There is no compelling reason for holding the line at psychiatric injury, all the more so since its boundaries are contested. We should take note of the following comments by Thomas J (dissenting) in a New Zealand Court of Appeal decision, *van Soest v Residual Health Management Unit*:

> The outcome of the restriction on recovery to recognisable psychiatric illness is to place the categories of mental and emotional harm for which damages may be recovered in the hands of psychiatry. Whatever that discipline chooses to identify and name as a psychiatric illness becomes the law's boundaries for damages in this area. Yet there is no necessary relationship between the fundamental concept of reasonable foreseeability and psychiatry's classification of psychiatric illnesses. A negligent wrongdoer may be able to reasonably foresee mental and emotional harm to a third person; he or she will not contemplate a particular or any psychiatric illness. This restriction, therefore, is simply an arbitrary means of limiting the number of claimants.[43]

The more we appreciate how disabling emotional harm can be, the more anomalous is the law's relative failure to provide redress when it is both serious and culpably caused. It is true that, for certain kinds of conduct, such as harassment and various discriminatory practices, there are now statutes that make compensation available for distress and injury to feelings.[44] However, apart from their piecemeal coverage, their broader significance is, as noted, in affirming the worth of individuals and the desire to advance social cohesion. The Protection from Harassment Act, for example, is important as a general statement about

---

[40] Scottish Law Commission, *Report on Damages for Psychiatric Injury*, (Edinburgh, The Stationery Office, 2004) No 196, paras 3.7–3.10. And see P Case, 'The Scottish Law Commission's *Discussion Paper on Damages for Psychiatric Injury*' (2003) 19 *Professional Negligence* 395, 396.

[41] See further below Ch 6, 171–4.

[42] See further below Ch 6, 177–9.

[43] *van Soest*, above n 5, 205.

[44] Eg, Protection from Harassment Act 1997, Race Relations Act 1976, Sex Discrimination Act 1975 and Disability Discrimination Act 1995.

respect for the individual, as well as for its more concrete goals of curbing persistent and menacing stalkers and compensating victims of intrusive behaviour. By the same token, anti-discrimination legislation affirms the importance of respect for the individual and social cohesion.

Such legislative developments, though intrinsically commendable, have introduced new anomalies in the way that the law distinguishes between different kinds and gradations of emotional and mental harm. For example, at its outer limits, the Protection from Harassment Act 1997 makes damages available for '*any anxiety*' caused by *apprehended, unintentional* harassment,[45] (emphasis added) without, one might add, providing a definition of 'harassment'. Causing emotional harm is not a precondition of liability,[46] but a claim for distress routinely features in such actions. Though most cases involve intentional behaviour, it suffices that a 'reasonable person' would think that the defendant's course of conduct amounted to harassment. Admittedly, the range of conduct meriting legal sanction under the rubric of 'harassment' defies concise definition, but the vagueness of the Act's approach leaves it open to criticism, especially as it also created three criminal offences.[47] If poorly drafted, it can at least be welcomed as an attempt to address the law's traditional undervaluation of emotional well-being. For our purposes, it is the contrast between the Act's broad scope and the general approach to 'non-physical' harm in the tort of negligence that is of particular interest. The availability of statutory redress for 'anxiety' from apprehended, unintentional harassment underlines the restrictive nature of the common law rules on 'mental harm' arising from demonstrably negligent conduct. Despite several opportunities to refashion these rules along more rational lines,[48] the House of Lords seems to have resigned itself to upholding a 'patchwork quilt of distinctions which are difficult to justify'.[49]

Underlying Hostility: Disparaging Intangible Harm and its Redress

Mind and Body

What underlying forces help to explain why the common law has been so reluctant to engage with the issue of intangible harm and provide redress for it? To

---

[45] Ss 1 (1), 1(2), 3(2) and 7(2). The House of Lords recently held that employers may be vicariously liable for breaches of the Act by their employees: *Majrowski v Guy's and St Thomas's NHS Trust* [2007] 1 AC 224.

[46] Under s 7(2), 'harassing' can *include* 'alarming' or 'causing distress' (emphasis added).

[47] Harassment of another; 'persuasive' harassment of others, and causing fear of violence: ss 1(1), 1(A) and 4(1), respectively. See further, AP Simister and GR Sullivan, *Criminal Law: Theory and Doctrine* (Oxford, Hart Publishing, 3rd edn, 2007) 410–13.

[48] *McLoughlin v O'Brian* [1983] 1 AC 410; *Alcock*, above n 11; *Page*, above n 9, and *White*, above n 12.

[49] *White*, above n 12, 500, *per* Lord Steyn.

begin with, there is the elusive nature of the 'mind' itself; the sense of mystery which has always surrounded it, reflected in the ancient use of the terms 'soul' and 'spirit' to signify the incorporeal. So far, we have referred to physical and mental harm as if they were wholly discrete phenomena. From at least the time of Plato onwards, scholars have posited various conceptions of the human mind as an enigmatic, non-physical entity, tenuously connected to the body in some obscure way. In the seventeenth century, Descartes formalised this intuition, in developing his dualistic account of mind and body as categorically distinct. They were, he maintained, separate thinking and physical substances, related by a special channel in the human brain (in the pineal gland), which carried influences from one to the other.[50] Though such details of Descartes' account were subjected to challenge[51] and ultimately abandoned, not only did dualism dominate scientific thought well into the nineteenth century, but its legacy survives, if in a more attenuated form. Among neurologists and psychiatrists differences persist over whether particular conditions are better described as presenting problems of the brain or of the mind. Meanwhile, the population at large still tends to think of mind and body as essentially distinct.[52]

Dualism is, however, very much at odds with the bulk of contemporary scientific thinking. The issue is, on one level, empirical. Advances in neuroscience have progressively demonstrated how closely physical and mental processes are related. There is mounting evidence that many mental disorders are attributable to an excess or deficiency of complex chemicals in the brain, and increasingly the brain, rather than the intangible 'mind', is being identified as the true site of much, if not all, mental illness:[53] 'the lack of obvious pathology does not necessitate reaching for a metaphysical explanation for symptoms', in preference to the 'lesion . . . in some recess of the brain, hidden from us at present but amenable to discovery in the fullness of time.'[54] There is a broad scientific consensus that, ultimately, all or virtually all 'mental' activity will be shown to be brain activity,[55] rendering the mind a redundant concept, 'the ghost in the machine'.[56]

Yet the idea of the mind as a separate entity remains deeply ingrained. Its cultural endurance is reflected in how naturally we still speak of the 'mind' and 'mental' attributes. The vocabulary of the non-physical 'mind' continues to hold

---

[50] Descartes, R, *Discourse on Method and the Meditations* (FE Sutcliffe (ed), London, Penguin Books, 1968).
[51] Spinoza, B, *Ethics* (1677) (Oxford, Oxford University Press, 4th edn, 1937, tr W Hale, revised edn, A Hutchinson Stirling).
[52] '[D]ualism still dominates popular thinking': N Humphrey, *Soul Searching: Human Nature and Supernatural Belief* (London, Chatto & Windus, 1995) 195.
[53] As increasingly recognised in the courts. Eg, *Morris v KLM Royal Dutch Airlines* [2002] QB 100, 113–114, *per* Lord Phillips MR.
[54] See B Mahendra, 'Mind and Body: Medicine and Law', in MDA Freeman and A Lewis (eds), *Law and Medicine: Current Legal Issues Vol 3* (Oxford, Oxford University Press, 2000) 559, at 567 and 559, respectively.
[55] R Gross, *Psychology: The Science of Mind and Behaviour* (London, Hodder & Stoughton, 3rd edn, 1996) 871–4.
[56] G Ryle, *The Concept of Mind* (London, Hutchinson, 1949).

sway, as does the use of the label 'mental illness' as a blanket term for disorders of the brain and nervous system.[57] We still balk at substituting 'brain illness' to describe various depressive and other disorders increasingly depicted in the medical literature as conditions of the brain.[58] In large measure, this is because the familiar language of the 'mind' conveys social meanings in ways which neurophysiological description cannot capture; just as the word 'signature' conveys a social meaning beyond the nerve activity and muscle movement involved in a given act of signing.[59] Mind language is still to be valued for its descriptive power, not least as a means of enabling patients to feel that their own attitude towards coping with their condition may help ameliorate it.

However useful and convenient for such purposes, mind language has served to bolster social and judicial resistance to compensation for those who suffer emotional harm. In this regard, the supposedly non-physical status of the mind has been an enduring stumbling block, its very intangibility often seized upon to assert that damage to it could not be quantified. It might be thought that scientific advance would, over time, consign outmoded social perceptions and legal analysis to history. Logically, if denial of liability rests on the absence of 'physical' damage, it cannot survive proof of such damage. Yet aversion to claims for 'emotional harm' has never been rooted in logic. Still bearing more than a trace of its historical and psychological legacy—an amalgam of religious beliefs, superstition, fear of the unknown and witchcraft—its prevailing modern rationale is an unsubstantiated fear of opening the floodgates. Whatever the explanatory power of brain science, the future scope of liability for mental and emotional harm will not, and should not, be determined by the chance discovery that particular stressors entail neurochemical damage and dysfunction. Any defensible legal regime for such harm should look to the social context in which it is experienced and make adequate provision for its disabling effects. For social and therefore legal purposes, the key questions today are whether harm has occurred for which legal redress is both appropriate and feasible. Unfortunately, the law's response to 'non-physical' harm still owes much to attitudes and policies that reflect a flawed socio-cultural legacy.[60]

The Stigmatisation of Mental Illness

Social stigma has always been at the heart of the diminished status accorded by the law to victims of mental and emotional harm. In the context of mental illness, the

---

[57] Cf '[t]he very name "Mental Health Act" ought to make us pause for thought. It implies that the domain of health and illness can validly be divided into separate categories of "mental" and "physical"': E Matthews, 'Mental and Physical Illness—An Unsustainable Separation?', in N Eastman and J Peay, *Law Without Enforcement: Integrating Mental Health and Justice* (Oxford, Hart Publishing, 1999) 47.

[58] MG Baker and M Menken, 'Time to abandon the term mental illness' *British Medical Journal* 2001; 322: 937.

[59] D Legge, *An Introduction to Psychological Science* (London, Methuen, 1975), cited in Gross, above n 55, 869.

[60] See P Bracken, *Trauma: culture, meaning and philosophy* (London, Whurr, 2002).

'unattractive and tenacious human trait of unfairly labelling and seriously disadvantaging others'[61] has a long history. In medieval times, mental suffering was routinely attributed to divine punishment or evil spirits.[62] Even when the worst excesses of the association with witchcraft began to fade, the belief persisted that mental suffering was punishment for sin and had to be fatalistically endured.[63] Although submissive resignation to divine providence declined during the Victorian era, it was succeeded by eulogies to self-help and moral fibre. This cultural shift served to legitimate the populist instinct that there is something inherently self-indulgent and frivolous, if not downright fraudulent, about claims for 'pure nervous shock'.[64] In the late nineteenth century:

> [e]ven doctors . . . took little interest in what was described as 'the vapours', and often refrained from giving treatment for many forms of mental disturbance which they rather contemptuously called 'nerves'.[65]

The early case law, from the 1880s onwards, reflected prevalent attitudes extolling the virtues of self-reliance, laced with mistrust of the fledgling discipline of psychiatry.

In one form or another, social stigma has continued to influence the law's approach to liability for psychiatric harm. Mental dysfunction remains a potent source of negative stereotyping,[66] ranging from lingering associations with 'madness' and violence to supposed lack of moral fibre, self-inflicted wounds and shamming. The demands of the 'abnormal' may be taken less seriously; the protestations of the 'whinger' and the 'malingerer' can readily be dismissed. This kind of hostility, which can exacerbate authentic suffering and any associated feelings of guilt, may also stem from a sense of unease in the presence of others unable to interact in a socially accepted manner.[67] Even when they are not perceived as threatening, their trials and tribulations seldom make for comfortable listening. Impatience in the presence of those who cannot cope or are incommunicative easily translates into scepticism about the extent or reality of their symptoms, fuelling resentment over the money, time and effort devoted to treating (let alone compensating) them.

---

[61] A Crisp, 'The tendency to stigmatise', *British Journal of Psychiatry* 2001; 178: 197,199.

[62] Mendelson, above n 34, ch 1.

[63] See, eg, VE Nolan and E Ursin, 'Negligent Infliction of Emotional Distress: Coherence Emerging from Chaos' (1982) 33 *Hastings Law Journal* 583, 604.

[64] H Teff, 'Liability for Negligently Inflicted Psychiatric Harm: Justifications and Boundaries' (1998) 57 *CLJ* 91, 92.

[65] WG Earengey, 'The Legal Consequences of Shock', reprinted in (1992) 60 *Medico-Legal Journal* 83, 85. This article first appeared in Vol 1 of the *Medico-Legal and Criminological Review* (1933). Earengey also suggested that the rule of evidence which until the mid-nineteenth century precluded direct testimony by plaintiffs could help explain the denial of a remedy for purely emotional suffering, since other witnesses would not have been able to give convincing proof of the plaintiff's state of mind. Ibid, 84.

[66] A Crisp, *et al*, 'Stigmatisation of people with mental illnesses', *British Journal of Psychiatry* 2000; 177: 4; P Hayward and J Bright, 'Stigma and mental illness: a review and critique', *Journal of Mental Health* 1997; 6: 345; Department of Health, *General Public Attitudes to Mental Health/Illness* (London, Department of Health, 1999).

[67] Cf E Goffman, *Stigma: Notes on the Management of Spoiled Identity* (New York, Prentice, 1963).

Subconsciously, at least, such reactions may mask more deep-seated concerns, including a common reluctance to confront our own vulnerability.[68] Psychological explanations along these lines seem necessary if we are to understand why claims to have been harmed emotionally, and, more specifically, attempts to obtain compensation for the harm, are so readily disparaged, often in extravagant terms.

When the stock criticism is levelled, in the media and elsewhere, that we have embraced a 'compensation culture',[69] actions for emotional trauma are very much to the fore, their denigration commonly taking the form of adverse comparison with claims for physical injury. Easy to portray as unworthy, they serve as a convenient symbol for the ills of the litigation process generally. One publication in 1999, itself bemoaning a growing 'culture of litigation',[70] inspired the following comment in a *Times* leader:

> Disability and pain resulting from *physical* injury, and certain extreme cases of psychological distress, clearly deserve compensation . . . But it does not follow that the ever-broadening spectrum of fusses and phobias can or should be remedied by a bulging bank balance.[71] (emphasis added)

One is tempted to ask why it is 'clear' that *any* physically induced suffering merits compensation, but only 'certain' *extreme* instances of psychological distress. Perhaps the existence of liability for minor physical harm is not seen as problematic because such claims are rarely pursued and, if trivial, can be excluded under the *de minimis* rule.[72] Yet the practical considerations which dissuade people from litigating apply at least as much, if not more, to claims for minor emotional harm.[73] It is not obvious that, if generally available, they would be any more frequently made. The passage quoted above is also revealing in implicitly labelling many victims of non-physical injury as mercenary hypochondriacs. Physical suffering is assumed to be authentic; much emotional disturbance is deemed suspect.

Negative perceptions of mental and emotional disturbance are not merely the stuff of casual conversation and the occasional newspaper column or television programme. They are sufficiently socially ingrained to influence both medical and legal decision-making. Psychiatric diagnoses plainly serve an important therapeutic purpose in authenticating the 'sick role'. However, as well as prejudicial attitudes towards psychiatry within the wider world of medicine,[74] within the

---

[68] Cf, 'As individuals, families or communities, we frequently wish to avoid the victims of trauma or disasters. These victims remind us of our own profound vulnerability to unexpected and unplanned for events.' RJ Ursano, BG Lang and CS Fullerton, 'The Structure of Human Chaos', in Ursano, Lang and Fullerton (eds), *Individual and Community Responses to Trauma and Disaster: The Structure of Human Chaos* (Cambridge, Cambridge University Press, 1994) ch 18, 405.

[69] See further below 18–20 and Ch 5, 149–51 and 158.

[70] F Furedi, *Courting Mistrust: The hidden growth of a culture of litigation in Britain* (London, Centre for Policy Studies, 1999).

[71] *The Times*, 24 Apr 1999.

[72] *De minimis non curat lex* (the law does not concern itself with trifles). See *Grieves v FT Everard & Sons*, above n 3 [71] *per* Lord Scott.

[73] See below Ch 5, 152. Cf *van Soest*, above n 5, 202–3, *per* Thomas J.

[74] P Byrne, 'Psychiatric Stigma: Past, Passing and to Come', *Journal of the Royal Society of Medicine* 1997; 90: 618.

discipline itself there is a lingering unease about the risks of 'over-medicalising' social problems.[75] As Summerfield puts it:

> [I]nsofar as the general public has come to associate such disagreeable features as lunacy, depravity and dangerousness with the day-to-day work of psychiatrists, it might be said that almost all psychiatric interventions carry a potential for stigmatization as a side-effect.[76]

The discipline may no longer be demonised, but criticism of lack of rigour and overreach persists.

For present purposes, the issue is not whether the psychiatric net is cast too wide in routine treatment, or open to abuse to achieve regulatory ends. It is rather the scope for overdiagnosis in the context of litigation, when certain mental states are imprecisely defined.[77] More especially in an adversarial system, making liability dependent on proof of a 'recognisable psychiatric illness' almost invites a measure of overdiagnosis on the part of expert witnesses. Of course, as doctors readily concede, medicine in general is not an exact science—the diagnosis of physical conditions can also be imprecise. To represent psychiatric disorders as uniquely problematic in this respect both perpetuates negative stereotyping and understates the specificity of many diagnostic categories within psychiatry. Be that as it may, when there is exaggeration of mental conditions in the court setting, it serves to reinforce any negative attitudes among the judiciary about psychiatry itself. It would be surprising if such attitudes had not influenced the law, encumbered as it is in this sphere by outmoded precedent, and shaped by judges whose own professional environment has traditionally favoured a robust, individualistic outlook. Underlying the policies which set the boundaries of liability for psychiatric illness, and for emotional harm in general, there is still more than a hint of what Jones has aptly dubbed the ' "pull yourself together" school of legal analysis'.[78]

It is true that, throughout the 100 years or so during which the courts have been grappling with compensation for psychiatric injury, there have been judges ready to question the unscientific premises on which the legal framework has rested, and to recognize the potential gravity of the harm. As early as 1915, in a workmen's compensation case, Lord Shaw observed that:

---

[75] See D Summerfield, 'Does psychiatry stigmatize?', *Journal of the Royal Society of Medicine* 2001; 94: 148, and D Summerfield, 'The invention of post-traumatic stress disorder and the social usefulness of a psychiatric category', *British Medical Journal* 2001; 322: 95–8. See also correspondence, *ibid*, 1301 ff.

[76] Summerfield, 'Does Psychiatry Stigmatize?', above n 75, 148.

[77] Eg, the difficulty of distinguishing between 'normal' grief and 'pathological grief disorder'. And see Law Com Rep No 249, above n 27, paras 3.27–3.29, and M Jones, 'Liability for Psychiatric Damage: Searching for a Path between Pragmatism and Principle', in J Neyers, E Chamberlain and S Peel (eds), *Emerging Issues in Tort Law* (Oxford, Hart Publishing, 2007) 130–34.

[78] M Jones, 'Liability for Psychiatric Illness—More Principle, Less Subtlety?' [1995] 4 *Web Journal of Current Legal Issues*, para 1. Cf 'For too long earlier generations of judges have regarded psychiatry and psychiatrists with suspicion, if not hostility': *McLoughlin v O'Brian*, above n 48, 433, *per* Lord Bridge.

[i]f compensation is to be recovered under the statute or at common law in respect of an occurrence which has caused dislocation of a limb, on what principle can it be denied if the same occurrence has caused unhinging of the mind? The personal injury in the latter case may be infinitely graver than in the former, and to what avail—in the incidence of justice, or the principle of law—is it to say that there is a distinction between things physical and mental? . . . Indeed it may be suggested that the proposition that injury so produced to the mind is unaccompanied by physical affection or change might itself be met by modern physiology or pathology with instant challenge.[79]

In 1941, one dissenting judge boldly referred to:

the erroneous notion that nervous shock was a purely subjective state of mind, a mental or emotional condition existing in the region of pure idea, instead of being, as in fact it is, an actual physical disorder of the nervous constitution of the body.[80]

Similar sentiments are increasingly to be found in leading judgments. For example, in *White v Chief Constable of South Yorkshire Police*, Lord Steyn acknowledged that:

Nowadays courts accept that there is no rigid distinction between body and mind. Courts accept that a recognisable psychiatric illness results from an impact on the central nervous system. In this sense therefore there is no qualitative difference between physical harm and psychiatric harm. And psychiatric harm may be far more debilitating than physical harm.[81]

However, Lord Steyn then proceeded to outline 'at least four distinctive features of claims for psychiatric harm which in combination may account for the differential treatment' in law.[82] These he identified as 'greater diagnostic uncertainty'; unconscious disincentive to rehabilitation; the potentially wide class of claimants, and the risk of defendants being burdened with liability disproportionate to their tortious conduct. How distinctive these features are, and to what extent, if at all, they justify the differential treatment, will be examined in detail later.[83] For the present, it is salutary to bear in mind the observation of Lord Nicholls that:

[d]enial of the existence of a cause of action is seldom, if ever, the appropriate response to fear of its abuse.[84]

That said, Lord Steyn's reservations about liability for psychiatric harm reflect the prevailing view in the House of Lords. They clearly indicate that, by itself, even

---

[79] *Coyle or Brown v John Watson Ltd* [1915] AC 1, 14. The case did not itself turn on liability for psychiatric injury. See also *Griffiths v R & H Green & Silley Weir Ltd* (1948) 81 Lloyd's L Rep 378, 380, *per* Birkett J.
[80] *Bourhill v Young* 1941 SC 395, 432, *per* Lord Justice-Clerk Aitchison.
[81] See *White*, above n 12, 492. Cf 'It is now accepted by medical science that recognisable and severe *physical* damage to the human body and system may be caused by the impact, through the senses, of external events on the mind': *McLoughlin v O'Brian*, above n 48, 418, *per* Lord Wilberforce; cf *Page v Smith*, above n 9, 181–3, *per* Lord Browne-Wilkinson.
[82] See *White*, above n 12, 493.
[83] See below Ch 5, 141–66.
[84] *Phelps v Hillingdon London Borough Council* [2001] 2 AC 619, 667.

overwhelming consensus in the scientific debate over the nature of psychiatric harm would not signal abandonment of the law's restrictive stance.

Nor, it should be said, are academic legal commentators at one in advocating a broader approach, although this does seem to be the majority view.[85] Indeed, Stapleton, in the context of a more general thesis about future priorities for tort law, has exhorted the courts to 'wipe out recovery for pure nervous shock', on the basis that 'no reasonable boundaries for the cause of action [can] be found, and this [is] an embarrassment to the law'.[86] Serious reservations were also voiced by Atiyah in his book, *The Damages Lottery*:

> By far the most worrying development in the law relating to the kind of harm for which you can recover damages, however, has been the huge growth of claims in recent years for damages for 'nervous or emotional shock' or, what nowadays tends to be called post-traumatic stress.[87]

In *White*,[88] Lord Steyn quotes the following passage from Weir's *Casebook on Tort*:

> [T]here is ... no doubt that the public ... draws a distinction between the neurotic and the cripple, between the man who loses his *concentration* and the man who loses his leg. It is widely felt that being frightened is less than being struck, that trauma to the mind is less than lesion to the body. Many people would consequently say that the duty to avoid injury to strangers is greater than the duty not to *upset* them. The law has reflected this distinction as one would expect, not only by refusing damages for grief altogether, but by granting recovery for other psychiatric harm only late and grudgingly, and then only in very clear cases.[89] (emphasis added)

When the distinction is drawn in such tendentious terms, doubtless many people would pronounce physical harm more serious than emotional harm. Major physical injury (loss of a leg) is contrasted with what is made to sound like relatively minor mental injury (loss of concentration), and the duty not to 'injure' strangers is contrasted with the duty not to 'upset' them. To say, without more, that it is 'widely felt ... that trauma to the mind is less than lesion to the body' is scarcely illuminating. In effect, Weir was saying that physical injury is *categorically*

---

[85] See *Mullany and Handford's Tort Liability for Psychiatric Damage* (Sydney, Lawbook Co, 2nd edn, 2006). Cf Jones, 'Liability for Psychiatric Illness—More Principle, Less Subtlety?', above n 78; Mendelson, *The Interfaces of Medicine and Law*, above n 34. And see Law Com Rep No 249, above n 27, para 1.7.

[86] J Stapleton, 'In Restraint of Tort', in P Birks (ed), *The Frontiers of Liability*, vol 2 (Oxford, Oxford University Press, 1994) 95–6. Contra H Teff, 'Liability for Negligently Inflicted Psychiatric Harm: Justifications and Boundaries', above n 64; NJ Mullany, 'Fear for the Future: Liability for Infliction of Psychiatric Disorder', in Mullany (ed) *Torts in the Nineties* (Sydney, LBC Information Services, 1997) 105–107, and Mullany, 'Negligently Inflicted Psychiatric Injury and the Means of Communication of Trauma—Should it Matter?', in NJ Mullany and The Honourable Justice AM Linden, *Torts Tomorrow—A Tribute to John Fleming* (Sydney, LBC Information Services, 1998) 162.

[87] *The Damages Lottery* (Oxford, Hart Publishing, 1997) 56. Cf A Weir, [1993] *CLJ* 520, 521 (review of Mullany and Handford, *Tort Liability for Psychiatric Damage*, 1st edn, 1993) and 'Errare Humanum Est', in P Birks (ed), *The Frontiers of Liability*, above n 86, 107.

[88] Above n 12, 493.

[89] T Weir, *A Casebook on Tort* (London, Sweet & Maxwell, 7th edn, 1992) 88. The passage does not appear in subsequent editions.

perceived as more 'real' and more serious: 'a broken leg is a broken leg is a broken leg'. Yet such a sweeping generalisation begins to unravel as soon as particular instances of harm are compared. The image of the 'cripple' in fact diverts our attention from the reality that much physical injury is relatively minor, does not take long to heal and, for that matter, over a wide range of conditions (whiplash, post-concussional syndrome, various back injuries, arthritis, migraine, etc) can be just as difficult to prove as the supposedly more impalpable forms of mental harm.

Nonetheless, a broad perception of harm to the psyche as less serious than physical harm continues to influence legal liability rules, its cultural and psychological roots fortified by persistent fears of proliferating claims. As regards liability in negligence, such fears were very evident in the early litigation on 'nervous shock', notably in cases concerned with the traumatic consequences of railway accidents.[90] Insistence on identifiable physical injury, so as not to leave 'a wide field open for imaginary claims',[91] was to prove something of a lifeline for the railway companies throughout the Victorian era. In what was then a high-risk activity, lack of third party insurance would have spelt ruin if shock from collisions had been perceived to have a physical effect on the spinal cord, thereby justifying compensation for the victims of what became known as 'railway spine'. Here, too, we see the mind-body controversy being played out. Did such shock indicate a form of physical injury, as Erichsen was claiming in the 1860s,[92] or was it a purely emotional reaction, which many late nineteenth century neuro-psychiatrists saw as afflicting only the psychologically predisposed? The latter view was put forward by Page,[93] himself a consulting physician for a railway company. It was naturally seized upon by the companies, whose anxieties about over-extensive liability found favour with those judges who were disposed to share the suspicions of Page and other doctors about malingering.[94]

The 'Blame and Claim' Culture

In both tone and substance, today's rhetoric of resistance to liability for emotional harm is not that far removed from the forebodings of the Victorian era. It is fashionable to assert that we have embraced an unhealthy 'culture of complaint' and a 'compensation culture'—a 'blame and claim' mind-set allegedly spawning a host of unjustifiable law-suits. We are told that 'people have embraced the stupid legalistic idea that the courts exist to indemnify them against life', and that 'the compensation culture is the culture of cowards'.[95] Typical of this libertarian genre is Furedi's lament for the passing of self-help, *Courting Mistrust: The hidden growth of a culture of litigation in Britain*:

[90] See, eg, *Victorian Railways Commissioners v Coultas* (1888) 13 App Cas 222 (PC).
[91] *Ibid*, 226.
[92] JE Erichsen, *On Railway and Other Injuries of the Nervous System* (Philadelphia, Henry C Lea, 1866).
[93] HW Page, *Injuries of the Spine and Spinal Cord Without Apparent Mechanical Lesion and Nervous Shock in their Surgical and Medical Aspects* (London, J and A Churchill, 1883).
[94] See further Mendelson, above n 34, ch 2.
[95] B Appleyard, 'Living Dangerously in our Dreams', *The Independent*, 26 Jul, 1995.

The tendency to blame others for one's predicament represents a profoundly disturbing statement about the way society regards the potential that human beings have for controlling their lives. It assumes that most of the time people are passive, pathetic creatures unable to make real choices and who therefore should not be expected to be responsible for their actions. From this perspective, suffering and injury are most likely to be presented as the fault of others. The culture of compensation encourages people to inflate these injuries and to present every traumatic experience as a 'life sentence'. It appears that people are so influenced by the negligent actions of others that they become 'scarred for life' and can rarely recover from their traumatic experience.[96]

In similar vein, asserts Polly Toynbee, a 'groundswell of litigation [is] . . . turning us into grasping whingers and self-pitying milksops'.[97]

With due allowance for poetic licence, it is telling that the decision to seek compensation for personal harm allegedly inflicted negligently can generate such invective and resentment. Most journalistic accounts of the 'compensation culture' follow a well-worn pattern. A litany of 'shock, horror' claims is retailed: the social worker who recovered £175,000 for 'stress at work'; the police officers who sued for trauma at Hillsborough; the doctor who, after inadvertently pricking herself on a needle left on a hospital trolley, received £460,000 for 'needle-phobia', and, inevitably, the American case of a customer scalded by McDonald's coffee who was awarded the equivalent of nearly £2 million. Much public disquiet is fuelled by incomplete accounts of untypically large awards and perceived distributive inequities. By omitting key factual details and skirting over relevant legal principles, notably on how damages are assessed, the claims are often presented in such a way as to evoke maximum disbelief and derision.

In the highly publicised McDonald's case, for example, the coffee, at a temperature of 190F was more than 20 degrees above the industry standard, and though the company had dealt with more than 700 claims from burned customers over 10 years, they did not reduce the temperature or issue warnings to customers. In this instance, the coffee spilt over an elderly woman's groin when, as a passenger in a stationary car, she opened the lid, causing third-degree burns. Her injuries necessitated two stays in hospital, painful skin grafts, with scarring and disability for over two years, and left her with initial medical expenses of $11,000. McDonald's offered her $800 and subsequently rejected a mediated settlement for $225,000. At trial, the jury's compensatory award of $200,000 was reduced to $160,000 for contributory negligence, but they also awarded $2.7 million punitive damages.[98] On appeal, the punitive damages were reduced to $480,000, a figure which attracted far less publicity than the amount originally awarded by the jury.[99]

---

[96] *Courting Mistrust*, above n 70, 38.

[97] P Toynbee, 'A culture of compensation makes victims of us all': *The Guardian*, 21 Apr, 1999.

[98] Punitive or exemplary damages are discretionary awards over and above the amount deemed appropriate for compensation, intended to punish and deter defendants for outrageous conduct. Controversial in a civil law context, in England they are available only in limited circumstances. Most importantly, these do not include negligence actions. See further *Aggravated, Exemplary and Restitutionary Damages*, Law Commission, Law Com Rep No 247 (1997).

[99] See B Glassner, *The Culture of Fear* Washington Center for Consumer Law (New York, Basic Books, 1999). For a detailed account of the case and its coverage in the media, see W Haltom and

Although, at least until very recently, there has been little by way of reliable data, there is a widespread belief that people are increasingly prone to seek compensation for personal injury.[100] Even if this be the case, constant use of the pejorative expression 'compensation culture', with its powerful image of rapacious claimants spurred on by equally rapacious lawyers, is apt to mislead. For example, as Peysner has argued, any greater disposition to sue could be less emotively portrayed as a rational reaction to the erosion of collective welfare provision.[101] More specifically, conventional assumptions about a thriving 'compensation culture' reflect the more explicitly commercial nature of the litigation process now that Legal Aid is no longer available for most personal injury claims. In its place, the 'conditional fee' system has been introduced, under which claimants' lawyers charge no fee if the case is lost but are entitled to a success fee over and above their normal costs if the claimant wins.[102] The conditional fee option is not the only sign of a move towards greater and more overt commercialisation. Also significant has been the lowering of restrictions on advertising by lawyers, coupled with the entry into the litigation market of claims management companies. Some of these companies have deployed 'hard sell' advertising and direct marketing tactics to attract clients, whose cases they then administer, before referring them on to firms of solicitors.[103] Doubtless, all these developments have enhanced claims-consciousness. However, it is easy to exaggerate the extent to which they influence the actual incidence of litigation. Solicitors who specialise in personal injury litigation may be reluctant to handle relatively small claims on a conditional fee basis, unless the evidence is compelling. It is their overall risk exposure, and the role played by insurers, that largely dictate which cases are pursued.[104]

Embracing Liability for Mental and Emotional Harm

Some Modern Statutory Developments

In an ordinary negligence claim, the barriers to recovery for 'pure' psychiatric harm now mainly hinge on fears of ever-increasing liability. Yet, in various pockets of the law, the right to sue for more common and often less severe forms of mental and emotional harm has been expanding. Much of this expansion has

---

M McCann, *Distorting the Law: Politics, Media and the Litigation Crisis* (Chicago, University of Chicago Press, 2004) ch 6.

[100] See further Ch 5, 149–51 and 158.
[101] J Peysner, 'Compensation Crazy: Do We Blame and Claim Too Much?', in E Lee, *et al*, *Compensation Crazy: Do we blame and claim too much?* (London, Hodder & Stoughton, 2002) 4.
[102] For more detailed examination of this system, see below Ch 5, 153–5.
[103] Claims management companies have recently been made subject to regulation. See below Ch 5, 153.
[104] See further below, Ch 5, 153–5.

resulted from legislation. 'Injury to feelings', for example, has been a basis for compensation under anti-racial and sex discrimination legislation since the mid-1970s,[105] and under the Disability Discrimination Act since 1995.[106] Since 1982, consolatory damages for grief and sorrow have been automatically available to bereaved spouses and parents of minors following wrongful death,[107] and, as we have seen, a broadly-conceived statutory notion of harassment now permits actions for 'any anxiety' or 'distress' caused.[108]

The structure of the anti-discrimination Acts is testimony to their social and symbolic significance. This is reflected in the strict nature of the liability, in that the unlawful conduct need not be intentional or even negligent; indeed, it can be 'indirect'—fair in form but discriminatory in effect. Some special provisions have also been introduced to ease the burden of proof in such claims.[109] The fact that the award for bereavement under the Fatal Accidents Act is a fixed sum,[110] and is available without proof of actual distress, indicates its primarily symbolic nature. Nonetheless, in addition to registering respect for the dignity and worth of those affected, all these statutes do provide compensation for emotional harm.[111] By contrast, the tort of negligence does not afford redress for much mental and emotional harm that may also seriously undermine the dignity and self-worth of those affected.

That modern statutes increasingly provide remedies for emotional harm is understandable. Perhaps more surprising, and easily overlooked, is the sheer extent of such redress at common law.[112] By no means limited to recent developments, it includes a diverse range of actions where emotional harm, in one form or another, can be a significant feature of the claim. In certain kinds of contract, in a number of torts, some of very ancient origin and, not least, in the general availability of damages for 'pain and suffering' in personal injury actions, the courts have viewed such recovery with equanimity, notwithstanding the cultural forces

---

[105] Race Relations Act 1976, s 57(4); Sex Discrimination Act 1975, s 66(4).
[106] Disability Discrimination Act 1995, s 8 (4).
[107] Fatal Accidents Act 1976 (as amended by the Administration of Justice Act 1982, s 3) s 1A.
[108] Protection from Harassment Act, 1997, ss 3(2) and 7(2), respectively.
[109] Eg, since 2001, new regulations reversing the burden of proof have made it easier to establish sex discrimination in employment. If the primary facts allow the tribunal to conclude that less favourable treatment resulted from a discriminatory act, it will uphold the complaint unless the employer can prove that it did not commit that act.
[110] Currently £10,000. See Damages for Bereavement (Variation of Sum) (England and Wales) Order 2002 (SI 2002/644). See also, Law Commission, No 263, *Claims for Wrongful Death* (London, HMSO 1999) and Department for Constitutional Affairs, *The Law on Damages*, Consultation Paper (CP 9) (London, Department for Constitutional Affairs, 2007), para 7. In Scotland, there is no fixed sum, and the claim for 'grief and sorrow' under the Damages (Scotland) Act 1976, s1(4) can cover both ordinary grief and a pathological grief reaction : *Gillies v Lynch* 2002 SLT 1420 (Outer House).
[111] 'Bereavement' is not defined in the Act, but it has been said that the award 'clearly encompasses both consolation of grief and sorrow and compensation for loss of society': *Bagley v North Herts Health Authority* (1986) 136 *NLJ* 1014, 1015, *per* Simon Brown J.
[112] See P Giliker, 'A "New" Head of Damages: Damages for Mental Distress in the English Law of Torts' (2000) 20 *Legal Studies* 19.

previously described.[113] Before outlining some common law instances of liability for emotional harm, broadly defined, we should take note of one particular category of claim: work-related *psychiatric* illness. Its central interest, for our purposes, lies in how the applicable law differs from the ordinary negligence regime for psychiatric harm. This is important for our general critique of that regime. Insofar as 'developments away from the nervous shock mainstream'[114] are not tainted by its unseemly distinctions,[115] they could prove influential in any reassessment of its more restrictive rules. In fact, as will emerge when we examine the 'mainstream' cases more fully,[116] those 'rules' are far from doctrinally secure,[117] despite the House of Lords' assertion that the courts are powerless to renounce them,[118] and despite subsequent cases that have cast further doubt on their soundness in law.[119]

The Special Case of Psychiatric Illness Caused by Stress at Work

In the past, claims for injury to health at work were overwhelmingly concerned with physical harm and its consequences. The setting was frequently industrial and the main focus of 'safety' in employment law was physical welfare. In the late twentieth century, the fast-growing service economy and rapid advances in information technology entailed new kinds of working environments and work patterns. Whether or not the resulting pressures have been more 'stressful' than those endured by earlier generations is highly debatable.[120] What is beyond dispute is the heightened sensitivity nowadays to occupational stress and, at least until recently, a corresponding growth in the number of claims to which it gave rise.[121]

Like any negligence action for 'pure' psychiatric harm, work stress claims require proof of a 'recognisable psychiatric illness'. They are, however, distinctive in bearing the mark of the multiple legal sources, statutory as well as common law,

---

[113] See below 26–31.
[114] A Sprince, '*Page v Smith*—being "primary" colours House of Lords' Judgment' (1995) 11 *Professional Negligence* 124, 126.
[115] See further, below Ch 4.
[116] See below Ch 3.
[117] See esp Lord Goff's powerful dissent in *White*, above n 12, and the conjoined decisions of the Australian High Court of Justice in *Tame v New South Wales; Annetts v Australian Stations Pty Ltd* [2002] 211 CLR 317.
[118] *White*, above n 12, 500, *per* Lord Steyn and 504, *per* Lord Hoffmann.
[119] Eg, *W v Essex County Council* [2001] 2 AC 592; *Leach v Chief Constable of Gloucestershire Constabulary* [1999] 1 WLR 1421, CA; *Farrell v Avon Health Authority* [2001] Lloyd's Rep Med 458; *Creutzfeld-Jakob Disease Litigation Group B Plaintiffs v Medical Research Council* [2000] Lloyd's Rep Med 161; *McLoughlin v Jones* [2002] 2 WLR 1279, CA, *North Glamorgan NHS Trust v Walters* [2003] Lloyd's Rep Med 49, CA. See further below Ch 4.
[120] See D Wainwright and M Calnan, *Work Stress: The making of a modern epidemic* (Buckingham, Open University Press, 2002).
[121] Cf the 'next growth area', NJ Mullany, 'Fear for the Future: Liability for Infliction of Psychiatric Disorder', in Mullany (ed), *Torts in the Nineties*, above n, 86, 107, at n 24. And see *Hatton v Sutherland* [2002] EWCA Civ 76 [3], *per* Hale LJ. For evidence of a decline in the incidence of such claims, see below Ch 5, 158–9 and 164–5.

which have shaped employer responsibility for the health and safety of the work force. Clearly, the harm in these cases is not *shock*-induced. By definition, illness due to occupational stress develops over time, through the cumulative effects of prolonged exposure to a distressing environment or set of circumstances. In this respect, it lacks what, in *Alcock*, was deemed a prerequisite of liability in the claims made by the Hillsborough relatives.[122] They, of course, were 'secondary victims', and it is possible, though this was not expressly asserted, that the House of Lords intended to confine the shock requirement to such cases.[123] In any event, the primary/secondary classification, if conceived of as spanning the entire range of actions for 'pure' psychiatric harm, seems unable to cater meaningfully for occupational stress claimants, since they are not necessarily exposed to foreseeable physical danger or the reasonable fear of it, a commonly asserted precondition of primary status.

Interestingly, not until the early 1990s was the requirement of shock-induced harm authoritatively presented as a legal rule for any claimants. Earlier on, it may have been no more than a contingent or often an assumed feature of the cases.[124] The emphasis placed on the need for 'sudden shock' in *Alcock*[125] revitalised the law's much-criticised but lingering attachment to the unscientific emphasis on fright as the cause of psychiatric harm—the isolated, traumatic event, encapsulated in the archaic terminology of 'nervous shock'. Its obligatory nature seemingly derives from its salience in *Alcock*, where it was boldly asserted that 'sudden and unexpected shock' had been an aspect of all the previous English authorities.[126] In reality, cumulative assaults on the nervous system more accurately describe the impact on the victim in a number of cases, not least *McLoughlin v O'Brian*,[127] decided by the House of Lords itself only a few years before *Alcock*. Since it is now well known that instant trauma is far from being the only possible cause of psychiatric illness, continued insistence on it as a requirement of liability, even if only in 'secondary' claims, is hard to explain, except as yet another artificial device for restricting their number.

At all events, the elaborate rule structure for 'nervous shock' in mainstream cases developed with scant reference to the employment setting, attracting little attention in claims for work-related non-physical harm. Such claims may now be based on various grounds: express or implied terms in individual contracts of employment,

---

[122] *Alcock*, above n 11.
[123] Several cases suggest that certain types of primary claimant must prove that their psychiatric illness was shock-induced. See, eg, *Hegarty v EE Caledonia Ltd* [1997] 2 Lloyd's Rep 259, 266, *per* Brooke LJ; *Young v Charles Church (Southern) Ltd* (1997) 39 BMLR 146, 150 and 152, *per* Evans LJ, and see Law Commission, No 249, *Liability for Psychiatric Illness* (London, HMSO, 1998), para 2.62. For a contrary view, see *Sion v Hampstead Health Authority* [1994] 5 Med LR 170, 173, *per* Staughton LJ and 176–7, *per* Peter Gibson LJ.
[124] See generally H Teff, 'The Requirement of "Sudden Shock" in Liability for Negligently Inflicted Psychiatric Damage' (1996) 4 *Tort Law Review* 44.
[125] See *Alcock*, above n 11, and below, Ch 4, 115.
[126] *Alcock* above n 11, 411, *per* Lord Oliver.
[127] *McLoughlin v O'Brian*, above n 48. See further below Ch 3, 59. See also *Chadwick v British Transport Commission* [1967] 1 WLR 912, 918, and *Jaensch v Coffey* (1984) 155 CLR 549.

and rights statutorily conferred on employees[128] or required by European law,[129] as well as the employer's basic common law duty, in negligence, to take reasonable care for the safety of workers.[130] The resultant competing lines of authority have produced some unresolved tensions and a degree of conceptual confusion.

In 1995, Northumberland County Council was sued for stress-induced psychiatric harm by John Walker, an overburdened social worker. The judge's finding of liability was based on breach of the employer's general duty, in negligence, to provide a safe system of work,[131] but he was also at pains to acknowledge an implied duty to like effect in the contract of employment.[132] *Walker v Northumberland County Council* was later expressly approved by the Court of Appeal in the important decision of *Hatton v Sutherland*, where it was described as a 'landmark' case.[133] In common with earlier cases involving a contract of employment,[134] the analysis in *Walker* did not refer to the special rules that had developed in 'nervous shock' cases and was manifestly not based on *shock*-induced injury. In fact, the Court of Appeal in *Hatton* confirmed that:

> [t]here are no special control mechanisms applying to claims for psychiatric ... injury arising from the stress of doing the work which the employee is required to do ... The ordinary principles of employers' liability apply.[135]

The comparative readiness, in this particular pocket of negligence law, to permit recovery for *stress*-induced psychiatric harm reflects, in part, the expectation that employers will take the mental aspects of 'health and safety at work' seriously due to the proximity of relationship inherent in the contractual nexus. As Lord Steyn has observed:

---

[128] See, eg, the Employment Rights Act 1996, and regulations under the Health and Safety at Work Act 1974. And see guidance provided by the Health and Safety Executive, aiming to 'secure the health, safety and welfare of persons at work': *Stress at Work : a guide for employees* (1995).

[129] See esp European Framework Directive on Health and Safety: Directive 89/391/EEC. And see K Wheat, 'Mental Health in the Workplace (1)—"Stress" Claims and Workplace Standards and the European Framework Directive on Health and Safety at Work' (2006) *Journal of Mental Health Law* 53.

[130] *Wilsons & Clyde Coal Co v English* [1938] AC 57.

[131] *Walker v Northumberland County Council* [1995] 1 All ER 737. An appeal resulted in an out-of-court settlement of £175,000.

[132] Eg, 'the scope of the duty of care owed to an employee to take reasonable steps to provide a safe system of work is *co-extensive* with the scope of the implied term as to the employee's safety in the contract of employment.' (Emphasis added) *Ibid*, 759. See further L Dolding and R Mullender, 'Law, Labour and Mental Health' (1996) 59 *MLR* 296.

[133] *Hatton v Sutherland*, above n 121 [20].

[134] In *Johnstone v Bloomsbury Health Authority* [1992] QB 333, the Court of Appeal refused to strike out a claim by a junior doctor that his contractual obligation to work very long hours had caused him exhaustion and depression. The case was later settled out of court: Croner's *Employment Briefing*, issue 82, 30 May, 1995. In *Petch v Customs and Excise Commissioners* [1993] ICR 789, a civil servant's claim failed for lack of reasonable foreseeability.

[135] *Hatton*, above n 121, [43]. This formulation is not easy to reconcile with the House of Lords' denial of a remedy to the traumatised on-duty police in *White*. They too, because of the Chief Constable's negligent crowd control, were exposed to the risk of psychiatric illness by doing the work that they were required to do. However, *White* decided that the duty of care in the employment relationship is subject to the 'ordinary rules of the law of tort', including the special limitations on claims by secondary victims, such as the police at Hillsborough. And see below Ch 3, 91.

Since 1909[136] our knowledge of the incidence of stress-related psychiatric and psychological problems of employees, albeit still imperfect, has greatly increased. What could in the early part of the last century dismissively be treated as mere 'injured feelings' is now sometimes accepted as a recognisable psychiatric illness ... Nowadays courts generally accept that they must act on the best medical insight of the day. Specifically, this realism has taken root in the field of employment law ... The need for protection of employees through their contractual rights, express and implied by law, is markedly greater than in the past.[137]

'One possible way of describing a contract of employment in modern terms', said Lord Steyn, 'is as a relational contract',[138] a term indicative of the modern legal approach to the employment relationship as one of mutual trust and confidence.[139] The case for allowing damages for stress-induced harm can only be strengthened by the law endorsing a more personalised conception of the relationship. Although there are some difficulties in reconciling *Walker* with *White*,[140] the line of authority stemming from *Walker* remains important in holding that stress-induced psychiatric harm is actionable in a setting where stress is not uncommon. It would become even more significant if it were to hasten the total demise of the single, shocking event requirement in negligence actions for psychiatric harm, a requirement which is increasingly subjected to judicial and academic criticism. As Lord Justice Henry put it:

> what matters is not the label on the trigger for psychiatric damage, but the fact and foreseeability of psychiatric damage, by whatever process.'[141]

So far, we have been considering the law's (limited) readiness to see stress as a legitimate 'trigger' for liability. It is important not to lose sight of the fact that, in the 'work stress' cases, the restrictive liability threshold of a 'recognisable psychiatric illness' remains. It could be argued that, as a matter of relativities, this high threshold is hard to square with judicial rhetoric about the dignity of labour. In one House of Lords decision, Lord Hoffmann observed that employment provides 'an identity and a sense of self-esteem', and Lord Millett endorsed the view

---

[136] Ie since the leading case of *Addis v Gramophone Ltd* [1909] AC 488, where the House of Lords established the general prohibition against damages for mental distress in contract.

[137] *Johnson v Unisys Ltd* [2003] 1 AC 518, 532. See also D Nolan, 'Recovering Damages for Psychiatric Injury at Work' (1995) 24 *Industrial Law Journal* 280.

[138] *Johnson v Unisys*, above n 137.

[139] See generally *Mahmud v Bank of Credit and Commerce International* [1998] AC 20, esp 46 and 50, per Lord Steyn, and *Johnson v Unisys Ltd*, above n 137, 532–3.

[140] See above n 135.

[141] *Frost v Chief Constable of South Yorkshire* [1997] 3 WLR 1194, 1208, CA. Cf *W v Essex CC*, above n 119, and the rejection of the sudden shock requirement in *Tame v New South Wales; Annetts v Australian Stations Pty Ltd* [2002] 211 CLR 317. Cf the Law Commission's conclusion that *Walker* 'represents a just development in the law'. Law Commission, *Liability for Psychiatric Illness* (1998), above n 27, para 7.22. And see *Tredget and Tredget v Bexley Health Authority* [1994] 5 Med LR 178 and other cases of elongated shock, esp *North Glamorgan NHS Trust v Walters*, above n 119, in which the requirement of a single 'horrifying event' was deemed satisfied by a series of events over 36 hours, each of which had an immediate impact. See further Ch 4 below, 118–20.

expressed in a Canadian case that 'work is one of the defining features of people's lives'.[142] In an earlier Canadian case, Chief Justice Dickson had stated that 'A person's employment is an essential component of his or her sense of identity, self-worth and emotional well-being.'[143] These sentiments seem to suggest that, in the work setting, respect for human dignity forms part of the rationale for compensation. If so, it is difficult to see why, in principle, the liability threshold for occupational stress should be so much higher than the statutory thresholds for unintentional harassment or discrimination. More generally, if we take the view that emotional well-being is intrinsically linked to sense of identity and self-worth, why should its negligent disruption, whether or not work-related, afford a remedy only for those whose affliction has reached the exacting threshold, mysteriously conjured up from nowhere, of a 'recognisable psychiatric illness'?[144]

The Scope for Liability at Common Law

Mental Distress resulting from Breach of Contract

Some broadening of liability for injured feelings and distress can be detected within the modern law of contract, where traditionally its scope was distinctly limited. In *Watts v Morrow*, Lord Justice Bingham said:

> A contract-breaker is not in general liable for any distress, frustration, anxiety, displeasure, vexation, tension or aggravation which his breach of contract may cause to the innocent party'.[145]

This was, he acknowledged, a rule based on considerations of policy rather than because such harmful consequences were not foreseeable. Until late into the twentieth century, the dominant view was that damages were never available *solely* for mental distress or injured feelings caused by a breach of contract, [146] but only when such harm resulted from *physical* injury or inconvenience.[147] The 1970s saw the Court of Appeal adopting a more receptive stance, initially in respect of contracts specifically for entertainment and enjoyment,[148] and then, if briefly,

---

[142] *Johnson v Unisys Ltd*, above n 137, 539, *per* Lord Hoffmann, and 549, *per* Lord Millett, citing *Wallace v United Grain Growers Ltd* (1977) 152 DLR (4th) 1, 33, *per* Iacobucci J.

[143] *Public Service Employee Relations Act* (Alberta) (1987) *re*, 1 SCR 313, 368, *per* Dickson CJ.

[144] See *Hinz v Berry*, above n 6, 42, *per* Lord Denning MR. See further below Ch 2, 52–4.

[145] *Watts v Morrow* [1991] 1 WLR 1421, 1445.

[146] *Hamlin v Great Northern Railway Co* (1856) 1 H & N 408, 411, *per* Pollock CB; *Hobbs v London & South Western Railway Co* (1875) 10 QB 111, 122; *Addis v Gramophone Co* [1909] AC 488; *Groom v Crocker* [1939] 1 KB 194. In an earlier case, damages had been awarded to smooth injured feelings when the plaintiff had been turned off a ferry before reaching his destination, 'with contumely' and 'in a contemptuous manner': *Coppin v Braithwaite* (1844) 8 Jur 875.

[147] *Burton v Pinkerton* (1867) LR 2 Ex 340; *Hobbs*, above n 146.

[148] *Jarvis v Swan Tours* (1973) QB 233, CA. Cf *Diesen v Samson* 1971 SLT 49 (wedding photos). In *Jackson v Horizon Holidays Ltd* [1975] 1 WLR 1468, CA, the award to the claimant extended to compensation, on his own behalf, for his family's loss of enjoyment.

for distress and anxiety from breach of a contract of employment.[149] Drawing back from this latter development, the Court was to hold that distress awards were available only in contracts intended 'to provide peace of mind or freedom from distress',[150] where the 'very object' of the contract was to provide pleasure, relaxation and objectives of a like nature.[151] In commercial cases, on the other hand:

> [c]ontract-breaking is treated as an incident of commercial life which players in the game are expected to meet with mental fortitude.[152]

The issue was revisited in *Farley v Skinner*,[153] a case concerning the purchase of a country house near Gatwick. In response to a specific question about aircraft noise, the defendant surveyor negligently stated in his report that the property was unlikely to be seriously affected. The House of Lords upheld an award of £10,000 for breach of contract in respect of discomfort, distress and inconvenience experienced by the purchaser, whose claim for diminution in value of the property had been dismissed on the facts. *Farley*,[154] then, adopts a relatively broad view of redress for emotional harm in contract. It sufficed that provision of the amenity was a major or important part of the contract, rather than its 'very object'. The purchaser had been denied the tranquillity which, to the knowledge of the defendant, he considered important in ensuring his pleasure, relaxation or peace of mind; he was entitled to damages for mental distress and disappointment.[155] There was no explicit finding of *physical* inconvenience and discomfort to which a claim for directly related mental suffering could have attached, though it was accepted that 'physical inconvenience' might be broadly construed so as to include the adverse consequences of aircraft noise.[156] In Lord Steyn's view, the exorbitant amount of time devoted to what was a comparatively simple case 'underlines the importance, in the quest for coherent and just solutions in such cases, of simple

---

[149] In a situation 'which within the contemplation of the parties would have given rise to vexation, distress and general disappointment and frustration': *Cox v Philips Industries Ltd* [1976] 1 WLR 638, 644, *per* Lord Denning MR.

[150] *Bliss v South East Thames Regional Health Authority* [1987] ICR 700, 718, *per* Dillon LJ. However, an award (subject to a statutory maximum) may be available for distress, under 'unfair dismissal' legislation.

[151] *Watts v Morrow*, above n 145, 1445, *per* Bingham LJ.

[152] *Johnson v Gore Wood & Co (a firm)* [2002] 2 AC 1, 49, *per* Lord Cooke.

[153] *Farley v Skinner* [2002] 2 AC 732.

[154] Applying *Ruxley Electronics and Construction Ltd v Forsyth* [1996] AC 344.

[155] See D Capper, 'Damages for Distress and Disappointment—Problem Solved?' (2002) 118 *LQR* 193; Capper, 'Damages for Distress and Disappointment—The Limits of *Watts v Morrow*' (2000) 116 *LQR* 553, 556.

[156] Several of the speeches in *Farley* point to uncertainty as to whether the aircraft noise could have been properly characterised as causing *physical inconvenience and discomfort*, such that damages would have been recoverable in contract, even in the absence of *physical injury*: *Hobbs*, above n 146. Lord Hutton, for example, was prepared to view the effect on the claimant's hearing as meeting this test: see above n 153, 762–4, and Lord Scott conjectured that being awoken at night by aircraft noise, and so being unable to sleep because of worry and anxiety, could be described as 'physical' phenomena: 768.

and practical rules'.[157] In contract, it seems, we need not resign ourselves to a 'patchwork quilt of distinctions which are difficult to justify.'[158]

Damages in Tort for Mental Distress

In tort, too, relatively 'simple and practical rules' apply to emotional harm when it results from physical injury. Damages for mental distress of the kind suffered in *Farley* are routinely awarded as general damages under the head of 'pain and suffering'. In the words of the Law Commission, '[t]he expression "pain and suffering" is now almost a term of art', and:

'[s]uffering' ... denotes the mental or emotional distress which the plaintiff may feel as a consequence of the injury: anxiety, worry, fear, torment, embarrassment and the like.[159]

Nothing better demonstrates that, in negligence, what now underpins resistance to liability for 'pure' psychiatric harm, and precludes recovery for 'mere' mental distress, is the floodgates fear. When this fear is assuaged because the claim is parasitic on one for physical injury, the other supposed justifications for denying or restricting liability seem to fade away. What would otherwise be seen as suspect and intangible becomes genuine and quantifiable.

Moreover, outside the realm of negligence, tort damages for 'mere' emotional distress are quite widely available, even in the absence of physical damage. They have, from very early times, been allowed as part of the general compensatory award when mental hurt of some kind was either an integral element of the tort, as in assault,[160] or commonly resulted from it, as when someone has been wrongfully deprived of their liberty (false imprisonment). Even the core medieval tort of battery only required unwanted physical *contact*, not injury, with compensation for mental distress being justified as a by-product of the interference with physical integrity. In defamation, although the main function of damages is to compensate for loss of reputation, the total award can also reflect injury to feelings.[161] In malicious prosecution, the willingness of courts to permit damages for emotional harm derives in part from the tort's affinity with the interests at stake in defamation and false imprisonment.

---

[157] *Farley v Skinner*, above n 153, 741. Cf *GW Atkins Ltd v Scott* (1991) 7 Const LR 215, 221: 'There may be many circumstances where a judge has nothing but his common sense to guide him in fixing the quantum of damages, for instance for pain and suffering, for loss of pleasurable activities or for inconvenience of one kind or another.' *Per* Sir David Cairns. Approved by Lord Lloyd in *Ruxley*, above n 154, 374, and endorsed by Lord Hutton in *Farley v Skinner*, above n 153, 760.

[158] *White*, above n 12, *per* Lord Steyn.

[159] Law Commission, Consultation Paper No 140, *Damages for Personal Injury: Non-Pecuniary Loss*, London, HMSO, 1995) 2.10. Such an award includes suffering or likely suffering from awareness of a reduced expectation of life: Administration of Justice Act, 1982, s 1 (1) (b).

[160] Putting someone in reasonable fear of immediate battery.

[161] Eg, 'the distress, hurt and humiliation which the defamatory publication has caused': *John v MGN Ltd* [1997] QB 586, 607, Sir Thomas Bingham MR, delivering the judgment of the Court.

Far from being aberrational, then, compensation for emotional distress is part of the normal award across a wide range of tortious conduct. It is also sometimes available as 'aggravated damages', for additional mental anguish, injury to feelings or humiliation caused by the outrageous or high-handed way in which the defendant has behaved. Such awards are most evident in torts strongly associated with injury to feelings and self-esteem.[162] They would seem not to be available in negligence,[163] partly due to confusion over whether their real purpose is punitive, as the need for outrageous conduct by the defendant would suggest.[164] However, when reviewing this abstruse area, the Law Commission strongly endorsed the view that such damages were remedial. They favoured substituting the rubric 'damages for mental distress' for 'the misleading phrase "aggravated damages"', in order that 'a more coherent perception, and so development of, the law on damages for mental distress should be possible'.[165] It would then be easier, the Commission noted, for such damages to become available in negligence.[166]

It is noteworthy that, as well as advocating use of the label 'mental distress' for the emotional impact of outrage or indignation, the Commission was at least prepared to contemplate its redress in negligence, the central and most extensive area of tort litigation. That said, aggravated damages constitute a relatively minor feature of tort law, and the scope for such awards in negligence would be limited. More telling is the half-hearted response, in negligence generally, to a category of harm more readily accommodated in other torts for centuries within the standard compensatory process. Surveying the tort field as a whole,[167] Giliker points to several factors which, even in the absence of physical injury, have been influential in encouraging redress for emotional hurt: notably whether the tort was intentional and/or seen as especially reprehensible, and whether it was actionable per se, implying the protection of interests other than or beyond physical integrity. The issue, she maintains, falls squarely within the realm of value judgement: the extent to which the perceived gravity of the wrongdoing should be deemed to outweigh the floodgates fear:

> [T]he floodgates argument may be seen to lie at the core of tort law in its attempt to provide a workable compensatory system of civil liability. Unless this objection can be overcome, damages for mental distress cannot stand as a legitimate head of damages in the law of tort.[168]

---

[162] Eg, battery, false imprisonment, defamation, deceit and statutory torts of discrimination on grounds of race or gender.
[163] *Kralj v McGrath* [1986] 1 All ER 54, 60–61, approved in *AB v South West Water Services Ltd* [1993] QB 507, though the position is not entirely clear since *AB* was overruled by *Kuddus v Chief Constable of Leicestershire* [2002] 2 AC 122.
[164] Cp punitive or exemplary damages. See *Thompson v Commissioner of Police for the Metropolis* [1998] QB 498.
[165] Law Commission, No 247, *Aggravated, Exemplary and Restitutionary Damages*, (London, HMSO, 1997) para 1.9.
[166] *Ibid*, para 2.43.
[167] P Giliker, 'A "New" Head of Damages: Damages for Mental Distress in the English Law of Torts', above n 112.
[168] *Ibid*, 22.

Undoubtedly the floodgates argument in its primary sense—fear of a proliferation of claims from a single event[169]—continues to exert great influence in the sphere of psychiatric illness. In *Page v Smith*, Lord Lloyd stated that a concern not to 'open the door too wide' was 'a very important consideration in claims by secondary victims. It is for this reason', he said:

> that the courts have, as a matter of policy, rightly insisted on a number of control mechanisms. Otherwise, a negligent defendant might find himself being made liable to all the world.[170]

Certainly the floodgates issue cannot simply be wished away. However, neither should its significance be exaggerated. Our contention is that this is precisely what has happened with claims in negligence for mental harm, prompting excessive judicial caution that has been reinforced by the indelible image of the mass disaster at Hillsborough. There is no cogent evidence that a more defensible formulation of the substantive law would be bound to broaden the scope of recovery to an unsustainable degree. Moreover, the cost of any resultant increase in litigation has to be weighed against the benefits of a legal regime that is more coherent and more responsive to the needs of deserving claimants. The challenge is to provide a proportionate legal response to serious suffering, taking into account the economic constraints on remedial demands. These constraints may require a liability threshold, but it is not self-evident that it should be as circumscribed as 'recognisable psychiatric illness'.[171] We will argue that, under a less restrictive liability model, fears of proliferating claims could be allayed by adjustments to the compensatory regime for personal injury cases generally.

Monetary recompense for personal injury can have several functions. Its most straightforward practical purpose is to replace lost income and expenses (pecuniary loss). In addition, there is compensation for the injury and its effects—pain and suffering, incapacity and loss of amenity or enjoyment of life (non-pecuniary loss). The common law requires 'full compensation' for pecuniary loss and, traditionally, did so for non-pecuniary loss; 'full' in the sense that, insofar as monetary redress would allow, wrongdoers must 'right the wrong' by making good the whole loss attributable to their conduct. However, whereas calculating lost income and expenses is a readily comprehensible and broadly achievable goal, putting a meaningful price on mental and emotional suffering is plainly more problematic. And incommensurability is not the only concern. Overwhelmingly, tort damages are, in the first instance, paid either by insurers or out of public funds, with the cost subsequently spread more widely within the community at large. It is unclear to what extent compensation for non-pecuniary loss should be seen as a social

---

[169] The argument is sometimes used to refer to the fear of many claims from a mass of separate events.
[170] See *Page* above n 9.
[171] See further below Ch 6, 171–85. See also, *van Soest*, above n 5, *per* Thomas J (dissenting), and *Mullany and Handford's Tort Liability for Psychiatric Damage* (Sydney, Lawbook Co, 2nd edn, 2006), ch 2.

priority in a system where, for the most part, it is ultimately funded by consumers and the general public, not by the individual wrongdoer.[172] Given scarce public resources, a cogent case can be made for introducing a threshold for recovering non-pecuniary damages in personal injury claims generally.

To expand the liability threshold for 'non-physical' harm beyond recognisable psychiatric illness *and* remove other restrictive controls on liability is not easily achievable. As a matter of practical politics, some quid pro quo would be needed to alleviate the unsubstantiated but commonly voiced fears that such reform would be unaffordable. We will argue that non-pecuniary loss should be subject to a monetary threshold; that tapered awards should be retained for moderately severe injuries, and more substantial awards for the most serious ones.[173] Within the general category of non-pecuniary loss, mental harm normally attracts much smaller amounts than physical harm, unsurprisingly, given conventional assumptions about their relative gravity. Consistent with our general theme, we would argue for some realignment in this respect.

Some Criminal Law Comparisons

The primacy accorded to 'physical' injury in tort has its criminal law counterpart in the traditional preoccupation with 'bodily' harm. Though our essential focus is on redress in the civil law, it is interesting to note a comparable, culturally-driven reluctance to criminalise the infliction of intangible harm—a further indication of assumptions about relative gravity. The reluctance is all the stronger because of the stigma and other potentially serious consequences of conviction. A related concern is that, since much everyday conduct can have adverse emotional effects on others, imposing penal sanctions too readily could inhibit socially defensible behaviour. It is no easy matter to gauge how far penal sanctions can justifiably, and efficaciously, be deployed to enhance social and emotional tranquillity, over and above what is required for the maintenance of social order. More clarity is needed as to the range of conduct; the mental element, and the degree of impairment of the victim's mental health, that justify criminalisation.[174] In the sphere of personal harm, parts of the substantive criminal law are still hampered by outmoded, mid-Victorian statutory provisions, which themselves echo the attitudes and terminology to be found in yet more distant case law.

The wording of the Offences against the Person Act, 1861, was designed to cater for basic forms of non-fatal physical injury: to '*wound* or *inflict* any grievous *bodily* harm',[175](emphasis added) and '*assault* occasioning *bodily* harm'[176](emphasis

---

[172] See further below Ch 6, 179–83.
[173] *Ibid*, 177–9.
[174] J Horder, 'Rethinking Non-Fatal Offences against the Person' (1994) 14 *OJLS* 335.
[175] Offences against the Person Act 1861, s 20.
[176] *Ibid*, s 47.

added). Such expressions are ill-suited to capture the nature and subtleties of emotional wounds, and recent judicial efforts to this end have a distinctly artificial tone. For example, some years ago, the House of Lords held, in *Ireland*, that repeated silent telephone calls which cause psychiatric illness can amount to 'occasioning actual *bodily* harm'[177](emphasis added). In *Burstow*, a conjoined decision, it held that 'stalking' which causes a serious psychiatric condition can amount to '*inflicting* grievous *bodily* harm'[178](emphasis added).

Although the underlying sentiments in the above cases are laudable, the reasoning looks suspiciously like a repudiation of the mind-body distinction in the face of statutory provisions which assert it. As it stands, the Offences Against the Person Act cannot satisfactorily accommodate emergent demands relating to emotional injury. A fresh vocabulary, more naturally applicable to broader conceptions of harm, is required, as was recognised by the Law Commission in a Report published 15 years ago, a few years before the decisions in *Ireland* and *Burstow*.[179] The Report was the basis of Home Office proposals for reform, in 1998,[180] which incorporated a new draft Offences Against the Person Bill. In the Bill, 'injury' was defined as including 'any impairment of a person's mental health'.[181] As yet, however, these proposals have not been implemented.

The criminal law is not, of course, immune to shifting social attitudes. In the Protection from Harassment Act 1997, we have already encountered an example of legislation that makes it a criminal offence to pursue a course of conduct that causes alarm or distress. As *Ireland* and *Burstow* demonstrate, although constrained by statutory wording and precedent, senior members of the judiciary have begun to take a more creative stance on non-physical injury. In another decision, at around the same time,[182] the then Lord Chief Justice, Lord Bingham, drew attention to the well-documented, and distinctive, psychological effects of burglary in a dwelling,[183] urging sentencers to take them into account. Such developments can only be fully understood in the broader context of a criminal justice system gradually becoming more attentive to the interests of victims and to crime's emotional impact on them.

From early times, the English criminal process has been conceptualised as a contest between the accused and the state. Characteristic of this adversarial model has been the development of due process rights for defendants; it had no role for victims, as such. In recent years, there has been much criticism that the system

---

[177] *Ireland* [1998] AC 147.
[178] *Burstow* confirmed the Court of Appeal decision in *Chan-Fook* [1994] 1 WLR 689. And see J Gardner, 'Stalking' (1998) 114 *LQR* 33; M Hirst, 'Assault, Battery and Indirect Violence' [1999] *Crim LR* 557.
[179] Law Commission, No 218, *Legislating the Criminal Code: Offences against the Person and General Principles*, (London, HMSO, 1993).
[180] Home Office, *Violence: Reforming the Offences Against the Person Act 1861* (London, Home Office, 1998).
[181] Offences Against the Person Bill, cl 15 (3).
[182] *Brewster* [1998] 1 Cr App R 220, 225–7.
[183] See M Maguire and T Bennett, *Burglary in a Dwelling* (London, Heinemann,1982).

often treats victims insensitively and is insufficiently attentive to their needs and concerns, a view that has gained added force from the growing tendency for international tribunals to recharacterise 'victims' rights' as 'human rights'.[184] Some shortcomings are relatively easily rectified. Examples include providing fuller information about the progress of cases, and more appropriate facilities at the court itself. More controversial is the call for victims to have a direct role in decision-making processes: allowing their feelings to feature in bail decisions and the charges brought, as well as, prior to sentence, admitting in evidence personal accounts of how offences have affected their lives.[185]

For courts to grant victims special procedural rights in the criminal process marks a further step towards attaching penal consequences to the infliction of emotional harm. Such recognition of crime's emotional impact on its victims has implications for the criminal justice system which could go well beyond modifying its essentially adversarial nature. Taken to its logical conclusion, the quest for more direct involvement of victims is a plea for alternative processes which either co-exist with standard procedures or by-pass the established criminal justice forum altogether. Mirroring developments in other common law jurisdictions, there have been experiments along these lines in the UK since the 1980s, using principles of 'restorative justice',[186] a problem-solving, participatory approach which involves the parties themselves and the wider community.[187] The growth of victim-offender mediation programmes illustrates the growing interest in exploring new ways of alleviating the emotional hurt of victims.

Caveat and Conclusion

Although considerations of justice, rationality and coherence favour broadening the scope of redress for harm to the psyche, a caveat needs to be entered. The perception that we have embraced a compensation culture that fosters excessive claiming must be openly addressed, and not solely because it is so widespread. There are also related concerns voiced about legal overreach fostering an unduly risk-averse society, in which beneficial risk-taking is discouraged and legitimate self-expression constrained. For example, given the range of social activities and

---

[184] See, eg, J Doak, 'The Victim and the Criminal Process: an analysis of recent trends in regional and international tribunals' (2003) 23 *Legal Studies* 1, 31–2.

[185] See eg, E Erez, 'Who's Afraid of the Big Bad Victim? Victim Impact Statements as Victim Empowerment and Enhancement of Justice' [1999] Crim LR 545; A Ashworth, 'Victim's Rights, Defendant's Rights and Criminal Procedure', in A Crawford and J Goodey (eds), *Integrating A Victim Perspective into Criminal Justice* (Aldershot, Ashgate, 2000) ch 9, and A Sanders *et al*, 'Victim Impact Statements: Don't Work, Can't Work' [2001] Crim LR 447.

[186] See A von Hirsch, *et al*, (eds), *Restorative Justice and Criminal Justice: Competing or Reconcilable Paradigms* (Oxford, Hart Publishing, 2003).

[187] Notably in schemes for the disposal of minor juvenile crime. See C Pollard, 'Victims and the Criminal Justice System: A new Vision' [2000] *Crim LR* 5.

commercial relations which foreseeably pose a threat to mental and emotional stability, there are a number of settings in which legal redress would often be inappropriate. Depending on the circumstances, these might include such diverse situations as the predictable psychic impact of a health authority conveying accurate but disturbing news and a television company reporting it; an employer announcing redundancies, or a partner ending a personal relationship. Routinely, unpalatable information has to be conveyed, often by officials working under pressure, to people already in a state of heightened anxiety. In an era characterised by rising expectations of frank as well as sensitive disclosure, the importance attached to free self-expression in personal relations, and to explicit coverage of newsworthy events, needs to be weighed against the equally legitimate assumption that unwelcome news should not be imparted in an insensitive and foreseeably damaging manner.

It will, however, be argued that the concerns about proliferating claims and legal overreach have been overstated, and that a reversion to established and more coherent negligence principles is achievable provided limited modifications are made to the compensatory regime. Meanwhile, manifestly deserving claimants are thwarted by rules that have long been a blot on the legal system, perpetuating a mismatch of law and medicine. Far from the judiciary being unaware of the mismatch, the case law is now replete with statements acknowledging the potential gravity of psychiatric harm and bemoaning the unscientific nature of the legal framework. In *Page v Smith*, Lord Lloyd went as far as to assert that, in a claim by a 'primary' victim, there was 'no justification for regarding physical and psychiatric injury as different "kinds" of injury',[188] in that they both constitute 'personal' injury.

Unfortunately, both from a medical and legal perspective, this essentially enlightened view is contestable when applied too literally. As Sprince points out, scientifically, it may be too reductivist to treat physical and psychiatric injury as 'one and the same',[189] and as a legal proposition it can create serious difficulties as regards the appropriate attribution of blame. For example, suppose that your negligent conduct could foreseeably have caused a very minor physical injury but instead caused a wholly unforeseeable major psychiatric disorder. It is far from clear that you should be held liable for the psychiatric disorder, as is now the case in claims by 'primary' victims, simply because 'personal' injury was foreseeable and has occurred.[190]

However, to the extent that Lord Lloyd's assertion indicates concern that mental well-being should not be devalued, it should be welcomed. Where the defendant *is* clearly blameworthy, it is invidious to insist on artificial barriers for want of a proven 'physical' link: it is neither desirable nor necessary to await definitive proof of neuro-chemical change in order for so-called secondary claimants to

---

[188] *Page*, above n 9, 190.
[189] See A Sprince, 'Negligently Inflicted Psychiatric Damage: a medical diagnosis and prognosis' (1998) 18 *Legal Studies* 59, 71.
[190] *Ibid*, 72–6. Cf Jones, above n 77, 119. And see below Ch 3 at n 130 and related text.

succeed. Equally, it is unreasonable to insist on proof of a 'recognisable psychiatric illness'. The prevailing liability threshold is too narrowly conceived and the scope for recovery by 'secondary' victims unduly limited. In contrast to the senior judiciary's defeatist stance, a more responsive approach began to emerge at the turn of the century in the reform proposals of the English and Scottish Law Commissions. Unfortunately, the Government's very recent, and belated, reaction to the English Commission's proposals does not augur well for change in the immediate future.[191] In the following chapters, we trace the major developments in civil liability for causing mental and emotional harm and propose an alternative approach towards determining when, and according to what priorities, compensation for such harm is warranted.

---

[191] Department for Constitutional Affairs, *The Law on Damages*, Consultation Paper (CP 9), (London Department for Constitutional Affairs, 2007). See further, below Ch 6, 188–9.

2

The Development of Redress for Emotional Harm and Nervous Shock

'Harm' at Common Law

Minimum Actionable Harm at Common Law

IN ANGLO-SAXON TIMES, when England effectively had no central government, different parts of the country were largely governed by local customary laws. A standardised ('common') law only began to emerge after the Norman Conquest, as a key element in the pursuit of centralised control and social cohesion. The primary goals of the emergent common law, civil as well as criminal, were to promote stability and prevent disruption. In these respects, most of the civil wrongdoing which constituted tort law in medieval times was barely distinguishable from crime. They both centred on the kinds of harm seen as most likely to disturb the 'King's Peace', namely, physically injuring people and seizing or damaging their property. As a precautionary measure, they also prohibited conduct which threatened such a train of events. One thing that the common law did not do, however, was to analyse in any depth what would suffice as actionable harm. Since it did not dwell on the outer limits of liability for harm in general, its relative disregard of the threshold for harm to the psyche is hardly surprising.

English tort law, as it began to develop during the thirteenth century, covered a wide range of wrongdoing for which the perpetrator could be required to provide redress. The most prominent and pervasive area of tort was trespass, and the threshold of liability for trespass, in its various forms,[1] was, and remains, very low. The conduct had to be direct, but actual damage or injury was not required. It was enough that someone had, without your consent, entered your land or touched your body (battery)[2] or interfered with your goods. As tangible damage was not a *necessary* ingredient of liability, there was simply no need for judges to define it when analysing trespassory conduct.[3]

---

[1] Trespass to land, trespass to the person, trespass to goods.
[2] Or had given you reason to believe that they were about to touch your body (assault).
[3] See P Catala and JA Weir, 'Delict and Torts: A Study in Parallel (Part III)' (1964) 38 *Tulane Law Review* 663, 665–70.

It is true that the extent of any damage could affect the level of compensation, but the linkage was somewhat imprecise. Although, for a wide range of violent injuries, monetary redress was specified as far back as the Anglo-Saxon era, it then took the form of a fixed tariff, akin to a fine, and was normally paid by a transfer of cattle or goods. Just as this system was largely designed to prevent blood feuds, so, too, in medieval times, the ultimate objective of damages for trespass to the person was to minimise the risk of retaliation and social disorder. The size of an award might sometimes have been influenced by the perceived degree of affront to the claimant and, doubtless in particular cases, by the gravity of the injury itself. However, all this was far removed from the much later conception of damages, as an individualised attempt to achieve 'full' compensation, insofar as money can, by restoring injured claimants to their pre-tort condition.

If concern to stamp out the merest potential threat to the 'King's Peace' made it unnecessary to explore the concept of damage in trespass, there was, at least in principle, scope for judicial analysis of minimum liability requirements in other areas of tort law. In a medieval action for harm caused *indirectly*, such as the various careless forms of civil wrongdoing that foreshadowed the now dominant tort of negligence, proof of actual damage was, and remains, essential. Precisely because 'damage' was a defining characteristic of such liability, it would have been natural enough for judges to decide what could count for this purpose. Similarly, in the tort of nuisance, damages were available, inter alia, for personal discomfort caused by someone who had indirectly interfered with another's right to the enjoyment of land. Here, the threshold requirement that the interference had to be 'substantial' and 'unreasonable' meant that judges would sometimes have indicated, at least in broad terms, what could amount to the requisite level of interference.

Yet even outside the confines of trespass, there was little sustained judicial focus on the meaning of damage.[4] This apparent gap in the system owes much to the distinctive nature of English civil procedure and, in particular, to the central role of the jury after the Norman Conquest. For many centuries, judges directed juries only on the general nature of the relevant law. Whether there was liability on the particular facts of a case, and, if so, how much to award by way of damages, were determined by the jury, who did not give reasons for their decisions.[5] In effect, then, unless 'damage' was a defining feature of a tort, judges did not need to give even cursory consideration to its meaning. Nor, in early times, did they pronounce on damages. Gradually, over several centuries, they first advised and later instructed juries on the measure of damages, eventually acquiring the authority to set aside jury awards as excessive or inadequate. Not until the mid-nineteenth century was the judge *required* to instruct the jury on the measure of damages, and

---

[4] A concept which, in English law, 'has never been a central topic of discussion': *ibid*, 665.

[5] '[T]he medieval jury had an almost unlimited flexibility to impose liability where it thought it appropriate': D Ibbetson, *A Historical Introduction to the Law of Obligations* (Oxford, Oxford University Press, 1999) 199.

misdirection in this respect became a ground for a new trial.[6] It was only in the late 1950s that the use of juries was abandoned for most types of civil action.

Although what counted even as physical damage was seldom tackled head-on or explored at length in the cases, it could have been addressed obliquely in several ways. In the development of the law of negligence, for example, a judicial determination that no 'duty of care' existed in the particular circumstances, or that the damage suffered was 'too remote', might reflect (or conceal) policy-driven doubts as to the appropriateness of providing compensation for the particular harm which had occurred.[7] The perceived triviality of a claim could itself be one such factor. It has long been the practice of the courts to overlook very trivial harm, whether carelessly or intentionally caused, by taking a 'de minimis' view of technically unlawful behaviour, such as minor physical contact in crowded places.[8]

Even in torts which do have a liability threshold, it is perhaps unsurprising that there has been limited judicial analysis of what it actually entails. As Stapleton has pointed out, in practice very few cases would reach the courts unless they had self-evidently passed the relevant threshold.[9] In negligence, a case involving marginal physical injury is now only likely to be fully litigated when it holds out the prospect of substantial damages for *non*-physical harm—damages often unavailable in the absence of 'physical' injury![10] In the past, if the threshold issue was addressed at all, it was largely treated as a matter of commonsense, requiring little by way of explanation, and the courts relied heavily on evidence of some physical manifestation. Increasingly, however, scientific and medical advance has forced them to consider afresh notions such as 'ascertainable', 'material', and 'physical' damage, nowadays in such diverse contexts as the contamination of land by radioactive waste[11] and the development of pleural plaques from asbestos dust, inducing clinical depression for fear of a future terminal disease.[12]

---

[6] *Blake v Midland Railway Co* (1852) 18 QB 93. See also McCormick, CT, *Handbook on the Law of Damages* (St Paul, Minn, West Publishing Co, 1935), ch 2; Law Commission, Consultation Paper No 140, *Damages for Personal Injury: Non-Pecuniary Loss* (London, HMSO,1995) 7 (at n 4).

[7] Cf 'What qualifies as actionable damage is a question of policy largely defined by the "duty" rules'. JG Fleming, *The Law of Torts* (Sydney, LBC Information Services, 9th edn, 1998) 216.

[8] Cf, in the criminal law context, the interpretation of 'actual bodily harm' under the Offences against the Person Act, 1861, s 47, as 'any hurt or injury calculated to interfere with the health or comfort of [the victim]', provided it is more than 'transient or trifling': *Donovan* [1934] 2 KB 498 (CCA). Cf to describe as 'actual bodily harm' minor abrasions and a bruise on the face 'went to the very margin of what was meant by that term': *Christopher Jones* [1981] Crim LR 119.

[9] 'This phenomenon of a clear sufficiency of actionable damage means that in the vast majority of cases the court is never required to assess what at the minimum is necessary to constitute actionable damage in negligence': J Stapleton, 'The Gist of Negligence' (1988) *LQR* 213, 214.

[10] Cf 'even the production of tears is a physical consequence and discomfort': *Brown v The Mount Barker Soldiers' Hospital Inc* [1934] SASR 128, 131, per Piper J. And see *Stephen v Riverside Health Authority* [1990] 1 Med LR 261 (minor symptoms, eg moist spots, tenderness and a rash on the breast following mammography, which caused the claimant to fear that an overdose of radiation had put her at increased risk of cancer).

[11] *Blue Circle Industries plc v Ministry of Defence* [1999] Ch 289. And see C Witting, 'Physical Damage in Negligence' (2002) 61 *CLJ* 189.

[12] See *Grieves v FT Everard* [2007] UKHL 39. And see below Ch 4, 110–13.

Early Legal Views on Intangible Harm

Several factors account for the law's historically limited engagement with emotional damage. Apart from its understandable preoccupation with physical injury and social disorder, its foundational concepts took shape long before the rise of science, let alone the emergence of psychiatry. That being so, it was virtually programmed to entrench primitive suspicions and prejudices about 'invisible', intangible harm. This is not to say that such harm was deemed an improper basis for damages. The point is rather that when it featured in claims for, say, assault, battery, nuisance or defamation, it was in a subsidiary and derivative capacity, tacked on to a claim for physical damage or for the infringement of a right.[13]

Just as with physical injury, the underlying impetus for assuaging hurt feelings was to prevent social upheaval. Concern about the emotional impact of wrongdoing on the claimant may well have influenced particular awards, but the law's acknowledgement of it in both civil and criminal sanctions:

> occurred remarkably early, not so much because it felt any singular tenderness for such claims, as that they happened to become identified with the early law's unremitting concern for public order.[14]

What was true for trespass to land applied also to assault: causing reasonable apprehension of imminent physical contact was both a crime and a tort, not due to the intrinsic fright or distress which it typically engendered, but because it constituted the kind of affront which threatened the King's Peace. In libel, and certain forms of slander, it was the attack on reputation which formed the gist of the action. If additional damages were awarded for injured feelings, it was also at least as much to minimise the risk of retaliation or duelling as to compensate for any accompanying emotional hurt.[15] Even in nuisance, damages for personal discomfort from interference with the use and enjoyment of land were indirectly geared to social stability. Being contingent on the claimant's proprietary amenity interest, their ultimate purpose was to reflect the diminished value of the land.

The above examples further suggest that, if and when they took emotional distress into account in awarding damages, juries, possibly with judicial encouragement, would have been influenced by the relative importance socially assigned to particular legal interests, and by the presumed sense of outrage, humiliation and hurt feelings which interference with them produced. Juries may well have been culturally attuned to the notion that emotional distress, or at least injured pride, would result from trespass or interference with a plaintiff's proprietary or reputational interests. There are parallels here with the longstanding discretion, in

---

[13] Cf 'We have to distinguish between the typical suffering and the interest which the law protects, for, though a judge charged with assessing an award must often have been much influenced by the distress, it was not the distress that triggered the liability': P Birks, *Harassment and Hubris: The Right to an Equality of Respect* (John Maurice Kelly Memorial Lecture, University College Dublin, 1996) 12.

[14] JG Fleming, *Introduction to the Law of Torts* (Oxford, Clarendon Press, 1967) 193.

[15] Ibid.

respect of certain torts, to award 'aggravated' damages, in the modern sense of additional compensation,[16] where injury to feelings has been exacerbated by the defendant's bad motive or otherwise outrageous, wilful conduct. The degree of distress so caused would normally influence the amount awarded, even if the ultimate justification for such damages may have been the denial of the right to respect.[17] As we have seen, it was to remove the punitive historical connotations of 'aggravated damages' that the Law Commission recommended changing the rubric to 'mental distress'.[18]

From the fourteenth century onwards, via the action on the case, the ambit of tortious liability expanded to include indirect, unintentional but careless conduct. Here, by contrast with trespass, the gist of the cause of action *was* damage. The need to prove damage meant that it had to be visibly apparent or demonstrable to the jury; to all intents and purposes, some physical manifestation was a prerequisite of liability,[19] not least because the parties were not deemed competent to give evidence.[20] 'Pure' emotional harm would not have sufficed, and there are good reasons to suppose that, even as an add-on to physical harm, 'injury to feelings' would often have been identified in terms of insult and affront rather than as emotional distress, let alone anything which would now be labelled mental illness. The very idea of claiming for what we would today call psychiatric harm was virtually unthinkable. For centuries, mental illness was not conceived of in biological or psychological terms. Nor, crucially for legal purposes, would its victims have blamed it on the wrongful conduct of others. Instead, it was conventionally attributed to the workings of divine will or evil spirits. To have questioned the former was tantamount to blasphemy; to have conceded the latter was to invite an accusation of witchcraft and the death penalty.[21]

The Victorian Era and 'Railway Spine'

Thus an amalgam of archaic civil procedure, superstition, religious beliefs and ignorance about the workings of the mind formed much of the backdrop to the rule that negligently inflicted emotional harm, of whatever kind, was not *in itself* a basis for the recovery of damages. This long-enduring stance was to gain added

---

[16] *Rookes v Barnard* [1964] AC 1129, *per* Lord Devlin. See above Ch 1, 29.
[17] Birks, above n 13, 22. In *Cassell & Co Ltd v Broome* [1972] AC 1027, the House of Lords took the view that mental distress, injury to feelings, insult, indignity, humiliation and a heightened sense of injury or grievance sufficed.
[18] Law Commission, No 247, *Aggravated, Exemplary and Restitutionary Damages* (London, HMSO, 1997) 3, 27. And see above Ch 1, n 165 and related text.
[19] Mendelson, *The Interfaces of Medicine and Law*, (Aldershot, Dartmouth Publishing Co, 1998) 11, 14.
[20] FH Bohlen, *Studies in the Law of Torts* (Indianapolis, Ind, Bobbs-Merrill, 1926) 254 (reprinted in (1902) 41 *American Law Register (NS)* 141); Earengay, WG, 'The Legal Consequences of Shock', reprinted in (1992) 60 *Medico-Legal Journal* 83 (first appeared in vol 1 of the *Medico-Legal and Criminological Review* (1933)), 84.
[21] Mendelson, *The Interfaces of Medicine and Law*, above n 19, 18–23.

resonance in Victorian times, and for a very particular reason—the advent of the train.[22]

In an age when third party liability insurance was not available, being viewed as contrary to public policy,[23] the numerous crashes attributable to this new mode of transport threatened the financial stability of the railway companies:

> Casualties on railways were so high that all major English railway companies employed their own teams of surgeons and physicians.[24]

From the mid-1840s onwards, many of these railway medical officers, having diagnosed and treated the injured passengers, would often also act as 'medical arbitrators' and offer them compensation on the company's behalf. Unsurprisingly, the prognoses were liable to be unduly optimistic, and the amounts obtained correspondingly inadequate. A number of patients successfully challenged such 'settlements' in the courts, where the way they had been arrived at prompted judicial criticism.

That said, the threat posed by collisions to the financial health of the railway companies concentrated judicial minds. Although many injured passengers would have suffered significant physical injury, a minority, though traumatised, were deemed physically unharmed. They discovered to their cost that mental disturbance 'alone' was, for legal purposes, too intangible to be quantified. The grieving relatives of a crash victim, pursuing a claim for loss of dependency and pain and suffering, fared no better:

> if a jury were to proceed to estimate the relative degree of mental anguish of a widow and twelve children from the death of the father of a family, a serious danger might arise of damages being given to the ruin of the defendants.[25]

Much reliance was to be placed on Lord Wensleydale's dictum that 'mental pain or anxiety the law cannot value'.[26] Again, however, he was expressly, if illogically, referring to situations where *only* such harm has occurred, for he continued:

> where a material damage occurs . . . it is impossible a jury, in estimating it, should altogether overlook the feelings of the party interested.[27]

---

[22] See RW Kostal, *Law and English Railway Capitalism 1825–1875* (Oxford, Oxford University Press, 1994) ch 7.

[23] Until the Employers' Liability Act 1880 paved the way for general liability insurance, gaining further momentum in the 1890s and 1900s with the arrival of the motor car. See further, M Davies, 'The End of the Affair: Duty of Care and Liability Insurance' (1989) 9 *Legal Studies* 67.

[24] D Mendelson, 'English Medical Experts and the Claims for Shock Occasioned by Railway Collisions in the 1860s—Issues of Law, Ethics, and Medicine' (2002) 25 *International Journal of Law and Psychiatry* 303, 305.

[25] *Blake v Midland Railway Co* (1852) 21 LJQB 233, 237; cf *Armsworth v South-Eastern Railway Co* (1847) 11 Jur (NP) 758, 760, *per* Parke B.

[26] *Lynch v Knight* (1861) 9 HL Cas 577, 598.

[27] *Ibid.* Among instances of recoverable *consequential* emotional harm, Mendelson cites a revealing mid-nineteenth century judgment on breach of a negative covenant against carrying on a business or calling: 'a person who stipulates that her neighbour shall not keep a school stipulates that she shall be relieved of all anxiety arising from a school being kept *and the feeling of anxiety is damage*': *Kemp v Sober* (1851) 61 ER 200 (emphasis added). See Mendelson, D, *The Interfaces of Medicine and Law*, above n 19, 117.

Nowadays, of course, compensation for emotional distress 'parasitic' on physical injury routinely attracts damages as suffering, under the head of 'pain and suffering'.[28]

That 'mental pain or anxiety' was deemed legally unquantifiable, although juries could, and would, have regard to the victim's 'feelings' serves to highlight how vague and unfocussed was the law's conception of remediable emotional harm. A major difficulty in all of this was the almost surreal nature of the law's attempts to address the issue. In the court setting, strongly held conflicting medical views about emotional harm, themselves marred by imperfect medical understanding, were being mediated through the judge and jury's still hazier grasp of such matters.

Development of Liability for 'Mental and Nervous Shock': The 'First Hundred Years'

The dispute over whether 'nervous shock' in the form of 'railway spine' was a *physical* condition caused by the violent shock of collision,[29] or a purely mental phenomenon,[30] persisted throughout the late nineteenth and early twentieth centuries. It was during this period that legal actions began to be formulated as 'nervous shock' claims, the expression having filtered down to the courts, partly, it would seem, via medical witnesses called to give expert evidence.[31] Its potential to cause confusion is amply demonstrated in cases from several common law jurisdictions at the time, mirroring the uncertainties and fluctuations of medical opinion.

In *Byrne v Great Southern and Western Railway Co* (1884),[32] the Irish Court of Appeal affirmed an award of £325 to a superintendent in the telegraph office at Limerick Junction, for 'great fright and shock', after a train had crashed through the wall of his office without touching him. Two years later, a 'near miss' incident occurred in the Australian State of Victoria, when a buggy, negligently allowed to proceed over a level crossing, narrowly avoided colliding with an oncoming train. A frightened passenger in the buggy fainted and 'received a severe nervous shock from the fright'. As a consequence, she suffered a miscarriage and was physically

---

[28] Eg, as 'mental anguish': *West (H) & Son Ltd v Shephard* [1964] AC 326.

[29] Erichsen, JE, *On the Concussion of the Spine, Nervous Shock and Other Obscure Injuries of the Nervous System* (New York, William Wood and Co, 1875); *On Railway and Other Injuries of the Nervous System* (Philadelphia, Henry C Lea, 1866).

[30] Page HW, *Injuries of the Spine and Spinal Cord Without Apparent Mechanical Lesion and Nervous Shock in their Surgical and Medical Aspects* (London, J and A Churchill,,1883). Page's analysis was, in turn, rejected by SV Clevenger, *Spinal Concussion* (Philadelphia & London, FA Davis, 1889).

[31] See D Butler, 'Identifying the compensable damage in "nervous shock" cases' (1997) 5 *Torts Law Journal* 67.

[32] *Byrne v Great Southern and Western Railway Co* (unreported, Irish CA, Feb 1884): cited in *Bell v Great Northern Railway Co of Ireland* (1890) 26 LR Ir 428.

ill for some months. The case, *Victorian Railways Commissioners v Coultas*, ultimately reached the Privy Council.[33]

Coultas can be seen as broadly reflecting English judicial attitudes when the courts were first confronted with 'nervous shock' claims. In a brief and somewhat opaque judgment, the damage was held to be too remote for the claimant to recover. Effectively equating 'nervous' and 'mental' shock, the Privy Council raised the spectre of 'a claim for damages on account of *mental* injury' in 'every case where an accident caused by negligence had given a person a serious nervous shock'[34] (emphasis added). Without categorically ruling out liability in the absence of physical 'impact',[35] it concluded that:

> Damages arising from mere sudden terror unaccompanied by any actual physical injury, but occasioning a nervous or mental shock, cannot under such circumstances . . . be considered a consequence which, in the ordinary course of things, would flow from the negligence of the gatekeeper.[36] (emphasis added)

Evidential concerns, shading into distrust, combined with fear of over-extensive liability, formed the driving force behind the Privy Council's decision not to uphold the claim:

> [T]he difficulty which now often exists in cases of alleged physical injuries of determining whether they were caused by the negligent act would be greatly increased, and a wide field opened for imaginary claims.[37]

Shortly afterwards, the conflation of 'nervous' and 'mental' shock in *Coultas* was rejected in *Bell v Great Northern Railway Co of Ireland*, on the ground that it assumed:

> as a matter of law, that nervous shock is something which affects merely the mental functions, and is not in itself a peculiar physical state of the body.[38]

This criticism was endorsed by the English High Court, in *Dulieu v White*,[39] which also dispelled an impression that had been gaining currency after *Coultas*, that fright had to be accompanied by actual impact for resultant nervous shock to ground a claim in negligence.

---

[33] *Victorian Railways Commissioners v Coultas* (1888) 13 App Cas 222 (PC). The Privy Council is the final court of appeal for certain Commonwealth jurisdictions. Its decisions, though authoritative, are not binding on the English Courts.

[34] Ibid, 225–6.

[35] Above n 33, 226.

[36] Above n 33, 225.

[37] Above n 33, 226.

[38] 'This error . . . pervades the entire judgment': *Bell* (1890) above n 32, 441, *per* Palles CB, drawing on the pre-*Coultas* decision of *Byrne*, above n 32. Cf '[A] nervous shock is distinct from mental anguish and falls within the physiological rather than the psychological branch of the human organism': *Sloane v Southern California Rail Co* 44 P 320 (Cal 1896).

[39] *Dulieu v White & Sons* [1901] 2 KB 669, 672–3, *per* Kennedy J, preferring the term 'nervous', 'where terror operates through parts of the physical organism to produce bodily illness . . . in view of the undoubted rule that merely mental pain unaccompanied by any injury to the person cannot sustain an action of this kind'. Cf *Henderson v Canadian Atlantic Railway Co* (1898) 25 OAR 437, 444 (Ontario CA).

It is significant that, as early as the mid-1880s, the Irish Court of Appeal was willing to affirm an award based on nervous shock,[40] and that, by the turn of the twentieth century, a number of judges were receptive to the view that adverse effects on the nervous system could be physically harmful. In *Dulieu v White*, for example, Kennedy J referred to someone 'made ill in body by such negligent driving as does not break his ribs but shocks his nerves'.[41] He went on to say:

> [I] should not like to assume it to be scientifically true that a nervous shock which causes serious bodily illness is not actually accompanied by physical injury, although it may be impossible, or at least difficult, to detect the injury at the time . . . I should not be surprised if the surgeon or the physiologist told us that nervous shock is or may be in itself an injurious affection of the physical organism.[42]

Even when not contemporaneous, physical injury which was a 'direct and natural effect' of shock would only have been too 'remote' in law if remoteness were viewed as a temporal rather than a causal concept, a point that had already been taken in *Bell*.[43] Endorsing the Irish decisions of *Bell* and *Byrne*, Kennedy J condemned the policy-based rationale in *Coultas* as involving 'the denial of redress in meritorious cases' and indicating unwarranted 'distrust' in the effectiveness of the legal process.[44] He did, however, suggest that liability should be restricted in one significant respect:

> [T]here is, I am inclined to think, at least one limitation. The shock, where it operates through the mind must be a shock which arises from a reasonable fear of immediate personal injury to oneself.[45]

The reason given—that nervous shock was not 'reasonably or naturally to be expected' from seeing someone else injured[46] was scarcely convincing.[47] The tentative locution ('I am inclined to think') perhaps betrays a sense that claims based on fear for others might indeed be just as, if not more, meritorious, and that their categorical exclusion was itself a concession to a contestable policy concern. In 1924, these very sentiments were to surface in the Court of Appeal's decision in *Hambrook v Stokes*,[48] the next major landmark extending liability for 'nervous shock'. It was a defining moment, partly because Atkin LJ emphatically repudiated

---

[40] *Byrne*, above n 32.
[41] *Dulieu*, above n 39, 672.
[42] *Ibid*, 677.
[43] 'As well might it be said that a death caused by poison is not to be attributed to the person who administered it, because the mortal effect is not produced contemporaneously with its administration.' *Bell*, above n 32, 439, per Palles CB.
[44] *Dulieu*, above n 39, 681.
[45] *Dulieu*, above n 39, 675.
[46] *Dulieu*, above n 39, 675.
[47] The High Court had previously held a practical joker liable for shock-induced physical illness after he had told a woman that her husband had been seriously injured in a road accident: *Wilkinson v Downton* [1897] 2 QB 57. This finding was reached on the basis that the statement was 'calculated' (ie likely) to cause physical harm. See further, *Wong v Parkside Health NHS Trust* [2003] 3 All ER 932, 935–7, per Hale LJ. Cf *Wainwright v Home Office* [2004] 2 AC 406. And see AL Goodhart, 'The Shock Cases and Area of Risk' (1953) 16 *MLR* 14, 17.
[48] *Hambrook v Stokes Bros* [1925] 1 KB 141.

the mind/body divide, but, crucially, because the Court rejected Kennedy J's 'fear for *oneself*' limitation on liability.[49]

By this time, psychiatry was beginning to establish itself as a discipline. There was mounting evidence that injury to the nervous system could have physical effects, graphically illustrated for the general public as the extent and severity of 'shell-shock' in the First World War began to emerge.[50] These developments helped shape legal thinking on nervous shock, in several jurisdictions.[51] We have already noted Lord Shaw's earlier conjecture, that 'modern physiology or pathology' might meet 'with instant challenge' the view that serious mental injury has no physical repercussions.[52] Ten years on, in *Hambrook v Stokes*, Atkin LJ was even more forthright:

> The legal effects of injury by shock have undoubtedly developed in the last thirty or forty years. At one time the theory was held that damage at law could not be proved in respect of personal injuries, unless there was some injury which was variously called 'bodily' or 'physical', but which necessarily excluded an injury which was only 'mental'. There can be no doubt at the present day that this theory is wrong . . . It may be due . . . in part to the law following a belated psychology which falsely removed mental phenomena from the world of physical phenomena.[53]

In the case itself, a mother saw a runaway lorry heading rapidly towards her round a bend where she had just left her children on their way to school. The Court of Appeal held that fear for *their* safety could ground liability in negligence for her fright-induced nervous shock. 'The cause of action', said Atkin LJ:

> appears to be created by breach of the ordinary duty to take reasonable care to avoid inflicting personal injuries, followed by damage, even though the type of damage may be unexpected—namely, shock.[54]

At the time, defendants were held liable for all the *direct* consequences of their negligent conduct, even if they could not have reasonably anticipated them:

> Once a breach of duty to the plaintiff is established[55] . . . [t]he question is whether the consequences causing damage are the direct result of the wrongful act or omission.[56]

---

[49] Described by Atkin LJ as a 'self-imposed restriction': *ibid*, 157.

[50] See Mendelson, *The Interfaces of Medicine and Law*, ch 5, 'Traumatic Neurosis, Shell-Shock, and Nervous Shock', above n 19.

[51] Eg, '[t]he development of modern science during the war has thrown new light on the subject of the nervous system, and nervous shock, and . . . it is now well established that a strong, robust man, may, as the result of nervous shock, become a helpless invalid, blind and paralysed, in fact a complete physical wreck, and not suffer any bruise, or even an abrasion of the skin': *Hogan v City of Regina* [1924] 2 WWR 307, 310 (Saskatchewan CA). See further, D Butler, 'Identifying the compensable damage in "nervous shock" cases' (1997) 5 *Torts Law Journal* 67.

[52] *Coyle or Brown v John Watson Ltd* [1915] AC 1, 14. Cf Kennedy J's dictum in *Dulieu v White*, above n 39.

[53] *Hambrook* [1925], above n 48, 153–4.

[54] Hambrook, above n 48, 158.

[55] In *Hambrook v Stokes*, according to Atkin LJ, when the lorry 'was left unattended in such a condition that it would run violently down the steep place': above n 48, 157.

[56] Hambrook, above n 48, 156. See *Polemis and Furness, Withy & Co, Re* [1921] 3 KB 560, CA. The 'direct' consequences test was effectively replaced, some 40 years later, by a test of 'reasonably foreseeable' consequences: *Overseas Tankship (UK) Ltd v Morts Dock and Engineering Co Ltd, The Wagon Mound* (No 1) [1961] AC 388, PC. See below, 52.

Subject to any reservations about the direct consequences test as such, on its particular facts, the decision was both morally compelling and consistent with the more progressive assumptions about possible causes of lasting trauma,[57] if at odds with conventional medical views then and for several decades to come.[58] Far from endorsing the 'fear for oneself' limitation, Atkin LJ saw no reason why liability should not extend even beyond the parent and child relationship, or 'why it did not eventually extend to bystanders'. Any risk of an increase in litigation, he thought, might be exaggerated, and to impose the limitation would deny meritorious claims, as in the instant case. To its critics, however, *Hambrook v Stokes* represented the gateway to an uncontrollable proliferation of questionable, relational claims by people whom English law would later classify as 'secondary victims'.[59]

Yet the majority in *Hambrook v Stokes* favoured one limiting device which ruled out many relational claims, namely, that the injury must have resulted from 'sight or sound of the accident',[60] that is, from experiencing it at the time with one's own unaided senses.[61] Taken literally, this limitation denied a remedy to traumatised family members who arrived later at the scene or the hospital and, by definition, it excluded anyone who was simply informed of what had happened. A requirement of direct perception helped to allay concerns about opening the floodgates, but it would become increasingly hard to justify in principle, not only because of advances in psychology but because of the way legal doctrine in negligence generally was developing.

In 1932, in *Donoghue v Stevenson*, Lord Atkin proclaimed his celebrated 'neighbour principle', as a *general* basis for determining the existence of a duty of care in negligence:[62]

> You must take reasonable care to avoid acts or omissions which you can reasonably foresee would be likely to injure your neighbour.[63]

Although the principle did not make much headway until the 1950s and 1960s, the courts then started to take a broader view of when a 'duty of care' existed and what should count as 'reasonably foreseeable' harm for the purposes of compensation.[64] The artificial limits in claims for nervous shock were conspicuously at odds with this widening ambit of liability.

---

[57] See Mendelson, above n 19, chs 2 and 3.

[58] See H Smith, 'Relation of Emotions to Injury and Disease: Legal Liability for Psychic Stimuli' (1944) 30 *Virginia Law Review* 193, and J Havard, 'Reasonable Foresight of Shock' (1956) 19 *MLR* 478, 482–3.

[59] Eg, 'the defendant is exposed to liability for a consequence which is only reached by a new and quite unusual link in the chain of causation, and which cannot therefore properly be held to have been within his ordinary and reasonable expectation. And the extent of this extra liability is necessarily both wide and indefinite'. *Hambrook v Stokes*, above n 48, 163, *per* Sargant LJ (dissenting). See also, D Howarth, *Textbook on Tort* (London, Butterworths, 1995) 254–9.

[60] *Hambrook*, above n 48, 159, *per* Atkin LJ.

[61] Presence at the aftermath of an accident, as a tenable basis for a claim, was not introduced until *McLoughlin v O'Brian* [1983] 1 AC 410. See below Ch 3, 61–2.

[62] Earlier findings of negligence, by way of the 'action on the case', were either 'one-off' decisions or cases covering specified categories of defendants, which included the drivers of vehicles.

[63] *Donoghue v Stevenson* (1932) AC 562, 580.

[64] See below, 49–50.

It is true that, when it addressed the issue of nervous shock for the first time, in 1943, the House of Lords appeared well-disposed towards Lord Atkin's approach. In *Bourhill v Young*,[65] commonly instanced as a paradigm of the 'unforeseeable plaintiff' problem, Lord Russell, Lord Wright and Lord Porter all expressly approved the 'neighbour principle',[66] and the other Law Lords gave it implicit support.[67] The case involved an eight month pregnant woman who, after stepping down from a tramcar, heard the sound of a collision some 45–50 feet away, while standing on the blind side of the tram. A negligent motor cyclist had collided with a car at a junction and had been killed. The claimant, who saw blood on the road after the body had been removed, suffered fright and severe nervous shock and a few weeks later delivered a stillborn child. She admitted that she had had no fear of immediate bodily injury, and the House of Lords unanimously held that, on the facts, no duty of care was owed to her. All five Law Lords considered her to be outside the range of the motor cyclist's reasonable contemplation, but there were significant differences in the way that they reached this conclusion. Lord Porter specifically said that no duty was owed to the claimant unless the defendant 'should reasonably have foreseen *emotional* injury to her as a result of his negligent driving',[68] (emphasis added) and Lord Wright indicated that being within the range of foreseeable *shock* would have sufficed.[69] The other speeches laid great stress on Mrs Bourhill not having been within the area of foreseeable *physical* danger, though not, it would seem, to the extent of making this a prerequisite of liability.[70]

In analysing reasonable foreseeability of nervous shock, both Lord Wright and Lord Porter were concerned about people's differing levels of susceptibility to emotional harm. Having alluded to Mrs Bourhill being eight months pregnant, Lord Wright posed the following question:

> Does the criterion of reasonable foresight extend beyond people of ordinary health or susceptibility, or does it take into account the peculiar susceptibilities or infirmities of those affected which the defendant neither knew of nor could reasonably be taken to have foreseen?[71]

Although concluding that liability for nervous shock must generally depend on a 'normal standard of susceptibility',[72] he conceded that this was a vague criterion, adding that:

---

[65] *Bourhill v Young* [1943] AC 92.
[66] Ibid, 101, 107 and 116–7, respectively.
[67] Lord Thankerton referred to a duty of reasonable care to persons reasonably foreseeably injured, which he identified with the 'test of proximity or remoteness'. Above n 65, 98. Lord Macmillan spoke of a duty to take care in respect of those to whom injury 'may reasonably and probably be anticipated'. Above n 65, 104.
[68] Above n 65, 119.
[69] Above n 65, 108–9.
[70] Lord Macmillan, above n 65 104–5, Lord Russell, 101–102 and Lord Thankerton, 98–9. See further, Goodhart, 'The Shock Cases and Area of Risk', above n 47.
[71] Above n 65, 109.
[72] Above n 65, 110.

definition involves limitation which it is desirable to avoid further than is necessary in a principle of law like negligence which is widely ranging and is still in the stage of development.

Lord Porter adopted a somewhat narrower stance:

> The driver of a car or vehicle, even though careless, is entitled to assume that the ordinary frequenter of the streets has sufficient fortitude to endure such incidents as may from time to time be expected to occur in them, including the noise of a collision and the sight of injury to others, and is not to be considered negligent towards one who does not possess the customary phlegm.[73]

Here we see what amounts to a further restriction on nervous shock claims.[74] In the ordinary law of negligence, what is 'reasonably foreseeable' can include relatively remote possibilities.[75] For you to be a foreseeable victim of *physical* injury, it suffices that injury to you is foreseeable or that you belong to a general class of people who would be within a reasonable person's contemplation.[76] Even on the assumption that Mrs Bourhill's condition could properly be described as one of 'abnormal susceptibility', it would not, on appropriate facts, have defeated a claim by her for *physical* injury.

Views may, of course, legitimately differ as to whether, on the particular facts, Mrs Bourhill's injuries were either reasonably foreseeable or, indeed, induced by shock.[77] At all events, in claims for physical harm, the mid-1950s saw the beginnings of a pronounced shift towards expansive and creative interpretation of Lord Atkin's 'neighbour principle'.[78] In one leading case, his formulation of the duty of care was said to extend to:

> any damage which [the defendant] can reasonably foresee may happen as a result of the breach however unlikely it may be, unless it can be brushed aside as farfetched.[79]

By 1970, Lord Reid felt able to assert that:

> the time has come when we can and should say that it ought to apply unless there is some justification or valid explanation for its exclusion.[80]

Yet in nervous shock cases, circumstantial details of little, if any, relevance to foreseeability of the claimant's condition could still rule out recovery. The emergence

---

[73] Above n 65, 117.
[74] A restriction which, in English Law, is now only applicable to secondary victims. See *Page v Smith* [1996] 1 AC 155, 189, *per* Lord Lloyd. See below Ch 3, 78–9.
[75] Eg, *Carmarthenshire County Council v Lewis* [1955] AC 549. Cf *Glasgow Corporation v Muir* [1943] AC 448, 457, *per* Lord MacMillan.
[76] See, eg, *Haley v London Electricity Board* [1965] AC 778 (safety of roadworks for blind people).
[77] See AL Goodhart, 'Emotional Shock and the Unimaginative Taxicab Driver' (1953) 69 *LQR* 347, 348.
[78] Eg, *Carmarthenshire CC v Lewis*, above n 75.
[79] *Koufos v C Czarnikow Ltd (The Heron II)* [1969] 1 AC 350, 422, *per* Lord Upjohn. Cf *Overseas Tankship (UK) Ltd v Miller Steamship Co Pty, The Wagon Mound (No 2)* [1967] 1 AC 617, 643–4, *per* Lord Reid.
[80] *Home Office v Dorset Yacht Co Ltd* [1970] AC 1004, 1027.

of a broad and flexible foreseeability formula for mainstream negligence further exposed the artificiality of the devices deployed to rein in liability in nervous shock cases, for which little was proffered by way of 'justification or valid explanation'.[81]

The point is well-demonstrated by the Court of Appeal's decision in *King v Phillips*.[82] A taxi driver backing into a side road without checking whether it was clear struck the tricycle of a child, who was slightly injured. The child's mother, standing at an upstairs window of her house, some 70 or 80 yards away, heard him scream and saw the tricycle disappear under the wheels of the taxi, though she did not see the child himself. She consequently 'suffered trembling fits, and became distressed and tearful'.[83] Given that her claim—unanimously rejected by the Court—was that her *emotional* injury was 'reasonably foreseeable', it is revealing how much emphasis was placed by the Court on her *physical* distance from the scene. In particular, Singleton LJ considered it:

> contrary to common sense to say that a taxicab driver ought reasonably to have contemplated ... injury by shock or any other injury, to a woman in a house *some 70 or 80 yards away* up a side street.[84] (emphasis added)

More bizarrely, Denning LJ held that, though in principle the taxi driver *did* owe a duty of care to the mother, the damage was too remote because:

> the slow backing of the taxicab was very different from the terrifying descent of the runaway lorry [in *Hambrook v Stokes*].[85]

Asserting that:

> [t]here can be no doubt since *Bourhill v Young* that the test of liability for shock is foreseeability of injury by shock[86]

he was firmly of the view that presence within the area of *physical* danger was not essential: '[i]n [*Hambrook v Stokes*] the mother was not herself in any *personal danger*. Nor was she here.'[87] (emphasis added)

---

[81] This is not to discount the emphasis put on foreseeability by some judges in the earlier case law. Eg, Kennedy J favoured the view that where a defendant did not do 'anything which could reasonably or naturally be expected to affect [the plaintiff] injuriously, there was no ... breach of legal duty' such as to constitute negligence: *Dulieu v White*, above n 39, 675. In *Hambrook v Stokes*, above n 48, Atkin LJ's finding of liability was ultimately based on 'breach of the ordinary duty to take reasonable care to avoid inflicting personal injuries': 158. In his concurring judgment, Bankes LJ spoke of '[w]hat the defendant ought to have anticipated ... when considering the extent of his duty': 151.

[82] *King v Phillips* [1953] 1 QB 429 (CA).

[83] *Ibid*, 430.

[84] Above n 82, 437. This comment should be read in conjunction with his earlier observation that, '[h]e could not know that she was at the window, nor was there any reason why he should anticipate that she would see his cab at all'. Above n 82, 436. Emphasis added. Contrast, however, Goodhart's proposed test: was it reasonably foreseeable that a person within direct view of the accident might receive an emotional shock? Goodhart, above n 77, 351. Denning LJ had also drawn attention to the lack of physical proximity: 'The taxicab driver cannot reasonably be expected to have foreseen that his backing would terrify a mother *70 yards away* ...' Above n 82, 442.

[85] Above n 82, 442.

[86] Above n 82, 441. Cf his earlier assertion that the test applied 'by each member of the House of Lords' in *Bourhill v Young* was 'foreseeability of emotional shock': Above n 82, 438.

[87] Above n 82, 441.

Whatever its defects, *King v Phillips* did seem to indicate that, in principle, the scope of foreseeable shock was the proper focus of nervous shock claims, and that it could therefore include instances of fear for one's child. These propositions were later applied in *Boardman v Sanderson*,[88] where an 8 year old boy's foot was trapped under the wheel of a car which his father's friend had negligently backed out of a garage. The father, recognising his son's screams, suffered a 'considerable shock' which caused him 'slight illness'. In contrast to *King v Phillips*, the careless driver knew that the father was only a few yards away, making it more readily foreseeable that he would almost immediately be at the scene and might suffer shock. Ormerod LJ said that a clear duty was owed to 'near relatives' known to be on the premises and within earshot, endorsing Lord Wright's observation in *Bourhill v Young* that negligence, based on reasonable foresight, is a 'fluid principle' that 'has to be fitted to the facts of the particular case'.[89]

One aspect of this fluidity, discernible in several cases, was a desire to reward altruism. Apparent in a number of decisions involving physical injury,[90] its influence in the nervous shock context was perhaps best exemplified by *Chadwick v British Railways Board*.[91] There, the judge was clearly affected by the horror and macabre nature of the Lewisham train disaster of 1957, in which 90 people were killed, and by the courage and selflessness of the claimant in immediately going to the scene of the accident and providing assistance to victims virtually throughout the night. Mr Chadwick's recovery of damages for anxiety neurosis rested on an untypically broad interpretation of reasonable foreseeability for a case of injury through shock. The Court endorsed Lord Justice Denning's view that foreseeability of shock (not physical injury) was the relevant test. The judge saw no reason in principle for confining recovery either to cases of fear for oneself or for one's immediate family. Although Chadwick had acted of his own volition, it was held that the defendants could have reasonably foreseen that someone might try to rescue passengers and might, in turn, 'suffer injury in the process'.[92] The conclusion that his resultant condition was reasonably foreseeable was also the

---

[88] *Boardman v Sanderson* [1964] 1 WLR 1317.

[89] *Bourhill v Young*, above n 65, 107. Cf 'the case satisfies the relevant test, being that of reasonable foreseeability discussed . . . in *Bourhill v Young*', *Boardman, ibid*, 1322, *per* Danckwerts LJ.

[90] Notably in *Carmarthenshire CC v Lewis*, above n 75, where a lorry driver was killed when swerving to avoid running over a child. The House of Lords deemed 'reasonably foreseeable' a series of events which had been described in the Court of Appeal as requiring 'almost superhuman vision': [1953] 2 All ER 1403, 1407, *per* Romer LJ. See also *Baker v TE Hopkins & Son Ltd* [1959] 1 WLR 966 (CA).

[91] *Chadwick v British Railways Board* [1967] 1 WLR 912. See also the suggestion by Bankes LJ (in *Hambrook v Stokes*, above n 48, 151) that, had the case concerned two mothers, one timid and concerned only for herself, the other courageous and concerned only for her child, a cause of action should equally lie for the 'more deserving one'.

[92] *Chadwick, ibid*, 921. Cf the broad interpretation of 'bodily injury' in *Dooley v Cammell Laird* (1951) 1 Lloyd's List Law Reports 271, 275, *per* Donovan J: 'No suggestion is made that the words "bodily injury" [in the context of shipbuilding regulations] . . . exclude injury to nerves, which after all are a part of the body.'

more easily reached by the judge taking a narrow view of 'extraordinary susceptibility'.[93]

Finally, reference should be made to another respect in which the 1960s saw 'reasonable foreseeability' being broadly interpreted in mainstream negligence. We have already noted that, under the rule in Re Polemis, wrongdoers had been liable for *all* the 'direct consequences' of their negligent conduct, but that, following the Privy Council decision in The Wagon Mound (1961), they were held liable only for reasonably foreseeable outcomes.[94] More precisely, liability was to depend on claimants proving that the harm to which they had been exposed was of a *type* or *kind* that was a foreseeable consequence of the defendant's negligence. On the face of it, this qualification might have been expected to reduce the incidence of liability, yet, if anything, it had the opposite effect. This is because the Polemis test had often been narrowly construed, the 'directness' of the consequences being denied for fear of imposing an undue burden of liability. By contrast, post-Wagon Mound, when insurance was widely available and in some contexts required, both 'reasonable foreseeability' and 'type of harm' tended to be generously construed, in part to facilitate compensation. The new willingness to expand liability in mainstream negligence did not, however, carry over to 'nervous shock' claims. Only a few years after The Wagon Mound, the Court of Appeal decision in Hinz v Berry[95] was to assert another special limiting device, setting 'nervous shock' yet further apart from the general trend.

Recoverable Harm: a 'recognisable psychiatric illness'

It is noticeable that the Court of Appeal's judgment in Boardman v Sanderson barely mentioned the nature of the harm suffered by the father, beyond describing it as 'slight shock'.[96] In this case, as in others, the cursory treatment of this key aspect of the claim is unfortunate.[97] It is true that, until late into the twentieth century, most judgments were, in their entirety, relatively short by today's standards. However, granted the contested nature of recoverable harm, some clarity and specificity is needed if there is to be minimally acceptable coherence in decision-making. Given that the ambit of 'nervous shock' had been vague and ill-defined from its inception, and that, even by the early 1960s, a cryptic finding of 'slight shock' or 'slight illness' could satisfy the Court of Appeal, the introduction, only a few years later, of a much narrower formulation—'recognisable psychiatric

---

[93] 'The community is not formed of normal citizens, with all those who are less susceptible or more susceptible to stress to be regarded as extraordinary. There is an infinite variety of creatures, all with varying susceptibilities.' *Chadwick*, above n 92, 922.
[94] See above, n 56.
[95] *Hinz v Berry* [1970] 2 QB 40.
[96] *Boardman v Sanderson*, above n 88, 1319–20. The judge at first instance referred to 'some slight illness' and awarded £75 in damages.
[97] See, eg, *King v Phillips* and *Dulieu v White*, above n 82 and n 39, respectively. Cf *Owens v Liverpool Corporation* [1939] 1 KB 394.

illness'—requires explanation, especially in view of the authoritative status which it has since acquired.

The Court of Appeal's decision in *Hinz v Berry* was seen as having established that a 'recognisable psychiatric illness' was *legally required* for compensation in 'nervous shock' cases. Lord Denning, having indicated that 'no damages are awarded for grief or sorrow', stated that:

> [d]amages are ... recoverable for nervous shock, or, to put it in medical terms, for any recognisable psychiatric illness caused by the breach of duty by the defendant.[98] (emphasis added)

If, as would appear to be the case, he meant that a 'recognisable psychiatric illness' was the liability threshold, he cited no supporting authority. As Thomas J was later to observe:

> no deliberative consideration seems to have accompanied the use of the expression. It can be traced to a statement by Lord Denning in *Hinz v Berry*... Subsequent Courts have adopted the phrase and embedded it in the law.[99]

It is possible that Lord Denning was simply replicating its use in evidence by the psychiatrist describing the particular plaintiff's condition.[100] In the very next paragraph of his judgment, he refers to damages being recoverable for 'nervous shock and psychiatric illness.'[101]

Consequently, though, since *Hinz v Berry*, 'recognisable psychiatric illness' has been accepted as the authoritative basis for liability in English law, its doctrinal authority is not beyond challenge.[102] There is growing support in various Commonwealth and United States jurisdictions for formulating the test in less restrictive terms.[103] Even if momentary fright and mild upset should be excluded,

---

[98] *Hinz v Berry*, above n 95, 42.

[99] *van Soest v Residual Health Management Unit* [2000] 1 NZLR 179, 204. It has been suggested that the definition 'any recognisable psychiatric illness' reflected a developing trend, as illustrated in an earlier Australian decision: 'Some form of medically recognised neurosis or damage to the mind going beyond ordinary human grief or anguish': *Storm v Geeves* [1965] Tas SR 252, 266. See D Butler, 'Identifying the compensable damage in "nervous shock" cases' (1997) 5 *Torts Law Journal* 67, 75.

[100] Cf 'It is important to bear in mind that what has resulted is described by the psychiatrist who gave evidence as a "recognisable psychiatric illness"', *per* Sir Gordon Willmer, *Hinz v Berry*, above n 95, 46. And see *McDermott v Ramadanovic* (1988) 27 BCLR (2nd) 45, 53, where Southin J rejected Lord Denning's limitation, 'if he intended it as a limitation of *law*' (emphasis added). Note, however, her subsequent observation that 'Lord Denning was giving his own meaning to the term "nervous shock"': *Rhodes v Canadian National Railway* (1990) 75 DLR (4th) 248, 283. Cf, 'One wonders ... how many of the pre-1970 plaintiffs actually suffered recognisable psychiatric illnesses': *Mullany and Handford's Tort Liability for Psychiatric Damage*, (Sydney, Lawbook Co, 2nd edn, 2006), 47.

[101] *Hinz v Berry*, above n 95, 43. Lord Justice Pearson, who also referred to the claimant's 'recognisable psychiatric illness', endorsed the conclusion of the judge at first instance that she was in a 'morbid state of depression' and was entitled to be compensated for her 'extreme mental anguish'. *Ibid*, 44.

[102] In one later case, though damages were excluded for worry, strain and distress, they were awarded for 'shock in the ordinary, general, everyday meaning of the word and not in any medical or psychiatric sense'—something more than emotional upset but less than medical incapacitation—'a shock, not psychiatric in character, which endured beyond the moment of impact': *Whitmore v Euroways Express Coaches Ltd, The Times*, 4 May 1984.

[103] See further below Ch 6, 172–5.

it does not follow that there should be no redress for serious mental suffering and emotional disturbance which, though not identifiable as 'recognisable psychiatric illness', is 'plainly outside the range of ordinary human experience'.[104]

An Overview of the Period

In the 'nervous shock' case law examined so far, the perceived demands of pragmatism largely withstood sporadic efforts to produce a more coherent rule structure. In line with many early twentieth century cases on negligent conduct, tensions between principle and policy were often either implicit or only obliquely articulated. So, for example, we see the extent of liability for shock limited by courts construing 'remoteness' of damage very broadly,[105] or taking a narrow view of 'direct' injury and of 'duty'.[106] Prior to *Donoghue v Stevenson*, there was little judicial theorising about the scope of negligence, and the courts dealt with such claims in a rather mechanical way. Successful actions were either single instances that closely resembled earlier ones, or they relied on precedents which had established that specified categories of defendant could be liable in negligence. Thus railway companies had long been held to owe a duty of care to physically injured passengers,[107] and comparable decisions applied to negligent users of vehicles on the highway and companies responsible for industrial injuries.

Most of the early nervous shock cases involved railway, road and workplace accidents. In the course of the twentieth century, the substantial growth of the liability insurance market was to have an important, if largely concealed, influence in widening the scope of liability for negligence generally.[108] The ensuing focus was increasingly on who fell within the sphere-of-risk, in the sense that the harm that they suffered could have reasonably been anticipated. That claims would, or could, have been covered by insurance was an additional, unspoken factor in routine actions,[109] which, in certain nervous shock cases, too, could help explain the

---

[104] *van Soest*, above n 99, 206, *per* Thomas J. And see further Ch 6 below. See also N Mullany and P Handford, 'Moving the Boundary Stone by Statute—the Law Commission on Psychiatric Illness' (1999) 22 *University of New South Wales Law Journal* 350, 361–75.

[105] Eg, *Coultas*, above n 33.

[106] Eg, *Dulieu v White*, above n 39. See also P Heffey, 'The Negligent Infliction of Nervous Shock in Road and Industrial Accidents (Part II)' (1974) 48 *Australian Law Journal* 240, 254–7.

[107] A comparable duty was established for 'level crossing' accidents in 1874: *North Eastern Railway Co v Wanless* [1874] LR 7 HL 12.

[108] The origins of this process can be traced back to the 1880s. As has been aptly said of Brett MR's general test for the duty of care in *Heaven v Pender* [1883] 11 QBD 503 (a precursor of the neighbour principle) 'the recasting of duty in terms of risk rather than personal responsibility was uncannily appropriate to the first burgeoning years of the liability insurance market in Britain.' See Davies, above n 23, 80.

[109] See Lord Denning's observations in *Nettleship v Weston* [1971] 2 QB 691, 699 and in *Morris v Ford Motor Co Ltd* [1973] QB 792, 798.

relatively relaxed view—at least prior to *Hinz v Berry*—of what needed to be established by way of harm.[110]

Broadly speaking, from *Coultas* until the latter part of the twentieth century, the legal framework for shock cases, and the judicial attitudes which it reflected, are well-captured in Goodhart's observation that they tended to 'vary in spirit from extreme caution to hesitant experimentation'.[111] For much of this period, the case law veered between denying liability via artificial restrictions and incrementally extending it. *Coultas*' virtual rejection of liability in the absence of physical impact was replaced by its gradual acceptance, subject to mostly arbitrary controls, such as fear for oneself,[112] perception through unaided senses and presence in the area of physical impact.[113] However, as these controls were not necessarily related to foreseeability, they began to look increasingly unsustainable during the 1960s and 1970s, when the 'neighbour principle' was acquiring authoritative status and the courts were adopting a more expansive attitude towards negligence in mainstream cases. A broader view was being taken of 'reasonably foreseeable' harm, both in deciding whether a duty of care existed[114] and in determining the extent of recoverable damage.[115] These doctrinal developments, combined with continuing advances in psychiatry,[116] further exposed the irrationality of the limiting devices as applied in cases such as *King v Phillips*.[117]

However, it is important to appreciate that the search for more conceptual coherence, from around the 1970s, was to have its own built-in limits. The open-textured nature of 'foreseeability', and of 'reasonableness' in qualifying it, left considerable room for judicial pragmatism, even in mainstream negligence cases. Lord Atkin himself, when first proclaiming the 'neighbour principle', had stressed the limits of its intended scope. As well as stating that a claimant had to be 'closely and directly affected' by the defendant's act, he observed that:

> acts or omissions which any moral code would censure cannot in a practical world be treated so as to give a right to every person injured by them to demand relief. In this way rules of law arise which *limit* the range of complainants and the extent of their remedy.[118] (emphasis added)

---

[110] Eg, *Boardman v Sanderson*, above n 88. Cf Fleming's suggestion that the insurance background explains why, in cases brought under the Workmen's Compensation Act for seeing a fellow worker killed, courts did not invoke 'remoteness' to deny claims as readily as when—before compulsory vehicle insurance—a comparable incident occurred in a street collision: JG Fleming, 'Remoteness and Duty: The Control Devices in Liability for Negligence' (1953) 31 *Canadian Bar Review* 471, 477–8, contrasting *Yates v South Kirkby Collieries Ltd* [1910] 2 KB 538 with *Smith v Johnson & Co* (1897) DC (unreported).

[111] AL Goodhart, 'The Shock Cases and Area of Risk' (1953) 16 *MLR* 14.

[112] Until *Hambrook v Stokes*, above n 48.

[113] *Bourhill v Young*, above n 65.

[114] Eg, *Hedley Byrne & Co Ltd v Heller & Partners Ltd* [1964] AC 465; *Home Office v Dorset Yacht Co Ltd* [1970] AC 1004, and *Anns v Merton LBC* [1978] AC 728.

[115] Eg, *Hughes v Lord Advocate* [1963] AC 837; *Robinson v Post Office* [1974] 1 WLR 1176.

[116] Cf 'It is, however, today a known medical fact that severe emotional distress can be the starting point of a lasting disorder of mind or body, some form of psychoneurosis or a psychosomatic illness': *Mount Isa Mines Ltd v Pusey* (1970) 125 CLR 383, 394, *per* Windeyer J.

[117] *King v Phillips*, above n 82.

[118] *Donoghue v Stevenson* above n 63, 580.

As we will see, the line between principle and pragmatism remains blurred under the prevailing triple formula for establishing a duty of care: 'reasonable foreseeability' and a relationship of 'sufficient proximity' between the parties, combined with 'fairness, justice and reasonableness.'[119]

Conclusion

Up to the decision in *McLoughlin v O'Brian* (1982), the most distinctive feature of the English case law on nervous shock was its resolute adherence to restrictive devices. Though the period can plausibly be portrayed as one of gradual liberalisation, ironically, the perceived need for such devices grew following acceptance, in the mid-1920s, that 'secondary' or relational victims could sue.[120] For that very gateway to expanded liability was seen as underlining the need for special controls, and helps to explain why they were not dislodged when, some 40 to 50 years later, foreseeability took centre stage in mainstream negligence law. The increased scope for suing heightened the fears of spurious or exaggerated claims, already prevalent among judges sceptical about psychiatric evidence and ambivalent about non-physical harm generally. On another, not unconnected, plane, the restrictions on liability were in line with the common law's historical legacy of fostering self-reliance and individualism. There was a widely-held belief, which had been reinforced in Victorian times, that the social and economic benefits of giving the individual free rein outweighed the adverse consequences from the concomitant risk of harm to others.[121] This sentiment was all the stronger where the harm in question was 'mere' nervous shock.

The barriers to redress were reinforced, in 1970, by Lord Denning's almost casual introduction of the 'recognisable psychiatric illness' test in *Hinz v Berry*. This high liability threshold may have served to alleviate some judicial fears and could be said to have articulated a minimum requirement of sorts, though, curiously, its effect was to entrust standard-setting to the very discipline which the courts had often viewed with scepticism. At the same time, the test has brought to the fore the extent of controversy over 'recognisable' psychiatric conditions, and the concern that even the outer boundaries of such classification can be insufficiently sensitive to serious instances of non-psychiatric emotional harm.[122]

Policy considerations were never far from the surface in the case law, and the imprecise language of the governing principles almost invited forced interpretations, producing some far from convincing outcomes. Too often, decisions on liability seemed to owe as much to assertion and 'intuitive evaluation'[123] as to analysis. In the early cases, claimants' injuries were often peremptorily deemed not

---

[119] *Caparo Industries plc v Dickman* [1990] 2 AC 605, 617–8, per Lord Bridge.
[120] *Hambrook v Stokes*, above n 48.
[121] Cf Fleming, above n 110, 474.
[122] Cf *van Soest, per* Thomas J, above n 99.
[123] Fleming, above n 110, 480.

to have been a 'direct' consequence of the defendant's conduct: they were simply adjudged 'too remote'. Later on, the focus shifted to whether a 'duty of care' existed and whether the claimant's injury was 'reasonably foreseeable'. Fleming cautioned against attaching undue significance to the particular terms used to establish liability criteria, because 'analysis is susceptible to the influence of deceptive connotations of the verbal formulas employed'.[124] However, importantly, he also pointed out that, in given contexts, some formulas are less deceptive than others. Though 'duty of care' and 'reasonable foreseeability' are malleable concepts, they are still more appropriate than 'remoteness' for resolving claims of negligence, especially claims based on 'nervous shock'. The language of duty and foreseeable risk, observed Fleming, 'has the merit of at least encouraging articulation of the policy values which determine judicial choice'.[125] 'Remoteness', by contrast, is more apt to divert attention from the real issues at stake. For example, though disarmingly neutral in tone, it 'carries an unfortunate connotation of proximity in time',[126] which may not adequately convey the scope for mental harm unreasonably created by a defendant's conduct.

In the period prior to the House of Lords decision in *McLoughlin v O'Brian*, the courts routinely offered cursory and superficial accounts of 'nervous shock'. Strongly wedded to artificial controls on liability, judges were unwilling to abandon them even when 'reasonable foreseeability' became the negligence norm. Unfortunately, however, as Fleming also noted, once the 'neighbour principle' had been firmly established, the limiting devices were increasingly presented as if they were actual *dimensions* of reasonable foreseeability, rather than a means of restricting its scope. The resultant doctrinal confusion and incoherence, all the more embarrassing in the light of continuing scientific advance, formed the backdrop to *McLoughlin v O'Brian*. There, for the first time, the House of Lords seriously addressed the key issue: should the traditional policy-driven stance on negligently inflicted psychiatric harm give way to a more principled approach?

---

[124] Above n 110, 498.
[125] Above n 110, 493.
[126] Above n 110, 493.

3

Contemporary Provision for 'Accident-Based' Psychiatric Illness

McLoughlin v O'Brian: Policy or Principle?

WHILE SHE WAS at home two miles away, Mrs McLoughlin's husband and three of her children were negligently injured in a very serious road accident.[1] Her youngest child, Gillian, who was 2 years old, died almost immediately. Some two hours later, a neighbour in a following car, who had not been involved in the crash, went to inform Mrs McLoughlin of the accident. He told her that he thought her elder son was dying and that he did not know where her husband was or what condition Gillian was in. He then drove her to the hospital, some 10 miles away, where her 11 year old son, Michael (who had been a passenger in his car), told her that Gillian was dead. At the hospital, she also saw her husband and the other children still covered in blood, dirt and oil, badly injured, in great pain and seriously traumatised. As a result of her own traumatic experience, Mrs McLoughlin brought a claim in negligence. For the purposes of the hearing, it was assumed, as pleaded, that she had subsequently suffered severe shock, organic depression and a change of personality; that her condition was caused or contributed to by shock, and that she was a person of normal susceptibility.

The judge dismissed the claim in the following terms:

> I feel bound by principle and what I conceive to be good sense . . . to conclude that in such circumstances injury to the mother is too remote a possibility to come within the ambit of the foresight of the reasonable bystander. Sorrow and hurt to her feelings and grief he would doubtless foresee but not, I think, injury by shock.[2]

Mrs McLoughlin fared no better before the Court of Appeal, even though it rejected this very narrow view of how she might foreseeably have been affected. To confine the range of a driver's foreseeability of injury by shock to persons 'on or near the highway', said Stephenson LJ, argued an 'abnormal degree of myopia'.[3]

---

[1] *McLoughlin v O'Brian* [1983] 1 AC 410.
[2] *McLoughlin v O'Brian* [1981] QB 599, 604.
[3] *Ibid*, 612. Cp 'readily foreseeable', 617, *per* Griffiths LJ.

Griffiths LJ acknowledged that it might be seen as illogical, but noted that almost all the reported nervous shock cases concerned accidents on the highway and stressed that physical proximity to the scene of the accident was 'the common thread running through all the judgments'.[4] He concluded that no duty was owed to anyone, not on the road at or close to the scene at the time the accident happened. '[T]he line', he said:

> has to be drawn somewhere and . . . it is inherently more likely that those present at the accident will suffer shock than those who have time to prepare themselves.[5]

There had previously been a few Commonwealth[6] and American[7] decisions granting a remedy in 'immediate aftermath' cases, but there was no clearcut English authority to this effect.[8] Stephenson LJ's analysis in *McLoughlin* centred on the then prevailing *Anns v Merton* 'two-stage' test for duty of care when new negligence issues came before the courts. If the proximity between the parties was such that damage was reasonably foreseeable, a duty was presumed to exist (stage 1), but it could be negated or restricted in scope if this was justified by considerations of public policy (stage 2).[9] Having conceded foreseeability, he concluded, 'not without some reluctance',[10] that the 'demands of society'[11] did not require liability to someone in Mrs McLoughlin's situation. 'Ask me why', he said:

> and I find some difficulty in stating a convincing reason. It is largely a matter of . . . 'judicial instinct' that the duty . . . must stop somewhere.[12]

Clearly, the floodgates fear loomed large in his mind—the 'economic consequences if the door is opened'.[13]

In the House of Lords, however, Mrs McLoughlin's appeal was unanimously allowed. None of their Lordships concluded that public policy considerations displaced the prima facie duty of care owed to her, and their dismissive treatment of the floodgates argument was particularly striking. Lord Edmund-Davies and Lord Bridge were fairly scathing, Lord Wilberforce and Lord Russell sceptical and only Lord Scarman was equivocal about it.[14]

Lord Wilberforce was at pains to assert that a decision in Mrs McLoughlin's favour did not introduce any new legal principle. Rather, he said, it represented:

---

[4] Above n 2, 619.
[5] Above n 2, 624.
[6] *Eg, Marshall v Lionel Enterprises Inc* (1971) 25 DLR (3rd) 141; *Benson v Lee* [1972] VR 879, and *Fenn v City of Peterborough* (1976) 73 DLR (3d) 177.
[7] *Eg, Dziokonski v Babineau*, 380 NE 2d 1295 (Mass, 1978) and *Archibald v Braverman*, 79 Cal Rptr 723 (1969).
[8] Though *Chadwick v British Railways Board* [1967] 1 WLR 912 and perhaps *Boardman v Sanderson* [1964] 1 WLR 1317 could be so construed. See above, Ch 2, 51.
[9] *Anns v Merton London Borough Council* [1978] AC 728, 751–2, *per* Lord Wilberforce.
[10] *McLoughlin v O'Brian*, above n 2, 613.
[11] Above n 2, 614. And see *Hedley Byrne v Heller* [1964] AC 465, 536, *per* Lord Pearce.
[12] *McLoughlin v O'Brian*, above n 2, 614.
[13] Above n 2, 614.
[14] *McLoughlin v O'Brian*, above n 1, 425, 442, 421, 429 and 430–1, respectively.

either the existing law, or the existing law with only such circumstantial extension as the common law process may legitimately make.[15]

Though sceptical about the floodgates fear, he was clearly resistant to any significant deviation from the special controls to be found in the earlier case law. Foreseeability alone did not suffice:

> there remains ... just because 'shock' in its nature is capable of affecting so wide a range of people, a real need for the law to place some limitation upon the extent of admissible claims. It is necessary to consider three elements *inherent* in any claim: the class of persons whose claims should be recognised; the proximity of such persons to the accident; and the means by which the shock is caused.[16] (emphasis added)

These three elements had featured prominently in the majority judgment of the California Supreme Court in *Dillon v Legg*,[17] a judgment referred to by Lord Wilberforce and considered at some length by Lord Bridge. The case concerned a mother who had recovered damages for emotional distress on seeing her infant daughter die when run over by a negligent driver. As the mother had not herself been in any physical danger, *Dillon v Legg* was a landmark decision, the first in the US to abolish the 'zone of danger' rule, still adhered to in many American States. The Court adopted a foreseeability test, to be determined on a case-by-case basis, by reference to 'such factors' as proximity to the scene, direct, contemporaneous perception, and closeness of relationship. Importantly, however, the majority judgment described these factors simply as '*guidelines*' to help resolve whether psychiatric harm was reasonably foreseeable,[18] (emphasis added) not as additional requirements. If, initially, some American courts did treat the '*Dillon* factors' as guidelines, there has been an increasing tendency in the US to make them legal *prerequisites* of liability.[19]

Lord Wilberforce did not advocate a rigid application of the '*Dillon* factors' as rules of law; rather, he concluded his speech by emphasising the need to apply such considerations 'with common sense to individual situations in their entirety'. However, he did clearly see 'proximity' as normally having a significant role in *restricting* liability for 'secondary' claimants, even when harm to them was reasonably foreseeable: '[a]s regards proximity to the accident, it is obvious that this must be close both in time and space'.[20] Yet, strictly speaking, Mrs McLoughlin was not obviously close to the *accident* in either respect. How, then, could Lord Wilberforce have reached the conclusion that she was entitled to recover?

---

[15] Above n 1, 423.
[16] Above n 1, 421–2.
[17] (1968) 29 ALR 3d 1316.
[18] *Ibid*, 1326–7.
[19] *Eg, Grotts v Zahner*, 989 P 2d 415 (Nev 1999) 416 (fiancé not within proximity of relationship); *Thing v La Chusa*, 771 P 2d 814 (Cal 1989), and see *Rabideau v City of Racine*, 627 NW 2d 795, 807 (Wis 2001).
[20] *McLoughlin v O'Brian*, above n 1, 422. See also H Teff, 'Liability for Negligently Inflicted Nervous Shock' (1983) 99 *LQR* 100, from which much of this section's analysis of the House of Lords decision is drawn.

Significantly, he felt able to do so, at least in part, by drawing an analogy between presence at the immediate aftermath and rescue. Just like many rescuers, other people who would be expected to:

> come immediately to the scene—normally a parent or a spouse—could be regarded as being within the scope of [the defendant's] foresight and duty.[21]

For this purpose, attendance at the aftermath in the hospital could be construed as being present at the 'accident' when the 'accident' is viewed as 'an entire event'.[22] From this standpoint, allowing Mrs McLoughlin to succeed was, Lord Wilberforce maintained, a practical and just extension of liability, albeit reaching 'the margin of what the process of logical progression would allow...'[23] The comparison with rescue[24] is instructive, if hardly compelling or 'logical'. Judicial recognition of a duty of care towards rescuers is a relatively modern development, owing much to a policy of encouraging and rewarding altruism. No such incentive is normally required to prompt close members of a family to visit one another in hospital. More importantly, as Lord Bridge pointed out, after *Hambrook v Stokes* had dispensed with the requirement that the claimant must have been physically endangered to succeed:

> there can be no *logical* reason whatever for limiting the defendant's duty to persons in physical proximity to the place where the accident... occurred.[25] (emphasis added)

One might add that, from a medical perspective, Lord Bridge's view would have been even more compelling by the early 1980s than in the mid-1920s. It is only because, for policy reasons, physical proximity to the actual scene of accidents had loomed so large in the case law, that some judges have resorted to artificial analogies such as rescue when such proximity is absent.

Lord Bridge warned against adopting 'hard and fast lines of policy', in an area of negligence:

> where we should resist the temptation to try yet once more to freeze the law in a rigid posture which would deny justice to some who... ought to succeed.[26]

He pointed to the arbitrariness of treating proximity factors and modes of experiencing accidents as legal requirements *additional* to reasonable foreseeability, rather than as considerations which might bear on the degree to which psychiatric illness was foreseeable. To alert us to the dangers, he envisaged the situation of a mother whose husband and children were, to her knowledge, staying in a hotel where there has been a disastrous fire. She learns about the fire from a newspaper

---

[21] *McLoughlin v O'Brian*, above n 1, 422.
[22] *McLoughlin v O'Brian*, above n 1, 422, citing *Benson v Lee* [1972] VR 879, 880 (Australia).
[23] *McLoughlin v O'Brian*, above n 1, 419.
[24] Made even more directly by Lord Edmund-Davies, who described Mrs McLoughlin's action as 'basically indistinguishable from that of a "rescuer"': *McLoughlin v O'Brian*, above n 1, 424.
[25] *McLoughlin v O'Brian*, above n 1, 439.
[26] *McLoughlin v O'Brian*, above n 1, 443.

where she also sees a photograph of trapped, unidentifiable victims, waving for help. On being told later that all her family have perished, she suffers an acute psychiatric illness. It is, said Lord Bridge, undeniable that such an illness would be reasonably foreseeable, and patently unjust if she were denied a remedy:

> simply on the ground that an important link in the chain of causation of her psychiatric illness was supplied by her imagination of the agonies of mind and body in which her family died, rather than by direct perception of the event.[27]

The speeches in the House of Lords reveal marked disagreement over the role of policy in negligence generally, and specifically with reference to psychiatric harm. According to Lord Bridge:

> in this area of the law there are no policy considerations sufficient to justify limiting the liability . . . by reference to some narrower criterion than that of reasonable foreseeability.[28]

Lord Scarman, who fully endorsed Lord Bridge's approach,[29] was even more emphatic in asserting the primacy of principle over policy:

> the objective of the judges is the formulation of principle. And, if principle inexorably requires a decision which entails a degree of policy risk, the court's function is to adjudicate according to principle, leaving policy *curtailment* to the judgment of Parliament.[30] (emphasis added)

And again, 'the policy issue as to where to draw the line is not justiciable'.[31] In their view, the proximity elements were 'factors to be weighed, but not legal limitations, when the test of reasonable foreseeability is to be applied'.[32] By contrast, Lord Edmund-Davies stressed the justiciability in principle of public policy issues. He agreed with Lord Wilberforce that the proximity factors were *additional* hurdles to be overcome, though he did concede that, once reasonable foreseeability has been established, 'the defendant would probably be hard put to escape liability'.[33] Lord Russell was prepared to let policy considerations 'feature' in an appropriate case, so as to 'inhibit' a decision in favour of liability, but he saw no policy justification for denying liability in cases like Mrs McLoughlin's, once reasonable foreseeability had been acknowledged.

Technically, these diverse opinions may be seen to produce a bare majority asserting that reasonable foreseeability can still be trumped by policy considerations. Yet four of the speeches, in differing degrees, favoured a flexible view of liability, rooted in reasonable foreseeability. Only Lord Wilberforce's incremental approach indicated that the proximity factors would often function as barriers to

---

[27] *McLoughlin v O'Brian*, above n 1, 442.
[28] *McLoughlin v O'Brian*, above n 1, 443.
[29] *McLoughlin v O'Brian*, above n 1, 429.
[30] *McLoughlin v O'Brian*, above n 1, 429.
[31] *McLoughlin v O'Brian*, above n 1, 431.
[32] *McLoughlin v O'Brian*, above n 1, 429, *per* Lord Scarman. Cf 'I accept, of course, the importance of the factors . . . as bearing on the *degree* of foreseeability': 442, *per* Lord Bridge.
[33] *McLoughlin v O'Brian*, above n 1, 426.

recovery, even when the harm caused was reasonably foreseeable. Yet, a decade later, it was his approach which was to prevail, as unanimously approved by the House of Lords, in *Alcock*.[34]

McLoughlin v O'Brian, then, was a tantalising decision in the history of 'secondary' claims for psychiatric harm. The House of Lords was torn between basing the duty of care on reasonable foreseeability and enabling additional, policy-driven restrictions to trump it. A few years on, Lord Justice Bingham saw the latter approach as correctly representing the majority position.[35] But then, in two first instance judgments just prior to *Alcock*,[36] parents not present at road accidents successfully sued for shock on being told about the death of a son shortly afterwards. The decision in both of these cases was based squarely on reasonable foreseeability.[37] As Lord Hoffmann was later to observe, *McLoughlin* had come 'within a hair's breadth' of applying the foreseeability test in the same way as in cases of physical injury. It was, he said:

> one of those cases in which one feels that a slight change in the composition of the Appellate Committee would have set the law on a different course.[38]

We should also recall that, in *McLoughlin*, the Law Lords had been generally dismissive of the floodgates argument. All this needs to be remembered in the light of the dispiriting message subsequently conveyed in both *Alcock* and *White*,[39] that it was too late for the courts to put the clock back. Is it really too late to heed Lord Scarman's dictum in *McLoughlin*, that:

> at each landmark stage common law principle, when considered in the context of developing medical science, has beckoned the judges on?[40]

If so, short of the ever-receding prospects of legislative change,[41] the House of Lords appears resigned to an incoherent framework.[42]

---

[34] See below, 67–74.
[35] *Attia v British Gas Plc.* [1988] QB 304, 319–20.
[36] *Hevican v Ruane* [1991] 3 All ER 65; *Ravenscroft v Rederiaktiebolaget Transatlantic* [1991] 3 All ER 73.
[37] Though one of them was later reversed on appeal, as inconsistent with *Alcock*: *Ravenscroft v Rederiaktiebolaget Transatlantic* [1992] 2 All ER 470.
[38] *White v Chief Constable of South Yorkshire* [1999] 2 AC 455, 502, *per* Lord Hoffmann.
[39] See below, 93–6.
[40] See above n 1, 430. See also NJ Mullany and P Handford, 'Moving the Boundary Stone by Statute—The Law Commission on Psychiatric Illness' (1999) 22 *University of New South Wales Law Journal* 350.
[41] Department for Constitutional Affairs, *The Law on Damages*, Consultation Paper (CP 9) (London, Department for Constitutional Affairs, 2007), ch 3, para 94. See further, below Ch 6, 188–9.
[42] See below, 93–4.

The 1990s: from *Alcock* to *Page* to *White*— 'Thus Far And No Further'?[43]

To understand judicial attitudes towards liability for psychiatric harm in the 1990s, one needs to bear in mind how, in general, liability for negligence had been evolving. At the end of the 1970s, the '2 stage' *Anns* test held sway: in novel situations, foreseeable harm was readily seen as imposing a duty of care unless policy dictated otherwise.[44] By the mid-1980s, appellate courts increasingly felt that liability for negligence was rising because judges were loath to deploy, or be seen to deploy, policy-based arguments, which would often have been social or economic in nature. In other words, the *Anns* test was rarely pursued beyond the first stage, courts generally preferring to justify decisions in terms of principle. When it came to psychiatric harm, of course, they had never broken free from the accumulated weight of policy-driven authority, and judicial forebodings of proliferating claims had been a constant feature of the relevant case law. In these respects, the finely-balanced decision in *McLoughlin* was itself somewhat aberrant; but the protestations and reservations in the case about resort to policy-based controls could not survive the growing concern in the late 1980s about indeterminate liability. By then, the floodgates fear had become more prominent in negligence across the board.[45] The combination of a new emphasis on judicial restraint and the sheer scale of the 1989 Hillsborough disaster—the next major testing-ground for psychiatric harm—did not augur well for legal analysis which spurned policy-driven restrictions on liability.

By 1990, the 'retreat from *Anns*' was more or less complete. The House of Lords had discarded the 'two stage' test for duty of care and substituted a triple, *composite* formula, combining reasonable foreseeability with 'sufficient proximity' and what is 'fair, just and reasonable'.[46] The more principled tone of this rebranding might seem paradoxical at the very time that policy concerns were gaining added momentum in the courts.[47] In fact, the 'fair, just and reasonable' limb has, to a degree, served as a vehicle for articulating policy.[48] 'Proximity', too, has proved sufficiently flexible as a concept to act as a cover for policy, nowhere more so than in the area of psychiatric harm. The new formula might be seen as a means of enabling judges to resolve novel issues with less overt recourse to policy when denying or restricting liability. At all events, what may have sounded like a shift towards more principled decision-making was to herald a general reversion to

---

[43] See *White*, above n 38, 500, *per* Lord Steyn.
[44] See above n 9 and related text.
[45] Eg, '[t]he pleading assumes . . . that for every mischance in an accident-prone world someone must be liable in damages': *CBS Songs Ltd v Amstrad Consumer Electronics plc* [1988] AC 1013, 1059, *per* Lord Templeman.
[46] See *Caparo Industries plc v Dickman* [1990] 2 AC 605.
[47] See J Steele, 'Scepticism and the Law of Negligence' (1993) 52 *CLJ* 437.
[48] Though, unlike *Anns* 'stage 2', it can be used to *impose*, as well as to negate, a duty of care.

incrementalism, confirming Lord Keith's contention that the question of duty in negligence is 'of an intensely pragmatic character'.[49] Unfortunately, in the context of psychiatric harm, what passes for pragmatism is liable to be little more than ill-informed supposition.

Alcock v Chief Constable of South Yorkshire Police[50]

The 16 claimants in *Alcock*, who were either relatives or friends of Hillsborough victims, sought damages for psychiatric illness, mainly in the form of PTSD. Several of them were in the stadium; one was just outside and saw what was happening on a television screen. Some were at home and saw live TV broadcasts; others who were only told about the disaster, or who had heard radio reports, saw recorded TV pictures later on. Psychiatric harm and causation were assumed for the purposes of the hearing, which centred on the scope for recovery when the claimant was neither a parent nor spouse of an immediate victim, and on whether communication other than by direct, unaided perception could ground a claim. The outcome for many other claimants would depend on success or failure in *Alcock*.[51]

At first instance, an incremental approach was taken. Nervous shock was deemed reasonably foreseeable in principle for claimants who had seen *live* TV but not for those who had been told of the disaster or had heard a live radio broadcast and only later saw recorded TV news items. Simultaneous television was deemed close enough to 'being there' to count as a medium of communication for purposes of liability:

> the visual image . . . is all-important. It is what is fed to the eyes which makes the instant effect upon the emotions, and the lasting effect upon the memory.[52]

The court's emphasis on the 'instant [visual] effect' is revealing. As previously indicated, in most situations such primary reactions rarely translate into compensable injury.[53]

The class of persons normally entitled to recover was held to include siblings, but no other categories beyond parent or spouse. On the particular facts, this ruled out recovery by a grandfather, uncles, a fiancée, a brother-in-law and a friend. According to Hidden J:

> once [the line] is *extended* to include brother and sister . . . it has reached the margin of what the process of *logical* progression would allow. [The other relationships] . . . are not so immediate . . . as to make it reasonably foreseeable to a defendant that psychiatric

---

[49] *Rowling v Takaro Properties* [1988] AC 473, 501.
[50] *Alcock v Chief Constable of South Yorkshire Police* [1992] 1 AC 310.
[51] See H Teff, 'Liability for Psychiatric Illness after Hillsborough' (1992) 12 *OJLS* 440, from which much of the material on pp 67–74 is drawn.
[52] *Alcock v Chief Constable of South Yorkshire* [1991] 2 WLR 814, 843.
[53] See above Ch 1, 6. See also *Hevican* and *Ravenscroft*, above n 36.

illness, rather than grief and sorrow, would follow death or damage to the loved one.[54] (emphasis added)

Several points arise. In the first place, inclusion of siblings in the category normally entitled to recover is scarcely an 'extension' of the line. Dicta abound envisaging recovery for 'near' or 'close' relatives and for 'loved ones'.[55] In one early case, a twin sister was awarded damages for shock, without any suggestion that she had a special status as a twin.[56] More generally, there is no 'logical' reason for presumptively excluding the claims of, say, a fiancée, partner or grandparent, just as there is no adequate explanation for ruling out claims *solely* on the basis of the particular means of communication. The court's conclusions were neither legally dictated nor medically compelling. They seem rather to represent a compromise reflecting the judge's position on the floodgates:

> the common law must be free to move on . . . But if the common law has the licence to move on with changing times, then that licence must also be subject to a certain degree of limitation if the defendant who is guilty of some negligence is not to be made liable to the world at large.[57]

Within a matter of weeks, *Hevican* and *Ravenscroft* were decided. In these first instance decisions, we find a straightforward application of reasonable foreseeability; several dicta referring to the legitimate claims of a 'loved one' and of 'near' relatives; indirect communication to claimants not at the scene or aftermath of the accident, and still a dismissive view of the floodgates argument. Significantly, in these judgments, close attention is paid to medical evidence about the causes of psychiatric illness,[58] and *Ravenscroft* refers approvingly to Lord Scarman's observation that, informed by 'developing medical science', common law principle has 'beckoned the judges on'.[59] In *Alcock*, both the Court of Appeal and the House of Lords were to decline the invitation.

Alcock on Appeal

The claimants who had won at first instance lost on appeal, and none of the others succeeded. They could not establish *all* of the proximity requirements—close ties and closeness in time and space to the accident. The overall impression conveyed by the appellate judgments is of a preference for restrictive interpretation driven by fear of the floodgates opening. In the House of Lords there was

---

[54] *Alcock*, above n 52, 839.
[55] In *McLoughlin*, Lord Wilberforce said that a 'near relative' may recover: [1983] 1 AC 410, 418. Cf *Bourhill v Young* [1943] AC 92, 117, 120, *per* Lord Porter; *King v Phillips* [1953] 1 QB 429, 441; *Boardman v Sanderson* [1964] 1 WLR 1317, 1318; *Hinz v Berry* [1970] 2 QB 40, 42.
[56] *Turbyfield v Great Western Railway Co* (1937) 54 TLR 221.
[57] *Alcock*, above n 52, 833.
[58] In *Ravenscroft*, the judge stressed Lord Bridge's criterion of ' "informed" judicial opinion' and his own indebtedness to the expert psychiatric evidence: [1991] 3 All ER 73, 79.
[59] *Ibid*, 87.

substantial endorsement of Lord Wilberforce's approach to proximity as a legal limitation on liability, if qualified by an ostensibly more flexible attitude on proximity of relationship. Lord Oliver, for example, could see:

> no logic and no virtue in seeking to lay down as a matter of 'policy' categories of relationship within which claims may succeed and without which they are doomed to failure in limine.[60]

'The source of the shock and distress in all these cases', he said, 'is the affectionate relationship which existed between the plaintiff and the victim'.[61] In similar vein, Lord Keith noted that: 'It is the existence of . . . ties [of love and affection] which leads to mental disturbance when the loved one suffers a catastrophe'.[62]

However, though the causal paramountcy of the *actual* relationship was recognised, there was no corresponding diminution in the significance attributed to other factors; they were still treated as dispositive without reference to closeness of tie. The 'immediate' aftermath was very narrowly construed; the attitude towards television as a medium of communication was more restrictive than at first instance, and much was made of the need for a 'sudden' and 'horrifying' impact on the claimant's mind.

Proximity of Relationship

In *McLoughlin*, Lord Wilberforce had said that restricting recovery to claimants with the closest of family ties—parent and child, husband and wife—could be justified, but that other categories, though not to be ruled out, would need very careful scrutiny:

> I cannot say that they should never be admitted. The closer the tie (not merely in relationship but in care) the greater the claim for consideration.[63]

In *Alcock*, the House of Lords recognized a rebuttable presumption in favour of a parent or spouse and required 'sufficiently close' ties of love and affection to be proved in the case of other relatives or friends. What precisely needs to be shown to establish such ties was not specified, though Lord Ackner would have required love and affection 'comparable to that of the *normal* parent, spouse or child of the victim',[64] (emphasis added) and Lord Jauncey, a relationship as close 'as might reasonably be expected in the case of spouses or parents and children'.[65] Given the determination not to confine recovery by reference to particular formal relationships, one is struck by the apparent eagerness to cling to categorical approaches of a distinctly restrictive nature. This can only produce sterile debate over what con-

---

[60] Ie failure to reach the liability threshold. *Alcock*, above n 50, 415.
[61] *Alcock*, above n 50, 416.
[62] Above n 50, 397.
[63] *McLoughlin*, above n 1, 422.
[64] *Alcock*, above n 50, 403.
[65] *Alcock*, above n 50, 422.

stitute 'normal' familial relationships. In the House's own terms, the cut-off point for the rebuttable presumption seems unduly strict, in particular by its exclusion of partners, fiancé(e)s[66] and siblings. It does not require great imaginative powers, or advanced understanding of psychiatry, to contemplate that, as members of a class, they might suffer from psychiatric illness when a serious accident occurs; all the more so since recovery of damages for such illness has been envisaged when it results from shock at seeing damage to one's property.[67]

Comparison with other categories needlessly obscures the issue. Why should we be sidetracked into deciding whether the claimant's relationship with the immediate victim is comparable to some other, imprecisely delineated, relationship, when we could be asking the more direct question: Was the claimant's condition a reasonably foreseeable result of the defendant's negligence? The House of Lords' unwieldy categorisation tends to undermine its commendable insistence on the critical importance of actual ties. Unfortunately, this is further undermined by the narrow stance taken on the 'immediate' aftermath, the mode of communication and the very nature of compensable shock.

The 'Immediate' Aftermath

Invidious distinctions are inevitable when the 'immediate' aftermath is treated in isolation, as a crude notion of temporal proximity. Mrs McLoughlin can succeed because she experiences shock only two hours after the crash, whereas a spectator at Hillsborough who identified a victim at the mortuary eight or nine hours after the disaster would almost certainly have failed on that basis alone.[68] A mother affected in precisely the same way as Mrs McLoughlin, but too far away or too overcome to reach the hospital quickly would likewise fail.[69] It may be objected that a broadly contemporaneous emotional response is a practical necessity. But this is primarily an argument about evidential uncertainty in regard to causation and foreseeability. Once the aftermath principle itself is accepted, it is more defensible for any cut-off point to be related to circumstances inextricably linked to the original incident than arbitrarily time limited.

The Mode of Communication

The Court of Appeal did not totally rule out claims based on communication of shock via live TV, but envisaged them only in the most exceptional circumstances. Concern was expressed that programmes going 'by satellite to millions' and

---

[66] Lord Keith expressly included fiancé(e)s: *Alcock*, above n 50, 397.
[67] *Attia v British Gas Plc*, above n 35.
[68] *Alcock*, above n 50, 405 and 424, *per* Lord Ackner and Lord Jauncey, respectively.
[69] See F Trindade, 'The Principles Governing the Recovery of Damages for Negligently Caused Nervous Shock' (1986) 45 *CLJ* 476, 490–3.

'viewed worldwide'[70] might create a floodgates problem; though ordinary viewers, of course, would be assumed to possess 'fortitude sufficient to enable them to endure the calamities of modern life'.[71] It was further suggested that the editing and commentary involved made the broadcast a *'novus actus'*[72] and that, being aware of the broadcasting code of ethics, 'the defendant could . . . reasonably expect that the television cameras would not show shocking pictures of suffering by recognisable individuals'.[73] But it was also conceded that the police knew that significant events at the match would have been shown live and seen by close relatives and friends of spectators, if anything, more clearly or vividly than from most parts of the ground. As Parker LJ put it, the cameras:

> may, and probably will, move from one part of the scene to another which seem best to convey the increasing horror of what was taking place.[74]

In such circumstances, it is far from clear that the defendant's knowledge of the code would have established a *'novus actus'*. The argument becomes weaker still in the House of Lords, because of the particular emphasis there on the causal importance of close ties.

In *Alcock*, the House of Lords said that the TV pictures were not capable of giving rise to 'shock' in the sense of a 'sudden assault on the nervous system' as distinct from 'feelings of the deepest anxiety and distress'.[75] Here, too, we see one factor, the mode of perception, artificially divorced from another, closeness of ties, as if they were entirely self-contained. By themselves, 'shocking' pictures might give rise only to primary reactions of transient, non-compensable 'nervous shock'; whereas the initial impact of 'deeply distressing' pictures seen in the context of understandable fears about loved ones could very well develop into secondary responses resulting in traumatic neurosis.

Sudden and Gradual Assaults on the Nervous System

The effect of the House of Lords' misconceived insistence on sudden shock in *Alcock*[76] was to vitiate manifestly deserving claims. Mr Copoc, for example, knew that his son was at the Hillsborough match and believed him to be in the danger zone. He and his wife watched the live TV presentation in a state of continuous fear. He then made telephone calls until 4.00 am the following morning to no avail, after which he went to Sheffield looking in vain for his son at the hospital.

---

[70] *Alcock*, above n 50, 362 and 379–80, *per* Parker LJ and Stocker LJ, respectively.
[71] *McLoughlin*, above n 1, 422, *per* Lord Wilberforce.
[72] A new intervening event, which would absolve the defendant from liability.
[73] *Alcock*, above n 50, 386, *per* Nolan LJ.
[74] *Alcock*, above n 50, 362.
[75] *Alcock*, above n 50, 398 and 405, *per* Lord Keith and Lord Ackner, respectively.
[76] Though Lord Ackner, *Alcock*, above n 50, 401, did say that the law did not *yet* include gradual, cumulative assaults, a qualification later seized upon by Clarke LJ in *North Glamorgan NHS Trust v Walters*, to indicate that he would have taken that 'incremental step' on the facts of *Walters*, had it been necessary: [2003] Lloyd's Rep Med 49, 60. See further below Ch 4, 119.

He finally identified his body at the mortuary on information received from the police. His claim failed.

In the Court of Appeal, Nolan LJ had gone some way towards acknowledging modern medical understanding, by conceding that an accumulation of more gradual assaults upon the nervous system might give rise to psychiatric illness as easily as an instant reaction. Lord Oliver, too, was troubled by the exclusion of claimants whose trauma resulted from a gradual, dawning realization. To extend the notion of proximity to them, he said, 'may seem a logical, analogical development'. But in the absence of express legal authority, the remedy made available to Mrs McLoughlin was denied to Mr Copoc.

Differentiation of this kind partly reflects the importance attached to immediacy of reaction in the formative case law,[77] coupled with the familiar causal potency in law of the single event.[78] But its endurance in the face of 'better understanding of mental illness and its relation to shock'[79] suggests that something more is at stake. Underlying the insistence on 'immediacy, closeness of time and space and direct visual or aural perception'[80] is another concern which has helped to shape the case law and to explain, if not necessarily justify, the spectre of 'virtually limitless liability'. It is the fear, forcefully expressed by Lord Oliver, that a legal regime for psychiatric illness which lacked such controls would have to compensate for such 'ordinary and inevitable incidents of life' as negligently caused grief and sorrow and the stress and strain suffered from caring for accident victims over a long period. The effect would be to extend the law in a direction for which there is, he said, 'no pressing policy need and in which there is no logical stopping point'.[81]

Lord Oliver saw the law on nervous shock as vulnerable to unprincipled line-drawing, encouraged by what he termed 'the essential but illusive concept of proximity'.[82] He could not see any 'readily discernible logical reason' for not compensating persons other than the 'primary victim' for inevitable and readily foreseeable injury. His was the only really sustained attempt to address the resultant anomalies. Yet, despite a certain coyness about using the word, 'policy' was to feature prominently in his analysis, in the speech most overtly concerned with the floodgates threat.

The absence of a legal duty to foreseeably injured persons cannot, he argued, be 'attributable to some arbitrary but unenunciated rule of 'policy' which draws a line as the outer boundary of the area of duty'.[83] It is rather that:

---

[77] Though Mrs McLoughlin's experience could have plausibly been portrayed as one of 'dawning realisation', and it would be invidious to assert that it was more harrowing than Mr Copoc's.
[78] See generally, J Stapleton, *Disease and the Compensation Debate* (Oxford, Clarendon Press, 1987).
[79] *Alcock*, above n 50, 399, *per* Lord Ackner.
[80] *Alcock*, above n 50, 416–7, *per* Lord Oliver. For the statutory exception as regards bereaved spouses and the parents of minors, see above Ch 1, 21.
[81] *Alcock*, above n 50, 416.
[82] *Alcock*, above n 50, 410.
[83] *Alcock*, above n 50, 410.

such persons are not, in contemplation of law, in a relationship of sufficient proximity to or directness with the tortfeasor as to give rise to a duty of care, though no doubt 'policy', if that is the right word, or perhaps the impracticability or unreasonableness of entertaining claims to the ultimate limits of the consequences of human activity, necessarily plays a part in the court's perception of what is sufficiently proximate.[84]

It is this alleged impracticability or unreasonableness that for Lord Oliver (and the other Law Lords in *Alcock*) ultimately justified their interpretation of the immediate aftermath and their insistence on sudden shock. In the instant case:

a dawning consciousness over an extended period that the imagined consequence had occurred, finally confirmed by news of the death and, in some cases, subsequent visual identification of the victim would not suffice.

There was not:

any pressing reason of policy for taking this further step along a road which must ultimately lead to virtually limitless liability.[85]

However, as some earlier Commonwealth decisions had demonstrated, the problem can be approached in a manner more consistent with general negligence principles, by reference to a distinction drawn by Deane J in *Jaensch v Coffey*. He contrasted psychiatric injury which 'results from the impact of matters which themselves formed part of the accident and its aftermath', with that which:

has resulted from contact with more remote consequences such as the subsequent effect of the accident upon an injured person.[86]

In *Beecham v Hughes*,[87] for example, the claimant suffered from reactive depression, signs of which began some time after a road accident in which his partner had sustained very severe brain damage, resulting in permanent disablement. His depression, which developed long after the accident, was held to have arisen not from seeing his partner injured or from the shock of experiencing the accident (in which he had also been injured), but from his subsequent sorrow and inability to accept that she would never be the same person again. The depression could thus be seen as an *indirect* consequence of the negligence. He was not, in respect of it, someone 'closely and directly affected' by the defendant's act. If due allowance is made for 'causal fade', 'causal proximity' can provide:

an objective basis for limiting the undue expansion of liability which would flow from the unfettered application of reasonable foreseeability.[88]

This approach is in keeping with Lord Atkin's observation that the duty of care based on reasonable foreseeability had to be 'limited by the notion of proximity', which he characterised as 'not confined to mere physical proximity' but as extend-

---

[84] *Alcock*, above n 50, 410.
[85] *Alcock*, above n 50, 417.
[86] *Jaensch v Coffey* (1984) 155 CLR 549, 607.
[87] *Beecham v Hughes* (1988) 52 DLR (4th) 625.
[88] *Ibid*, 663, *per* Taggart JA.

ing to 'such close and direct relations that the act complained of directly affects a person'.[89] Lord Bridge's assertion that:

> [h]owever liberally the criterion of reasonable foreseeability is interpreted . . . the number of successful claims in this field . . . [is] likely to be moderate[90]

needs to be understood in the light of his reference to 'the classic principles of negligence derived from *Donoghue v Stevenson*'.

It is true that there has been much scepticism about the usefulness of proximity as a legal concept.[91] It has, for example, been described as a notion which 'tends to conceal and prevent discussion of the policy choices which are determinative'.[92] To this extent, 'causal proximity' could be seen as yet another 'convenient label' which may permit, and disguise, pragmatic decision-making. But the issue has never been whether policy considerations should be eliminated from the analysis. In *McLoughlin*, Lord Bridge and Lord Scarman were as concerned as Lord Wilberforce that there should be limitations on liability. Focussing on causal proximity simply provides a more rational and principled framework for analysing specific situations than 'mechanical considerations of geographical or temporal proximity'.

This is not to deny that, as elsewhere in negligence, the issue of causation may be difficult to resolve. In *Rhodes v Canadian National Railway*,[93] the claimant heard on the radio of a train crash involving her son as a passenger. She made numerous telephone enquiries and saw newspaper pictures of the wreckage. For reasons unconnected with the defendant, she had to endure a very distressful period of eight days before reaching the scene of the collision, during which time she came to realize that her son had died. She never saw his body, which had been consumed by fire. In the event, the appellate court rejected her claim for reactive depression. In the words of Taylor, JA:

> someone who suffers psychological injury as a result of being informed of the death of a relative, or of ruminating on the circumstances of the relative's death, or of visiting the scene some days later cannot, in the absence of any unexpected alarming or horrifying experience caused by the circumstances of the accident, be said to have been closely and directly affected by the negligence which caused it.[94]

The Court was much influenced by the fact that Mrs Rhodes had not been directly exposed to a specific experience 'of an alarming, startling or frightening nature', attributable to the defendant, but had heard of the death from other people. It is open to debate on which side of the line this case should fall. It bears

---

[89] *Donoghue v Stevenson* [1932] AC 562, 581.
[90] *McLoughlin*, above n 1, 441.
[91] See, eg, Justice McHugh, 'Neighbourhood, Proximity and Reliance,' in PD Finn (ed), *Essays on Torts* (Sydney, The Law Book Co Ltd, 1989) ch 2, especially at 27–33; J Steele, 'Scepticism and the Law of Negligence', above n 47, esp at 450–53; D Butler, 'Proximity as a Determinant of Duty: The Nervous Shock Litmus Test' (1995) 21 *Monash University Law Review* 159. See also *Hill v Van Erp* (1997) 188 CLR 159. But see C Witting, 'Duty of Care: An Analytical Approach' (2005) 25 *OJLS* 33.
[92] See Justice McHugh, *ibid*, 39.
[93] (1990) 75 DLR (4th) 248.
[94] *Ibid*, 298.

a strong resemblance to Lord Bridge's example, in *McLoughlin*, of the hotel fire.[95] Though the extrinsic factors which prolonged Mrs Rhodes' ordeal plainly complicated the issue of causation, too much stress may have been laid on the absence of a specific shock and on third party communication. Several aftermath cases deemed to turn on the direct perception of a specific event in reality seem to involve a more extended process of dawning realization, as the full horror unfolds, in which third party communication may have been the first stage.[96] Only in the last decade or so have the English courts begun to be more receptive of medical evidence which perceives a causal link through cumulative shock.[97]

In retrospect, it is unfortunate that the first opportunity, after *McLoughlin*, for the House of Lords to reconsider the ambit of liability for nervous shock should have arisen from a televised mass disaster. It was all the more inopportune coming at a time when several such disasters were in the news, one of which—the Zeebrugge ferry incident—also raised the question of potential liability to television viewers. The topicality of PTSD, the number of people injured at Hillsborough and the heightened traumatic potential of such highly publicised events could only have reinforced traditional judicial concerns about the floodgates. Perhaps, too, the fact that communication via television was a major issue served to foster a sense of inappropriateness, even trivialisation, regarding secondary claims.[98] The contrast with *McLoughlin* is striking: in *Alcock*, the House of Lords unanimously endorsed Lord Wilberforce's insistence on special controls.

Page v Smith and *White v Chief Constable Of South Yorkshire*: the 'Patchwork Quilt' Embedded

If *Alcock* appeared to signal the triumph of pragmatism over principle, it did not bring an end to controversy. The old tensions resurfaced in two other key House of Lords decisions of the 1990s, *Page v Smith*[99] and *White v Chief Constable of the South Yorkshire Police*.[100] On one level, *Page* seemed to hold out the promise of more coherence, with Lord Lloyd's assertion, in the leading speech, that '[t]here is no justification for regarding physical and psychiatric injury as different "kinds" of injury'.[101] Yet, in certain respects, the case served to muddy the waters still further; while, in *White*, Lord Hoffmann declared that 'in this area of the law, the search for principle was called off in *Alcock*'.[102] Despite this defeatist message, the

---

[95] See above n 27 and related text.
[96] Eg, *McLoughlin* itself, and *Jaensch v Coffey*, above n 86.
[97] See further below Ch 4, 118–21.
[98] Eg, 'Watching television, like living itself, is something to be done at one's own risk': *The Times*, Editorial, 29 Nov 1991.
[99] *Page v Smith* [1996] AC 155.
[100] See above n 38.
[101] See above n 99, 190.
[102] *White*, above n 38, 511.

proper scope of liability for psychiatric harm continues to exercise the appellate courts.[103]

Much of the current confusion stems from attempts to label all claimants as either 'primary' or 'secondary' victims, by reference to how directly involved they were in the circumstances which caused an accident. Within this framework, primary victims need only prove psychiatric harm as a result of reasonably foreseeable exposure to the risk of 'personal' injury; by contrast, claims by secondary victims remain subject to the traditional control mechanisms. This dual approach was first mooted by Lord Oliver in *Alcock*, where, in broad terms, he attributed primary status to 'involved participants' and secondary status to 'passive witnesses'. A few years later, in *Page*, Lord Lloyd endorsed the primary/secondary divide but he appeared to introduce a more restrictive interpretation of primary status, that would *confine* it to persons who have been *physically* injured or imperilled. This restrictive, if contested, definition, seemingly endorsed by the House of Lords in *White*, has substantially disadvantaged claimants outside the zone of physical danger.

Any *accident*-based model of liability, whether predicated on direct involvement or physical endangerment, prompts several objections. First, it perpetuates the medically unsound assumption that instant, 'on the spot' experience of an event (or of its immediate aftermath) is bound to be more causally significant than other triggers of psychiatric harm.[104] Secondly, it cannot cater for meritorious claims arising from situations where there has been no discrete 'accident' in the form of a collision or other disastrous event. For example, psychiatric illness resulting from negligent misinformation, work-related stress or a prolonged bedside vigil following hospital negligence does not entail exposure to physical danger. Thirdly, even in ordinary road and railway accidents, it can be far from easy to determine, as a matter of fact, whether particular claimants were 'directly' involved or physically endangered. And if physical endangerment *is* required for primary status, the stringent rules for secondary victims will often result in the arbitrary denial of deserving claims. The upshot has been yet more convoluted distinctions, uncertainty and inconsistency in the case law. In order to appreciate the overall impact of *Page* and *White*, it is first necessary to take a closer look at the 'primary'/'secondary' divide.

Primary/Secondary/Both/Neither?

In *Page*, Lord Lloyd could hardly have been more emphatic or candid:

> In cases involving nervous shock, it is essential to distinguish between the primary victim and secondary victims . . . In claims by secondary victims the law insists on certain

---

[103] See below Ch 4.
[104] See, eg, C Tennant, 'Liability for Psychiatric Injury: an Evidence-based Approach' (2002) 76 *Australian Law Journal* 73.

control mechanisms, in order as a matter of policy to limit the number of potential claimants.[105] (emphasis added)

Though this supposedly essential distinction still looms large in the case law, there has been considerable judicial disagreement over how to apply it in practice, and increasing acknowledgement of its shortcomings. Use of the pejorative label 'secondary' highlights a claim's dependence on what has happened to someone else. It diverts attention from the foreseeability of harm to the claimant, whom we are invited to think of as inherently more peripheral and less entitled to legal redress than someone 'directly' imperilled in an untoward incident. Yet, precisely because the strength of a person's bond with an immediate victim is often the key predictor of ensuing psychiatric illness, the essence of the 'secondary' claim is *experiential*, not remote. Of course, the narrower the definition of 'primary' status, and the more demanding the legal obstacles which 'secondary' victims must overcome, the easier it is to assuage concerns about proliferating claims. The majority of the Law Lords in both *Page* and *White* would have granted 'primary' status to a much more limited range of claimants than Lord Oliver had envisaged in *Alcock*.

In *Alcock*, Lord Oliver had described psychiatric injury claims in the following way:

Broadly they divide into two categories . . . cases in which the injured plaintiff was involved, either mediately or immediately, as a participant, and those in which the plaintiff was no more than the passive and unwilling witness of injury caused to others.[106] (emphasis added)

Two points should be made at the outset. First, *Alcock* itself (unlike the car crash in *Page*) did not concern 'involved participants', so that Lord Oliver's observations on 'primary' victims do not technically constitute a binding statement of law. Secondly, he was merely proffering a broad categorisation, not a comprehensive definition, of primary and secondary victims.[107] That said, 'participants', almost by definition, would satisfy the proximity criteria at the heart of liability for negligence: their direct personal involvement itself could be said to create the relationship that establishes a duty. In other words, they should be owed a duty of care without having to satisfy the special, additional requirements demanded of secondary victims.

Importantly, under Lord Oliver's classification, you can be a participant without being (or reasonably believing yourself to be) in *physical* danger. He expressly refers to rescuers, whether or not physically at risk, and to involuntary agents of injury to others.[108] In *Page*, Lord Lloyd appeared to define primary victims more narrowly, when he described the claimant as a 'participant', who had been 'directly involved in the accident and well within the range of foreseeable physical

---

[105] *Page*, above n 99, 197.
[106] *Alcock*, above n 50, 407.
[107] See *White*, above n 38, 472, *per* Lord Goff.
[108] Eg, *Dooley v Cammell Laird & Co Ltd* [1951] 1 Lloyd's Rep 271. Cf *Galt v British Railways Board* (1983) 133 *New Law Journal* 870.

injury'.[109] As a practical matter, the physical boundaries of the 'zone of danger' might be difficult to identify, so that the obvious advantage of establishing primary status is prone to generate litigation over an often tenuous divide. Suppose, for example, that negligent conduct or design causes a coach, train or bus to crash, or the seating in an auditorium or stadium to give way. How many traumatised but physically unharmed passengers, members of the audience or spectators, as the case may be, will recover for psychiatric illness because they are deemed to have been within the range of foreseeable physical injury?[110]

Such is the imprecision of the divide that, in some of the cases, the same claimant has been plausibly described as primary, secondary, both or neither! In *Frost*, (*White* at the Court of Appeal stage) Rose LJ considered the four police officer claimants on crowd control at Hillsborough to be primary victims, because they were on duty at the ground and directly involved through their employer's negligence; Judge LJ saw them as secondary victims, because they were not exposed to the risk of *physical* injury from that negligence, and Henry LJ said: 'I am not sure that the labelling of each plaintiff as a primary or secondary victim really matters'![111] In allowing their appeals, the Court, by a majority, found that they had a primary, or at least special, status such that the additional control mechanisms did not apply. In *Page*, Lord Lloyd said that claimants could sometimes be both primary and secondary victims.[112]

The Mixed Messages of *Page v Smith*

Confused Legal Doctrine

In *Page v Smith* there was a collision of 'moderate severity', when the defendant drove negligently across the path of Mr Page, who was driving at around 30 miles per hour. He did not sustain any external bodily injury but claimed that, due to the collision, the post-viral fatigue syndrome from which he had suffered intermittently in the past had recurred, in a chronic and permanent form. Having concluded that the condition, also known as CFS or ME,[113] was a genuine, if 'elusive', illness and that Mr Page 'did suffer nervous shock in the broad sense of the word', the judge found the defendant liable.[114] His decision was reversed by a unanimous

---

[109] But see below, 80–82.
[110] Cf 'What is so magical about being within the range of foreseeable physical injury, except perhaps the mistaken view that the number of potential claimants will be limited by the nature of the case?' F Trindade, 'Nervous Shock and Negligent Conduct' (1996) 112 *LQR* 22, 24–5.
[111] *Frost v Chief Constable of South Yorkshire* [1997] 3 WLR 1194, 1213, CA.
[112] See above n 99, 190, citing *Schneider v Eisovitch* [1960] 2 QB 430; *Malcolm v Broadhurst* [1970] 3 All ER 508, and *Brice v Brown* [1984] 1 All ER 997. See also *Hunter v British Coal Corp* [1999] QB 140, CA.
[113] Chronic fatigue syndrome and myalgic encephalomyelitis, respectively.
[114] The condition is not listed in DSM-IV or ICD-10. Though predominantly seen as a psychiatric disorder, the symptoms can sometimes suggest a neurological origin. See *Page*, above n 99, 185 and 197, *per* Lord Lloyd.

Court of Appeal, applying Lord Denning's dictum that 'the test of liability for shock is foreseeability of injury by shock'.[115] The Court held that such injury had to have been reasonably foreseeable in a person of normal fortitude,[116] a requirement it did not deem satisfied by a relatively minor car accident in which no one had been physically injured.

The House of Lords, however, by a majority of three to two, found in favour of Mr Page.[117] Lord Lloyd held that only *secondary* claimants had to prove foreseeability of injury *by* shock in order to establish liability *for* shock. In *King v Phillips*, the context of Lord Denning's dictum, the claimant was a 'secondary' victim and this was true also, said Lord Lloyd, of all the other cases in which the rule had been applied. By contrast, Mr Page was 'directly involved in the accident and well within the range of foreseeable physical injury. He was the primary victim'. 'Is it', asked Lord Lloyd rhetorically, 'to become necessary, in ordinary personal injury claims, where the plaintiff is the primary victim, for the court to concern itself with different "kinds" of injury?'[118] In such cases, he maintained, as regards the nature of the harm, it suffices for claimants to show that some kind of *personal* injury to them, physical or psychiatric, was reasonably foreseeable:

> where the plaintiff is the primary victim of the defendant's negligence, the nervous shock cases . . . are not in point. Since the defendant was admittedly under a duty of care not to cause the plaintiff foreseeable physical injury, it was unnecessary to ask whether he was under a separate duty of care not to cause foreseeable psychiatric injury.[119]

Physical injury to Mr Page was held to be reasonably foreseeable, and though *it* did not occur, personal (psychiatric) injury did. As for the rule that the injury had to be reasonably foreseeable in claimants of 'normal fortitude', this, too, was held to be inappropriate in the case of primary victims:[120] it did not matter that Mr Page was unusually susceptible to psychiatric injury.[121] Nor did it matter that the recurrence of the condition proved to be unforeseeably severe. As *some* kind of personal injury to him was foreseeable, he was owed a duty of care and, said Lord Lloyd, the 'eggshell skull' principle applied—the defendant had to take his victim as he found him and was liable to the full extent of his personal injury.[122]

---

[115] In *King v Phillips* [1953] 1 QB 429, endorsed by the Privy Council in *Overseas Tankship (UK) Ltd v Morts Dock and Engineering Co Ltd (The Wagon Mound (No 1))* [1961] AC 388, PC, 426, *per* Viscount Simonds. See above Ch 2, 50.

[116] See *Bourhill v Young* [1943] AC 92, 117, *per* Lord Porter. See also *Malcolm v Broadhurst* and *Brice v Brown*, above n 112. And see above Ch 2, 48–9.

[117] Subject only to proof of causation, which was later established: *Page v Smith* (No 2) [1996] 1 WLR 855.

[118] *Page*, above n 99, 187.

[119] Above n 99. And again: 'Nothing will be gained by treating them as different "kinds" of personal injury, so as to require the application of different tests in law.' *Ibid*, 188.

[120] At least in 'zone of danger' cases. See D Howarth, in K Oliphant (ed), *The Law of Tort* (London, LexisNexis Butterworths, 2nd edn 2007), Ch 12, para 12.159.

[121] Cf '[i]t was not relevant to ask whether psychiatric illness was reasonably foreseeable either to the plaintiff (who had a history of CFS) or to a person of normal fortitude': Law Commission, No 249, *Liability for Psychiatric Illness* (London, HMSO, 1998), para 2.14, 13–14.

[122] See *Malcolm v Broadhurst*, above n 112.

The decision was controversial in several respects. To begin with, there was the 'ill-defined' nature of the medical condition itself, the uncertainty as to its causes, and its absence from the leading international classificatory systems: nowhere in the judgment was it explicitly stated that Mr Page's condition met the legal requirement of a 'recognised' or 'recognisable' psychiatric illness. Its impact on him, however, was so severe that he was considered unlikely to be capable of future full-time work. *Page* is a salutary reminder that, as a guide to the appropriateness of redress, the severity of a condition may sometimes be more compelling than its formal designation. In fact, Lord Lloyd's treatment of established legal doctrine attracted much unfavourable analysis, most notably the formidable criticism by Lord Goff in *White v Chief Constable of South Yorkshire Police*. In a powerful dissent, he described *Page* as 'a remarkable departure from . . . generally accepted principles'.[123] The controversy is complicated by elements of ambiguity in Lord Lloyd's speech, and it may be useful at this point to summarise some of the main areas of contention.

According to Lord Lloyd, only 'secondary' claimants had to prove that their psychiatric harm was foreseeably caused by shock. Yet, though any diminution of the 'shock' requirement is to be welcomed, many previous decisions and authoritative dicta are more naturally understood as having assumed shock to be a general feature of psychiatric harm claims.[124] Similarly, there is no indication in the earlier case law that the 'normal fortitude' requirement was intended as an obstacle only for secondary victims.[125] Lord Lloyd's deployment of the 'eggshell skull' principle is also problematic. He said that as *some* kind of personal injury to Mr Page was foreseeable, he was owed a duty of care and entitled to damages to the full extent of his injury. But the 'eggshell skull' principle—'taking your victim as you find him'—is purely concerned with the amount of compensation to be awarded *once liability has been established*. There can be no liability at all without breach of duty, which entails causing a reasonably foreseeable kind of injury.[126] Mr Page was held not to have been physically *injured*, and it was not *decided* that any kind of *psychiatric* illness was *reasonably foreseeable*.[127] Therefore no breach of a duty to prevent him from suffering psychiatric harm occurred. In the absence of *any* breach of duty, there was no basis for invoking the eggshell skull principle.[128]

---

[123] *White*, above n 38, 473. And see *Corr v IBC Vehicles Ltd* [2008] UKHL 13 [54], *per* Lord Neuberger. See also NJ Mullany, 'Psychiatric damage in the House of Lords—Fourth time unlucky: *Page v Smith*' (1995) 3 *Journal of Law and Medicine* 112; F Trindade, 'Nervous Shock and Negligent Conduct', above n 110.

[124] See eg, *Bourhill v Young*, above n 116, 101–2, 105 and 117; *King v Phillips*, above n 115 and related text; *The Wagon Mound (No 1)*, above n 115, 426; *Brice v Brown*, above n 112, 1006–7.

[125] See above n 116 and related text. See also *McLoughlin*, above n 1, 422, *per* Lord Wilberforce; *Page*, above n 99, *per* Lord Keith (diss), 169 and *per* Lord Jauncey (diss) 178.

[126] See *White*, above n 38, 476, *per* Lord Goff.

[127] 'It was unnecessary to ask, as a separate question, whether the defendant should reasonably have foreseen injury by shock.' *Page*, above n 99, 190, *per* Lord Lloyd. Though Lords Lloyd and Ackner did consider that injury by shock was foreseeable on the facts, they did not regard this as the correct test.

[128] Scottish Law Commission, *Discussion Paper on Damages for Psychiatric Injury* (Edinburgh, The Stationery Office, 2002) No 120, 17, para 3.16.

In addition, though symbolically appealing if seen as an attempt to decry the belittling of psychiatric harm,[129] to insist that physical and psychiatric harm are not to be treated in law as 'different "kinds"' of personal injury is problematic. As Jones has persuasively argued, to conflate them is too sweeping from a medical standpoint and can be singularly unhelpful for courts tasked with deciding what is reasonably foreseeable for the purpose of attributing blame:

> *Page* does not fit with medical understanding of the causes of psychiatric harm. The mere fact that minor or trivial physical injury has occurred—let alone has not occurred but was reasonably foreseeable—is not an indicator for developing a psychiatric reaction.[130]

Most importantly, *Page* was open to the interpretation that presence within the range of foreseeable *physical* injury is a *necessary* attribute of primary status. It was interpreted to this effect in several Court of Appeal decisions and would appear to have been so construed by Lord Steyn in *White*, where he said that, in *Page*:

> [t]he plaintiff was directly involved in a motor car accident. He was within the range of potential physical injury. As a result of the accident he suffered from chronic fatigue syndrome. In this context Lord Lloyd . . . adopted a distinction between primary and secondary victims: Lord Ackner and Lord Browne-Wilkinson agreed. Lord Lloyd said that a plaintiff who had been within the range of foreseeable injury was a primary victim. Mr Page fulfilled this requirement and could in principle recover compensation for psychiatric loss. In my view it follows that all other victims, who suffer pure psychiatric harm, are secondary victims and must satisfy the control mechanisms laid down in the *Alcock* case . . . [I]f the narrow formulation by Lord Lloyd . . . of who may be a primary victim is kept in mind, this classification ought not to produce inconsistent results.[131]

In the other leading speech in *White*, Lord Hoffmann, if more guardedly, also conveyed the impression that he saw physical endangerment as integral to primary status. In particular, one might draw this inference from his analysis of the claim that the on-duty police were akin to rescuers.[132]

---

[129] At least as regards primary victims.

[130] M Jones, 'Liability for Psychiatric Damage: Searching for a Path between Pragmatism and Principle', in J Neyers, E Chamberlain and S Pitel (eds), *Emerging Issues in Tort Law* (Oxford, Hart Publishing, 2007) ch 5, 113, 119. See also A Sprince, 'Negligently Inflicted Psychiatric Damage: a Medical Diagnosis and Prognosis' (1998) 18 *Legal Studies* 59.

[131] *White*, above n 38, 496–7. For examples of Court of Appeal judgments applying Lord Lloyd's 'narrow formulation,' see Lord Goff's dissenting speech, especially at 478, where he instanced the Court of Appeal judgments in *Young v Charles Church (Southern) Ltd* (1997) 39 BMLR 146 and in *Frost/White* itself. He also noted that the Law Commission had interpreted Lord Lloyd's speech in the same way: Law Commission, No 249, *Liability for Psychiatric Illness* (London, HMSO, 1998), para 5.46. Cf '[A]ccording to Lord Lloyd . . . it is only when the pursuer [claimant] is within the zone of potential physical danger that the general duty not to cause him personal, including psychiatric, injury arises': Scottish Law Commission, *Discussion Paper*, above n 128, 3.18.

[132] Lord Hoffmann viewed the argument that the claimants were secondary victims because they were not 'within the range of foreseeable physical injury' as having had 'some support from the speeches in *Page*': *White*, above n 38, 505. He went on to say that '[t]here is no authority which decides that a rescuer is in any special position in relation to liability for psychiatric injury', and that he did not see 'any logical reason why the normal treatment of rescuers on the issues of foreseeability and causation should lead to the conclusion that, for the purpose of liability for psychiatric injury, they should be given special treatment as primary victims when they were not within the range of foreseeable

That *Page* can be understood as having made physical endangerment a *precondition* of primary status is apparent from several passages in Lord Lloyd's speech. We have already noted his observation that Mr Page was 'directly involved in the accident, and well within the range of foreseeable physical injury. He was the primary victim'. In addition, he said that:

> the secondary victim is almost always outside the area of physical impact, and therefore outside the area of foreseeable physical injury. But where the plaintiff is the primary victim ... [s]ince the defendant was admittedly under a duty of care not to cause the plaintiff foreseeable physical injury, it was unnecessary to ask whether he was under a separate duty of care not to cause foreseeable psychiatric injury.[133]

However, as Lord Goff pointed out in *White*, Lord Lloyd had 'accepted the distinction between primary and secondary victims drawn by Lord Oliver in the *Alcock* case'.[134] Lord Oliver, it will be recalled, far from limiting primary status to the 'physically endangered', saw it as covering 'involved participants', including those 'coming to the aid of others injured or threatened', whether or not they were physically threatened themselves, and involuntary agents of injury to others. Moreover, Lord Lloyd, in summarising his conclusions, said that (aside from the special controls for secondary claims):

> the approach in all cases should be the same, namely, whether the defendant can reasonably foresee that his conduct will expose the plaintiff to the risk of personal injury, whether physical or psychiatric.

The natural inference, said Lord Goff, is that Lord Lloyd saw reasonable foreseeability of physical injury as a 'sufficient' but not a 'necessary' condition of liability for psychiatric injury. On this view, the references to being within the range of foreseeable physical injury should be understood as descriptive of the situation Mr Page was in as the victim of a car accident—not prescriptive of primary victims as a class. However, Lord Goff was a lone voice in pursuing the above analysis in *White*.[135] It

---

physical injury and their psychiatric injury was caused by witnessing or participating in the aftermath of accidents which caused death or injury to others': *ibid*, 509. Lord Browne-Wilkinson concurred with Lord Steyn and Lord Hoffmann.

[133] *Page*, above n 99, 187. Lord Lloyd also said that 'None of [the *Alcock* control] mechanisms are required in the case of a primary victim. Since liability depends on foreseeability of physical injury, there could be no question of the defendant finding himself liable to all the world.' And again, 'Before a defendant can be held liable for psychiatric injury suffered by a primary victim, he must at least have foreseen the risk of physical injury': 189.

[134] See above n 38, 478, *per* Lord Goff.

[135] Though it is true that Lord Steyn prefaced a seemingly unqualified definition of primary status by saying that Mr Page 'was directly involved in a motor car accident. He was within the range of potential physical injury ... *In this context* Lord Lloyd ... adopted a distinction between primary and secondary victims': see above n 131 and related text (emphasis added). Cf 'in circumstances such as a road accident': *White*, above n 38, 463 *per* Lord Griffiths. And see below Ch 4 for decisions which treat the restrictive interpretation of primary status in *Page* as limited to traditional accident-based cases involving immediate or imminent danger; eg, *The Creutzfeldt-Jacob Disease Litigation Group B Plaintiffs v Medical Research Council* [2000] Lloyd's Law Rep Med 161, 164, *per* Morland J; *Grieves v FT Everard* [2007] UKHL 39, [32] and [33], *per* Lord Hoffmann. And see *Leach v Chief Constable of Gloucestershire Constabulary* [1999] 1 WLR, 1421, 1429, *per* Pill LJ.

is, to say the least, unfortunate that several passages in Lord Lloyd's speech conveyed the impression that he saw physical endangerment as a precondition of primary status, and that Lord Steyn, too, could be seen as having attempted 'an exhaustive definition of primary victims'.[136]

The Unfulfilled Promise of 'Law Marching with Medicine'

To confine primary status to the physically imperilled is to mark a retreat to the early twentieth century fixation on the 'zone of danger', a refusal to engage with modern science at odds with the protestations that the legal rules need to reflect advances in psychiatry. The inconsistency has added salience given the shaky doctrinal foundations of the majority analysis in *Page* more generally. Certainly the case contained some positive-sounding pronouncements by Lord Lloyd and Lord Browne-Wilkinson. Yet at the heart of the decision lies a profound contradiction. Rhetorically it asserts a bold assimilation of physical and psychiatric harm; in substance, it appeared to reinforce the unscientific nature of the legal framework by insisting on physical imperilment as the key to primary status. As a consequence, many claimants relegated to 'secondary' status may be denied redress for unsubstantiated reasons of policy.

Lord Lloyd had professed himself anxious to rid the law of ill-informed differentiation between physical and psychiatric injury:

> In an age when medical knowledge is expanding fast, and psychiatric knowledge with it, it would not be sensible to commit the law to a distinction between physical and psychiatric injury, which may already seem somewhat artificial, and may soon be altogether outmoded. Nothing will be gained by treating them as different 'kinds' of personal injury, so as to require the application of different tests in law.[137]

His concern that physical and psychiatric injury should be *treated* as the same 'kind' of 'personal injury' may have served a specific doctrinal purpose—a purported, if misconceived, application of the 'eggshell skull' rule.[138] But, putting the doctrinal issue to one side, it is not unreasonable to assume that his conflation of the physical and the psychiatric did have a broader import. He had, after all, just commended both Lord Macmillan's dictum that '[t]he distinction between mental shock and bodily injury was never a scientific one',[139] and Kennedy J's surmise that 'nervous shock is or may be in itself an injurious affection of the physical organism'.[140] More tellingly, in the very same paragraph as the passage cited

---

[136] See *Campbell v North Lanarkshire Council* [1999] ScotCS 163 [42].
[137] *Page*, above n 99, 188. Lord Browne-Wilkinson was also at pains to assert the close relationship between physical and mental processes. By contrast, the dissenting speeches suggest a more disparaging attitude towards harm to the psyche, as in Lord Jauncey's reference to 'a plaintiff who suffers *merely* nervous shock': *ibid*, 171, (emphasis added), as well as evident scepticism about the gravity of the claimant's condition: 169–70, *per* Lord Keith and 180, *per* Lord Jauncey.
[138] See above 78–9.
[139] *Bourhill v Young* [1943] AC 92, 103.
[140] *Dulieu v White & Sons* [1901] 2 KB 669, 677. See above Ch 2, 45.

above, there is a lengthy extract from Lord Bridge's speech in *McLoughlin*, expressing similar sentiments to support the argument that reasonable foreseeability should be the basis of liability for *all* psychiatric harm claims in negligence. Lord Lloyd's position would seem to point more naturally to liability for *all* recognisable personal harm being rooted in reasonable foreseeability, yet he was firmly of the view that, for policy reasons, special controls were essential in claims by secondary victims.

As is apparent, the reconfiguration of liability rules in *Page* provoked much controversy. Ironically, had it been decided on more orthodox lines, the outcome would have been the same, since the majority did consider psychiatric illness reasonably foreseeable to someone of normal fortitude, on the facts.[141] As Lord Lloyd put it:

> When cars collide at 30 miles per hour, the possibility that those involved will suffer nervous shock, resulting in some form of psychiatric illness, is not something to be brushed aside.

Lord Ackner, in a terse speech, was more forthright:

> the risk of injury by nervous shock was clearly foreseeable. A person of 'normal fortitude', whatever that imprecise phrase may mean, could well have been terrified by the event and the resultant assault on his or her nervous system could well have caused a post-traumatic neurosis.[142]

However, Lord Ackner's stance on what was foreseeable in *Page* is not easy to reconcile with his more sanguine view of the likely effects on parents and spouses of the simultaneous TV broadcasts at Hillsborough.[143]

Hillsborough Revisited

Soon after the decision in *Page*, 14 police officers who had been physically present in the enclosures at Hillsborough, trying to save crushed fans, received out-of-court settlements for psychiatric harm. But what of the officers not exposed to the risk of physical injury, who had performed emotionally exacting tasks either during or in the aftermath of the disaster? This was the issue in *Frost/White*.[144] Of the five claimants,[145] four were at the ground, helping to carry the dead or attempting

---

[141] *Page*, above n 99, 197, *per* Lord Lloyd; 170, *per* Lord Ackner, and 181–2, *per* Lord Browne-Wilkinson.

[142] *Page*, above n 99, 170. It is of interest that several of the appellate judges in *Page* were unwilling to concede the foreseeability of injury through 'nervous shock' when cars collide at 30 miles per hour.

[143] See *Alcock*, above n 50, 405.

[144] *Frost* at first instance and in the Court of Appeal (above n 111), *White*, above n 38, in the House of Lords.

[145] Selected as representative of the various roles discharged by 23 claimants.

to resuscitate spectators, in horrifying circumstances.[146] The fifth officer had been on duty at the local hospital mortuary and went to the ground only later in the evening. Once again, the judicial response was mixed. All the claimants lost at first instance; the four officers on duty at the ground succeeded in a divided Court of Appeal, only to lose by a majority in the House of Lords.

The officers claimed that they were owed a duty of care on at least one of two possible grounds: as 'employees',[147] acting under the direction of an employer whose negligence had put them at foreseeable risk of psychiatric injury,[148] or as 'rescuers'. On either basis, they contended, the special proximity controls did not apply. Waller J dismissed both arguments. As employees, he saw the claimants as secondary victims, since any psychiatric injury resulted from their witnessing death or injury to others. On the facts, he considered only one of them to have been a rescuer but, in any event, he saw 'professional' rescuers as persons 'of extraordinary phlegm', hardened to circumstances which would cause an ordinary person distress.[149] They should not, he said, recover damages unless the nature of their rescuing activity made it just and reasonable for them to do so when a spectator who viewed the horrific scene had no remedy. Nor, for that matter, was he satisfied that their psychiatric injury was 'shock-induced'.

By the time the case reached the Court of Appeal, the House of Lords had decided *Page v Smith*. If the narrow interpretation of 'primary victim' in *Page* were to be applied, none of the claimants could succeed. Not physically endangered, they would only have had secondary status, and they lacked close ties with the immediate victims.[150] Understandably, the Court felt constrained to dwell at length on whether the appellants had 'primary' or 'secondary' status.[151] Yet, as the judgments of Rose and Henry LJJ indicate, such an approach is far from satisfactory. It diverts attention from a more open, direct and natural inquiry into whether, on the particular facts, the defendant should have foreseen the harm. The limited value, and deceptive potential, of bare labels is equally apparent in the Court's treatment of 'rescuer' and 'employee' status. The point is not that a claimant's rescuing function or employment role should be disregarded, rather that the designation 'rescuer' or 'employee' without more is insufficiently precise and informative to guarantee defensible outcomes.

---

[146] 'It was truly gruesome. The victims were blue, cyanotic, incontinent: their mouths open, vomiting: their eyes staring. A pile of dead bodies lay and grew outside gate three. Extending further and further onto the pitch, the injured were laid down and attempts made to revive them . . . The scene was emotive and chaotic as well as gruesome.' Taylor LJ, *Interim Report on the Hillsborough Stadium Disaster* (London, HMSO, 1989) Cmnd 3878, 15. Cited by Rose LJ in *Frost*, above n 111, 1198.

[147] In functional terms. Ie, strictly speaking they were office holders, essentially owed the same duty as employees.

[148] Cf *Knightley v Johns* [1982] 1 WLR 349.

[149] Cf the 'fireman's rule', applied in a few United States jurisdictions, precluding recovery for negligence, an approach rejected unanimously by the Court of Appeal. And see *Ogwo* v *Taylor* [1988] AC 431.

[150] This was the position adopted in the Court of Appeal by Judge LJ, dissenting.

[151] See above 77.

Having noted that, in *Alcock*, rescuers formed Lord Oliver's first category of 'involved participants', Rose LJ concluded that whether or not a particular claimant is a rescuer is a question of fact in all the circumstances. These would include the character and extent of the incident; whether it had finished; whether there was any danger, continuing or otherwise, to the accident victim or the claimant; the character of the claimant's conduct, both intrinsically and vis-à-vis the accident victim, and how proximate the claimant's conduct was to the incident in time and place.[152] Professional rescuers might, in general, be 'more hardened' than others, but whether they are at foreseeable risk of psychiatric harm is, also, simply a question of degree on the particular facts.[153] In similar vein, his Lordship said that the standard of care required of an employer and the requisite degree of proximity:

> will of course vary from case to case according, among other matters, to the nature of the job and the degree of fortitude to be expected of the employee.[154]

Significantly, Rose LJ ruled that a number of officers whom he did not deem rescuers on the facts were entitled to succeed as employees: the defendant's negligence, he said, had exposed them to 'excessively horrific events such as were likely to cause psychiatric illness even in a police officer'.[155]

The judgment of Henry LJ also conveys a sense of mounting impatience with the surfeit of labels and intricate distinctions which have plagued this area of law, turning it into a taxonomist's paradise. His doubts as to whether the 'primary'/'secondary' labelling really mattered were, in effect, a plea for a more direct focus on the foreseeability of the harm. For example, he considered that a duty of care should be owed to the claimants 'by *any* defendant who caused such a disaster', employer or otherwise.[156] (emphasis added). If claims by employees or rescuers did require some additional element of proximity, he said, their active involvement would normally provide it. In the case of the appellants in *Frost*, there was no doubting their foreseeable, direct and close involvement, as participants who 'had no choice but to be there and be involved'.[157] The South Yorkshire Police standing order on PTSD, introduced in 1988, and its provision of a force welfare officer and psychologist at the stadium, were strong additional indicators, if such were needed, that the Chief Constable recognised the foreseeability of psychiatric harm to them. 'Here', said Henry LJ:

> it seems to me obvious that the chief constable must have had police officers on crowd control duty in mind, and must have contemplated them as being directly affected.[158]

---

[152] *Frost*, above n 111, 1203.
[153] *Frost*, above n 111, 1199. Cf Lord Goff's observation that greater expectations of resilience should not affect the result in the 'wholly exceptional circumstances of the present case.' *White*, above n 38, 471.
[154] *Frost*, above n 111, 1204.
[155] *Frost*, above n 111, 1205.
[156] *Frost*, above n 111, 1220.
[157] *Frost*, above n 111, 1212.
[158] *Frost*, above n 111, 1217.

Henry LJ was acutely conscious of the need to bridge the gap between medical and lay, including legal, understanding. Deriding judicial use of the expression 'customary phlegm', as 'the law significantly falling back on the language of ancient physiology',[159] he observed that:

> the numbers [of officers] affected strongly suggest that ordinary police robustness is not protection against an experience such as this, a conclusion that would not surprise the doctors.[160]

A notable feature of his judgment was the importance which he attached to the medical evidence of Professor Sims, whose report was accepted by the Court for the purposes of deciding the relevant legal issues. In particular, he drew attention to Professor Sims' explanation that the trauma at Hillsborough did not take the form of 'instantaneous horror' but rather 'prolonged exposure to horrifying and uncontrollable circumstances':

> In fiction, and perhaps in a layman's view of shock as a psychological event, the individual experiences a grossly untoward event or situation with one or more sensory modalities but almost always vision and is instantaneously 'shocked' or traumatised. *In practice this almost never occurs* . . . and it is in the nature of psychological trauma that exposure for several hours results in much more severe long-term symptoms than the instantaneous exposure to shock and then the removal of the aversive stimulus.[161] (emphasis added)

This insight helps to explain Henry LJ's comprehensive repudiation of the 'sudden shock' requirement, when he asserted that:

> what matters is not the label on the trigger for psychiatric damage, but the fact and foreseeability of psychiatric damage by whatever process . . . Clearly the law should accept PTSD rather than exclude it whether it is caused by sudden shock (properly defined) or not.[162]

For good measure, he rejected the policy-based arguments put forward by Lord Wilberforce, in *McLoughlin v O'Brian*, for not extending the scope of liability for psychiatric harm.[163]

Had the approach of Lord Justice Henry been endorsed by the House of Lords, some of the more discreditable features of the modern law on psychiatric harm would have been jettisoned. However, it was not to be. Despite Lord Goff's powerful dissent, itself an eloquent exposition of the direction the law might have taken, the House, by a majority, reversed the Court of Appeal's decision. It held that the police officers, not having been exposed to, or in reasonable fear of,

---

[159] *Frost*, above n 111, 1209.
[160] *Frost*, above n 111. Cf drawing on the report of Professor Sims, Lord Goff noted recurring themes of police officers' feelings of helplessness, guilt and shame, concluding that any significance of their 'professional' role was 'offset by a combination of the nature and scale of the catastrophe and the hostility and shame resulting from police responsibility for the tragedy', *White*, above n 38, 489.
[161] *Frost*, above n 111, 1207.
[162] *Frost*, above n 111, 1208–9.
[163] *Frost*, above n 111, 1217. See generally, below Ch 5.

physical danger were not primary victims, and that neither employee nor rescuer status could relieve them of the general obligation to satisfy all the 'Alcock controls'.[164] This they could not do, most obviously for lack of close ties with the immediate victims.

Lord Steyn's speech, in its general tenor, has much in common with that of Lord Lloyd in *Page*. At the outset, he acknowledged that:

> [c]ourts of law must act on the best medical insight of the day. Nowadays . . . [they] accept that a recognisable psychiatric illness results from an impact on the central nervous system. In this sense therefore there is no qualitative difference between physical harm and psychiatric harm.[165]

Then, under the rubric *Policy considerations and psychiatric harm*, he explored several 'distinctive features' of such claims which, 'in combination', helped to account for and 'justify' differential treatment 'in a practical world'. We will address these policy concerns later.[166] At this point, suffice it to say that the perceived danger of uncontainable liability was a dominant theme. The assumption in *McLoughlin v O'Brian* that the floodgates fear might have been exaggerated was, said Lord Steyn, no longer tenable, having been 'falsified by the growth of claims . . . in the last 10 years'.[167] As for the facts of the case itself, he said that 'the awarding of damages to these police officers sits uneasily with the denial of the claims of bereaved relatives . . . in *Alcock*.' The Court of Appeal's decision, he added, 'introduced an imbalance in the law of tort which might perplex the man on the Underground'.[168] Having thus set the scene, Lord Steyn briefly considered the decisions in *Alcock* and *Page*. Endorsing the prescriptive interpretation of Lord Lloyd's categorisation of 'primary victims', he confined them to the physically endangered, adding:

> In my view it follows that all other victims, who suffer pure psychiatric harm, are secondary victims and must satisfy the control mechanisms laid down in the *Alcock* case.[169]

After finding that the officers were secondary victims, he went on to address the claim that they were special cases, either as employees or rescuers.

Lord Steyn discerned two strands to the employment argument: first, the obligation to protect the workforce from 'harm'; secondly, the demands of justice. His starting point was that any duty owed to employees in tort could not derive from their employee status, as if there were some discrete field of 'employment tort law'. Rather, it depended on the ordinary rules of tort. So the general duty not to negligently cause employees injury did not entail a duty to protect *secondary* victims against *psychiatric* harm, unless they satisfied the control mechanisms which apply to such victims. As for the demands of justice, they presented a 'weighty

---

[164] The majority consisted of Lord Steyn and Lord Hoffmann, Lord Browne-Wilkinson concurring. Lord Goff dissented on both the employment and rescue issues, Lord Griffiths on rescue.
[165] *White*, above n 38, 492.
[166] See below Ch 5, 141–55.
[167] *White*, above n 38, 495.
[168] *White*, above n 38, 495.
[169] *White*, above n 38, 497.

moral argument', given that the officers had suffered serious psychiatric harm from performing their duties in harrowing circumstances. However, if the employer's duty were enlarged in this way:

> the new principle would be available in many different situations, eg doctors and hospital workers who are exposed to the sight of grievous injuries and suffering.[170]

This particular image of potentially far-reaching liability further illustrates how heavily the floodgates argument weighed with Lord Steyn. Whatever the general potential for rising claims in the employment context,[171] one might have thought that claims by health professionals for purely psychiatric harm from *negligent* exposure to injury and suffering would be relatively rare.

More importantly, Lord Steyn may have understated the extent of an employer's personal duty as regards the health and safety of employees. It is conceptually distinct from any duty owed to them as secondary victims[172] and, in principle, applies to psychiatric as well as physical harm.[173] Where there is a pre-tort 'special relationship'—in the employment context, the obligation of 'mutual trust and confidence'—claimants unable to satisfy the *Alcock* controls are increasingly seen as able to rely on the broad tort principle of assumption of responsibility.[174] In the leading Australian case of *Annetts v Australian Stations Pty Ltd*, McHugh J observed that:

> [i]n *White*, the House of Lords appears to have overlooked that the employer's duty of care arises from an implied term of the contract as well as from the general law of negligence.

and he pointed to a wealth of authority indicating that it covered psychiatric injury under both heads.[175]

As to whether the conduct of some officers entitled them to claim as 'rescuers', Lord Steyn considered that the majority in the Court of Appeal had used the concept in 'an undefined but very wide sense'[176]. A rescuer, he said, unlike any of the claimants, 'must at least satisfy the threshold requirement that he objectively

---

[170] *White*, above n 38, 498.

[171] Lord Steyn had cited Mullany and Handford's comment that 'workplace claims loom [large] as the next growth area of psychiatric injury law': 'Hillsborough Replayed' (1997) 113 *LQR* 410, 415. But see further below Ch 5, 161–5.

[172] See S Deakin, A Johnston, and B Markesinis, *Markesinis and Deakin's Tort Law* (Oxford, Oxford University Press, 6th edn, 2008) 155–157 and 655–6.

[173] See Rose LJ at the Court of Appeal stage in *Frost*, above n 111, 1204. Cf a leading Australian decision, *Mount Isa Mines Ltd v Pusey*: 'in the present case, the duty of care is not based simply on duty to a neighbour. It includes that but arises also *independently* from the legal relationship between the plaintiff and the defendant. It is the duty of care which a master has for the safety of his servant. Foreseeable harm caused by a master to the mind of his servant is just as much a breach of his duty of care for him as harm to his body would be.' (1970) 125 CLR 383, 404, *per* Windeyer J. (emphasis added)

[174] S Deakin, A Johnston, and B Markesinis, above n 172, 152, 653–656. And see M Lunney and K Oliphant, *Tort Law: Text and Materials* (Oxford, Oxford University Press, 3rd edn, 2007) 366–7.

[175] *Annetts v Australian Stations Pty Ltd* (2002) 211 CLR 317 [140]. And see P Handford, 'Psychiatric Injury in the Workplace' (1999) 7 *Tort Law Review* 126.

[176] *White*, above n 38, 498.

exposed himself to danger or reasonably believed that he was doing so.'[177] This restrictive view is hard to square with *Chadwick v British Railways Board*,[178] a decision that had received unqualified approval in the House of Lords in both *McLoughlin* and *Alcock*. Mr Chadwick had gone to the scene of a major rail disaster to aid and comfort the injured, which he did for some 12 hours. He entered a wrecked carriage where passengers were trapped and, said Lord Steyn, 'there was clearly a risk that the carriage might collapse'.[179] He saw Mr Chadwick as a primary victim, entitled to recover damages for his subsequent psychiatric illness *because* he had been physically endangered. However, this was not the actual basis of the decision. As Waller J had said, in a passage cited by Lord Steyn:

> although there was clearly an element of personal danger in what Mr Chadwick was doing, I think I must deal with this case on the basis that it was the *horror of the whole experience* which caused his reaction.[180] (emphasis added)

It seems a strained interpretation of Waller J's reasoning to suggest that *Chadwick* requires objective exposure to danger, or a reasonable belief in such exposure, 'in order', as Lord Steyn put it, 'to contain the concept of rescuer in reasonable bounds'.[181] 'Without such limitation', he maintained:

> one would have the unedifying spectacle that, while bereaved relatives are not allowed to recover as in the *Alcock* case, ghoulishly curious spectators who assisted in some peripheral way in the aftermath of a disaster, might recover.[182]

It would, he said, have been 'an unwarranted *extension* of the law' to have allowed the officers to succeed as 'rescuers'.[183] (emphasis added). So the relatives' failure in *Alcock* and the narrow interpretation of primary victims in *Page*, both controversial in their own right, are here compounded by a contestably narrow and artificial interpretation of *Chadwick*.

It is true that, within a spectrum that can encompass both heroic endeavour and peripheral assistance, a clearcut definition of 'rescue' is elusive. We might recall that both Lord Wilberforce and Lord Edmund-Davies invoked the analogy of rescue in describing Mrs McLoughlin's arrival at the hospital to see her family.[184] How, for example, should those who search for survivors be characterised? Asking such questions again underlines the danger of attaching too much significance

---

[177] *White*, above n 38, 499.
[178] *Chadwick v British Railways Board*, above n 8.
[179] *White*, above n 38, 499.
[180] *Chadwick*, above n 8, 918 and described as the basis of the decision by Rose LJ, in *Frost*, above n 111, 1202.
[181] *White*, above n 38, 499, an interpretation described as 'bizarre' in DR Howarth and JA O'Sullivan, *Hepple, Howarth and Matthews' Tort: Cases and Materials* (London, Butterworths, 5th edn, 2000) 147. In *Alcock*, Lord Oliver described Mr Chadwick as 'rescuing and comforting' victims: *Alcock*, above n 50, 408.
[182] *White*, above n 38, 499.
[183] *White*, above n 38, 499–500. But see Lord Goff, *ibid*, 486–7.
[184] See above n 24 and related text.

to labels and too little to the foreseeable traumatic consequences of particular circumstances.[185] As Lord Goff observed:

> we must not be prisoners of our concepts, here the concept of rescue. Mr Chadwick was not attempting to rescue anybody.[186]

Doubtless, most 'professional rescuers' and many people who voluntarily assist others in need, are less likely to be traumatised by the experience than the population at large. Yet this reasonable assumption should not distract us from the intense impact, on *anyone*, of prolonged active assistance at a disaster such as Lewisham or Hillsborough. In such circumstances, ensuing mental trauma might readily result from the 'horror of the whole experience' rather than from physical danger, or the fear of it.

In common with Lord Steyn, Lord Hoffmann stressed that the officers were subject to the general principles of tort law. He, too, could not countenance the police succeeding 'while the bereaved relatives are sent away with nothing'. It was the belief that such an outcome would offend against the ordinary person's 'notions of distributive justice' that seems to have been his key concern,[187] more so than the supposed dictates of legal doctrine. On several issues, Lord Hoffmann conceded that the authorities were open to differing interpretations.[188] In fact, he accepted that the case law would have permitted what he described as the 'incremental step of extending liability for psychiatric injury to "rescuers"' even in the absence of physical imperilment, but, he insisted, the result would have been 'quite unacceptable'.[189]

Lord Hoffmann's anxiety to avoid the 'unacceptable' result is also apparent in his approach to the employment issue, on which, as we have seen, different lines of legal authority have proved to be a source of some confusion. The degree of interplay between tort and contract principles in the employment sphere is readily apparent in the relevant case law. For example, in *Walker*, the case of the overburdened social worker, the judge said that:

> the scope of the duty of care owed to an employee to take reasonable care to provide a safe system of work is co-extensive with implied terms as to the employee's safety in the contract of employment.[190]

---

[185] In *Alcock* it was asserted that, in exceptionally horrific circumstances, even claims by unrelated bystanders could succeed: *Alcock*, above n 50, 403, *per* Lord Ackner and 397, *per* Lord Keith. *Contra McFarlane v E E Caledonia Ltd* [1994] 2 All ER 1, 14, *per* Stuart-Smith LJ.

[186] *White*, above n 38, 484.

[187] *White*, above n 38, 510. *Contra* Lord Griffiths: 'I do not share the view that the public would find it in some way offensive': 465.

[188] In his own (Court of Appeal) judgment in *Page*, he had said that foreseeability of *physical* injury was neither necessary nor sufficient for damage caused by mental trauma: *Page v Smith* [1994] 4 All ER 522, 551.

[189] *White*, above n 38, 510.

[190] *Walker v Northumberland County Council* [1995] 1 All ER 737, 759. See also L Dolding and R Mullender, 'Law, Labour and Mental Health' (1996) 59 *MLR* 296.

In *Hatton v Sutherland*,[191] the Court of Appeal approved a line of cases under which psychiatric illness arising from employment was governed by ordinary employers' liability principles, as '*[c]ontractual* claims by *primary* victims'[192] (emphasis added). The Court concluded that:

> [t]here are, therefore, no special control mechanisms applying to claims for psychiatric ... injury or illness *arising from the stress of doing the work which the employee is required to do*.[193] (emphasis added)

This formulation is not easy to reconcile with *White*. True, in *White*, the majority found that, within the 'ordinary rules of the law of tort', the officers were secondary victims subject to the special control mechanisms, which Lord Hoffmann saw as applicable only to trauma suffered as a result of injury to *others*.[194] By contrast, he said, the social worker in *Walker*[195]:

> was in no sense a secondary victim. His mental breakdown was caused by the strain of doing the work which his employer had required him to do.[196]

On the facts of *White*, doing the job which the Chief Constable required officers to do happened to involve attending to the needs of *others*. But why should this chance factor displace the employer's personal duty to have regard to the health and safety of employees, a duty reinforced by a growing array of contractual and regulatory obligations?

A Misconceived Public Relations Exercise in the Name of Distributive Justice?

In *White*, the majority's apparent stance that physical endangerment was required for primary status was vigorously opposed by Lord Goff, as contrary to authority and an artificial barrier to recovery.[197] Having voiced his fundamental objection to the narrow interpretation of *Page* by reference to prior case law, he proceeded to reject the restrictive approach to the 'employee' and 'rescuer' arguments. Essentially, he drew on precedents which had treated actively involved employees and rescuers as primary victims, the position outlined by Lord Oliver in *Alcock*.[198] As regards the 'rescuer' category, he placed considerable stress on *Chadwick*,[199] a

---

[191] *Hatton v Sutherland* [2002] EWCA Civ 76.
[192] Ibid, [21]. See *Petch v Customs and Excise Commissioners* [1993] ICR 789, and *Walker*, above n 190, both approved by the Court of Appeal in *Garrett v Camden London Borough Council* [2001] EWCA Civ 395.
[193] *Hatton*, above n 191, [22].
[194] *White*, above n 38, 504.
[195] See above Ch 1, 24.
[196] *White*, above n 38, 505.
[197] *White*, above n 38, 486–8.
[198] *White*, above n 38, 481–4. See also *Young v Charles Church*, above n 131, as contrasted with *Robertson v Forth Road Bridge Joint Board*, 1995 SCLR 466.
[199] Incorporating within the category persons actively assisting in exceptionally stressful situations.

case which he also deployed to telling effect in demonstrating the artificiality and potential for unfairness implicit in the majority's position. Imagine, he said, two Chadwick brothers, one working on the front half of the train, where there was some physical danger, the other on the rear half, where there was none. Only the former would recover, and this would be so even if he were unaware of the danger, as long as it objectively existed![200]

There was a further, more general, reason why Lord Goff rejected the majority's insistence on physical imperilment. It seemed, he said, to have been driven by a misconceived underlying concern: that, without this control mechanism, the police would be, and be seen to be, 'better off' than the relatives in *Alcock*.[201] Concern at such an outcome, said Lord Goff, would only be justified if, like the relatives, the police were no more than passive witnesses. In that event, he would have accepted that they, too, would not have recovered. Lord Hoffmann characterised the underlying concern in *White* as one of fairness between citizens. Was liability in negligence essentially about corrective justice—a principled 'righting of wrongs' by the wrongdoer within established legal rules—or should broader considerations of public policy and social justice be allowed to influence or determine outcomes? Though, historically, the pursuit of corrective justice held sway, and is still often portrayed as the dominant function,[202] considerations of what is sometimes described as 'distributive justice' increasingly intrude.[203] In negligence, they are effectively built into the prevailing formulation of the duty of care, via the 'fair, just or reasonable' requirement.[204]

As we have seen, such considerations seem to have been paramount for Lord Hoffmann, concerned that the ordinary person would find it unacceptable for the police to succeed 'while the bereaved relatives are sent away with nothing'.[205] And again:

> your Lordships are now engaged, not in the bold development of principle, but in a practical attempt, under adverse conditions, to preserve the general perception of the law as [a] system of rules which is fair between one citizen and another.[206]

Lord Steyn, who expressed similar sentiments, later said of *White*, in a non-judicial capacity: 'It is a hard case. But reasons of distributive justice were *decisive*'[207]

---

[200] *White*, above n 38, 487–8.
[201] *White*, above n 38, 488.
[202] See, eg, *X (Minors) v Bedfordshire County Council* [1995] 2 AC 633, 749, *per* Lord Browne-Wilkinson.
[203] See *White*, above n 38, 503–4, *per* Lord Hoffmann. Cf 'The truth is that tort law is a mosaic in which the principles of corrective justice and distributive justice are interwoven. And in situations of uncertainty and difficulty a choice has to be made between the two approaches.' *McFarlane v Tayside Health Board* [2000] 2 AC 59, 83, *per* Lord Steyn.
[204] See *Caparo Industries plc v Dickman* [1990] 2 AC 605, 617, *per* Lord Bridge. Cf The 'fair, just or reasonable' test 'expresses the same idea' as distributive justice: *Rees v Darlington Memorial Hospital NHS Trust* [2004] 1 AC 309, 344, *per* Lord Millett.
[205] *White*, above n 38, 510.
[206] *White*, above n 38, 511.
[207] Lord Steyn, *Perspectives of Corrective and Distributive Justice in Tort Law*: John Maurice Kelly Memorial Lecture (University College Dublin, Faculty of Law, 2002) 7.

(emphasis added). We would take issue with the somewhat grandiose use of the term 'distributive justice' as a rationale for the decision. As a concept, distributive justice is most appropriately understood in systemic terms, as a model for achieving greater fairness in the overall pattern of resource allocation. By contrast, tinkering with the liability rules on psychiatric harm in *White* merely limits the class of those who can obtain a remedy within the framework of a system rooted in corrective justice.

Even as a proclaimed exercise in 'fairness', *White* is far from convincing. As Mullender and Speirs[208] pertinently ask: why were the bereaved relatives, rather than persons such as Mr Chadwick, seen as the appropriate comparator for the police officers? Though easy enough to understand in terms of the 'politics' of Hillsborough, the choice of the relatives ignores two salient considerations. First, the active participation of the police was more akin to the conduct of a Mr Chadwick. Secondly, to have allowed their claims would have reflected modern law's general tendency to encourage and reward altruistic behaviour—both as commendable in its own right and as an instrumental aspect of public policy.[209] Though one would not normally describe what the police do in the course of their duty as 'altruistic', the term may be seen as fitting in exceptionally harrowing circumstances.[210] In this respect, the argument mirrors English law's rejection of the 'fireman's rule'.[211] At all events, the 'more acceptable' solution in *White* was bound to store up further trouble, as subsequent case law has demonstrated.[212]

White v Chief Constable of South Yorkshire: Weary Resignation?

The most disquieting feature of *White* is the air of weary resignation that pervades the majority speeches. The arbitrary nature of the applicable law is openly acknowledged, but we are told that there is little or nothing that the courts can do about it. In the words of Lord Steyn:

> [t]here are no refined analytical tools which will enable the courts to draw lines by way of compromise solution in a way which is coherent and morally defensible. It must be left to Parliament to undertake the task of radical law reform.[213]

If, said Lord Hoffmann, *McLoughlin* brought us within a 'hair's breadth' of a simple foreseeability test:

---

[208] See R Mullender and A Speirs, 'Negligence, Psychiatric Injury, and the Altruism Principle' (2000) 20 *OJLS* 645.
[209] See, eg, the rescue cases, such as *Baker v TE Hopkins & Son Ltd* [1959] 1 WLR 966; *Wagner v International Railway Co* 133 NE 437 (NY 1921), and cognate decisions such as *Carmarthenshire County Council v Lewis* [1955] AC 549. See also *Dooley v Cammell Laird & Co Ltd*, above n 108.
[210] See Mullender and Speirs, above n 208, esp 655–6 and 664–6.
[211] See *Ogwo v Taylor*, above n 149. See also above n 160, and related text.
[212] See further below Ch 4.
[213] *White*, above n 38, 500.

the moment passed and when the question next came before [the House of Lords] in *Alcock* . . . judicial attitudes had changed.[214]

'It is', he said:

> too late to go back on the control mechanisms as stated in the Alcock case. Until there is legislative change, the courts must live with them[215]

There are several objections to this defeatism. First of all, does not the claim that 'judicial attitudes had changed' between the decisions in *McLoughlin* and *Alcock* imply that they could change again? It might be said that, at least in the specific context of psychiatric harm, the Court of Appeal's decision in *Frost* and Lord Goff's dissent in *White* themselves indicate some support among the senior judiciary for a change of direction. What, apart from the alleged 'unacceptability' of finding in favour of the police officers, could have prompted the majority to depict the House of Lords as powerless to renew the search for principle?[216] When, in *McLoughlin*, Lord Bridge concluded that 'this whole area of English Law stands in urgent need of review',[217] he set out a very different vision of the judicial function:

> To attempt to draw a line at the furthest point which any of the decided cases happen to have reached, and to say that it is for the legislature, not the courts, to extend the limits of liability any further, would be, to my mind, an unwarranted abdication of the court's function of developing and adapting principles of the common law to changing conditions, in a particular corner of the common law which exemplifies, par excellence, the important and indeed necessary part which that function has to play.[218]

Self-evidently, the prime responsibility for discharging this judicial function rests with the House of Lords.[219] Lord Steyn frankly acknowledged that the law on emotional injury results in 'imperfect justice'. However, his conclusion that it is 'by and large the best that the common law can do'[220] is unduly pessimistic. As a wealth of judicial and other analysis has shown, it understates the 'doctrinal fragility' of the new orthodoxy.[221] Lord Lloyd's 'narrow formulation', insofar as it requires physical imperilment for primary status, like other key concepts of liabil-

---

[214] *White*, above n 38, 502 *per* Lord Hoffmann.
[215] *White*, above n 38, 504.
[216] '[A] defeatist disposition which is incompatible with the role and obligation of appellate judges': NJ Mullany and P Handford, 'Moving the Boundary Stone by Statute—The Law Commission on Psychiatric Illness' (1999), above n 40, 355. It was reiterated in *North Glamorgan NHS Trust v Walters*: if change is needed, 'Parliament must do it': [2003] Lloyd's Rep Med 49, 60, *per* Ward LJ.
[217] *McLoughlin*, above n 1, 431.
[218] *McLoughlin*, above n 1, 441.
[219] Below this level in the judicial hierarchy a more circumspect approach is more common: 'If judges are to don a legislative mantle in this controversial field again, this . . . is the proper function of the House of Lords and not of this court.' *Hunter v British Coal Corp* [1999] QB 140, 155, *per* Brooke LJ. As a very last resort, the House of Lords could have exercised its freedom to depart from its previous decisions when they are deemed to be obstructing the proper development of the law: *Practice Statement (Judicial Precedent)* [1966] 1 WLR 1234.
[220] *White*, above n 38, 491.
[221] See JG Fleming, (1994) 2 *Tort Law Rev* 202, 203 (review of Mullany and Handford, *Tort Liability for Psychiatric Damage*, 1st edn, 1993).

ity for psychiatric harm, remains highly contestable, as a matter of common law. There are good reasons for maintaining that *Alcock* was wrongly decided, and that, at the very least, liability in *White* could have been justified by reference to Lord Oliver's description of primary status and reliance on *Chadwick*.[222] After its extensive exploration of the whole area, the Law Commission concluded that 'in some respects, and most notably in . . . *Alcock* . . . the common law has taken a wrong turn'.[223] The Commission, of course, was advocating reform via legislation, its essential remit. However, it was both disingenuous and premature for the majority in the House of Lords to say that further judicial development was not an available option. Within a year or so of *White*, further doubts were to be expressed in the House itself about the nature of primary and secondary status, Lord Slynn describing the question of classification as a 'a concept still to be developed in different factual circumstances'.[224]

The fatalism of *White* was doubly unfortunate, given the relatively slim prospect of Parliamentary time being devoted to reform in this area.[225] *Alcock*, and *Page v Smith* as construed in *White*, were policy-based decisions which consciously rejected the opportunity to re-root liability in reasonable foreseeability, the principled outcome so nearly achieved in *McLoughlin* and established by the Australian High Court in *Tame v New South Wales*.[226] It is a matter of concern that *White* stands as the most authoritative general statement of the current law on liability for negligently inflicted psychiatric harm. This is so not just because of an incoherence which the majority speeches freely concede, but because an entire segment of negligence liability has been shaped to accommodate the perceived needs of an 'acceptable' outcome to problems posed by a wholly untypical disaster. And the sheer fact of yet another House of Lords decision with restrictive implications for psychiatric harm claims in general, and those of rescuers and employees in particular, can only constitute an additional obstacle to reform—whether via the common law or legislation.

Not only was the decision in *White* controversial, but there was a measure of disagreement in the majority speeches as to the policy concerns which underpinned it. The floodgates argument, and some related issues, seem to have been the driving force behind Lord Steyn's analysis, though he also subscribed to the 'unacceptability' argument. For Lord Hoffmann, the 'unacceptability' argument was crucial, and he professed himself agnostic about the floodgates. Interestingly, this agnosticism was based on the difficulty of producing 'concrete evidence' on the matter. Yet his belief that the public would have found it offensive for the police to succeed where the relatives had failed, a view vigorously challenged by

---

[222] It is of interest that a number of earlier claims by police officers similarly affected at Hillsborough had been settled out of court.
[223] *Liability for Psychiatric Illness*, above n 131, para 4.2.
[224] *W v Essex County Council* [2001] 2 AC 592, 601. Cf '[T]his part of the law is still in a state of development': *White*, above n 38, 473, *per* Lord Goff.
[225] See above n 41 and below Ch 6, 188–9.
[226] (2002) 211 CLR 317. But see further, below, Ch 4, 135–7.

Lord Griffiths,[227] can scarcely be described as rooted in hard evidence. We will consider the force of the various policy considerations after examining the post-*White* case law. What is apparent from a number of recent decisions is that, faced with contestable doctrine and a range of policy concerns, some judges will find ways of circumventing rules which they or others have deemed incoherent. Inevitably, however, such piecemeal change leaves the essential arbitrariness intact.

[227] *White*, above n 38, 465.

4

Liability for Psychiatric Harm 'Beyond the Mainstream'

Introduction

THE LIABILITY RULES for negligently caused mental harm were essentially crafted with *accident*-based claims in mind.[1] Whether one thinks of the rail or road crashes which shaped the early law, or mass disasters at particular venues, the paradigm is an untoward physical event causing shock-induced psychiatric illness.[2] Throughout the twentieth century, presence in the 'zone of danger' and instant fright were stock features of the case law. The primary/secondary divide is but the latest construct to confirm the law's preoccupation with physical proximity to a particular physical incident.

Yet there are numerous types of situation in which the accident-driven rule structure has little or no meaningful purchase. Often the negligent conduct complained of is not 'accident-based' as described above, so that there is no one who fits the narrow *Page/White* formula for primary victims, or who could satisfy the full range of legal criteria for secondary victims.[3] When the negligent delivery of services[4] or of bad news[5] causes psychiatric harm, there is no 'accident scene' and only in exceptional circumstances would the recipient have been physically endangered.[6] Similarly, if psychiatric harm is induced over time by work-related stress, there is by definition no single causative incident involving exposure to physical danger. So, too, when the harm results from a prolonged hospital vigil for negligently treated, dying family members.[7] In many contexts, to insist that the

---

[1] Cf '[the case] is not the normal psychiatric damage case . . . not a case which involved either a near-accident to the plaintiff, or the plaintiff witnessing an accident or anticipated accident to another, or its aftermath.': *Leach v Chief Constable of Gloucestershire Constabulary* [1999] 1 WLR 1421, 1440, *per* Henry LJ.
[2] See above Ch 1, 2–3.
[3] Eg, *Farrell v Avon Health Authority* [2001] Lloyd's Rep Med 458, and *Walters v North Glamorgan NHS Trust* [2002] Lloyd's Rep Med 227. See below 106–8 and 115–6, respectively.
[4] Eg, *W v Essex County Council* [2001] 2 AC 592 (Social Services), below 99–101; *McLoughlin v Jones* [2002] 2 WLR 1279, CA (solicitors), below 101–3.
[5] Eg, *Allin v City & Hackney Health Authority* [1996] 7 Med LR 167, below 106.
[6] See, eg, *McLoughlin v Jones*, above n 4, 1296–7, *per* Hale LJ.
[7] *Sion v Hampstead Health Authority* [1994] 5 Med LR 170, CA. Ie as distinct from experiencing a single traumatic incident—the 'sudden shock' of a 'horrifying event'. But see below 113–21.

claimant fit within the accident-driven format either rules out liability arbitrarily or prompts yet more artificial legal analysis.

The legal framework is problematic enough in the situations for which it was devised; nominal adherence to rules which are literally inapplicable is indefensible. Especially in non-accident-based cases, there has been mounting judicial unease about the supposedly all-embracing nature of the primary/secondary divide and, increasingly, the special rules as reformulated in *Page* and *White* have been either grudgingly applied,[8] implausibly reinterpreted[9] or even cast aside altogether. One of the more striking recent developments has been the virtual elimination of the 'sudden shock' requirement for 'secondary' victims of medical negligence.[10] Another is the expanding interpretation of 'personal injury', to include diminished wellbeing as a result of inadequate educational and welfare provision. A number of actions have reached the appellate courts alleging that negligent conduct by teachers, educational psychologists[11] and social workers[12] has caused children to suffer psychological detriment. Prominent among these actions are claims for untreated dyslexia, and it may well be that the relevant law now provides a remedy for psychological injury without proof of a recognisable psychiatric disorder.[13] If so, it could in theory herald an enlarged scope for emotional harm claims.

In this chapter, our main focus is on how the courts have approached actions 'away from the nervous shock mainstream'.[14] Many such actions have a distinguishing feature absent from the standard road accident, namely, a prior link of some kind between claimant and defendant. Where not literally contractual in nature, the link may have strong affinities with contract or at least suggest that the defendant has assumed a degree of responsibility for the claimant's well-being, on which the latter might reasonably have relied. This relational element has, on occasion, been invoked to justify strained interpretations of the doctrinal barriers to recovery, while some judges have been emboldened either to disregard a particular restrictive device or even to dispense with all the special controls in favour of broader negligence criteria. In the more radical judgments, they have openly asserted that certain categories of claim are more appropriately analysed by

---

[8] Eg, '[w]hether we like it or not, we are constrained [to apply the control mechanisms]': *Galli-Atkinson v Seghal* [2003] Lloyd's Rep Med 285, CA, 290 [23], per Latham LJ. As regards the 'primary/secondary victim dichotomy', see *AB v Leeds Teaching Hospital NHS Trust & Cardiff and Vale NHS Trust* [2005] Lloyd's Rep Med 1, 32 [197].

[9] Eg, *Farrell* and *Walters*, above n 3.

[10] See below 113–21.

[11] Eg, *Phelps v Hillingdon London Borough Council* [2001] 2 AC 619; *Robinson v St Helens Metropolitan Borough Council* [2002] EWCA Civ 1099, *Adams v Bracknell Forest Borough Council* [2005] 1 AC 76. And see *Carty v Croydon London Borough Council* [2005] EWCA Civ 19 (education officer). See below 122.

[12] Eg, *Barrett v Enfield London Borough Council* [2001] 2 AC 550.

[13] See below 123–4.

[14] Sprince, A, '*Page v Smith*—being "primary" colours House of Lords' Judgment' (1995) 11 *Professional Negligence* 124, 126.

reference to general negligence criteria for duty of care and reasonable foreseeability of harm.[15]

Negligent Provision of Services

Only a few months after *White* was decided, Lord Slynn questioned the assumption that physical endangerment was necessary for primary status. He also criticised the inflexible way in which primary and secondary status were being interpreted generally, but without challenging the accepted view that this dual categorisation covered all psychiatric harm claims. In *W v Essex County Council*,[16] he described the question of classification as 'not . . . finally closed'. It was, he said, 'a concept still to be developed in different factual circumstances'.[17] In *W*, the claimants, who had four children and were approved foster carers, had expressly informed the Council and the relevant social worker that they were not willing to foster any child known to be (or suspected of being) a sexual abuser. Despite this stipulation, and an express assurance to honour it, the Council, through the social worker, negligently placed with them a 15-year-old boy who had admitted and been cautioned for an indecent assault on his sister and was also under investigation for an alleged rape. These facts had been recorded on the Council's files and were known to the social worker. Within a month, all four of the claimants' children had been sexually abused by the foster child, and the parents sued the Council for psychiatric illness caused by their guilt feelings as unwitting agents of the abuse. The Council sought to have this claim struck out as disclosing no cause of action,[18] but the House of Lords unanimously allowed it to go to trial. In the only substantive speech, Lord Slynn described it as 'plainly a claim which is arguable'.

In general, unless novel claims seem virtually bound to fail in law, the courts have been slow to dispose of them without addressing the disputed questions of fact.[19] However, in the late twentieth century, notably in claims against public authorities, they began to use the striking out power more freely, thereby putting themselves on a collision course with the European Court of Human Rights (ECtHR). Initially, at least, the ECtHR viewed recourse to striking out as effectively granting public bodies immunity from suit in negligence, denying litigants

---

[15] Eg, Brooke LJ in *McLoughlin v Jones*, above n 4 and in *Leach*, above n 1; Morland J in *The Creutzfeldt-Jacob Disease Litigation Group B Plaintiffs v Medical Research Council* [2000] Lloyd's Law Rep Med 161, and Ward LJ in *Swinney v Chief Constable of Northumbria* [1997] QB 464, CA. And see below, 128–30.

[16] *W*, above n 4.

[17] *W*, above n 4, 601. And see *Farrell v Merton, Sutton and Wandsworth Health Authority* (2000) 57 BMLR 158, 163, *per* Steel J.

[18] Using a preliminary procedure, under which the court considers whether there is an arguable case in law, without trying the particular factual issues: Civil Procedure Rules 1998, rule 3.4.

[19] See, eg, *X (Minors) v Bedfordshire County Council* [1995] 2 AC 633, 740–1, *per* Lord Browne-Wilkinson.

the right to a fair trial as provided for under Article 6 of the European Convention.[20] *W v Essex County Council* reached the House of Lords at a delicate stage in this controversy, when the appellate courts had begun to be more restrained in their use of the power to strike out.[21] Yet, when every allowance is made for this reversion to the traditional approach, and for the leeway it can grant to relatively tenuous arguments, the decision in *W*, and Lord Slynn's call for greater flexibility on the primary/secondary divide, are hard to square with the position that the House of Lords apparently adopted in *White*.

Though there was nothing in *W* to suggest that the parents had been physically endangered, Lord Slynn did not rule out the possibility of them being treated as primary victims. He noted Lord Goff's observation in *White*, that Lord Oliver[22] 'did not attempt any definition of this category, but simply referred to a number of examples',[23] and these included involuntary or unwilling participants. Lord Slynn thought it conceivable that feelings of guilt for bringing the abuser to the home, or for failing to detect what was happening, could have entitled the parents to primary status, a view seemingly at odds with the majority position in *White*. Alternatively, he suggested that though the parents only learnt about the abuse some time after it had occurred, their experience might be construed as close enough to it in time and space for them to be deemed secondary victims. Adopting Lord Scarman's call in *McLoughlin v O'Brian* for flexibility in dealing with 'new situations',[24] he said that 'the concept of the "immediate aftermath" of the incident has to be assessed *in the particular factual situation*'[25] (emphasis added). Yet, whatever their intrinsic merits, dicta in dissenting speeches from *White* and *McLoughlin v O'Brian*, and a broad conception of the 'immediate aftermath', do not reflect the new orthodoxy as proclaimed in *White* for *all* psychiatric injury claims. The parents did not directly perceive the abuse or its immediate aftermath;[26] nor can they be said to have suffered psychiatric harm from shock in the form of the 'sudden appreciation by sight or sound of a horrifying event'.[27] In short, if the new orthodoxy had been adhered to in *W*, the parents could not have succeeded either as primary or secondary victims.

W was not an 'accident' case. To confine analysis of it within the straitjacket, even when loosened, of the special liability rules for psychiatric harm was to distract attention from the availability of more naturally applicable negligence criteria. In an insightful critique,[28] Wightman criticises the narrowness of the House of

---

[20] *Osman v United Kingdom* (1998) 29 EHRR 245.
[21] See especially, *Barrett*, above n 12, cited by Lord Slynn in *W*, above n 4 and *Phelps*, above n 11. Cf the description of *Osman, ibid*, as an ECHR decision 'which if nothing else engendered great caution in the use of striking out': *A v Essex County Council* [2004] 1 WLR 1881, 1892, *per* Hale LJ.
[22] In *Alcock v Chief Constable of South Yorkshire Police* [1992] 1 AC 310, 407.
[23] *White v Chief Constable of South Yorkshire Police* [1999] 2 AC 455, 472.
[24] *McLoughlin v O'Brian* [1983] 1 AC 410, 430.
[25] *W* above n 4, 601.
[26] 'I am not persuaded that in a situation like the present the parents must come across the abuser or the abused "immediately" after the sexual incident has terminated': *W*, above n 4, *per* Lord Slynn.
[27] *Alcock*, above n 22, 401, *per* Lord Ackner.
[28] J Wightman, 'The Limits of the Rules on Recovery for Psychiatric Damage in the United Kingdom' (2000) 8 *Tort Law Review* 169.

Lords' focus in *W* as 'arguably the least satisfactory way of handling the novel claims which were brought.'[29] In substance, *W* was a case where a public body's failure to comply with a specific undertaking to parents had predictably devastating consequences for the entire family, including, in the event, marital breakdown.[30] Unlike the situation in routine accident cases, there was a clear pre-existing relationship between the parties, and prior discussion of the very risk which materialised. In such circumstances, it is eminently reasonable to posit an 'assumption of responsibility' on the part of the defendant Council. Though the fostering agreement was not, in law, a contract,[31] 'the [parents'] stipulation', as a Scottish judge would later observe, 'gave the case a contractual flavour.'[32] In fact, precisely because they had relied on the Council's assurances, the parents included a claim for negligent misstatement, a cause of action available in circumstances 'equivalent to contract',[33] but Lord Slynn's analysis obviated any need for it to be pursued. In principle, however, the express assurances which the parents were given would have made such a claim, grounded in assumption of responsibility, entirely credible.[34]

There are certain affinities between *W* and another striking out action, *McLoughlin v Jones*. There,[35] the Court of Appeal held that a client has an actionable claim if, due to a solicitor's negligent handling of his defence, he has foreseeably suffered psychiatric injury from wrongful conviction and imprisonment. *McLoughlin v Jones* resembled *W* in several respects. It, too, was not accident-based, involved professional services[36] and had a contractual dimension—in this instance not merely a flavour, as the claim was grounded in both breach of contract and negligence. In *McLoughlin v Jones*, Brooke LJ drew a distinction between standard psychiatric harm claims and cases 'in which the defendant had neither imperilled nor caused physical illness to anyone'.[37] Yet, without expressly describing the claimant as a 'primary victim', he clearly saw him in that light, despite the absence of any reference to physical imperilment in the case as pleaded. Instancing Lord Hoffmann's readiness to view the social worker in *Walker* as a primary victim,[38] he distinguished Mr McLoughlin's position from that of secondary

---

[29] Ibid.
[30] See also *A v Essex County Council*, above n 21 (negligent failure of adoption agency to provide relevant information to prospective adoptive parents).
[31] It was regulated by the provisions of a statutory scheme.
[32] *Salter v UB Frozen and Chilled Foods Ltd* 2003 SLT 1011, 1013.
[33] *Hedley Byrne v Heller* [1964] AC 465, 529, per Lord Devlin. It is noteworthy that the children's claim for negligence had been deemed arguable at first instance, and in the Court of Appeal, where Judge LJ strongly advanced the 'assumption of responsibility' rationale both for liability in ordinary negligence and for negligent misstatement: *W v Essex County Council* [1998] 3 WLR 534, 552–61.
[34] See further, below 103, 126.
[35] *McLoughlin v Jones*, above n 4.
[36] Cf *Al-Kandari v JR Brown & Co* [1988] QB 665.
[37] *McLoughlin v Jones*, above n 4, 1288 [27], per Brooke LJ, reiterating views that he had expressed in *Leach*, above n 1, 1434–5.
[38] It will be recalled that, in *White*, Lord Hoffmann described the physically unendangered (but successful) employee-claimant in *Walker* as 'in no sense a secondary victim.' See Ch 3, 91.

victims,[39] saying that the special rules which apply to them were inapplicable when the claimant relies on a 'breach of a duty of care arising out of the parties' contractual relationship which sounds in damages in tort.'[40] In such cases, said Brooke LJ, it was 'necessary to go back to first principles'.[41] As Hilson has observed, his central focus was on the 'standard negligence tests for determining whether a duty of care exists in a novel situation',[42] and again:

> his overall approach to the duty of care . . . suggests that psychiatric injury cases which do not involve the 'standard' accident/disaster scenario . . . should be decided on the basis of the general law of negligence rather than a *sui generis* law on psychiatric injury.[43]

In the only other substantive judgment, Hale LJ considered it 'quite clear that the claimant in this case should . . . be regarded as a primary victim', despite accepting that, in *White*, Lord Steyn and Lord Hoffmann had confined primary status to the physically imperilled.[44] She also provided a glimpse of how the law could develop, at least in cases analogous to *McLoughlin v Jones*, if Lord Lloyd's assertion that '[t]here is no justification for regarding physical and psychiatric injury as different "kinds" of damage' was taken seriously.[45] In an intriguing, if speculative, alternative analysis, she declared that '[l]oss of liberty is just as much an interference in bodily integrity as loss of a limb.'[46] Since it was 'obviously foreseeable' that negligence in conducting the defence of someone wrongly accused of serious crimes could result in wrongful imprisonment, consequential psychiatric injury was, she said, recoverable. 'Why', she added:

> should this be any different from the person who suffers physical injury in a road accident with consequential psychiatric illness?[47]

An instinctive reaction might be that, as an outcome of the defendant's negligence, the foreseeable interference with Mr McLoughlin's bodily integrity and its potential psychiatric consequences lacked the immediacy or imminence associated with physical injury in a road accident.[48] However, physical injury need not always be

---

[39] *McLoughlin v Jones*, above n 4, 1287–8.
[40] *McLoughlin v Jones*, above n 4, 1288 [26] and [27].
[41] *McLoughlin v Jones*, above n 4 [26].
[42] C Hilson, 'Liability for psychiatric injury: primary and secondary victims revisited' (2002) 18 *Professional Negligence* 167, 171.
[43] *Ibid*. And see J O'Sullivan, 'Liability for fear of the onset of future medical conditions' (1999) 15 *Professional Negligence* 96, 100–104, for an incisive analysis of Morland J's approach in *The Creutzfeldt-Jacob Disease Litigation*, above n 15.
[44] *McLoughlin v Jones*, above n 4, 1296 [55] and [56]. She, too, cited Lord Hoffmann's analysis of *Walker*.
[45] *Page v Smith* [1996] AC 155, 190.
[46] *McLoughlin v Jones*, above n 4, 1296.
[47] *McLoughlin v Jones*, above n 4, 1297.
[48] Such a reaction is not without judicial support. Eg, 'In the *Page v Smith* primary victim situation, breach of duty, the primary victim's awareness of danger and his participation in the traumatic event, his shock and resultant psychiatric illness happen simultaneously or almost contemporaneously': *CJD Litigation Group B v Medical Research Council*, above n 15, 164, *per* Morland J. Cf '[t]he requirement of the infliction of some physical injury or apprehension of it introduces an element of immediacy which restricts the category of potential plaintiffs': *White*, above n 23, 494, *per* Lord Steyn.

contemporaneous with the negligent conduct that causes it in order to permit recovery. The key issue is causal, not temporal, proximity.[49]

McLoughlin v Jones, like *W v Essex*, was distinguishable from the accident cases by virtue of the pre-tort 'special relationship' between the parties. Mr McLoughlin could have plausibly argued that he had reasonably relied on the knowledge and skill of the solicitor-defendants who had assumed a responsibility not to cause him harm by handling his case in a negligent manner. We have here the basic ingredients for a claim under the 'extended *Hedley Byrne* principle',[50] whereby liability for negligent misstatement has, by way of analogy, expanded in recent years to cover the negligent provision of services.[51] Though overwhelmingly associated with claims for pure economic loss, the *Hedley-Byrne* principle is not wholly confined to such claims.[52] It has been applied to personal injury in the form of physical damage,[53] and is, in principle, applicable to psychiatric harm. In fact, at the Court of Appeal level in *W*,[54] Judge LJ went as far as to say that '[t]he ingredients for a claim under the *Hedley Byrne* case are established'.[55] To deny such liability sits uncomfortably with Lord Lloyd's assertion, in *Page*, that '[t]here is no justification for regarding physical and psychiatric injury as different "kinds" of damage'.[56]

Communicating Bad News

Negligent Communication of Information

If the negligent supply of services can ground a claim for psychiatric harm, why not the negligent supply of information, whether or not it takes the form of a

---

[49] See J O'Sullivan, above n 43, 101–2, citing *Wieland v Cyril Lord Carpets Ltd* [1969] 3 All ER 1006.
[50] See *Williams v Natural Life Health Foods Ltd* [1998] 1 WLR 830, 834, *per* Lord Steyn. And see above n 33 and related text.
[51] *Williams*, ibid. Cf *Henderson v Merrett Syndicates Ltd* [1995] 2 AC 145; *White v Jones* [1995] 2 AC 207. See also, C Witting, *Liability for Negligent Misstatements* (Oxford, Oxford University Press, 2004) 7, para 1.09.
[52] Eg, '[t]he fact that these tests are usually deployed in cases involving pure financial loss does not mean that they are inappropriate for use when the only damage in question is psychiatric illness': *McLoughlin v Jones*, above n 4, *per* Brooke LJ, 1288, referring, *inter alia*, to the 'assumption of responsibility' test, and citing *Henderson v Merrett*, ibid. Cf 'there is no sign that the Law Lords in *Hedley Byrne* meant their remarks as to when one person will owe another a duty of care to be confined to cases where a defendant has caused another to suffer a form of pure economic loss': NJ McBride and R Bagshaw, *Tort Law* (Harlow, Longman, 2nd edn, 2005) 139.
[53] *Clay v AJ Crump & Sons Ltd* (1964) 1 QB 533; *T (A Minor) v Surrey County Council* (1994) 4 All ER 577.
[54] See *W v Essex County Council*, above n 33.
[55] *W v Essex County Council*, above n 33, 561. In the event, it did not prove necessary for the House of Lords to pursue the issue.
[56] Cf 'If psychiatric harm is to be treated as a species of physical harm, then it also enjoys priority over pure economic loss claims': P Case, 'Curiouser and Curiouser: Psychiatric damage caused by negligent misinformation' (2002) 18 *Professional Negligence* 248, 258.

misstatement? If bad news is conveyed in such an insensitive and inappropriate manner that it foreseeably causes psychiatric illness, should not the injured recipient be entitled to sue?[57] The dearth of such claims in the past was almost inevitable, given the dominance of the accident paradigm. In cases hinging entirely on how bad news was transmitted, would-be claimants could not have pointed to an accident in which they had been directly involved, let alone physically endangered; nor one that they had directly perceived by their own unaided senses. 'Being told' did not suffice; in the well-known words of Windeyer J, there was 'no duty in law to break bad news gently'.[58] It is true that, in some Commonwealth jurisdictions, such a duty had occasionally been acknowledged quite early on,[59] notably where there was a pre-existing relationship, such as doctor and patient.[60] Perhaps more importantly, as the Law Commission has pointed out, the requirement of direct perception was:

> formulated in respect of claims by secondary victims against the person responsible for the accident itself and was presumably not intended to rule out claims for negligent communication.[61]

The requirement simply did not address the circumstances in which a *communicator*, as distinct from a prior wrongdoer, might be liable in negligence for causing foreseeable psychiatric harm.

The nub of such an action is whether there has been a lack of reasonable care in the *manner* of communicating distressing news. This may prove difficult to determine, not least because the way information should have been conveyed is often linked to various aspects of its content. Beyond the intrinsic gravity of the message, a traumatic statement may be true or false; it may be about the recipient or other people, and it may concern something that has already happened or some serious future risk. Equally, what might count as a negligent mode of communicating is not confined to questions of tone or wording; it could include failure to provide information face to face, or inadequate explanation and advice by an appropriate professional.[62] To this day, there have been relatively few reported English cases on negligent communication. These have mainly arisen in health care settings,[63]

---

[57] See generally, NJ Mullany, 'Negligently Inflicted Psychiatric Injury and the Means of Communication of Trauma—Should it Matter?' in NJ Mullany and AM Linden (eds), *Torts Tomorrow: A Tribute to John Fleming* (Sydney, LBC Information Services, 1998).

[58] *Mount Isa Mines Ltd v Pusey* (1970) 125 CLR 383, 407. Cf *Guay v Sun Publishing Co* [1953] 4 DLR 577 (Canada): newspaper held not liable for psychiatric harm caused by reading a false report of family's death published negligently.

[59] *Mullany and Handford's Tort Liability for Psychiatric* Damage, (Sydney, Lawbook Co, 2nd edn, 2006), ch 26.

[60] Eg, *Furniss v Fitchett* [1958] NZLR 396, 403–4, *per* Barrowclough CJ (New Zealand). Cf *Brown v Mount Barker Soldiers' Hospital* [1934] SASR 128 (Australia).

[61] Law Commission, Consultation Paper No 137, *Liability for Psychiatric Illness* (London, HMSO, 1995). para 2.45.

[62] See *Leach*, above n 1, and below 105, on failure to offer timely counselling.

[63] See below 105–9. See especially *Farrell v Avon HA*, above n 3, and Case's illuminating article, 'Curiouser and Curiouser: Psychiatric damage caused by negligent misinformation', above n 56, 249.

and forced attempts to fit the facts within the special rule structure have only pointed up the artificiality of the analysis. In an atmosphere of mounting judicial disquiet about the intricate nature of the structure,[64] 'bad news' claims constitute yet one more category for which the orthodox liability rules for psychiatric harm are not just ill-suited but inapplicable. Given that there was a measure of support for a negligent misstatement approach in *W v Essex CC*,[65] some negligent misinformation cases might be amenable to similar analysis.[66] Alternatively, by analogy with *McLoughlin v Jones*, claims of this kind could be seen to merit a return to first principles, grounded in reasonable foreseeability. Consideration of the relevant case law indicates how such approaches might provide a more defensible framework for liability.

As late as 1996, in *AB v Tameside and Glossop Health Authority*,[67] Brooke LJ could observe that:

> there appears to have been no previous reported English case in which liability in negligence has been imposed on someone for communicating accurate, but distressing, news in a careless manner.[68]

AB itself concerned obstetric treatment received by 928 women from a health worker later found to have been HIV-positive. The two hospitals involved informed the women by letter of the very remote risk that they had been infected, stating that advice, counselling and blood-testing were available. 114 women subsequently sued the health authorities, the essence of their claim being that they had suffered psychiatric injury from a negligent failure to inform them face to face.[69] Counsel for the defendants conceded that, in principle:

> a duty to take reasonable care exists where the relevant relationship is between health authorities and their patients and former patients[70]

but the Court of Appeal reversed the judge's finding that the defendants were in breach of any such duty. It acknowledged that face to face communication would have been the optimum solution but held that, on the particular facts, the method adopted did not constitute unreasonable care.[71] Since counsel had conceded that the pre-existing relationship gave rise to a duty of care, the Court of Appeal itself chose not to make a definitive statement on the matter:

---

[64] See, eg, *Galli-Atkinson v Seghal*, above n 8.
[65] Ie in the Court of Appeal and at first instance; see above, n 33.
[66] See Case, above n 56, 256–8.
[67] *AB v Tameside & Glossop HA* [1997] 8 Med LR 91(CA).
[68] *Ibid*, 93, citing Mullany, NJ, and Handford, P, *Tort Liability for Psychiatric Damage* (Sydney, Lawbook Co, 1st edn, 1993), 183–4. Cf *Alcock*, above n 22, 398, *per* Lord Keith, and 363, *per* Parker LJ (CA).
[69] A related, if subsidiary, argument was that the facilities offered were inadequate. For example, the letters were sent before a telephone counselling service became operational.
[70] *AB*, above n 67, 93.
[71] *AB*, above n 67. Had there been a finding of unreasonable care, the claimants would still have had to prove that the method, and not just distress about the news itself, was a substantial causal factor in the onset of a recognisable psychiatric illness.

[w]e do not have to decide this point, or to consider whether such a duty exists, or the parameters of that duty, where there is no pre-existing relationship of care.[72]

In *Allin v City and Hackney Health Authority*,[73] a mother who had just undergone a very difficult labour and birth was incorrectly, though not insensitively, told by two doctors that her baby was dead. Some 6 hours later, the mother learned that the baby had survived, and she subsequently sued for post traumatic stress disorder. As in *AB*, it was conceded that a duty of care was owed when such information was communicated; in fact, said the judge:

> It would have been an extraordinarily negligent thing to do, to inform a mother that her baby was dead when it was not.[74]

In psychological terms, it would be simplistic to assume that subsequently hearing the good news would have prevented the onset of PTSD. The period of misinformation was held to be a substantial cause of the mother's disorder, and her claim succeeded.

In both *Allin* and *AB*, counsel's concession that a duty of care existed may have been premature. As regards *AB*, we have noted the absence of English authority for such a duty where the information was accurate. *Allin*, in common with *AB*, was a claim for psychiatric injury decided after *Alcock* and *Page v Smith*; it is therefore curious that the defendant Authority did not contend that the claimant had neither primary nor secondary status within the special rule structure, as envisaged in those decisions. What Ms Allin had been negligently *told* would not have entitled her to recover as a secondary victim. As for primary status, she could not have been convincingly described as an involved participant in an accident, let alone someone physically imperilled. Now that the latter requirement has apparently been endorsed by *White*, resort to broader negligence principles is needed to find a convincing justification for imposing a duty of care in a case such as *Allin*.

The need is well-illustrated by the questionable analysis in *Farrell v Avon Health Authority*,[75] a post-*White* case which also concerned erroneous information. A nurse had mistakenly told Mr Farrell that his newborn baby had died. He was given the body of a dead baby to hold and was not informed of the error for some 20 minutes, after which he briefly saw his own child. He, too, succeeded in a claim for post traumatic stress disorder, on the basis that he was owed a duty of care as a primary victim. The judge acknowledged that, on a 'literal reading' of Lord Lloyd's 'narrow formulation', Mr Farrell would have had 'to be regarded as a secondary victim', as he had 'neither sustained nor was it reasonably foreseeable that [he] would sustain any physical injury from the events complained of'.[76] However, expressly invoking Lord Oliver, in *Alcock*,[77] he concluded that 'the claimant here

---

[72] *AB*, above n 67, 93, *per* Brooke LJ.
[73] *Allin*, above n 5.
[74] *Allin*, above n 5, 170.
[75] *Farrell v Avon HA*, above n 3.
[76] *Farrell v Avon HA*, above n 3, 465.
[77] *Alcock*, above n 22, 407.

is clearly a primary victim as he was physically involved in the incident itself.'[78] In addition, he was its only victim. As a matter of commonsense, said Bursell J:

> [h]ow can there be a secondary victim if there is no other person who was physically involved as a potential victim?[79]

However rhetorically appealing and commonsensical, the characterisation of Mr Farrell as a primary victim when he was not in a zone of physical danger would seem incompatible with the analysis in *White*. Its practical significance was that if, instead, he had been deemed a secondary victim, he would probably not have succeeded on the facts. He would have had to show that it was reasonably foreseeable that a person of 'normal fortitude' would have suffered psychiatric illness in the circumstances, something which the court appeared to doubt. In addition, he had had very little contact with the mother during the pregnancy; apparently never saw the child again after the birth, and, in the judge's opinion, had never intended to form an ordinary father and son relationship. Consequently, the presumption that, as a parent, he had the close bond with his son required of secondary victims might well have been rebutted. Viewed as a primary victim, however, he had only to prove psychiatric harm of a kind that would have been reasonably foreseeable in the context of an ordinary paternal relationship. Interestingly, Bursell J sought to bolster Mr Farrell's claim to primary status by reference to Lord Slynn's speech in *W*.[80] If the physically unendangered parents in *W* could feasibly be accorded such status, why not Mr Farrell? However, even if *they* could arguably have relied on their 'feeling of responsibility' for the abuse suffered by their children, no such justification would have been available to Mr Farrell.

As noted, Bursell J described Mr Farrell as having been 'physically involved in the *incident* itself'[81](emphasis added). As Case points out, this terminology alerts us to a difficulty about the precise nature of his claim. Seen purely as someone traumatised by being *informed* that his son was dead, he would have fitted naturally into the category of (unsuccessful) 'secondary' victims who have not directly perceived a shocking *event* with their own unaided senses. On the other hand, the sequence of events taken in their entirety, especially the macabre kissing of the corpse and holding it for some twenty minutes, have an altogether more direct, experiential quality. From this perspective, had the case been decided before *White*, Mr Farrell, though not physically endangered, could certainly have satisfied Lord Oliver's 'involved participant' test for primary status, and arguably Lord Lloyd's formulation in *Page*, insofar as he emphasised 'physical involvement' in the incident.[82] However, after *White*, such an interpretation was surprising in a court of first instance. Mr Farrell may have succeeded, but the doomed attempt to fit the facts convincingly within orthodox doctrinal boundaries for psychiatric

---

[78] *Farrell v Avon HA*, above n 3, 471.
[79] *Farrell v Avon HA*, above n 3, 471.
[80] *Farrell v Avon HA*, above n 3, 471 and see above 100.
[81] See above n 78 and related text.
[82] See above Ch 3, 76, and Case, above n 56, 252–4.

harm is succinctly characterised by Case as 'a haphazard strike at the present framework.'[83]

If *Farrell v Avon* demonstrated the perils of purporting to accommodate 'bad news' claims within a rule structure designed for accidents, *AB* and *Allin* simply sidestepped that structure, on the back of the defendants' concession that a duty of care existed. The legal battleground immediately shifted to the conventional terrain of more general negligence principles, and how to apply them in the absence of clear authority. This broader approach is welcome, not only to free deserving claimants from artificial barriers to recovery, but because it permits fuller exploration of underlying policy concerns than the rigid primary/secondary divide would allow. Particular problems arise when what is in issue is not the conduct for which the primary wrongdoer was directly responsible, but the way that someone else has described it or conveyed its implications. Such claims immediately suggest several reasons which might give one pause before asserting that liability is justified when, under the prevailing special structure, 'primary' victims might succeed too readily. Prominent among these reasons is an instinctive 'don't shoot the messenger' reaction, reflecting both the peripheral role and unenviable but necessary task of the defendant. In the commonplace road accident, no necessary purpose is normally served by what the defendant has done. Often, there is simply negligent driving which has, inter alia, caused psychiatric harm. By contrast, conveying bad news is a necessary social function, obligatory for services personnel and other employees, which often has to be discharged in fraught circumstances. It is also often desirable that it be conveyed without delay, in which case it is appropriate for the law to encourage 'the free and prompt supply of the relevant information.'[84] In some contexts, such as the termination of personal relationships, it may raise issues about authenticity of behaviour, free expression and candour, just as dissemination of information by the media raises the issue of honest and accurate reporting. More generally, it might be argued that, in a world of proliferating mobile phones, routinised use of e mail and fax machines, where instant communication is the norm, to facilitate 'bad news' claims could be seen as inviting the floodgates of litigation to open.

That said, the *way* news is conveyed is rarely an effective or substantial cause of psychiatric illness. As a potential causal agent, it normally pales into insignificance by comparison with the impact of the negligent conduct itself, the claimant's constitutional make-up and, in 'secondary' claims, the intimacy of relationship between the claimant and primary victim. Subject to the caveats noted above, it is self-evidently desirable that bad news, even if accurate, should not be conveyed in such a hurtful or insensitive manner that psychiatric injury foreseeably ensues.[85] In principle, then, it is appropriate to characterise such behaviour as potentially

---

[83] Case, above n 56, 254.
[84] *Annetts v Australian Stations Pty Ltd* (2002) 211 CLR 317 [228], *per* Gummow and Kirby JJ.
[85] Cf 'it cannot make any difference in the attribution of legal responsibility that the information happened to be correct. It is foreseeability, not falsity, which matters': *Mullany and Handford's Tort Liability for Psychiatric Damage*, above n 59, 644 [26.270].

a breach of the duty to take reasonable care not to cause injury, provided due regard is paid to the pressures and difficulties faced by the conveyer as well as the recipient, when deciding whether the defendant has acted reasonably in all the circumstances.

Fear for the Future

Suppose that you have learnt that negligent treatment undergone many years earlier has put you at risk of a terminal illness at some time in the future. If you then develop a psychiatric disorder through fear that the risk will materialise, can the negligent party be held liable for this disorder? 'Fear for the future' litigation, which has spawned a considerable body of case law in the United States,[86] attracted attention in the UK after it became known that injecting children with human growth hormone created a risk of their developing Creutzfeld-Jakob Disease (CJD), a devastating and fatal condition. In a hearing on preliminary issues of law,[87] Morland J held that the Department of Health, who were responsible for the relevant clinical trials, owed a duty of care to any of the claimants who had foreseeably suffered psychiatric illness.[88] Though the trigger for this illness was communication of the risk, the 'physical event' of the injection many years previously was described as a 'potent causative factor'. How was the situation to be analysed in light of the decision in *Page v Smith*?[89]

Plainly the claimants were not secondary victims, as it would have been meaningless to describe them as having had a relationship with other accident victims. Nor did Morland J see them as primary victims in a traumatic incident as envisaged in *Page v Smith*, there having been no immediate or imminent physical danger from a physical event.[90] '[T]he factual situation', he said:

> is so far removed from the factual situation in Page v Smith or any factual situation envisaged by their Lordships in their speeches that Page v Smith is not applicable.[91]

However, 'it was', he said:

> reasonably foreseeable that [claimants] would receive the shocking news that [they were] at risk of CJD over a very wide time span.

---

[86] NJ Mullany, 'Fear for the Future: Liability for Infliction of Psychiatric Disorder', in Mullany (ed), *Torts in the Nineties* (Sydney, LBC Information Services, 1997) ch 5.

[87] *CJD Litigation*, above n 15. See also *Aston v Imperial Chemical Industries Group* (unreported, 21 May 1992). And see O'Sullivan, above n 43.

[88] Several of the claimants later obtained damages: *Andrews v Secretary of State for Health* (1998) 54 BMLR 111.

[89] The case predates the House of Lords decision in *White*.

[90] 'The *Page v Smith* primary victim becomes aware of imminent danger and is a participant in the traumatic event': *CJD Litigation*, above n 15, 164; cf above n 48. But see also O'Sullivan, n 49 and related text.

[91] *CJD Litigation*, above n 15, 164.

Invoking Lord Scarman, he declared: 'If the psychiatric injury was reasonably foreseeable it should be untrammelled by spatial, physical or temporal limits.'[92] Furthermore, he did:

> not consider that a delay between the shock of the news of the first cases of CJD and the onset of the psychiatric injury should defeat a plaintiff's claim. A psychiatric injury can be readily induced by an accumulative awareness or drip-feed of information over a prolonged period of time.[93]

Morland J also reasserted the pre-*Page v Smith* understanding that shock-induced psychiatric injury to someone of ordinary fortitude has to be foreseeable in primary as well as secondary victims,[94] a stance consistent with the view that:

> the law on primary victims is merely the application of the general law of negligence to the specific area of directly induced psychiatric harm.[95]

It is of interest that he also described the relationship between the claimants and the defendant as 'akin to that of doctor and patient, one of close proximity.'[96] This observation has prompted the suggestion that the decision in such 'fear for the future' cases is based on the narrower ground of 'assumption of responsibility' for the claimants' mental health.[97] However, this latter rationale is not explicitly asserted. The reference to the nature of the relationship might be better understood as an indicator of the established proximity requirement for a duty of care in novel negligence situations,[98] an interpretation more in keeping with the general tenor of the judgment.

Morland J's unwillingness to confer primary status on the claimants was reinforced by an additional concern. He was troubled by the potential consequences of the rule in *Page v Smith* that, in respect of primary victims, foreseeability of physical injury that might but does not occur can ground liability for unforeseeable psychiatric injury that does. He accepted the argument that to treat the CJD claimants as primary victims would be a novel step that could, for example, open the floodgates to claims by people exposed to asbestos or radiation:

> The asbestos worker will inhale or ingest asbestos fibres. Radiation causes physical insult by gamma rays or alpha particles striking cells. There is the potential for many thousands of claims from the victims of asbestos or radiation who could assert possibly years after that they learnt that they were at risk from mesothelioma or leukaemia and as a result suffered psychiatric illness.[99]

---

[92] *CJD Litigation*, above n 15, 168.
[93] *CJD Litigation*, above n 15, 168.
[94] See above Ch 3, n 125 and related text.
[95] O'Sullivan, above n 43, 103–4.
[96] *CJD Litigation*, above n 15, 165.
[97] M Lunney and K Oliphant, *Tort Law: Text and Materials* (Oxford, Oxford University Press, 3rd edn, 2007) 367–8.
[98] Ie as part of the triple composite formula set out in *Caparo Industries plc v Dickman* [1990] 2 AC 605. See above Ch 3, n 46 and related text.
[99] *CJD Litigation*, above n 15, 165.

An issue of this kind recently reached the House of Lords in *Grieves v FT Everard*, one of a number of test cases in which compensation had been sought by claimants who had developed pleural plaques.[100] For some eight years during the 1960s, Mr Grieves had been negligently exposed to asbestos dust at work. Following an X-ray in 2000, he was diagnosed as having developed asymptomatic pleural plaques, indicating the presence in the lungs and pleura of asbestos fibres that could independently cause diseases such as lung cancer or mesothelioma. Though the plaques do not themselves cause the development of such diseases, they signal a level of exposure to asbestos that, exceptionally, can increase susceptibility to them and shorten life expectancy. Having been told by his doctor that the plaques indicated significant exposure to asbestos and the risk of future disease, Mr Grieves was later diagnosed with clinical depression, in respect of which he sued his former employers. The plaques were held not to constitute an actionable injury, and no asbestos-related disease had occurred. The clinical depression, on the other hand, being a 'recognisable psychiatric illness', was in principle actionable damage. However, there was held to be no evidence that, on the particular facts, the risk of an asbestosis-related disease would have caused psychiatric illness to a person of 'ordinary fortitude', the applicable test in negligence where an employer has no actual or constructive knowledge of an employee's special vulnerability.[101]

To the extent that a potentially life-threatening disease was in issue, it was readily foreseeable that even a very low level of risk would have caused anxiety to someone of normal fortitude in Mr Grieves' position. Yet it is not necessarily the case that his former employers should have foreseen a psychiatric condition. He had worked for them between 1961 and 1969, after which he was employed elsewhere until 2002. He first had anticipatory anxieties about his exposure to asbestos in the 1960s, when knowledge of its dangers began to emerge. These anxieties were alleviated by X-rays taken in 1979, 1982 and 1984, which reported no abnormalities, but after he was informed of the X-ray results in 2000, he began to suffer from depression, developed irritable bowel syndrome and retired in 2002. A further X-ray at that time showed no signs of pleural thickening or asbestosis, but 'possible minimal pleural plaques formation', and a CT Scan in 2003 revealed 'very small bilateral pleural plaques formation.' He was then told that he had a 2 per cent risk of disabling breathlessness; a 2 per cent risk of developing asbestosis, a 5 per cent risk of developing mesothelioma and that his existing risk of lung cancer (from smoking earlier in life) had increased to 5 per cent. His condition was described as much improved after the diagnosis and prognosis and by the extent of medical reassurance that he then received, but which appears not to have been provided after the X-ray in 2000. The House of Lords unanimously rejected his appeal.

---

[100] *Grieves v FT Everard* [2007] UKHL 39.
[101] *Ibid*, Lord Hoffmann, [24] and [25], who invoked the principles set out by Hale LJ in *Hatton v Sutherland* [2002] EWCA Civ 76, as approved in *Barber v Somerset County Council* [2004] UKHL 13.

The finding that Mr Grieves' clinical depression was not reasonably foreseeable to his former employers may have been defensible on the facts, though it could be argued that, in its current form, the law demands considerable stoicism of someone in his position. The reality is that, in this type of case, it can be very difficult to gauge the relative causal significance (if any) of the employer's negligent conduct, as against the manner of subsequent medical communication, the constitutional make-up of the employee and the impact of what can be sensationalised accounts of future risk. In addition, there is the difficulty of identifying whose judgment is the most appropriate measure of whether a particular outcome was reasonably foreseeable, in a field where there may be a significant gap between expert and lay understanding of what is predictable. Since the law's focus is on culpability, it would be unreasonable to hold a defendant to the highest attainable scientific understanding of cause and effect. The prevailing yardstick, as formulated by Lord Bridge in *McLoughlin v O'Brian*, was reaffirmed by Lord Hoffmann in *Grieves*:

> [T]he judge, relying on his own opinion of the operation of cause and effect in psychiatric medicine, as fairly representative of that of the educated layman, should treat himself as the reasonable man and form his own view from the primary facts as to whether the proven chain of cause and effect was reasonably foreseeable.[102]

Inevitably this approach means that some findings will be at variance with advances in psychiatric medicine, and occasionally with the foresight that can realistically be expected of the notionally reasonable person. However, it seems an acceptable compromise, paying due attention to the limits of culpability while at the same time reflecting law's role as a standard-seeking agency. It should not be assumed that Lord Bridge's wording was intended to discourage the use of expert evidence in psychiatric cases. In practice, such evidence will normally assist the judge in reaching a defensible conclusion as to the level of foresight that can reasonably be expected on a matter which, within an adversarial structure, it is ultimately for the court to determine.

Of most interest, for our purposes, is that Mr Grieves also invoked the rule in *Page v Smith*, claiming that he was a 'primary victim' at foreseeable risk of *physical* injury, who did not need to establish foreseeability of *psychiatric* harm. However, the House of Lords held that this rule applied only when there was exposure to a risk of physical injury that was immediate or imminent. Lord Hoffmann said of *Page v Smith*:

> It does not appear to have caused any practical difficulties and is not, I think, likely to do so if confined to the kind of situation which the majority in that case had in mind. That was a foreseeable event (a collision).

---

[102] *McLoughlin v O'Brian*, above n 24, 432. Cf *Grieves*, above n 100, [28], *per* Lord Hoffmann.

And again:

> [i]t would be an unwarranted extension of the principle in *Page v Smith* to apply it to psychiatric illness caused by apprehension of the possibility of an unfavourable event which had not actually happened.[103]

Yet it is only to the extent that 'exposure to physical risk' has been so narrowly and artificially conceived—as entailing an accident-based 'zone of danger' and the risk of immediate or imminent physical injury—that liability in *Grieves* could have been deemed an extension of the rule.[104] Finally, it should not be overlooked that the broader implications of the litigation would have probably played a significant part in the outcome. Certainly, policy considerations were central to the Court of Appeal's rejection of all the test cases.[105] The fact that many thousands of workers have developed pleural plaques raised precisely the kind of floodgates fear alluded to by Mr Justice Morland in the CJD Litigation.[106]

Medical Negligence: the Declining Significance of the 'Sudden Shock' of a 'Horrifying Event'[107]

Introduction

An important dilution of the special rule structure has been very apparent of late, most notably in secondary claims arising from medical negligence. It is the marked decline in insistence on psychiatric illness being shock-induced, as described by Lord Ackner—the 'sudden appreciation by sight or sound of a horrifying event'.[108] Neither presence at an incident nor immediacy of reaction are necessary

---

[103] *Grieves*, above n 100, [32] and [33], respectively. Cf Lord Rodger, who noted that the claimant in *Page* suffered psychiatric injury from 'being exposed to, but escaping, instant physical harm': *Grieves*, [95]. And see above n 48 and related text.

[104] See above Ch 3, 80–82. See also J Steele, *Tort Law: Text, Cases, and Materials* (Oxford, Oxford University Press, 2007) 309–10.

[105] *Rothwell v Chemical & Insulating Co Ltd* [2006] EWCA Civ 27 [67], per Lord Phillips CJ and Longmore LJ. And see J Steele, ' "Breach of Duty Causing Harm?" Recent Encounters between Negligence and Risk', in *Current Legal Problems 2007* (Oxford, Oxford University Press, 2007) Vol 60, 331–7.

[106] In 2006, within the insurance industry, estimates of the potential cost of successful claims were put at up to £1.5 billion over the next 25 to 30 years. Lord Rodger, however, noted that previous successful claims and many settlements, made over the last 20 years or so, had 'not resulted in an unmanageable flood of claims': *Grieves*, above n 100, [79]. More recently, The Ministry of Justice has estimated the total potential cost at between £3.7bn and 28.6bn, depending on the number of claims: Ministry of Justice, *Pleural Plaques*, Consultation Paper (CP 14) (London, Ministry of Justice, 2008) para 33.

[107] See generally, H Teff, 'No More "Shock, Horror"? The Declining Significance of "Sudden Shock" and the "Horrifying Event" in Psychiatric Injury Claims', in S McLean (ed), *First Do No Harm: Law, Ethics and Healthcare* (Aldershot, Ashgate, 2006) ch 19, from which much of the material on pp 113–21 is drawn.

[108] See *Alcock*, above n 22, 401, per Lord Ackner.

triggers for psychiatric illness, and 'sudden shock' is often a poor predictor of it. Empirical evidence has demonstrated how important the duration, as well as the severity, of a distress reaction can be in inducing psychiatric illness, especially, though not exclusively, when the illness takes the form of depression.[109] Responding to the English Law Commission on the issue, the Royal College of Psychiatrists' Mental Health Law Group was scathing:

> For psychiatrists the 'shock-induced' requirement causes serious problems. The term is vague, has no psychiatric meaning and is emotively misleading. The requirement should be abandoned. Psychiatric evidence should require demonstration, or not, of a psychiatric disorder distinct from a normal mental reaction and, if present, its relationship with the index event. This is usually possible. The requirement to fit the evidence around the concept of whether or not the disorder is 'shock-induced' has no scientific or clinical merit. It is simply playing with words.[110]

Quite apart from being scientifically and clinically misconceived, even as a *legal* requirement 'shock' is high on the list of doctrinally fragile concepts. As we have seen, prior to *Alcock* there was no clear indication that the instant display of emotional shock had ever been a prerequisite of liability in English law.[111] This development can be traced to Brennan J's assertion, in the leading Australian case of *Jaensch v Coffey*, that there had to be a 'sudden sensory perception . . . that . . . affronts or insults the plaintiff's mind',[112] which may have prompted Lord Ackner's graphic depiction, though he gave no authority for it.[113] It is true that, in *Alcock*, Lord Oliver described 'sudden and unexpected shock' as one of the 'common features' of all the previous English authorities on secondary claims,[114] but this leaves open the question whether 'suddenness' had been a requirement or a mere contingency. In the first half of the twentieth century, many judges would doubtless have assumed that serious mental conditions normally resulted from momentary fright or terror—a 'shock to the system'.[115] Yet, in a number of pre-*Alcock* decisions, the onset of psychiatric illness is more plausibly explained by gradual, cumulative assaults on the nervous system.[116]

---

[109] C Tennant, 'Liability for Psychiatric Injury: an Evidence-based Approach' (2002) 76 *Australian Law Journal* 73.

[110] Law Commission, No 249, *Liability for Psychiatric Illness* (London, HMSO, 1998), para 5.29 (2).

[111] See above Ch 1, n 124. Cf 'Whilst the requirement for "shock" to induce the psychiatric illness was not explicit in English case law until the *Alcock* case, it has been applied since that decision with some rigour by the Court of Appeal': *Tan v East London and City Health Authority* [1999] Lloyd's Rep Med 389, 395, *per* Ludlow J. See further, H Teff, 'The Requirement of "Sudden Shock" in Liability for Negligently Inflicted Psychiatric Damage' (1996) 4 *Tort Law Review* 44.

[112] *Jaensch v Coffey* (1984) 155 CLR 549, 567.

[113] See *North Glamorgan NHS Trust v Walters* [2003] Lloyd's Rep Med 49, 55–6 [25], CA, *per* Ward LJ.

[114] *Alcock*, above n 22, 411.

[115] See *Rhodes v Canadian National Railway* (1990) 75 DLR (4th) 248, 280, *per* Southin JA.

[116] Eg, *McLoughlin v O'Brian*, above n 24, and *Chadwick v British Railways Board* [1967] 1 WLR 912, decided on the basis that it was 'the horror of the whole experience which caused the [claimant's] reaction': 918 (over some 12 hours). And see above Ch 3, n 180 and related text.

The traditional preoccupation with momentary shock was a corollary of the road/rail crash paradigm. The later emergence of liability for psychiatric injury induced over time has undermined any assumption that shock, in the sense of fright or terror, is universally required. This development, most obvious in regard to claims arising from work-related stress, is also prominent in the hospital setting; as when patients, or those close to them, suffer psychiatric harm not from involvement in a single incident but from the strains of a prolonged process or the cumulative effect of a series of events.

Lord Ackner's Conception of Shock

The courts have generally accepted as authoritative Lord Ackner's depiction of the shock requirement in *Alcock*:

> 'Shock', in the context of this cause of action, involves the sudden appreciation by sight or sound of a horrifying event, which violently agitates the mind. It has yet to include psychiatric illness caused by the accumulation over a period of time of more gradual assaults on the nervous system.[117]

This formulation evokes an image of a dramatic occurrence, eliciting an instant reaction—an arresting, if stereotypical, image of what triggers psychiatric harm. Before examining its various threads, a few preliminary observations should be made. First, Lord Ackner alone described shock in precisely these terms. Secondly, this was one of several propositions on the then prevailing liability criteria for psychiatric harm, all of which he prefaced by the words, '[w]hatever may be the pattern of the future development of the law in relation to this cause of action'[118]. The force of the qualification that the law 'has yet' to include more gradual, cumulative assaults on the nervous system is unclear. Though he possibly intended it as a plain factual statement, Lord Ackner may have been counselling against such a development, anticipating it or both.

The Event

Just as, in earlier case law, the 'event' was considered as a virtually instantaneous occurrence, so, too, was its perception. However, if a broader view is taken of what can constitute an event, Lord Ackner's wording may allow for more flexibility than appears at first sight. In *McLoughlin v O'Brian*, Lord Wilberforce had described an Australian decision as 'based soundly' on:

> direct perception of some of the events which go to make up the accident as an entire event [including] the immediate aftermath.[119]

---

[117] *Alcock*, above n 22, 401.
[118] *Alcock*, above n 22, 400. And see *North Glamorgan NHS Trust v Walters*, above n 113, 60, *per* Clarke LJ.
[119] *McLoughlin v O'Brian*, above n 24, 422, in reference to *Benson v Lee* [1972] VR 879, 880.

In *North Glamorgan NHS Trust v Walters*, Ward LJ invoked this interpretation to construe a series of incidents over a 36 hour period in a hospital as the 'entire event.' 'One looks', he said, 'to the totality of the circumstances which bring the claimant into proximity... to the accident'.[120] He also said that what the claimant is *told* may be relevant. Whereas it has long been the law that 'merely being informed of, or reading, or hearing about the accident' does not ground liability:

> [i]nformation given *as the events unfold before one's eyes* is part of the circumstances of the case to which the court is entitled to have regard.[121] (emphasis added)

If a series of 'mini-events' or a single elongated process, together with oral communications along the way, can be construed as the 'entire event', does not the phrase '*sudden* appreciation of a *horrifying* event' part company with its more natural meaning? Admittedly, there has been a finding that the issue is not whether the defendant's conduct was 'shocking' in the sense of the claimant witnessing a sudden and violent incident, but rather the *unexpected* nature of what the claimant sees or experiences.[122] Still, it remains artificial to describe claimants who have reacted to a series of events in a process[123] as having 'suddenly' been 'horrified'.

Suddenness

It is clear from his explicit contrast with gradual assaults that, for Lord Ackner, 'suddenness' was a key ingredient of liability. After *Alcock*, it was routinely required in standard 'accident' cases and, initially, when denying claims involving a prolonged 'process'.[124] Yet only a year or so after *Alcock*, a more pragmatic approach began to emerge as regards negligence in the hospital setting,[125] and, over the last decade or so, the courts have come close to abandoning the shock requirement where there have been long drawn-out medical processes.[126] There have also been signs of a similar shift in respect of other professional services[127] and, more importantly, on occasion even in mainstream 'accident' cases.[128]

It is significant that several judges have begun to use more neutral, less emotive terminology. By the mid-1990s, in *Page v Smith*, we find Hoffman LJ referring to 'damage caused by mental trauma',[129] and Henry LJ, in *Frost*, also preferring

---

[120] *Walters*, above n 113, 55 [23]. Cf *Tredget and Tredget v Bexley Health Authority* [1994] 5 Med LR 178 (48 hours), and *Chadwick*, above n 116.

[121] *Walters*, above n 113, 58 [35].

[122] *Sion*, above n 7, 176, *per* Peter Gibson LJ. In *Jaensch*, above n 112, 567, Brennan J referred to the plaintiff's perception of a 'phenomenon', which would not necessarily connote an event.

[123] As in the hospital cases below, 117–21.

[124] See *Sion*, above n 7, and *Taylorson v Shieldness Produce Ltd* [1994] PIQR P329 (CA).

[125] See *Tredget and Tredget*, above n 120.

[126] Eg, *Walters*, above n 113, and *Froggatt v Chesterfield and North Derbyshire Royal Hospital NHS Trust* [2002] All ER (D) 218. *Aliter, Tan v East London and City Health Authority* [1999] Lloyd's Rep Med 389. See further below, 118–19.

[127] *McLoughlin v Jones*, above n 4.

[128] Eg, *Galli-Atkinson v Seghal*, above n 8.

[129] *Page v Smith* [1994] 4 All ER 522, CA, 549–50.

'trauma' to 'shock', stressing that 'what matters is not the label on the trigger for psychiatric damage, but the fact and foreseeability of psychiatric damage, by whatever process.'[130]

Horror Violently Agitating the Mind

Though the main focus of the shock requirement has been on 'suddenness', the issue of whether the occurrence is sufficiently 'horrifying' has also proved capable of limiting the scope of 'secondary' claims,[131] due mainly to Lord Ackner's reference to the need for a 'horrifying' event.[132] Although instant horror and fright are of limited significance as indicators of psychiatric illness, it may well be that the contemporary prominence and graphic media portrayals of PTSD have hindered a more rational approach. When PTSD is thought of as almost synonymous with psychiatric harm, it is easy to assume that all such harm entails exposure to an event which is both 'sudden' and 'horrifying', such as to precipitate the 'violent agitation' associated with 'flashbacks' as a characteristic symptom of PTSD.[133] In one relatively recent case, the only substantive judgment in the Court of Appeal referred to 'negligently caused psychiatric injury or nervous shock, now more commonly referred to as post traumatic stress disorder'.[134] It is precisely this kind of equation that invites dubious, often invidious, judicial exploration of how macabre the scene must be to justify recovery, and speculation on whether the immediate traumatic stressor was truly 'horrifying' or *merely* very distressing—as if this distinction were the key to ensuing psychiatric damage.

Claims resulting from Medical Negligence

In the fraught environment of the hospital, the natural anxieties of patients and people intimately connected with them are often heightened by inadequate information or mixed messages. The traumatic experience of a long-drawn-out vigil, with intermittent crises and hopes raised only to be dashed, or an extended process of dawning realisation culminating in the trauma of attendance at the mortuary, can provide ample evidence of '*causal* proximity'.[135] Yet under *Alcock*, whatever the surrounding circumstances, secondary claims would appear to require a specific traumatic incident.

Taylor v Somerset Health Authority[136] was a case in point. Mr Taylor's fatal heart attack at work, months after the negligent diagnosis and treatment which had

---

[130] *Frost v Chief Constable of South Yorkshire* [1997] 3 WLR 1194, 1208.
[131] See *Ward v Leeds Teaching Hospitals NHS Trust* [2004] Lloyd's Rep Med 530, below 120–21.
[132] None of the other Law Lords in *Alcock* used this term, though, in the Court of Appeal, Nolan LJ had said that 'the expression "nervous shock," as used in the decided cases, connotes a reaction to an immediate and horrifying impact'. *Alcock* [1991] 3 WLR, 1057, 1095, CA.
[133] See Tennant, above n 109, 77.
[134] *Chief Constable of West Yorkshire v Schofield* [1998] 43 BMLR 28, 33, *per* Hutchinson LJ.
[135] See *Jaensch v Coffey*, above n 112, 606–607, *per* Deane J.
[136] (1993) 4 Med LR 34.

caused it, was the culmination of a deteriorating heart condition. His wife, informed that he had been taken ill, went straight to the hospital where a doctor told her that he had died. A few minutes later, she went to the mortuary, mainly to settle her disbelief. Her claim for psychiatric injury was dismissed for want of any 'event' to which the 'immediate aftermath' principle could be applied. Even if the death could have been so construed, her illness did not result from exposure to an 'external traumatic event, in the nature of an accident or violent happening'.[137] For good measure, we are told that, in the mortuary, the dead body 'bore no marks or signs to her of the sort that would have conjured up for her the circumstances of his fatal attack'.[138] This insistence on instant reaction to a discrete, traumatic event was unsurprising, coming so soon after *Alcock*. It was reinforced by the Court of Appeal, in *Sion*, where due to an allegedly negligent hospital diagnosis, the claimant's son deteriorated, fell into a coma and died. His father's claim for psychiatric illness, following an 18 hour a day vigil for 14 days, which included a series of traumatising events, was struck out. There was, said Staughton LJ, 'no trace in [the medical] report of "shock" *as defined by Lord Ackner*'. Rather, it was:

> a process continuing for some time, from first arrival at the hospital to the appreciation of medical negligence after the inquest.[139] (emphasis added)

It is true that, by this time, hints of a more flexible approach were evident, most notably in *Tredget and Tredget v Bexley Health Authority*.[140] *Tredget* involved a claim by parents for psychiatric illness, when, due to medical negligence, a prolonged, difficult labour and traumatic delivery had culminated in their child's death. According to White J, '[a]lthough lasting for over 48 hours from the onset of labour to the death, this effectively was one event'.[141] However, as late as 1999, we find a striking example of more restrictive analysis in *Tan v East London and City Health Authority*,[142] despite overwhelming evidence of the claimant's foreseeable presence. Mr Tan's wife had been admitted to hospital for an elective caesarean. Before this could take place, he received a telephone call from the consultant informing him of the baby's death, which, it was later conceded, was due to negligence. Mr Tan went to the hospital immediately, arriving an hour and a half later, and for nearly two hours he comforted his distressed and 'obviously extremely shocked' wife. There was then a caesarean delivery (just under four hours after the death). Mr Tan briefly held the dead child, kept vigil overnight and saw her being placed in a metal box. In dismissing his claim for psychiatric illness, the court held that the death *in utero*, or its immediate aftermath, constituted the accident or event at which he needed to have been present. He was not present at the death, and the phone call did not involve direct perception. The death,

---

[137] (1993) 4 Med LR 37. But see above n 122 and related text.
[138] Above n 136, 37.
[139] *Sion*, above n 7, 174.
[140] *Tredget and Tredget*, above n 120.
[141] Above n 120, 184.
[142] *Tan v East London and City Health Authority* [1999] Lloyd's Rep Med 389.

stillbirth, overnight vigil and removal of the baby were not construed as all one event such as to satisfy the aftermath test. Though death in the womb and stillbirth are two events that are 'inextricably linked', the stillbirth was unrelated to the actual *circumstances*, as distinct from the *fact*, of the death. Furthermore, the *Alcock* 'shock' requirement was deemed not to have been met, for several reasons: the foreknowledge, planning and timing of the stillbirth (just under four hours after the death apparently not satisfying the immediate aftermath test); the ordinary way in which the operation was conducted, and the appearance of the baby, looking normal as if asleep.

Over the last few years, the declining insistence on 'sudden shock' in the hospital setting has become more pronounced. In *North Glamorgan NHS Trust v Walters*,[143] the hospital failed to diagnose acute hepatitis in a 10 month old baby, whose epileptic fit, witnessed by his mother, was more serious than the staff had indicated. Told later that his severe brain damage ruled out any quality of life, she agreed to the withdrawal of life support, and he died in her arms, some 36 hours after the seizure. She suffered a pathological grief reaction from witnessing, experiencing and participating in these events, and the Court of Appeal endorsed the finding that the 36 hour period could be construed as 'one horrifying event'.[144] Because each traumatic event had an instant impact, the need for 'sudden' appreciation was deemed satisfied, but Clarke LJ intimated that even if the decision had involved an incremental step advancing the frontiers of liability, he would have taken it.[145] Similarly, in *Froggatt v Chesterfield and North Derbyshire Royal Hospital NHS Trust*,[146] where a woman had been negligently misdiagnosed with cancer, her husband's first sight of her body after a mastectomy was treated as sudden appreciation of a horrifying, shocking event—not something 'expected'.[147] This was so, despite his advance knowledge of the operation and the inevitable delay before he saw her, suggesting a conception of the 'immediate aftermath' that goes well beyond what was envisaged in *McLoughlin v O'Brian* and *Alcock*.[148] It is also of interest that, in apparent disregard of the direct perception requirement, Mr Froggatt's 10 year old son recovered for shock from *overhearing* a telephone conversation in which his mother had referred to her 'cancer'. These more liberal interpretations of the sudden event, immediate aftermath and unaided perception, in the hospital context, are beginning to have a broader resonance. In a mainstream road accident case, decided a few months after *Walters*, Latham LJ drew on the decision to assert that a sudden event did not require a 'frozen moment in

---

[143] See above n 113.
[144] '[A] seamless tale with an obvious beginning and an equally obvious end': above n 113, 58 [34], *per* Ward LJ. Cf *Farrell v Merton, Sutton and Wandsworth Health Authority*, above n 17, 164.
[145] *North Glamorgan NHS Trust v Walters*, above n 113, 60 [51].
[146] [2002] All ER (D) 218.
[147] Cf *Sion*, above n 7, 174, *per* Peter Gibson LJ.
[148] See M Jones, *Medical Negligence* (London, Sweet & Maxwell, 3rd edn, 2003) 147, para 2-129. In the Personal Injury Bar Association Annual Lecture (2004), 'Liability for Psychiatric Injury', Lord Phillips referred to *Froggatt*, as evidence of the 'considerable elasticity' of the aftermath concept.

time'; rather, he said, both an event and its aftermath could be made up of a number of components.[149]

This is not to say that the potential for restrictive analysis in the medical sphere, as elsewhere, is entirely a thing of the past, as is illustrated by *Ward v Leeds Teaching Hospitals NHS Trust*.[150] In *Ward*, the claimant's 22 year old daughter was admitted to hospital for the extraction of wisdom teeth. Due to negligence, she failed to regain consciousness after the surgery and was pronounced dead some 48 hours later. Mrs Ward claimed for psychiatric injury in the form of PTSD, on the basis of various events surrounding the death. These included initially having seen her daughter in the recovery room; then in the intensive care unit; after the ventilator was switched off, and finally at the mortuary. However, the court accepted the defence expert's analysis that a severe and prolonged bereavement reaction was the overwhelming cause of her condition and that there was no 'shocking event of a particularly horrific nature'[151] to justify a diagnosis of PTSD.

Ward is of interest primarily for its observations on shock-induced injury, more specifically, the 'horror' component of the requirement. Adopting Lord Ackner's definition, the judge observed that death of a loved one in hospital was not:

> [a]n event outside the range of human experience ... unless also accompanied by circumstances which were wholly exceptional in some way so as to shock or horrify. Mrs Ward's own descriptions of these incidents did not strike me as shocking at the time in that sense, although undoubtedly they were distressing. To describe an event as shocking in common parlance is to use an epithet so devalued that it can embrace a very wide range of circumstances. But the sense in which it is used in the diagnostic criteria for PTSD must carry more than that colloquial meaning.[152]

In *Walters*, it was said of the claimant that:

> [h]er hopes were lifted then they were dashed and finally destroyed when ... she was advised to terminate treatment on the life-support machine.[153]

The events which caused her pathological grief reaction 'must have been *chilling moments*, truly shocking events ... distressing in the extreme'[154](emphasis added) Yet Mrs Ward, too, had her hopes lifted and dashed. When present in the recovery room, 'she still thought she would be taking her daughter home'.[155] She, too, experienced some traumatic, even perhaps 'chilling', moments, as when, before she had internalised the possibility of her daughter dying, she was told in the ICU to keep talking to her, because the hearing was the last thing to go,[156] or when she

---

[149] *Galli-Atkinson v Seghal*, above n 8, 290, para 25. Cf *Walters*, above n 113, 55 [23], *per* Ward LJ.
[150] *Ward v Leeds Teaching Hospitals NHS Trust* [2004] Lloyd's Rep Med 530.
[151] *Ibid*, 535 [21].
[152] Above n 150 [21].
[153] *Walters*, above n 113, 58–9 [36].
[154] *Walters*, above n 113 [36].
[155] *Ward*, above n 150, 532 [10].
[156] *Ward*, above n 150, 533 [11]; another instance of third party communication contributing to the total experience of someone present and directly perceiving events? Cf *Walters*, above n 113 and related text.

saw her in the mortuary with some blood in her ears and some bruising around her neck.

None of this is to take issue with the finding in *Ward*, where *Walters* was plausibly distinguished as based on agreed psychiatric evidence. *Ward* was essentially pleaded as a case of PTSD, for which the evidence seemed slim: in a sense, pleading PTSD ups the stakes by requiring a particularly severe stressor.[157] To the limited extent that pathological grief reaction was also invoked, the argument was undermined by the claimant's expert initially conceding that it was explicable by various predisposing and other factors unrelated to events at the hospital.[158] The real indictment of *Ward* is giving undue salience to horror, narrowly defined, as a determinant of liability for psychiatric harm generally. Insofar as it is now conceded that shock need no longer be 'sudden', the case for it being 'horrifying' would seem to evaporate too. 'Horror' too readily conjures up an image of someone shuddering with terror, transfixed by a sudden event, which 'violently agitates the mind'. If Lord Ackner's comment that the law had yet to include gradual assaults on the nervous system was meant as a portent of things to come, it would indeed have been ironic since, at the outset of his speech, he noted that liability for the cause of action had 'greatly expanded . . . largely . . . due to a better understanding of mental illness and its relation to shock.'[159]

The 'shock, horror' model of how psychiatric harm is induced, with its enduring hold on the popular imagination, has long been mirrored in the legal setting.[160] If deprecated of late in the case law, it still has undue capacity to determine legal outcomes.[161] The inclination towards more liberal interpretation in the hospital cases seems in part attributable to judicial empathy, a tacit recognition of the narrowness and rigidity of the liability rules. It also reflects the fact that, in this setting, the case for restricting 'secondary' claims for want of 'sufficient proximity' looks distinctly thin. There is commonly a nexus between the hospital and those closest to the patient, whose 'presence', when not actually known about as a fact, is readily foreseeable, even if they seldom directly perceive a shocking event. Abandonment of the shock requirement would be both an important symbolic and practical demonstration of the progressive understanding of psychiatric harm which the House of Lords has asserted in recent years.

---

[157] See M Horne's commentary on *Ward*, above n 150, 536.
[158] *Ward*, above n 150, 535 [21].
[159] *Alcock*, above n 22, 399.
[160] See D Mendelson, *The Interfaces of Medicine and Law*, (Aldershot, Dartmouth Publishing Co, 1998).
[161] Cf *Tan*, above n 142.

Negligence Causing Psychological Detriment[162]

The early 1990s saw the gradual emergence of a new kind of personal injury action,[163] which does not seem to fit naturally within the established criteria in tort for physical or psychiatric harm. Difficult to formulate with precision, the action spans various forms of psychological detriment, ranging from loss of self-worth and wellbeing to diminution in life chances, both social and economic. It has come to prominence in educational and social care settings, in claims that educational psychologists, teachers and social workers have, variously, failed to identify certain conditions, ameliorate learning difficulties or make appropriate care decisions.

The seminal case, *Phelps v Hillingdon London Borough Council*,[164] as well as being a House of Lords decision, is noteworthy as a precedent for at least three reasons. First, unlike most of the cases in this novel area, it was not a pre-trial striking out application, to determine whether the claim was 'arguable' in principle, but a decision of the House on the facts.[165] Secondly, it is a leading authority on the liability of public authorities in negligence, seen to have warranted a hearing by seven rather than five Law Lords. Thirdly, and importantly for our purposes, it is open to the interpretation that, in a common law negligence claim for mental suffering, a 'recognisable psychiatric illness' is not always a threshold requirement.[166]

Dyslexia, a specific form of learning difficulty affecting reading, writing and spelling, is generally considered to be a congenital, neurological condition.[167] In *Phelps*, the local education authority was held vicariously liable for the negligence of an educational psychologist, whose failure to diagnose the claimant's dyslexia denied her the appropriate treatment, or educational provision, needed to mitigate its adverse consequences. In such circumstances, it is not easy to pinpoint the precise basis of the duty owed, the legal nature of the loss or damage, or the causal significance of the defendant's failure to diagnose and alleviate the condition.

First, let us consider the causation issue. Unlike the position in contract, damages are normally available in tort only for harm caused; that is to say, an inflicted loss as opposed to a lost gain through failure to confer a benefit by improving the claimant's

---

[162] T Kerr, 'The Broadening Notion of Psychological Injury in Tort Subsequent to the *Phelps* Litigation' (2004): http://www.11kbw.com. .

[163] See *X (minors) v Bedfordshire County Council* [1995] 2 AC 633.

[164] *Phelps*, above n 11. .

[165] 2 of the 3 learning disability cases reported under *Phelps*—*G (A Minor) v Bromley LBC* and *Jarvis v Hampshire CC*—were striking out actions. The third, *Anderton v Clwyd County Council*, which concerned a pre-trial procedural issue (pre-action discovery) turned on a broad *statutory* definition of 'personal injuries': 'any impairment of a person's physical or mental condition': Supreme Court Act 1981, s 35 (5).

[166] D Fairgrieve, 'Pushing back the Boundaries of Public Authority Liability: Tort Law Enters the Classroom' (2002) *PL* 288, 293.

[167] 'Today, developmental dyslexia is seen as a complex neurological condition occurring in about 4 per cent of the population and is a legally recognised disability': MN Haslum, in RL Gregory (ed), *The Oxford Companion to the Mind* (Oxford, Oxford University Press, 2nd edn, 2004) 272.

situation.[168] Nevertheless, the House of Lords decided that damages are available for the adverse consequences of negligent failure to diagnose and treat conditions such as dyslexia,[169] by analogy with the liability of doctors who negligently fail to treat their patients, itself an exception to the general requirement of inflicted loss.[170]

As regards the nature of the loss or damage in *Phelps*, after noting that an educational psychologist's failure to exercise care could cause a child '*emotional* or *psychological* harm', Lord Slynn continued:

> There can be no doubt that if foreseeability and causation are established, psychological injury may constitute damage for the purpose of the common law. But so in my view can a failure to diagnose a congenital condition and to take appropriate action as a result of which failure a child's level of achievement is reduced, which leads to loss of employment and wages.[171]

It has been suggested that Lord Slynn's use of the term 'psychological injury' must have been intended as shorthand for 'recognised psychiatric illness'.[172] However, this is far from clear, at least in the sphere of educational development, and possibly beyond it. First, there is the introductory reference to 'emotional or psychological harm', which more naturally suggests conditions such as anxiety, disappointment and distress where there is no medically recognised pathology.[173]

---

[168] 'The Court of Appeal therefore held that failure to mitigate or ameliorate the consequences of the condition could not be an injury': *Phelps*, above n 11, 663, *per* Lord Slynn.

[169] '[F]ailure to diagnose a congenital condition and to take appropriate action as a result of which a child's level of achievement is reduced' may 'constitute damage for the purpose of the common law': *Phelps*, ibid, 654, *per* Lord Slynn. And see *Adams v Bracknell Forest Borough Council* [2005] 1 AC 76, 83 [20], *per* Lord Hoffmann.

[170] See *Keating v London Borough of Bromley*, a striking out application, reported under *X (minors) v Bedfordshire County*, above n 163, 705–6, *per* Evans LJ, and 703, *per* Sir Thomas Bingham MR. See generally, Kerr, above n 162.

[171] *Phelps*, above n 11, 654. Cf '[T]he mental or psychological effects of negligent advice may in themselves be able to constitute a proper head of damages, such as post-traumatic stress disorder or a psychological illness': ibid, 670, *per* Lord Clyde.

[172] D Nolan, 'New Forms of Damage in Negligence' (2007) 70 *MLR* 59, 80–86. Cf nothing 'short of identifiable psychological illness', *Nicholls v Rushton* (1992) *The Times*, 19 Jun, *per* Croom-Johnson LJ. See also, '[t]he expression "pure psychiatric or psychological injury" is intended to refer to a recognisable psychiatric illness which is neither caused by nor related to a physical injury sustained by the person concerned': *Tame v New South Wales; Annetts v Australian Stations Pty Ltd* (2002) 211 CLR 317, [44, n 25], *per* Gaudron J.

[173] See Freckleton, I, 'New Directions in Compensability for Psychiatric Injuries', *Psychiatry, Psychology and Law*, vol 9; 2002, 271. Cf 'He [the child psychiatrist] had not diagnosed psychological harm, let alone mental disorder': *A v Essex CC*, above n 21, 1901[57], *per* Hale LJ. But note the Scottish Law Commission's approach to terminology in this area: 'the main terms in current use are recognised psychiatric injury, illness or disorder . . . We understand that there is some doubt as to the precise scope of the terms "psychiatric" and "psychological". In order to ensure that all kinds of psychiatric *and psychological injuries or illnesses* are included we have decided to adopt, after consultation with some members of the Scottish Division of the Royal College of Psychiatrists, the general term "medically recognised mental disorder"': Scottish Law Commission, *Report on Damages for Psychiatric Injury* (Edinburgh, The Stationery Office, 2004) No 196,3, para 1.7(Emphasis added). There was no indication that any substantive change in the law was envisaged by this formulation, which may have been 'simply a repackaging of the common law rule that restricts recovery to cases involving a recognised psychiatric illness': D Nolan, 'Reforming Liability for Psychiatric Injury in Scotland: A Recipe for Uncertainty?' (2005) *MLR* 983, 986.

Secondly, the context of *Phelps* and other cognate cases[174] was that of distress, disappointment, lack of self-worth and a sense of under-achievement, due to an untreated congenital condition—not the infliction of psychiatric injury. This reading of *Phelps* is reinforced by that of Brooke LJ in the later case of *Robinson v St Helens Metropolitan Borough Council*:

> [T]he present appeal shows that the House of Lords has now recognised the existence of a legal duty of care concerned with a person's well being where the foreseeable (and recoverable) damage resulting from a breach is not necessarily a physical or recognisable psychiatric injury.[175]

The duty, as established in *Phelps*, was, he said:

> a duty to take care in relation to the diagnosis of a particular kind of congenital condition. A negligent failure to diagnose this condition [dyslexia] could foreseeably lead to damage in the sense of economic loss (stemming, for instance, from the failure of a child to achieve the level of educational attainment reasonably to be expected) *and/or* to damage in the sense of emotional or psychological harm *which would usually fall short of developing into a recognisable psychiatric injury*. This is the kind of damage which the duty exists to prevent... A claimant is therefore entitled to recover that kind of damage when the duty of care is broken.[176] (emphasis added)

It has been suggested that *Phelps* opens the way to recovery for 'free-standing' mental distress in the absence of psychiatric harm, that is, for '[i]nadequate education provision leading to mere "psychological damage"'.[177] Though the distinction between having a specific 'learning disability', on the one hand, and having poor literacy or numeracy skills, on the other, may sometimes be a source of evidential difficulty, *Phelps* does not assert that educational under-development could constitute actionable damage in its own right.[178] Nonetheless, in allowing a right to claim for 'educational neglect', the courts have clearly not confined the action to economic loss for negligent provision of services.[179] Nor do they appear to have confined the recovery threshold to that of a recognisable psychiatric illness.

---

[174] The conjoined cases, above n 165.
[175] *Robinson v St Helens Metropolitan Borough Council* [2002] EWCA Civ 1099 [36].
[176] Ibid.
[177] Fairgrieve, above n 166, 293. Though note *Younger (Katie) v Dorset & Somerset Strategic Health Authority and South East London Strategic Health Authority* [2006] LS Law Medical 489, where, on a preliminary issue, *Phelps* was held to apply only to claimants who suffered from a *pre-existing or congenital condition* capable of amelioration.
[178] See above n 169.
[179] 'Such a claim in a post-Cartesian world', said Lord Hoffmann, 'is for personal injury': *Adams v Bracknell*, above n 169, 81[10].

The Doctrinal Basis for Exceptions to the Special Rule Structure

It is apparent that, beyond the realm of standard accidents and disasters, judges have not always adhered to the special rules devised for negligently inflicted psychiatric harm; nor to the primary/secondary framework as authoritatively laid down, despite initial indications that both the framework and the rules were meant to cover all such cases. In contexts as diverse as communication of bad news, delivery of professional services and the duties of governmental authorities, courts have sometimes deployed alternative approaches. Nor are the types of claim examined above exhaustive. For example, psychiatric harm due to negligently conducted criminal investigation has been recognised as warranting redress, despite the fact that such liability reduces the extensive immunity from suit formerly afforded to the police on grounds of public policy.[180] In *Swinney v Chief Constable of Northumbria*,[181] a claim for psychiatric harm based on police failure to safeguard confidential documents which revealed an informant's identity was allowed to proceed to trial. So, too, was the claim in *Leach v Chief Constable of Gloucestershire*,[182] that the psychiatric condition of a volunteer 'appropriate adult'[183] was, at least in part, attributable to undue delay in her being offered counselling. In *Leach*, the particular circumstances were unusually harrowing. The claimant had been present during the investigation and interviews of a suspect, who, unknown to her at the time, turned out to be the notorious serial killer, Frederick West. She had accompanied him to the murder scenes and was often left alone with him in a cell. '*In this context*', said Pill LJ:

> I do not find helpful the distinction between primary and secondary victims considered by the House of Lords in *Page v Smith* . . . in the context of road traffic accidents.[184] (emphasis added)

If, in accident-based cases, the rule structure for psychiatric harm is a 'patchwork quilt', the disparate nature of non-accident claims, and the varied solutions devised for them, might seem to offer little prospect of enhancing coherence.

---

[180] *Hill v Chief Constable of West Yorkshire Police* [1989] AC 53. .
[181] *Swinney*, above n 15. .
[182] *Leach*, above n 1.
[183] The presence of an 'appropriate adult' is statutorily required at interviews of suspects whom the police believe to be mentally disordered.
[184] *Leach*, above n 1, 1429. Another context in which the distinction is plainly unhelpful, if intelligible at all, is that of psychiatric harm caused by seeing one's property negligently destroyed. The leading authority is *Attia v British Gas plc* [1987] 3 WLR 1101, a striking out action in which the Court of Appeal acknowledged that, in principle, liability was possible. Bingham LJ said that it was 'necessary to apply the tests of proximity and foreseeability derived from Lord Atkin's classic statement in *Donoghue v Stevenson* . . . in order to define the class to whom the defendant owes a duty': 1111. Though the case was decided prior to the formulation of the primary/secondary divide in *Alcock* and its subsequent modifications in *Page* and *White*, it has not been expressly overruled.

Several are open to more than one line of legal analysis;[185] some, such as the psychological detriment cases, do not fit comfortably within any settled legal doctrine. None of them can or should be artificially accommodated within a conceptual framework (badly) designed for different circumstances. They are of particular interest, however, to the extent that they offer a way out of the morass of unintelligible rules by stressing the explanatory power of more general negligence concepts. In this respect, the most significant themes to emerge from cases beyond the mainstream are 'assumption of responsibility' and reversion to 'first principles'.

'Assumption of Responsibility'

In many non-standard cases, one plausible rationale for liability is that obligations stemming from a pre-existing relationship between the parties justify forgoing the full rigour of the formal regime. Put another way, their 'special' relationship satisfies, or is a surrogate for, the element of 'sufficient proximity', which in 'secondary' accident-based claims can only be legally established by control mechanisms mainly rooted in physical nearness. Even in the absence of a contract, the defendant might be seen as having voluntarily assumed a responsibility not to cause the claimant psychiatric harm, either because of express assurances or, more often, due to the very nature of the relationship. By the same token, the claimant might be seen as having reasonably relied on the defendant not to cause such harm.

As the Court of Appeal judgment in *W v Essex County Council* indicates,[186] sometimes 'assumption of responsibility' and/or 'reasonable reliance' would appear to justify a claim for negligent misstatement or negligent provision of services. However, various doctrinal considerations might stand in the way of such a claim. It is not wholly clear, for example, whether, under the *Hedley Byrne* principle of liability for negligent misstatement, the defendant's assumption of responsibility must be positively demonstrated or may be inferred from the circumstances. Similarly, in a typical *Hedley Byrne* situation, the claimant must prove that the damage suffered resulted from having acted in reliance on the defendant's statement. In addition, one cannot ignore the evident reluctance of the courts to apply *Hedley Byrne* beyond claims for economic loss, as shown by the relative dearth of such authority for physical, let alone psychiatric, damage, and by the lack of analysis along such lines even in claims based on negligent communication. Consequently, in the minority of non-standard cases that are theoretically amenable to such analysis, claimants might find that they have escaped the restrictions of the special rule structure only to fall foul of restrictive elements within the *Hedley Byrne* principle itself.

When acknowledging a duty of care in non-standard claims, the courts have seldom disowned the special rules altogether; rather, they have highlighted particular aspects of a claim as justifying a certain leeway in applying them. This

---

[185] Eg, *W v Essex County Council*, above n 4. And see above 98–101.
[186] *W v Essex County Council* [1998] 3 WLR 534. See above n 33.

approach is apparent in a number of the hospital cases, both as regards the meaning of 'shock' and in the attribution of primary and secondary status. Here, as elsewhere, the notion of an assumed responsibility, if not always articulated, often seems to underpin the judicial approach. A relational link, such as doctor and patient, or even doctor and close relative, may persuade the court to dispense with one or more of the limiting devices.[187] The same holds true in the sphere of work-related stress, where emphasis on the contractual relationship, and an expanded interpretation of the obligation to protect employees from 'personal injury', have been the spur to recent doctrinal development.[188] Many such cases are decided as contractual claims by primary victims, whose psychiatric injury need not be shock-induced and who need not have been physically endangered.[189] At the same time, to some extent the courts still feel constrained by the primary/secondary divide in the employment context, as can be seen in the categorisation of the bases for liability set out in *Hatton*,[190] and from the House of Lords' classification of the police officers in *White*.

There are distinct signs of judicial readiness to invoke 'assumption of responsibility', broadly construed, when finding public authorities liable. In *Phelps*, for example, Lord Slynn said that:

> where an educational psychologist is specifically called in to advise in relation to the assessment and future provision for a specific child, and it is clear that the parents acting for the child and the teachers will follow that advice, prima facie a duty of care arises. It is sometimes said that there has to be an *assumption of responsibility* by the person concerned. That phrase can be misleading in that it can suggest that the professional person must knowingly and deliberately accept responsibility. It is, however, clear that the test is an objective one: *Henderson v Merrett Syndicates Ltd* [1995] 2 AC 145, 181. The phrase means simply that the law recognises that there is a duty of care. It is not so much that responsibility is assumed as that it is recognised or imposed by the law.
>
> The question is thus whether in the particular circumstances the necessary nexus has been shown.[191] (emphasis added)

Increasingly, then, 'assumption of responsibility' is seen as having considerable explanatory power when there is a prior relationship between the parties.[192]

---

[187] Eg, respectively, *Farrell v Merton, Sutton and Wandsworth HA*, above n 17, and *Farrell v Avon HA*, above n 3.

[188] As reinforced by statutory developments and EC Directives. See above Ch 1, 23–5. But see also below Ch 5, 161–5.

[189] See *Hartman v South Essex Mental Health and Community Care NHS Trust* [2005] ICR 782.

[190] *Hatton v Sutherland* [2002] Civ 76, per Hale LJ, [19]–[21].

[191] *Phelps*, above n 11, 654. As regards child welfare, see *X (Minors) v Bedfordshire County Council* [1995] 2 AC 633, 663–4, per Sir Thomas Bingham MR (diss), CA. See also *Leach*, above n 1, 1434, per Brooke LJ and 1429, per Pill LJ (diss); *R v Deputy Governor of Parkhurst Prison, Ex parte Hague* [1992] 1 AC 58, 165–6, per Lord Bridge.

[192] S Deakin, A Johnston, and B Markesinis, *Markesinis and Deakin's Tort Law* (Oxford, Oxford University Press, 6th edn, 2008) 152–5. But as regards psychiatric illness due to the communication of distressing information, note Witting's observation that '[t]he law in this area is nascent' and 'liability, if it arises, is likely to be restricted to cases in which the defendant communicator has "assumed a responsibility" for the well-being of the claimant': *Liability for Negligent Misstatements*, above n 51, 6.02. Cf Lunney and Oliphant, above n 97.

A Reversion to First Principles

Granted that it is possible to rationalise certain non-standard cases by reference to 'assumption of responsibility', to what extent is it appropriate to do so? The term's relative imprecision means that it is liable to be applied in a haphazard and inconsistent manner. Beyond the realm of economic loss, it lacks a sure footing in negligence doctrine, conspicuously so as regards psychiatric harm claims based on negligent misstatement.[193] What should not be overlooked, however, is that 'assumption of responsibility' could play a significant role as one possible ingredient in a reversion to first principles in negligence. It already performs this function in ordinary negligence law, when it provides the 'sufficient proximity' element in the triple formula for the duty of care, establishing the necessary closeness of relationship between the parties. It is easy to lose sight of this fact, partly because, when *physical* injury is positively inflicted, proof of sufficient proximity is for most practical purposes redundant. For example, in the commonest negligence context of all, the road accident, 'proximity' is self-evident and rarely involves a *prior* relational element. And because *physical* nearness is the primary lay meaning of 'proximity', the word itself immediately conveys an image of presence at or nearby some occurrence. Thus it sounds entirely natural to say of accident-based psychiatric harm cases that '[l]iability flows from proximity of the claimant to the event caused by the defendant or its physical aftermath.'[194] Put another way, it is easy to lose sight of the fact that it is in closeness of *relationship* (which frequently includes spatial relationship) that the essence of legal proximity resides.[195]

If, in non-standard psychiatric harm claims, proximity conceived of as *physical* closeness to a harm-inducing event generally lacks explanatory power, would it not be preferable to decide such cases according to ordinary negligence principles, where 'assumption of responsibility' may usefully feature as part of a multi-layered approach? The very fact that it is a malleable concept, which can be deployed as a cloak for policy, is all the more reason for resisting the temptation to elevate it almost to the status of a 'one club' solution. In an area as open-ended as negligence, no brief formula can encapsulate all eventualities. A broadly based conceptual framework seems better suited to deliver the nuanced analysis that the subtleties of psychiatric harm often demand, and to encourage more explicit articulation of any relevant policy issues. In the employment context, for example, a general assumption of responsibility on the part of the employer as to health and

---

[193] Cf '[T]he difficulty with treating [assumption of responsibility] as a self-contained alternative approach to duty is that it is clear that the issue is not always simply whether the defendant assumed responsibility for something but whether the law will regard him as having done so in a way which attracts liability in tort': WVH Rogers, *Winfield and Jolowicz on Tort* (London, Sweet & Maxwell, 17th edn, 2006) 145–6.

[194] Witting, above n 51, 6.02.

[195] Cf 'In so far as this rather ambiguous term can be given a general meaning, it normally signifies the presence of a pre-tort relationship of some kind between claimant and defendant arising *prior to* the infliction of damage': Deakin, Johnston, and Markesinis, above n 192, 128.

safety clearly features, but the applicable law for most work-related psychiatric harm is grounded in a duty of reasonable care, the extent and limits of which were elaborately spelt out by Hale LJ, in *Hatton*.[196]

Several other non-standard claims for psychiatric harm, such as the *CJD Litigation*, *Swinney* and *Leach*,[197] also illustrate how 'assumption of responsibility' has at times been deployed in the same way as it would be in an ordinary (non-psychiatric) negligence claim. *Swinney*, where it was alleged that police negligence had put an informant and her husband at risk, is a good example. In dismissing an attempt to have the action struck out, the Court of Appeal made no reference to any psychiatric damage cases, and none of the judgments suggested that any special considerations arose from the claim being for psychiatric harm.[198] As succinctly summarised by Ward LJ, the judicial analysis mirrors that of a standard claim for personal injury. On the facts as pleaded, the theft of documents identifying the informant was foreseeable, as was the risk of consequent harm to her and her husband. There was a special relationship of sufficient proximity between the claimants and the police, since the police had assumed responsibility for preserving confidentiality, on which they had relied. It was deemed fair, just and reasonable for the law to impose a duty, provided that there was 'no overwhelming dictate of public policy' to exclude the claim.[199] In the *CJD Litigation*,[200] Morland J's description of the relationship between the parties—'akin to that of doctor and patient, one of close proximity'—suggests that the notion of assumption of responsibility influenced his rejection of the special rule structure, but seemingly as part of a reversion to first principles, rather than as an exclusive test. In *Leach*, Pill LJ was similarly persuaded that the police had assumed a responsibility towards Frederick West's 'appropriate adult', and that they had failed to discharge it by not providing counselling. However, he expressly stated that this argument had to be seen as an ingredient of the orthodox triple test in negligence for duty of care: foreseeability, sufficient proximity and the 'fair, just and reasonable' criterion.

A comparable broadening of the basis for liability was apparent in the more recent case of *Home Office v Butchart*.[201] There, a prisoner on remand alleged that the authorities, though aware that he was in a depressed and unstable condition, placed him in a cell with a remand prisoner who they knew was a suicide risk, and who in fact committed suicide. The claimant, who discovered the body, also alleged that a prison officer had blamed him for the death. In addition, he was later briefly put in the same cell as another prisoner, who had just attempted suicide.

---

[196] *Hatton v Sutherland*, above n 190.

[197] *CJD Litigation*, and *Swinney*, above n 15, and *Leach*, above n 1. And cf Brooke LJ in *McLoughlin v Jones*, above n 4.

[198] True, the plaintiffs were physically endangered, if not in the sense of exposure to immediate peril akin to the situation in *Page*. See also the decision (post-*White*) of *L (A Child) v Reading Borough Council* [2001] 1 WLR 1575, CA.

[199] *Swinney*, above n 15, 486, *per* Ward LJ.

[200] See above 109–10.

[201] [2006] 1 WLR 1155, CA. See further, C McIvor, 'Liability for Psychiatric Harm' (2007) 23 *Professional Negligence* 249.

The cumulative effect of these events, said the claimant, caused him psychiatric illness, for which he sued the Home Office in negligence. They sought to characterise his claim as one of psychiatric damage due to his previous cell mate's suicide, maintaining that, in line with *Alcock* and *White*, he was a secondary victim who could not prove close ties with the deceased.

The Court of Appeal refused to strike out the claim. This was not, said Longmore LJ, a 'nervous shock' case 'narrowly based' on the effects of the suicide; rather, it was an alleged breach of the 'duty to take reasonable steps to ensure the health and safety of a prisoner' in the care and custody of the authorities. Treating the relational dimension as central, and drawing an analogy with the employment cases in particular, he concluded that there was a duty in the custodial context to 'prevent or minimise psychiatric harm' where it was reasonably foreseeable. This effective reversion to negligence first principles, whereby the action was seen to involve a 'primary duty' to the claimant, would also preclude a defence based on the absence of 'sudden shock' as the alleged trigger for his condition.

In 'non-standard' cases, then, the overall picture is of courts, constrained by precedent, artificially conforming to a perverse rule structure through forced interpretation, subject to the occasional reasoned resistance. Yet the resultant climate of judicial embarrassment, whether in feeling obliged to apply or defy the rules, could serve a constructive purpose. The reasoned departures, in particular, could have an important function in persuading the courts that to revert to first principles is also appropriate in typical, accident-based claims. They could help pave the way for the further erosion, if not demise, of the special structure in the heartland of liability for psychiatric harm. In certain other common law jurisdictions, courts have been far from impressed by the special controls which the House of Lords still deems indispensable. Particularly instructive in this respect are certain recent, if short-lived, judicial developments in Australia.

An Australian Exemplar: *Tame v New South Wales; Annetts v Australian Stations Pty Ltd*[202]

Australian common law has been much influenced by English precedents and, for much of the twentieth century, its liability rules for psychiatric harm developed along broadly similar lines.[203] Both systems require proof of a 'recognisable psy-

---

[202] *Tame v New South Wales; Annetts v Australian Stations Pty Ltd* (2002) 211 CLR 317.

[203] Even its inauspicious beginnings in *Victorian Railways Commissioners v Coultas* is testimony of a kind to a shared ancestry: above ch 2, 43–4. If anything, the Privy Council's rejection of Mrs Coultas' claim for fear of opening 'a wide field . . . for imaginary claims' was initially a greater barrier to development in the Australian courts which, unlike their English counterparts, were then technically bound by Privy Council decisions. Interestingly, the Victorian Supreme Court had upheld Mrs Coultas' claim, seemingly treating the nervous shock as a physical injury: *Coultas v Victorian Railways Commissioners* (1886) 12 VLR 895.

chiatric illness';[204] several modern Australian decisions mirrored the English case law on the need for a shock-induced condition,[205] and, in *Jaensch v Coffey*,[206] the Australian High Court adopted the 'aftermath' doctrine, a year or so after it had been established by the House of Lords in *McLoughlin v O'Brian*.

The key issue of whether 'untrammelled' reasonable foreseeability should displace control mechanisms was extensively explored in both of the above cases, though neither satisfactorily resolved the matter. However, whereas the English courts were to become increasingly wedded to artificial controls, Australian law had already been showing signs of greater flexibility.[207] In *Jaensch* itself, the High Court rejected its previous insistence on contemporaneous, unaided perception;[208] and though the majority did not abandon control mechanisms, Brennan J effectively treated reasonable foreseeability and causation as exclusive criteria of liability,[209] while Deane J pointed to the merits of causal, as against physical, proximity as a test of reasonable foreseeability.[210] The force of the analysis in the sustained judgments of Brennan and Deane JJ may have helped to ensure that Australia did not adopt the rigid primary/secondary divide or the restrictive liability regime apparently established in *Page* and *White*.[211]

The judicial parting of the ways reached its high point in the conjoined decisions of *Tame* and *Annetts*,[212] a notable landmark in Australian law on psychiatric injury, and a telling contrast to the approach of the House of Lords in *White*. *White* reinforced what it acknowledged to be a deeply flawed rule structure. In *Tame* and *Annetts*, the general tone of the judgments was noticeably free from the aura of resignation pervading the majority speeches in *White*.[213] The Court largely repudiated the use of limiting devices as preconditions of liability in favour of a more principled and rational approach, firmly grounded in reasonable foreseeability. More specifically, direct perception, sudden shock and harm that would have been

---

[204] *Hinz v Berry* [1970] 2 QB 40, 42, *per* Lord Denning MR; *Mount Isa Mines Ltd v Pusey* (1970) 125 CLR 383, 394, *per* Windeyer J. As noted earlier, this threshold requirement was foreshadowed in the Australian decision of *Storm v Geeves* [1965] Tas SR 252.

[205] 'Sudden sensory perception': *Jaensch v Coffey*, above n 112, 567, *per* Brennan J. Cf *Campbelltown City Council v Mackay* (1989) 15 NSWLR 501; *Anderson v Smith* (1990) 101 FLR 34.

[206] *Jaensch v Coffey*, above n 112.

[207] Eg, in 1970 the High Court had rejected the notion that 'secondary' claimants need to have been physically imperilled to succeed: *Mount Isa Ltd v Pusey*, above n 204, and there were conflicting views in Australian jurisdictions on whether, or to what extent, 'secondary' claimants needed to have 'close ties' with the primary victim.

[208] In *Coates v Government Insurance Office of New South Wales*, Kirby P was especially dismissive of the direct perception requirement as 'hopelessly out of contact with the modern world of telecommunications': (1995) 36 NSWLR 1, 10.

[209] *Jaensch*, above n 112, 572.

[210] *Jaensch*, above n 112, 606–7. Neither of them categorically ruled out recovery by unrelated bystanders: 570, *per* Brennan J; 605–6, *per* Deane J.

[211] McHugh J would later cast doubt on whether the primary/secondary divide would survive in England: *Tame*, above n 202, [93].

[212] Above n 202. .

[213] Except, perhaps, for Callinan J: 'Courts should be slow to do what legislators have abstained from doing': above n 202 [334].

foreseeable in a person of 'normal fortitude' were no longer to be seen as prerequisites of liability but only as factors that might help determine foreseeability.

In *Tame*, due to a police officer's clerical error, an incorrect blood alcohol reading was entered for Mrs Tame on a Traffic Collision Report. On learning about the mistake, some 17 months later, she phoned the police station and was told that the records had in fact been rectified within a few weeks. However, as someone who had rarely drunk alcohol for some 20 years, who was 'personally horrified' by the very idea of drink driving, she became 'obsessed' by the initial error. She experienced guilt and stress, and was ultimately diagnosed with a psychotic depressive illness, a condition to which she was apparently predisposed. The High Court held that a reasonable person in the position of the police officer would not have foreseen that careless completion of the Report would cause such an 'extreme and idiosyncratic' reaction. In short, the risk was 'far-fetched or fanciful', and no duty of care was owed to Mrs Tame in the circumstances.[214]

Annetts concerned psychiatric injury suffered by Mr and Mrs Annetts on hearing of the disappearance, and subsequently the death, of their 16 year old son. He had left home to begin work as a jackaroo (apprentice farm hand) in Western Australia. On the assumed facts,[215] his parents had agreed to their son taking the job only after they had received assurances from the defendant company that he would be well cared for and would be working under constant supervision. In the event, after only seven weeks in the job, he was sent to work on his own, as caretaker of an isolated property. Two months later, when the police informed his parents by phone that he had gone missing, his father collapsed. After a further 5 months of searching, in which the parents had taken some part, their son's remains were found in the desert, and they were duly informed, again by phone. The High Court held that a duty of care was owed to them in respect of their psychiatric injury.

Both *Tame* and *Annetts* were 'non-standard' cases. Neither claim involved physical presence at an accident or its immediate aftermath, or the direct experience of a shock-inducing incident. However, there was a large measure of agreement in the High Court that sudden shock and direct perception should not be prerequisites of liability. The only restriction to attract significant minority support was that psychiatric harm should have been foreseeable in a person of 'normal fortitude'.[216] Yet the notion of 'normal fortitude', apart from being 'scientifically untenable'[217] and bearing a disarmingly objective tone that belies its scope for conflicting judicial interpretation,[218] is largely embodied in the test of '*reasonable* foreseeability', insofar as this test restricts recovery for harm caused by 'abnormal sensitivity'.

---

[214] Above n 202[233] *per* Gummow and Kirby JJ.
[215] Duty of care was addressed as a preliminary issue.
[216] McHugh J [112]–[114], Callinan J [366] and possibly Hayne J [296] and [300], *Tame* above n 202.
[217] JG Fleming, *The Law of Torts* (Sydney, LBC Information Services, 9th edn, 1998) 179.
[218] Cf the sharply contrasting views of the Law Lords in *Page v Smith*, above n 45, on the foreseeability of injury through 'nervous shock' to a driver of 'normal fortitude' when cars collide at 30 miles per hour. The Court of Appeal was unanimously of the view that it was reasonably foreseeable: *Page v Smith* [1994] 4 All ER 522.

An Australian Exemplar: Tame and Annetts

In *Tame* and *Annetts*, reasonable foreseeability and other fundamental negligence principles took centre stage. There is copious reference to general principle, including many allusions to *Donoghue v Stevenson* and Lord Atkin's neighbour principle. As Gummow and Kirby JJ put it in the leading judgment, it was 'unsound' to view the 'normal fortitude' assumption, 'sudden shock' and 'direct perception' as *preconditions* of liability. Though, in a given case, such considerations might have a bearing on the likelihood of psychiatric harm, they were no substitute for the 'general requirements of duty of care, reasonable foreseeability, causation and remoteness of damage.'[219] And again:

> [in *Annetts*] The Full Court [of the Supreme Court of Western Australia] erred in failing to apply the ordinary principles of the tort of negligence, unhindered by artificial constrictions based on the circumstance that the illness for which redress was sought was purely psychiatric.[220]

Effectively, they applied ordinary negligence principles; and liability in negligence, as expressed in the various judicial formulations that have held sway at different times, is essentially geared to a broad conception of reasonable conduct.

It is, of course, a truism to say that *reasonableness* is the overarching consideration in the general law of negligence. The very term 'reasonable' itself conditions foreseeability of harm, in establishing whether a duty of care exists and whether it has been broken; while failure to take 'reasonable care in the particular circumstances' to avoid harm is the measure of breach. Yet, given the longstanding history of resort to controls when it comes to psychiatric harm, the constant refrain in *Tame* and *Annetts* that reasonableness reigns supreme still resonates:

> [T]he law of negligence already supplies its own limiting devices... [T]he ordinary principles of negligence circumscribe recovery. Further, the tort of negligence requires no more than reasonable care to avert reasonably foreseeable risks. Breach will not be established if a reasonable person in the defendant's position would not have acted differently. The touchstone of liability remains reasonableness of conduct.[221]

It is only the status of control mechanisms as an *absolute*, unprincipled, bar to recovery to which Gummow and Kirby JJ take exception. For example, having rejected 'normal fortitude' as a 'free-standing criterion of liability', they nonetheless describe it as:

> a postulate which assists in the assessment, at the stage of breach, of the reasonable foreseeability of the risk of psychiatric harm.[222]

---

[219] See *Tame* and *Annetts*, above n 202 [187] and [188].

[220] *Annetts*, above n 202 [236].

[221] *Tame* and *Annetts*, above n 202, [195], *per* Gummow and Kirby JJ. Cf Reasonableness 'is at the heart of the law of negligence': [14], *per* Gleeson CJ, and '[i]n the law of nervous shock, as in other areas of negligence law, the notion of reasonableness should condition the duty to exercise reasonable care for the safety of others': [113], *per* McHugh J.

[222] *Tame* and *Annetts*, above n 202 [189]. Cf 'ordinarily "normal fortitude" will be a convenient means of determining whether a risk of psychiatric injury is foreseeable': [62], *per* Gaudron J. See also *Gifford v Strang Patrick Stevedoring Pty Ltd* (2003) 214 CLR 269, confirming the High Court's commitment to reasonableness in the light of community standards: 'The limiting consideration is

Whether or not one embraces *Tame* and *Annetts* in every particular,[223] recasting what are often arbitrary limits on liability as only *potentially* relevant to foreseeability of harm has much to commend it, not least as a means of injecting an air of reality into legal analysis. With or without control mechanisms, it seems surprising that *Tame* ever reached the Australian High Court. In essence, it concerned a promptly corrected error that had never been acted upon, brought to the claimant's attention long after it had been made, for which an apology was given. All seven judges viewed Mrs Tame's psychotic depression as simply not a risk 'which the law of negligence required a reasonable person to avoid.'[224] The case was cogently resolved on straightforward negligence principles, rooted in reasonable foreseeability and reasonableness.

In *Annetts*, a court wedded to the traditional barriers to recovery could easily have produced an unreasonable outcome, by denying an intrinsically meritorious claim. Consider 'direct perception'. On any normal understanding of the concept, the parents had not directly perceived the accident or its immediate aftermath with their own unaided senses; yet that purported requirement was decisively rejected by the Court.[225] The only judge who deemed it essential felt constrained to define 'direct perception' in exceptionally broad and convoluted terms, far removed from its doctrinal and commonsense meaning. It was, said Callinan J:

> no more than a requirement that, by one or other of the senses, a 'bilaterally related person' perceive, or come to know of, or realise, at the time of, or as soon as is practicable after its occurrence, a shocking event or its shocking aftermath.[226]

However, from the perspective of what was reasonably foreseeable, and what would have been reasonable conduct, the key consideration in *Annetts* was the nature of the pre-existing relationship between the parties. The High Court concluded that the assurances of safety and constant supervision given to the parents of a minor established that they were owed a duty of care. As McHugh J observed:

> They could have sued in contract, but they elected to sue in negligence under the general law. The result is the same.[227]

Crucially, then, the relational element is seen to fulfil one of the first principles of ordinary negligence liability. In effect, assumption of responsibility dictated

---

reasonableness, which requires that account be taken both of interests of plaintiffs and of burdens on defendants. Rejection of a "control mechanism", such as the need for direct perception of an incident or its aftermath, originally devised as a means of giving practical content to that consideration does not involve rejection of the consideration itself': [9] *per* Gleeson CJ.

[223] Eg, there was no readiness to broaden the liability threshold beyond that of a recognisable psychiatric illness; though some concerns about the prevailing rule were explored by Hayne J, under the rubric *Psychiatric injury and emotional distress* [285]–[296].

[224] See above n 202, [233] *per* Gummow and Kirby JJ.

[225] *Annetts*, above n 202 [18] *per* Gleeson CJ; [51] *per* Gaudron J; [221]–[222] *per* Gummow and Kirby JJ, and [267] *per* Hayne J.

[226] *Annetts*, above n 202 [365].

[227] *Annetts*, above n 202 [144]. Cf 'They, like an employee, gave his safety into the hands of the employer': [304] *per* Hayne J.

proximity. In quintessential negligence terms, it was acknowledged that the parents were clearly persons so closely and directly affected by the company's conduct that it should reasonably have contemplated the kind of injury which they suffered.[228]

Within a year, the High Court was to consider a claim for psychiatric injury by children whose father had been negligently crushed to death in a workplace accident.[229] Though they did not witness the accident or its aftermath, they were informed about it later the same day. Applying *Tame* and *Annetts*, the Court held that they could, in principle, recover. The duty owed to them, said Gummow and Kirby JJ, 'emerges by application of the ordinary principles of the law of negligence.'[230]

Legislative Developments

Yet the seemingly decisive departure from prevailing English law on psychiatric harm was to prove short-lived. At the turn of the century, Australia saw a dramatic rise in the cost of personal injury liability insurance and corresponding reductions in risk coverage. What was widely perceived as an 'insurance crisis', symbolised by the collapse of a major general insurer, HIH, generated much political and media-driven debate about litigation rates, the breadth of negligence liability and the level of awards, concerns endorsed by some members of the judiciary.[231] Tort law reform was already on the agenda in several States when, in 2002, the Federal government instituted a major review of negligence law, chaired by Justice Ipp.[232] The Ipp Report noted that:

> [T]he Ministerial communiqué, the Terms of Reference, and the breadth and range of the responses received in submissions and consultations, indicate that there is *a widely held view in the Australian community* that there are problems with the law [on negligence].[233] (emphasis added)

The problems were described as 'stemming from perceptions' of unclear and unpredictable decisions; liability for personal injury being too easily established, and damages that were often too high.[234] The reviewing Panel acknowledged that,

---

[228] *Annetts*, above n 202 [37] *per* Gleeson CJ; [51] and [54] *per* Gaudron J; [144]–[146] *per* McHugh J, and [237] *per* Gummow and Kirby JJ [237], who drew attention to the similarity with *W v Essex County Council*, above n 4.

[229] *Gifford v Strang Patrick Stevedoring Pty Ltd*, above n 222.

[230] Above n 222 [85].

[231] The most prominent and forthright judicial contribution has been that of Spigelman AC, Chief Justice of New South Wales, in a series of speeches: 'Negligence: The Last Outpost of the Welfare State' (2002) 76 *Australian Law Journal* 432; 'Negligence and Insurance Premiums: Recent Changes in Australian Law' (2003) 11 *Torts Law Journal* 91, and 'Tort Law Reform: An Overview' (2006) 14 *Tort Law Review* 5, where he suggests that the New South Wales restrictions may have been excessive.

[232] Department of the Treasury, *Review of the Law of Negligence: Final Report* (Canberra, Department of the Treasury, 2002) (The *Ipp Report*).

[233] *Ipp Report*, ibid, para 1.4.

[234] Above n 232, para 1.4.

typically, the submissions it had received were 'not supported by reliable and convincing empirical evidence', and that there was a 'dearth of hard evidence in the areas in which decisions are called for.'[235] Nonetheless, as regards the 'insurance crisis', it proceeded on the basis that:

> [p]ersonal injury law has contributed to this state of affairs, and ... reducing liability and damages would make a significant contribution to resolving the crisis.[236]

As a direct consequence of the Ipp Report's recommendations, substantial, wide-ranging reforms were implemented, mainly between 2002 and 2004, in all Australian jurisdictions.[237] *Tame* and *Annetts* were 'immediately partially overturned by legislative amendment in New South Wales'.[238] There, as in several other States, a test based on a claimant of 'normal fortitude' has been designated a *precondition* of foreseeability in psychiatric injury cases,[239] and some new statutory provisions are more restrictive still than the recommendations in the Ipp Report. In particular, as regards secondary victims, several States have confined recovery to claimants who are either present at the *scene* of an accident and see another person being killed, injured or imperilled,[240] or who are in a 'close relationship' with such a person.[241]

The diminishing scope for psychiatric harm claims is not only the result of provisions specifically directed at this sub-area of the law. It is also implicit in new restrictions of a more general nature, notably on foreseeability and compensation. The open texture of 'reasonable foreseeability' was more easily portrayed as a vice rather than a virtue when the realm of the foreseeable was anything not 'far fetched or fanciful', the dominant test in the case law towards the end of the twentieth century.[242] Disparaged in several recent cases,[243] this test was dubbed by Spigelman AC as one of 'conceivable' rather than 'reasonable' foreseeability.[244] It has now been disowned by several States, in favour of the Ipp Report's more stringent recommendation that for a risk to be deemed foreseeable it must be 'not insignificant'.[245] In addition, as regards compensation, various restrictive devices have been either introduced or strengthened, such as liability thresholds for non-pecuniary loss,[246] caps on recoverable damages and higher discount rates for future loss.

---

[235] Above n 232, paras 1.38, 1.39.
[236] Above n 232, para 1.36.
[237] See L Skene and H Luntz, 'Effects of Tort Law Reform on Medical Liability' (2005) 79 *Australian Law Journal* 345.
[238] I Freckleton, 'New Directions in Compensability for Psychiatric Injuries', *Psychiatry, Psychology and Law*, Vol 9; 2002: 271, 272.
[239] Civil Liability Amendment (Personal Responsibility) Act 2002 (NSW) s 32.
[240] Seemingly this excludes aftermath cases.
[241] Civil Liability Act 2002 (NSW), s 30.
[242] *Wyong Shire Council v Shirt* (1980) 146 CLR 40, 47.
[243] Eg, *Swain v Waverley Municipal Council* (2005) 79 ALJR 565 [80], per McHugh J; *Koehler v Cerebos (Australia) Ltd* (2005) 79 ALJR 845, 850 [54], per Callinan J.
[244] 'Negligence: The Last Outpost of the Welfare State', above n 231, 441.
[245] Eg, Civil Liability Act 2002 (NSW) s 5B.
[246] Expressed either in monetary terms or as a percentage of an extreme case (15% in New South Wales: Civil Liability Act 2002, s 16 (1)) or, in some jurisdictions, as a 'significant injury'.

A recent report on trends in Australian personal injury litigation[247] found that, 'contrary to widespread belief, litigation rates had not, generally, been increasing in the period leading to the Ipp Review';[248] nor were data available to confirm that personal injury claims were becoming increasingly successful and producing increasingly large awards.[249] In short, it found no evidence that personal injury litigation was 'the root cause of the insurance crisis.'[250] It did, however, find that since the introduction of the reforms there has been a substantial decline in personal injury litigation rates in most jurisdictions. Indeed, in a recent overview, Spigelman J observed that '[a] number of persons, including myself, have indicated that in various respects the statutory changes have gone too far' and that:

> the speed, some would say haste, with which the changes were introduced . . . was such that there are substantial pressures emerging for some changes to be reversed.[251]

Conclusions

What lessons might be derived from the Australian experience, and what bearing does it have on recent developments in English law? First, one might note that, apart from some narrowing of the criterion for 'reasonable foreseeability', the *substantive* concept of negligence appears largely unaltered by the reforms. In particular, the 'negligence calculus', the factors that the courts must now take account of when determining breach of duty, largely replicates familiar common law criteria: probability and gravity of harm, the burden of taking adequate precautions and the social utility of the defendant's conduct. However, given the explicit aims of the reforms, their general tenor, the limits placed on compensation, and the widespread belief that they were dictated by an increase in litigation rates, it would not be surprising if they were to act as a spur for seriously restrictive judicial interpretation.

Like all common law jurisdictions, England and Australia have found it very difficult to formulate convincing unifying principles, let alone a universal criterion, for the existence of a legal duty of care in negligence.[252] Not long ago, the *Caparo* triple formula—reasonable foreseeability, proximity and what is fair, just and reasonable—was unanimously discarded by the Australian High Court. In *Sullivan v Moody*,[253] it dismissed 'proximity' as lacking in explanatory power, and resort to

---

[247] E Wright, *National Trends in Personal Injury Litigation: Before and After 'Ipp'* (Canberra, Australia, 2006). This study was commissioned by the Law Council of Australia, the national organisation of the legal profession.
[248] *Ibid*, 3.
[249] Above n 247, 29.
[250] Above n 247, 29.
[251] The Hon JJ Spigelman AC, 'Tort Law Reform: An Overview', above n 231, 14.
[252] See *Graham Barclay Oysters Pty Ltd v Ryan* (2003) 211 CLR 540, [229]–[244], per Kirby J. Cf 'It is reaching for the moon . . . to expect to accommodate every circumstance which may arise within a single short abstract formulation': *Merrett v Babb* [2001] 3 WLR 1 [41], per May LJ.
[253] *Sullivan v Moody* (2001) 207 CLR 562.

what is 'fair, just and reasonable' as a recipe for discretionary decision-making. 'The contemporary Australian approach ... is to engage in a multi-factorial or salient features analysis.'[254] Increasingly there is resort to notions of 'control' and 'vulnerability': the extent of the defendant's control over the situation serving as an indicator of whether reasonable precautions had been taken, and the level of claimant vulnerability as an indicator of capacity for self-protection.

Whatever the terminology, an evaluative role is inescapable when one is trying to assess what is or is not reasonable in the particular circumstances. As Kirby J has observed:

> Excessive analysis and undue intellectual subdivision of what is basically a unitary concept can lead a decision maker into over-sophisticated elaboration of a notion that is, at its heart, a reflection of practicality and common sense.[255]

In *Tame* and *Annetts*, Gummow and Kirby JJ made a powerful case for a negligence framework rooted in reasonable foreseeability and the primacy of reasonableness, as judged by community standards. Evaluation of reasonableness by reference to 'community standards' is, by definition, shaped by the temper of the times. And in a climate of concern over the breadth of liability, it is not difficult to detect a renewed emphasis on the personal responsibility of claimants, and expectations of self-reliance in negligence generally,[256] sentiments commonly voiced in reference to claims for psychiatric harm. However, it is important to distinguish 'community standards' from 'public sentiment', insofar as the latter too easily suggests mere populist attitudes or feelings. Standards imply values that have been thought through and implicitly entail consideration of broad social and moral concerns as a backdrop to the facts of the particular case.[257]

In the sphere of psychiatric harm, it is easy to see how the open texture of reasonable foreseeability and reasonableness readily evokes a floodgates fear and the perception of a system that has become unduly burdensome for defendants. Such concerns were not entirely absent from *Tame* and *Annetts*. As McHugh J put it:

---

[254] Spigelman AC, above n 251, 10. See also *Perre v Apand Pty Ltd* (1999) 198 CLR 180, 253 [198], *per* Gummow J. Cf 'vulnerability, power, control, generality or particularity of the class, the resources of, and demands upon the authority, the "core, or ... non-core" functions or relation to "a matter of policy or executive action"': *Graham Barclay Oysters Pty Ltd v Ryan*, above n 252 [321], *per* Callinan J.

[255] *Graham Barclay Oysters*, above n 252 [230].

[256] Eg, *Pyrenees Shire Council v Day* (1998) 192 CLR 330, 409 [226]–[227] *per* Kirby J. See also *Perre v Apand Pty Ltd* (1999) above n 254, and *Agar v Hyde* (2000) 201 CLR 552. Cf, in the English context, *Reeves v Commissioner of Police of the Metropolis* [2000] 1 AC 360, 368, *per* Lord Hoffmann, and *Tomlinson v Congleton Borough Council* [2004] 1 AC 46, especially [81] *per* Lord Hobhouse, and see [47] *per* Lord Hoffmann and [94] *per* Lord Scott. See further below Ch 5, 167–8.

[257] Commenting on Lord Atkin's famous description of 'liability in negligence' as based upon a 'general public sentiment of moral wrongdoing for which the offender must pay': *Donoghue v Stevenson* [1932] AC 562, 580, Ipp J observed that '[o]f course, "public sentiment" in this sense does not mean attitudes that change with the whim of fashion. It does not mean transient beliefs in some political platform, or media driven public anger or approval in regard to issues of the moment. Rather, public sentiment is a reflection of deep-seated moral, political, social and economic values; a reflection of the values of society itself.' D Ipp, 'Policy and the Swing of the Negligence Pendulum' (2003) 77 *Australian Law Journal* 732, 734.

I think that the time has come when this Court should retrace its steps so that the law of negligence accords with what people really do, or can be expected to do, in real life situations. Negligence law will fall—perhaps it already has fallen—into public disrepute if it produces results that ordinary members of the public regards as unreasonable.[258]

Yet there is also a compelling argument that it is precisely to prevent the law falling, or falling further, into disrepute that the courts should seek to achieve as intelligible and coherent a framework as is consistent with the practical constraints and imperfections inevitable in any legal system. That goal is not best served by a liability regime based on crude, mechanical cut-off points that traduce the medical determinants of psychiatric damage and entail unjust consequences.

The English cases 'beyond the mainstream' have the virtue of concentrating the mind on the challenges posed to a decision-maker when the mainstream structure is itself seriously flawed. They bring into sharp relief the policy considerations that have been so influential in the emotive and doctrinally fragile sphere of compensation for harm to the psyche. Superficially, their very diversity has added new layers to the incoherence of the rules as stated in *White*. Yet 'assumption of responsibility' has some claims to a footing in the established law, and the cases that advocate a return to 'first principles' offer the hope of a more defensible framework. It is salutary to reflect that in *Tame* and *Annetts*, from essentially the same doctrinal origins, a distinguished supreme court was able to produce a broadly coherent structure for psychiatric harm, rejecting the conventional wisdom that the policy concerns are so overwhelming as to make arbitrary rules unavoidable. Our contention is that much more coherence is attainable than English law currently affords, and that it is attainable without the dire consequences commonly envisaged. At the same time, it remains a sobering thought that, essentially for policy reasons, the fruits of *Tame* and *Annetts* could be so swiftly abandoned in hastily drawn up legislation. The quest should be for maximal coherence consistent with any substantiated or cogent policy concerns. Whether, or to what extent, the commonly expressed concerns are well-founded must now be more fully examined.

---

[258] *Tame*, above n 202, *per* McHugh J [101].

5

Policy Concerns

IN *WHITE*, LORD Steyn declared that:

> Courts of law must act on the best medical insight of the day... And psychiatric harm may be far more debilitating than physical harm.[1]

Yet the liability rules and relatively low awards continue to convey a very different message; one that undervalues mental well-being, often to the psychological as well as financial detriment of deserving claimants. Such undervaluation seems all the more misplaced at a time when optimum mental faculties are integral to everyday functioning and the ability to cope with changing patterns of work. Adverse consequences extend beyond the difficulties experienced by those whose financial and care needs are not met. Additional burdens commonly fall on others, and the law's effectiveness as a just compensatory mechanism is undermined. Are there nonetheless cogent reasons for the law as it stands? Putting to one side the constraints of precedent, real or perceived, we now consider various policy concerns often invoked in the case law in defence of the prevailing dispensation. In particular, it would appear that an exaggerated fear of proliferating claims is the main barrier to rational reform.

Some Common Policy Justifications for Special Controls

An instructive contemporary explanation of the status quo, at the highest judicial level, has been offered by Lord Steyn, under the explicit rubric *Policy considerations and psychiatric harm*.[2] In *White*, having noted that 'public perception has played a substantial role in the development of this branch of the law', he reiterates his

---

[1] *White v Chief Constable of South Yorkshire Police* [1999] 2 AC 455, 492.
[2] Broadly the same issues were considered in *McLoughlin v O'Brian* [1983] 1 AC 410, by Lord Wilberforce, 421 and Lord Bridge, 441–2. Cf *Tame v New South Wales; Annetts v Australian Stations Pty Ltd* (2002) 211 CLR 317 [192–3], *per* Gummow and Kirby JJ. See also, Law Commission, No 249, *Liability for Psychiatric Illness* (London, HMSO, 1998) 81–3, paras 6.5–6.8. And see D Howarth, in K Oliphant, (ed), *The Law of Tort* (London, LexisNexis Butterworths, 2nd edn, 2007) 12.137–12.142. Some of the material in this section is drawn from H Teff, 'Liability for Negligently Inflicted Psychiatric Harm: Justifications and Boundaries' (1998) 57 *CLJ* 91.

belief that 'nowadays we must accept the medical reality that psychiatric harm may be more serious than physical harm.'[3] Yet he endorses the restrictive approach, suggesting that psychiatric harm has 'at least four distinctive features . . . which in combination may account for the differential treatment.'[4] These can be summarised as greater diagnostic uncertainty, the prospect of compensation as a disincentive to rehabilitation, the potential to greatly increase the class of claimants, and to impose a burden of liability disproportionate to the defendant's blameworthiness.

'If claims for psychiatric harm were to be treated as generally on a par with physical injury it would', says Lord Steyn, 'have implications for the administration of justice'.[5] Given the legal requirement of a 'recognisable psychiatric illness', the 'complexity of drawing the line between acute grief and psychiatric harm' entails 'greater diagnostic uncertainty', requiring 'costly and time consuming' expert evidence.[6] As regards the litigation process and rehabilitation, and with industrial accidents particularly in mind, he is troubled by the '*unconscious* effect of the prospect of compensation'.[7] He then singles out as 'important' the concern that:

> [t]he abolition or a relaxation of the special rules . . . would greatly increase the class of persons who can recover damages in tort.[8]

Finally, instancing car accidents, Lord Steyn argues that wide-ranging redress for pure psychiatric harm could result in 'a burden of liability disproportionate to tortious conduct involving perhaps momentary lapses of concentration.'[9]

Before exploring these arguments in detail, we would question the 'distinctiveness' of the link between psychiatric harm and three of the four specified features, namely, diagnostic uncertainty, the impact on claimants of compensation prospects, and the potential for disproportionate liability. All of these features may be present in negligence claims for *physical* harm,[10] without any suggestion being made that they warrant denial of the duty of care or the imposition of special controls. This is particularly evident as regards 'disproportionate liability'. Compensation for personal injury is not based on the *degree* of the defendant's negligence, but on the victim's financial loss and the severity of the harm suffered.[11]

---

[3] *White*, above n 1, 493.
[4] *White*, above n 1, 493.
[5] *White*, above n 1, 493.
[6] *White*, above n 1. For further consideration of whether the prevailing liability threshold is appropriate, see below Ch 6, 171–5.
[7] *White*, above n 1, 494.
[8] *White*, above n 1, 494.
[9] *White*, above n 1, 494.
[10] Although the *class* of claimants has not widened in actions for physical injury, some such actions can also be said to have 'floodgates' implications of a sort. Scientific and technological advances have substantially increased the numbers of people at risk from negligently caused physical injury, eg, from nuclear, chemical (including pharmaceutical) and environmental disasters: see D Butler, *Damages for Psychiatric Injuries* (Sydney, The Federation Press, 2004) 75–6 [422]. In such contexts, legislative measures have been introduced to impose 'strict liability' regimes on defendants. See, eg, the Nuclear Installations Act 1965, and the Consumer Protection Act 1987.
[11] See below, 148–9.

Consequently, substantial damages are frequently awarded for serious *physical* injury arising from 'momentary lapses of concentration', car accidents having long been the paradigm case.

Diagnostic Uncertainty

The supposed need for controls because of the 'costly and time-consuming exercise' of establishing a recognisable psychiatric illness is, we would argue, a largely self-inflicted wound, which rests on very slender authority.[12] In any event, Lord Steyn himself sees the potential administrative costs of expert evidence as a factor which:

> on its own ... may not be entitled to great weight and may not outweigh the considerations of justice supporting genuine claims.[13]

In an adversarial system, conflicting evidence inevitably looms large in complex areas and is commonplace across the whole spectrum of professional negligence litigation. Doubtless, as a broad generalisation, diagnostic boundaries are more uncertain in psychiatric than in general medicine,[14] and psychiatry is perhaps more liable to produce dogmatic schools of thought, on the one hand, and more vulnerable to shifting attitudes on the other.[15] Yet it has also been observed that:

> [f]or most of the major psychiatric disorders, the agreement reached by psychiatrists is as high or higher than for many general medical conditions[16]

and it is common knowledge that precise explanations are unattainable for many physical ills.[17] The case law on medical negligence, workplace injuries and environmental hazards is replete with conflicting evidence and uncertainty about the nature of various physical conditions. Yet there is no call in these areas for restrictions comparable to those which apply to psychiatric harm, a domain in which biomedical advance has progressively weakened the argument that its imprecision uniquely justifies special legal constraints, ungrounded in medicine or science.[18]

In the forensic setting, psychiatrists are often broadly in agreement as to the extent of a claimant's disturbance, disability and dysfunction, even if they disagree

---

[12] See *Hinz v Berry* [1970] 2 QB 40, and *van Soest v Residual Health Management Unit* [2000] 1 NZLR 179, 204–5 [97]–[99], per Thomas J. And see above Ch 2, 53–4.

[13] *White*, above n 1, 493.

[14] *White*, above n 1, 493.

[15] See Lord Rodger, 'Law and Medicine: an Odd Couple?', Personal Injuries Bar Association, *Newsline* (2006) 3. .

[16] T Rogers, 'Diagnostic validity and psychiatric expert testimony' *International Journal of Law and Psychiatry* (2004) 27, 281, 285. See also, T Sartorius, *et al*, 'Progress towards achieving a common language in psychiatry' *American Journal of Psychiatry* (1995) 152, 1427.

[17] Cf '[S]ome physical injuries, such as whiplash, back pain and other soft tissue damage, probably are feigned more easily than complex psychoneurotic reactions': P Bell, 'The Bell Tolls: Toward Full Tort Recovery for Psychic Injury' (1984) 36 *University of Florida Law Review* 333, 352.

[18] RE Kendell, 'The distinction between mental and physical illness', (2001) *British Journal of Psychiatry*, 178, 490.

about the appropriate diagnostic label.[19] Ultimately, the issue for them is not whether particular symptoms irrefutably constitute a conceptually distinct 'disease entity', provable, say, by a laboratory test. '[T]he central defining point of psychiatry', observes Rogers, 'has to be "mental suffering" or "abnormal behaviour." '[20] Up to a point, the law reflects a similar approach. As we have seen, DSM and ICD psychiatric classifications are not dispositive in law;[21] however cogent and respected, for legal purposes they are still only guidelines. In essence, the law requires an illness or condition that is *identifiable* as psychiatric in nature, which would seem to allow some leeway for advances in scientific knowledge not yet reflected in the standard works of reference. Herein, perhaps, lies the force of a *recognisable* rather than *recognised* psychiatric illness as the common law test, though the two terms are often used interchangeably. Lord Denning may well have used the particular expression 'recognisable psychiatric illness' without 'deliberative consideration',[22] but it is at least clear that his concern was to exclude liability for transient distress of minimal impact. In law, as in psychiatry, it is the level of morbidity that is central: 'the psychiatric illness does not have to have any particular label or term of art applied to it'.[23] As we have seen, the Scottish Law Commission initially favoured a formula that focussed explicitly on the impact of the harm—a 'significantly disabling psychiatric injury'.[24] However, the majority of its consultees considered 'significantly disabling' too *high* a liability threshold, and the Commission's Report recommended 'medically recognised mental disorder', a formula designed to include psychological as well psychiatric disorders.[25]

When expert witnesses do disagree as to whether a claimant has suffered from a 'recognisable psychiatric illness', it is ultimately for the judge to decide the matter, on the balance of probabilities, in the light of the totality of the evidence.[26] Even under the prevailing liability threshold, concern that diagnostic uncertainty is a threat to the administration of justice would diminish if judicial interpretation could address more directly the substantive seriousness of a claimant's condition and was less preoccupied with contestable technical labels.[27] It is true that much

[19] Cf Scottish Law Commission, *Discussion Paper on Damages for Psychiatric Injury* (Edinburgh, The Stationery Office, 2002) No 120, 7–8, para 2.8.

[20] See above n 16, 286.

[21] Above Ch 1, 6–7.

[22] See above Ch 2, n 99 and related text. In Australia, recent statutory reforms have used the arguably narrower term 'recognised', which appears in the Ipp Report, Department of the Treasury, *Review of the Law of Negligence: Final Report* (Canberra, Department of the Treasury, 2002) (The *Ipp Report*), rec 34.

[23] *Brice v Brown* [1984] 1 All ER 997, 1006, per Stuart-Smith J. Cf 'a condition which can reasonably be described as an illness': *Simpson v Imperial Chemical Industries Ltd* 1983 SLT 601, 609, per Lord Grieve.

[24] Scottish Law Commission, *Discussion Paper*, above n 19, para 2.8. And see above Ch 1, 9.

[25] Scottish Law Commission, *Report on Damages for Psychiatric Injury* (Edinburgh, The Stationery Office, 2004) No 196, rec 3(b), paras 3.9, 3.10; Draft Bill, cl 4(1) (a). And see above Ch 4, n 173.

[26] Cf 'to gauge the weight and usefulness of such assistance as he is given and to reach his own conclusions accordingly': *Vernon v Bosley (No 1)* [1997] 1 All ER 577, 603, per Evans LJ. See Lord Bridge's exposition of the 'educated layman' criterion: *McLoughlin v O'Brian* [1983] 1 AC 410, 432–3.

[27] Cf D Butler, 'Identifying the Compensable Damage in "Nervous Shock" cases' (1997) 5 *Torts Law Journal* 67. And see further below Ch 6, 172–5.

of the time and money spent on expert evidence is concerned with causation, that is, on whether the defendant's conduct caused the claimant's alleged psychiatric condition. And the issue of causation can be difficult to resolve.[28] However, this issue, which is also for the judge to determine, may be just as problematic in claims that physical harm resulted from, say, medical negligence, environmental hazards, or shortcomings in health and safety provisions.

Litigation and Rehabilitation

At the Court of Appeal stage in *McLoughlin v O'Brian*,[29] Stephenson LJ observed:

> I derive some comfort from reflecting that to encourage such claims ... would ... do a grave disservice to many sufferers from nervous shock and mental injury, which may be exacerbated and prolonged or even made incurable by the anxieties of litigation.[30]

It is this well-intentioned, if paternalistic, sentiment that constitutes Lord Steyn's second reason for the differential treatment of psychiatric harm. The term 'compensation neurosis'[31] commonly features in this context, unfortunately so, since it has also been used to describe claims based on feigned illness and dismissively described as malingering and 'compensationitis'.[32] Lord Steyn is clearly not alluding to the phenomenon in its pejorative sense but to authentic psychological problems linked to the process of claiming compensation. He makes no reference to the scientific evidence on this issue and, at least as a general proposition, his endorsement of its significance is both qualified and speculative: '[t]he litigation is *sometimes* an unconscious disincentive to rehabilitation', a factor that '*may* play a larger role in cases of pure psychiatric harm'(emphasis added).[33] He does, however, single out industrial accidents as an area where 'psychiatric harm is repeatedly encountered and often endures until the process of claiming comes to an end.'[34]

In fact, there is good reason to suppose that, in its non-pejorative sense, the significance of 'compensation neurosis', both as a medical phenomenon and an influence on judicial policy, has been much exaggerated.[35] If a major reason for judicial aversion to broader liability rules had been fear of inhibiting the recuperation of growing numbers of authentic claimants, one might have expected to find

---

[28] Commenting on the Law Commission's Consultation Paper No 137, *Liability for Psychiatric Illness* (London HMSO,1995), Wessely observed that the Commission's approach to causation implied 'greater confidence about our knowledge of the aetiology of psychiatric disorders than is justified': S Wessely, 'Liability for Psychiatric Illness' (1995) 39 *Journal of Psychosomatic Research* 659, 667.
[29] *McLoughlin v O'Brian* [1981] QB 599.
[30] *Ibid*, 616.
[31] Sometimes called 'litigation neurosis' or 'accident neurosis'.
[32] See Law Commission, *Liability for Psychiatric Illness*, above n 2, 52–3, paras 3.30 and 3.31.
[33] *White*, above n 1, 494.
[34] *White*, above n 1.
[35] The Law Commission has acknowledged that 'compensation neurosis' has been re-evaluated in recent years and its practical significance minimised: above n 2, para 3.31.

more articulation of this concern than appears in the case law. It would have been a less contentious basis for denying liability than the supposed danger of numerous fraudulent claims, which did loom large in the early case law.[36] By the mid-twentieth century, as psychological techniques for exposing bogus claims improved, judicial concern about fraud was beginning to recede. However, from the 1960s onwards, it saw a resurgence, largely due to an influential study by the leading neurologist of the day, Henry Miller.[37]

Miller's conclusions on what he termed 'accident neurosis' were based on personal examination of some 4,000 patients over 12 years for post-accident medico-legal assessment. He maintained that prospective litigation was an important source of malingering and perpetuation of symptoms, especially after industrial accidents, by contrast, for example, with injuries on the hunting field or in rugby football, where compensation was not in issue. His follow-up of 50 (out of 200) head injury cases, in which the patients developed 'neurotic symptoms' after trauma, indicated that within two years of their claims being settled the vast majority had returned to work. In claims of 'accident neurosis', said Miller:

> many of the complainants are not only *consciously* but even frankly and obsessively preoccupied with the question of financial compensation . . . In my considered opinion these cases are much closer to malingering than to any form of mental disease genuinely outside the patient's control.[38] (emphasis added)

Miller's views found considerable support among the judiciary, notably so in the Court of Appeal decision of *James v Woodall Duckham Construction Co Ltd*.[39] Echoing his contrast between industrial and sporting injuries, Lord Steyn chooses this case to illustrate the *unconscious* effect of the prospect of compensation in industrial injury litigation.[40] It should however be noted that, in the case itself, 'compensation neurosis' was equated with malingering, and Lord Justice Winn quoted approvingly Sir Francis Walshe, Miller's mentor, to the effect that:

> wherever compensation need or compensation greed was involved in the total subconscious mentality and mental state of a patient, it must be diagnosed that his neurosis was at least in part purposive.[41]

Walshe himself reputedly described traumatic neurosis as a unique disease or condition in medicine, being the only one he knew which could be cured by gold.[42]

Despite Miller's undoubted influence, there has been little by way of confirmation of his findings in later studies. Several commentators questioned his methodology,

---

[36] Eg, *Victorian Railways Commissioners v Coultas* (1888) 13 App Cas 222. And see G Mendelson, 'Outcome-related compensation: in search of a new paradigm', in PW Halligan, C Bass and DA Oakley (eds), *Malingering and Illness Deception* (New York, Oxford University Press, 2003) ch 17, 226.

[37] 'Accident Neurosis' *British Medical Journal* 1, 919–25, 992–8 (1961).

[38] H Miller, 'Mental After-effects of Head Injury', *Proceedings of the Royal Society of Medicine* 59, 257, 259 (1966).

[39] *James v Woodall Duckham Construction Co Ltd* [1969] 1 WLR 903.

[40] *White*, above n 1, 494.

[41] *James v Woodall Duckham*, above n 39, 908.

[42] Sir F Lawton, 'A Judicial View of Traumatic Neurosis' (1979) 47 *Medico-Legal Journal* 6, 8.

dismissed his more forthright pronouncements as unduly subjective and deprecated the impact of his study on litigation. In 1985, Tarsh and Royston went as far as to say that it had 'held sway in the Courts since its publication in 1961, in spite of subsequent work which refutes it'.[43] More recent research, as well as doubting the prevalence of malingering and fraud in the forensic context, is circumspect about the alleged link between compensation processes and recovery from psychiatric illness. At most, any such link is accorded no more than a minor role among numerous other factors.[44] Taking the medical literature as a whole:

> compensation and litigation should probably not be considered as primary determinants of the recovery process, and ... 'compensation neurosis' is comparatively rare.[45]

Miller himself said that accident neurosis is 'characteristically a complication of minor or trivial injury and is rare after serious accidents.'[46] Though the litigation process may affect prognosis, as one of a range of influences that reinforce and prolong psychiatric disorder, most modern research attributes greater significance to considerations such as personality, environmental factors, employment prospects and, critically, the time when psychological management of symptoms commences. If doctors assume too readily that symptoms are a function of litigation which will disappear when it has ended, some patients risk having potentially valuable interventions denied or deferred, such that their condition endures or becomes less amenable to treatment.[47]

Plainly there is ample opportunity for expert witnesses to apprise the courts of current medical understanding in these matters. For example, in *Arrowsmith v Beeston*, Brooke LJ summarised the expert evidence as follows:

> One old belief, which featured so prominently in adversarial personal injuries litigation up to the 1980s (and perhaps beyond) that an award of compensation is likely to bring an end to a depressed patient's symptoms, was firmly rejected by both [doctors]. Dr [X] told the judge that a series of authoritative studies had shown conclusively that the actual rate at which people recover after they receive compensation on settling their litigation is low and that the prognosis is generally poor if a patient's symptoms have gone on for more than a couple of years.[48]

---

[43] MJ Tarsh and C Royston, 'A Follow-up Study of Accident Neurosis', (1985) *British Journal of Psychiatry*, 146, 18.

[44] Eg, as regards malingering, the 'basic postulate [of 'compensation neurosis']—that litigating patients improve when the case is finalized—is incorrect.' G Mendelson, above n 36, ch 17, 225.

[45] C Vincent and IH Robertson, 'Recovering from a Medical Accident: the Consequences for Patients and their Families', in C Vincent, M Ennis and RJ Audley, *Medical Accidents* (Oxford, Oxford University Press 1993)163. Cf Tarsh and Royston, above n 43, RI Cohen and JM Pfeffer, 'Accident Neurosis Revisited' (1987) 27 *Medicine, Science, and the Law* 177. See also B Bryant, R Mayou and S Lloyd-Bostock (1997), 'Compensation Claims following Road Accidents: a six-year follow-up study' (1997) 37 *Medicine, Science, and the Law* 326, 335 and R Mayou, S Tyndel and B Bryant, 'Long-term outcome of motor vehicle accident injury' (1997) *Psychosomatic Medicine* 59 (6) 578.

[46] Miller, above n 38, 258.

[47] RW Evans, 'The Effects of Litigation on Treatment Outcome with Personal Injury Patients' (1994) *American Journal of Forensic Psychology* 12;4: 19, 20–23, 30.

[48] *Arrowsmith v Beeston*, unreported, CA, Jun 1998, 14–15. Cited in NJ Mullany and PR Handford, 'Moving the Boundary Stone by Statute—The Law Commission on Psychiatric Illness' (1999) 22

Insofar as the compensation neurosis argument still resonates in the courts, it seems likely that it owes much to residual suspicions of malingering—an amalgam of conventional wisdom and the 'tendency for lawyers in practice to take a somewhat robust, often cynical, attitude to apparently "unexplained" symptoms',[49] reinforced by media coverage of exceptional cases. Just as it needs only one Hillsborough to stir up a floodgates fear, it takes only one well-publicised instance of suspect psychiatric evidence, however unusual, to bolster or revive judicial mistrust of intangible symptoms and misgivings about 'secondary' claims of psychiatric harm.[50]

Liability Disproportionate to Culpability

Before we explore the reason most commonly advanced for judicial refusal to relax the rule structure—the 'floodgates fear'—mention should be made of Lord Steyn's fourth explanation: that defendants might be burdened with damages disproportionate to their blameworthiness. The problem with this argument can be briefly stated. It has long been the basic principle of damages for personal injury that, as far as is possible, successful claimants should be restored to the position that they would have been in but for the defendant's tortious conduct.[51] If negligence and causation have been established, a claimant is entitled to such compensation for financial loss, pain and suffering and disability as is deemed appropriate to achieve that aim. There is no attempt to refine the award to reflect the gravity of the defendant's negligence: the actual extent of the claimant's financial loss and injuries is the only calculation. Though one can, of course, debate the merits of an approach so influenced by chance factors, any potential for a 'disproportionate' burden[52] is no greater in respect of psychiatric harm than for physical injuries arising from momentary carelessness at the wheel, or from any number of routine activities.

In *McLoughlin v O'Brian*, Lord Bridge emphatically dismissed the disproportionality argument:

> I can see no grounds whatever for suggesting that to make the defendant liable for reasonably foreseeable psychiatric illness caused by his negligence would be to impose a crushing burden on him out of proportion to his moral responsibility. However liberally

---

University of New South Wales Law Journal 350, 377, at n 175, where the authors describe the old belief as a 'long-held false premise [that] belies the most complex of human processes and the seriousness of chronic disorder.' See further A Sprince, 'Malingering and the law: a third way?', in Halligan *et al*, above n 36, ch 18, and K Wheat, *Napier and Wheat's Recovering Damages for Psychiatric Injury* (Oxford, Oxford University Press, 2nd edn, 2002) 82–5. But see also J Stapleton, 'In Restraint of Tort', in P Birks (ed), *The Frontiers of Liability* vol 2 (Oxford, Oxford University Press, 1994) ch 7, 95.

[49] Sprince, *ibid*, 239.
[50] See *Vernon v Bosley* (No 1) 1997 1 All ER 577 and *Vernon v Bosley* (No 2) [1999] QB 18, CA. And see J Dwyer, 'The Vernon Saga' (1998) 6 *Tort Law Review* 91.
[51] *Livingstone v Rawyards* (1880) 5 App Cas 25. And see below Ch 6, 000.
[52] In practice, the burden is largely discharged via insurance and loss-spreading. See below Ch 6, 180.

the criterion of reasonable foreseeability is interpreted, both the number of successful claims in this field and the quantum of damages they will attract are likely to be moderate.[53]

Fleming was equally sceptical, describing the risk of inordinate burdens as a factor that is:

> largely speculative, prone to be promoted by the often hyperbolic rhetoric of defendants and the all too reticent prejudices of judges.[54]

The Potential for Proliferating Claims

The Potency of the 'Floodgates Fear'

For every person physically injured by another's negligent conduct there will commonly be many more who could have conceivably suffered mental harm. It should therefore not surprise us to find a judge declaring that, of all the reasons typically advanced, it is:

> the fear of 'opening the floodgates' which motivated the Courts to depart from basic principle and seek to limit or control the circumstances in which damages for mental harm may be recovered.[55]

Towards the end of the twentieth century, the English judiciary's increasing concern about negligence liability expanding[56] was underlined, as regards psychiatric harm, by reflection on the sheer number of people who might, in pure theory, have claimed for mental trauma after the events at Hillsborough; though, according to a member of the Hillsborough solicitors' steering committee, no strangers to the primary victims sought legal advice about suing, apart from the police officers on duty.[57] The prospect of future mass disasters helped to generate a 'floodgates fear', which gained added momentum from extensive media coverage of PTSD as an emergent basis for claims, and from rising concern that work-related stress might become 'the next growth area'. There was, however, little overt judicial reference to the flood of 'imaginary claims' envisioned in *Coultas*.[58] By acknowledging that he did not see bogus claims as posing a substantial problem for the courts, Lord

---

[53] *McLoughlin v O'Brian*, above n 2, 441. Lord Bridge also rejected the other 3 policy rationales presently under discussion.

[54] (1994) 2 *Tort Law Review* 202, 204 (review of Mullany and Handford, *Tort Liability for Psychiatric Damage*, 1st edn, 1993).

[55] *van Soest*, above n 12, 201, *per* Thomas J (diss). Cf *Page v Smith* [1996] AC 155, 189, *per* Lord Lloyd, and *Alcock v Chief Constable of South Yorkshire Police* [1992] 1 AC 310, 417, *per* Lord Oliver. Cf 'nearly all arguments for restricting negligence liability are at bottom versions of the floodgates argument': Sir Robin Cooke, 'Tort Illusions', in P Finn (ed), *Essays on Torts* (Sydney, Law Book Co, 1989) ch 4, 74.

[56] Eg, '[s]ince *Anns* put the floodgates on the jar, a fashionable plaintiff alleges negligence.' *CBS Songs Ltd v Amstrad Consumer Electronics Plc* [1988] AC 1013, 1059, *per* Lord Templeman.

[57] *The Independent*, 4th Oct, 1991.

[58] See above Ch 2, n 37 and related text.

Steyn seemed to identify excessive litigation over genuine suffering as the real threat.

In its detailed Report on *Liability for Psychiatric Illness*, published shortly before the decision in *White*, the Law Commission had explored substantially the same policy concerns as Lord Steyn was about to address. The Commission had found only one of them convincing,[59] and their endorsement of it was scarcely wholehearted:

> After much deliberation, we do, however, remain persuaded that *at this point in time...* the 'floodgates argument' requires special policy limitations to be imposed over and above the test of reasonable foreseeability.[60] (emphasis added)

Their declared aim was to remove unnecessary constraints, 'but without giving rise to *fears* of uncontrolled liability'[61](emphasis added). The inference that the overriding anxiety was about perception, and the guarded nature of the conclusion, are not without interest. Moreover, the Commission deplored the consequences of attaching practical significance to the primary/secondary distinction; recommended abandonment of the 'sudden shock' requirement for all types of claimant, and removal of the need for closeness in time and space and direct perception in 'secondary' claims. However, their proposed retention of the 'close ties' requirement in such cases was expressly driven by the floodgates argument.[62]

As the dominant contemporary judicial policy concern, the only one relied on by the Law Commission and the one that appears to resonate most with the public, the floodgates argument requires close scrutiny. Primarily a fear of claims proliferating from a single event,[63] it is also applicable to the possibility of a mass of claims arising from a mass of separate events. 'Both possibilities', said the Commission:

> give rise to the concern that such a proliferation of claims would clog the court system and divert too many of society's resources into compensating the victims of psychiatric illness at the expense of other equally or more deserving plaintiffs. If the system fails to cope, the law will fall into disrepute.[64]

Thus formulated, the argument can be seen to have several different strands, including the forebodings already noted of administrative overload and a 'disproportionate burden' on defendants. Of particular importance for present purposes is its powerful general appeal: dispense with the controls and there will be an unacceptable increase in the number of claims.

A fear of numerous claims allows a superficially plausible, and largely unexamined, assumption to exert a hold on people's minds. This is mainly achieved

---

[59] They, too, did not see fraudulent and exaggerated claims as posing a serious risk: Law Com Report, above n 2, paras 3.31–3.32.

[60] And again: '[W]e accept that it is difficult to be sure that a move to a pure reasonable foreseeability test would open the floodgates of litigation.' Law Com Rep, above n 2, para 6.8.

[61] Law Com Rep, above n 2, para 1.3.

[62] Law Com Rep, above n 2, para 6.10.

[63] '[P]robably the argument's central force,' Law Com Rep, above n 2, para 6.6, n 9.

[64] Law Com Rep, above n 2, para 6.6, n 9.

through mere repetition via media scare stories, in which exaggerated or fraudulent claiming is often the underlying theme. It is not difficult to raise alarm and indignation by invoking the spectre of countless would-be litigants inundating the courts and succeeding on the back of flimsy claims. The desired effect is the more easily achieved because, as well as instilling resentment, the message builds on populist scepticism about non-physical symptoms. At the crudest level, generalisations about 'opportunistic' claimants and 'ambulance-chasing' lawyers, coupled with anecdotal accounts of extravagant claims, a stab at the 'compensation culture' and dire predictions of an impending crisis make good copy.[65] Between 1993 and 2006, national newspapers carried approximately 2,300, mostly negative, articles featuring the term 'compensation culture'.[66] And insurance industry lobbyists are generally better-placed to have such material publicised than individual claimants or pressure groups are to counteract it.[67] For a more dispassionate assessment of how cogent the floodgates argument is, it is necessary to take due account of the significant disincentives to claiming and, as far as available data allow, to explore its actual and potential frequency.

Disincentives to Claiming

The kind of media influence just described, reinforced by constant advertising encouraging people to pursue claims, helps to explain why the floodgates fear retains such general appeal, *despite* the lack of hard evidence of a present-day litigation explosion, and despite the fact that involvement with lawyers and the courts is widely assumed to be costly, unpredictable, often long drawn out and emotionally draining. Of course, hopes of a quick settlement may often be the claimant's objective; but somewhere in the popular imagination there also seems to lurk an assumption that litigants can easily dupe medical experts, walk straight into the courtroom and persuade judge and counsel that a relatively minor upset has caused them serious psychiatric harm which merits substantial redress.[68] Absent from this characterisation is any sense that there are more basic and powerful disincentives to litigating than abstruse, restrictive liability rules, of which most

---

[65] Cf 'The public conscience, an elusive thing, as often as not turns out to be an echo-chamber inhabited by journalists and public moralists': *Vellino v Chief Constable of Greater Manchester* [2002] 1 WLR 218, 233, per Sedley LJ.

[66] See A Morris, 'Spiralling or Stabilising? The Compensation Culture and Our Propensity to Claim Damages for Personal Injury' (2007) 70 *MLR* 349, 353, at n 30.

[67] Australia's speedy adoption, nation-wide, of major reforms to its personal injury laws was facilitated by media identification of the insurance industry's perceived needs with the public interest. See T White and A Melville, 'Hey, but who's counting?: the metrics and politics of trends in civil litigation', in W Prest and SR Anleu (eds), *Litigation: Past and Present* (Sydney, University of New South Wales Press, 2004) ch 6.

[68] There is little public awareness of the preliminary stages in the civil law process, in particular the substantial development of pre-trial case management under the Civil Procedure Rules 1998, including meetings or discussions between medical experts that might expose unfounded claims. On the other hand, of course, such preliminary processes may establish common ground that facilitates early settlement.

people are in any event oblivious. A general aversion to lawyers and legal processes might be one; the fact that a prospective defendant is uninsured and without means would be another. The potential or perceived cost of suing, inhibiting factors for many would-be litigants, may loom especially large in pure psychiatric harm claims, where awards are still low in relative terms.[69]

If the financial risk, inconvenience and unpleasantness of becoming embroiled in the unfamiliar workings of the law are not off-putting enough, the experience is liable to be particularly daunting for those already suffering from mental trauma.[70] If an early settlement is not achieved, they may, over several months, have to undergo multiple, searching interviews by lawyers and psychiatrists or psychologists, reliving the original traumatic occurrence, an experience which can itself play some part in impeding the process of trauma resolution.[71] They may also be fearful of the prospect, however remote in reality, that the ordeal will be repeated in the alien environment of a public, adversarial court hearing. More generally, they may have concerns about keeping their job or jeopardising their job prospects. In addition, some 'secondary' victims who had a very close relationship with an immediate accident victim might consider it distasteful or unseemly to sue.

One way or another, then, it is reasonable to assume that a sizeable number of potential claimants either exclude from the outset the option of suing, or, often on the advice of others, decide not to follow it through. In the first instance, family, close friends and doctors would be the most natural sources of such advice. A less intuitively obvious source is the high street lawyer, given the common belief that solicitors offering the enticing prospect of claiming on a 'no win no fee' basis are major contributors to an upward trend in litigation. Let us assume that nowadays people are more disposed to sue than in the past. Surely, the argument runs, persistent portrayal of suing as a largely painless, routine administrative process, in which there is much to gain and little or nothing to lose, is destined to translate into higher rates of litigation.[72] Yet examination of the structural context within which personal injury claims are now pursued, as well as some recent empirical data, cast doubt on this hypothesis.

---

[69] See Judicial Studies Board, *Guidelines for the Assessment of General Damages in Personal Injury Cases* (Oxford, Oxford University Press, 8th edn, 2006), below Ch 6, 178–9, 184. As regards personal injury more generally, there is 'some recent evidence that fear of costs is not a major barrier to claiming': P Cane, *Atiyah's Accidents, Compensation and the Law* (Cambridge, Cambridge University Press, 7th edn, 2006) 214. See Millward Brown, *Effects of Advertising in respect of Compensation Claims for Personal Injuries* (London, Department for Constitutional Affairs, 2006) para 2.4.9.

[70] See, eg, P Handford, *Mullany and Handford's Tort Liability for Psychiatric Damage*, (Sydney, Lawbook Co, 2nd edn (2006) 735–8.

[71] G Fulcher, 'Litigation-induced Trauma Sensitisation (LITS)—A Potential Negative Outcome of the Process of Litigation' (2004) *Psychiatry, Psychology and Law*, vol 11, 79.

[72] Cf 'The language of many ads reinforces the views of many that claiming might not actually involve entering a legal process.' Millward Brown, above n 69, 4.

The Claims-handling Process

The availability of legal aid[73] declined markedly towards the end of the twentieth century,[74] culminating in its abolition for most personal injury claims in 2000.[75] By the early 1990s, there was a shift from state-funded to market provision, initially by non-legally-qualified claims assessors, entitled to negotiate settlements but not to litigate. They would normally act on a contingency basis, taking a percentage of the *amount recovered* but nothing at all if unsuccessful.[76] Before long, claims assessors were largely superseded by claims management companies (CMCs) which, operating mainly as brokers for firms of solicitors, expanded rapidly in response to the new marketing opportunities that arose in 2000. Initially, CMCs were not regulated, and a minority adopted 'hard-sell' tactics, such as accosting passers-by in the street or cold calling in person, raising expectations of substantial compensation at little or no cost. Using mass advertising and direct marketing, some CMCs would take on numerous cases, with scant regard to their strength. To remain viable, they would hope to sell clients after-the-event (ATE) insurance policies,[77] as well as obtaining non-refundable signing-on fees and charging for referrals to solicitors' firms. Though many CMCs have survived, others fell by the wayside and, in 2003, the two main ones, Claims Direct and The Accident Group, went into liquidation. CMCs were recently made subject to regulation,[78] and the Department for Constitutional Affairs[79] initiated a review of the personal injury claims process.[80]

The withdrawal of legal aid provision heralded a major increase in the use by solicitors of Conditional Fee Agreements (CFAs), commonly referred to as 'no win no-fee' arrangements.[81] In broad outline, the arrangements are now as follows. Losing claimants do not pay their own solicitor's costs but will normally be liable for those of the other side, and for their own expenses.[82] To protect against this eventuality, they commonly buy ATE insurance. If they win, or the case is settled,

---

[73] Now 'Community Legal Service funding'.

[74] Whereas some 80% of the population were eligible for at least some legal aid in 1979, by 1999 the proportion had dropped to around 40%: P Cane, *Atiyah's Accidents, Compensation and the Law* (London, Butterworths, 6th edn, 1999) 218.

[75] Access to Justice Act 1999. It remains available for clinical negligence claims.

[76] Their inability to threaten court proceedings would seem to encourage low offers, but any incentive for them to accept undervalue offers must be weighed against their own hopes of obtaining a larger sum. At the same time, some clients might prefer speedy resolution to the chance of higher compensation. See Department for Constitutional Affairs, *The Report of the Lord Chancellor's Committee to Investigate the Activities of Non-Legally Qualified Claims Assessors and Employment Advisers* (London, Department for Constitutional Affairs, 2000) para 80.

[77] To cover the defendant's costs if the case was unsuccessfully litigated.

[78] Under Pt II of the Compensation Act 2006.

[79] Now the Ministry of Justice.

[80] See M Geffin, 'Practice trends: personal injury', *Solicitors Journal*, 13 Apr, 2007, 448.

[81] Provision for solicitors to offer CFAs was officially proclaimed in an enabling Act, in 1990: Courts and Legal Services Act 1990, s 58. They were formally introduced in 1995: Conditional Fee Agreements Order 1995 SI 1995/1674. See further, M Lunney and K Oliphant, *Tort Law: Text and Materials*, (Oxford, Oxford University Press, 3rd edn, 2007), 949–51.

[82] Eg, medical report fees and court fees.

the defendant usually has to pay their legal costs and expenses, and is also liable for any 'success' fee charged by their solicitor.[83] Nowadays, approximately 90 per cent of solicitors' (non-medical) personal injury work is based on CFAs,[84] much of it via referrals from claims management companies and Trade Unions, or through their own advertising on television, in the press and, increasingly, on the internet.[85]

The catchphrase, 'no win no fee', has predictably been seized upon by some journalists to condemn CFAs as an open invitation to sue, a metaphor for the 'compensation culture', and a sure sign of a claims explosion:

> It seems that legal action is expected of anyone involved in a minor accident. It has somehow become a matter of course ... You can now sue for damages after almost any accident, with zero risk of a liability and the prospect of a financial windfall. Another guilty party is the 'no-win no-fee' industry, which has become expert at dangling carrots in front of the greedy public.[86]

Yet, even if 'no win no fee' is an inducement for a sizeable proportion of potential claimants, a moment's reflection suggests that whether the introduction of CFAs has led to an upsurge in litigation is a function of how law firms and insurers view them as a commercial proposition.

The *overall* strategy of law firms, itself often heavily influenced by the attitude of insurance companies, is important in determining the number and type of personal injury cases that they take on and litigate.[87] Several factors may come into play, such as their size and degree of specialisation, as well as the perceived strength of the particular case, an important factor especially for small firms with a limited throughput. Clearly, the system provides an incentive for firms generally to prioritise cases with a high prospect of success:

> lawyers faced with funding disbursements themselves, delays in payment and the possibility of no payment at all will be inclined to be over-cautious.[88]

The more complex and elaborate the case (or category of case), the higher is the premium to cover the costs payable to the defendant's lawyer should the claimant lose. When these costs were covered by legal aid, an otherwise eligible applicant normally had to show only a reasonable prospect of success; with CFAs, the claimant needs a lawyer willing to act and an ATE insurer who will cover the risk of losing.[89] So quite strong claims may either not be brought or may be settled at

---

[83] An uplift to a maximum of 100% of normal costs, depending on various risk factors associated with the case.

[84] See P Fenn *et al*, *The Funding of Personal Injury Litigation: comparisons over time and across jurisdictions* (Department for Constitutional Affairs Research Series, Feb 2006) para 5.1.1.

[85] In 1984, they were granted the right to advertise by amendment of the Law Society's Practice Rules.

[86] G Adams, 'The Greed behind our Compensation Culture', *The Independent*, 14 Mar, 2005, 33.

[87] 'The insurers monitor the firms, not the individual cases': R Moorhead, 'Conditional Fee Agreements, Legal Aid and Access to Justice' (2000) 33(2) *University of British Columbia Law Review* 471, 485.

[88] N Block and B Doherty, 'Personal Injury: a cultural myth' (youclaim.co.uk).

[89] See A Morris, above n 66, 362. If the claimant loses, the ATE insurer pays the defendant's costs, and the ATE insurance premium may be reimbursed or waived. And see Cane, above n 69, 264.

undervalue to secure an order for costs. Such evidence as is available confirms the rational assumption that solicitors will take a risk-averse approach to CFAs in any complex and potentially expensive area of work,[90] a category which would include psychiatric harm. ATE insurers who underwrite cases on an individual basis have shown some reluctance to insure claims with prospects of success of between 50 and 60 per cent,[91] and a few years ago, some insurers were said to have expected success rates as high as 95 per cent from their panel solicitors.[92] A number of law firms belong to tied panels and are at risk of being dropped from them if they are not seen to be sufficiently selective.

In short, 'no win, no fee' conjures up a false image. If, in practice, it is not the claimant's desire to sue but the profit calculations of law firms that largely dictate their approach to CFAs, one would hardly expect them to encourage irresponsible claiming. By the same token, CMCs, conscious of spectacular failures in the past, and now subject to regulation, may prove more risk-averse in the future. The easy assumption that a market dominated by CFAs is bound to produce a substantial, or even a significant, rise in the number of claims may have no foundation in fact. Admittedly, the operative word here is 'may'. As regards both personal injury claims generally and psychiatric harm in particular, the most troubling aspect of the 'floodgates' debate is the sweeping nature of assertions that have been made in the absence of hard data. However, there are now more reliable data on the frequency of claims generally, as well as certain pointers to the likely incidence of claims for psychiatric harm.

The Frequency of Claims

Personal Injury Claims in General

Unsurprisingly, journalists are rarely inclined, or encouraged, to ask why there are not *more* personal injury claims, though it seems as appropriate a question to ask as why there are 'so many', which is the subject of countless articles. If most injured people in the UK never resort to law, as was indicated in the survey conducted by the Pearson Commission,[93] and by other, subsequent studies,[94] one

---

[90] Eg, S Yarrow, *The Price of Success: Lawyers, Clients and Conditional Fees* (London: Policy Studies Institute, 1997) 5. Cf RCA White and R Atkinson, 'Personal Injury Litigation, Conditional Fees and After-the-Event Insurance' (2000) *Civil Justice Quarterly* 118, cited in Morris, above n 66, 362.
[91] E Gilbert, 'The ATE Legal Expenses Insurance Marketplace: An Overview' (2004) *Journal of Personal Injury Law* 99, 101.
[92] Moorhead, above n 87, 485.
[93] 'Only 11% of the injured took any steps towards making a claim for tort compensation, even to the extent of discussing the possibility with someone else': Royal Commission on Civil Liability and Compensation for Personal Injury ('Pearson Report') (London, HMSO, 1978) Cmnd 7054 vol 2, 119, para 389.
[94] See D Harris *et al, Compensation and Support for Illness and Injury* (Oxford, Clarendon Press, 1984) 65; H Genn, *Paths to Justice* (Oxford, Hart Publishing, 1999) 52, and P Pleasance *et al, Causes of Action: Civil Law and Social Justice* (London, Legal Services Commission, 2004) 50.

might wonder whether it is the absence of a compensation culture that requires an explanation.[95]

For various reasons, it has not been possible to establish with precision either the incidence of personal injury claims or the reasons for fluctuations over time. Until recently, the data were far from revealing. The official publication, *Judicial Statistics*, records only claims in which proceedings were issued, and it only separates out as *personal* injury claims the small minority brought in the High Court. The much greater number heard in county courts are not identified as such.[96] Popular accounts of the number of 'claims' made commonly fail to distinguish between different stages of the claiming process,[97] and hardly ever point out that only around 1 per cent are heard to judgment.[98] Comparisons of claiming patterns over time are especially problematic, as the figures can easily become skewed by particular, time-specific, phenomena, such as large scale disasters or epidemics, or significant changes in substantive or procedural law.[99] By selective use of a given timeframe, sectional interests can make use of such occurrences in order to influence public opinion.

However, data compiled over the last decade or so can now shed more light on the floodgates issue than was previously possible. In an illuminating article,[100] Lewis, Morris and Oliphant have scrutinised key sources founded on a very wide statistical base—the Compensation Recovery Unit (CRU) statistics, actuarial analyses commissioned by the Association of British Insurers (ABI), and NHS statistics on clinical negligence compensation—to test the validity of the assumption that the UK is in the grip of a damaging compensation culture.

As regards personal injury claims generally, since 1997–8, CRU, which administers state recovery of social security benefits from tort damages, has been the most comprehensive and reliable new source. Compensators are legally required to report details of claims received within 14 days,[101] and the insurers and other bodies who, in practice, are the real defendants operate standardised reporting procedures. As a result, an acceptably accurate picture of the number of claims each year is now attainable, whether proceedings are issued or not and whether the claim is won, lost

---

[95] K Williams, 'State of Fear: Britain's "Compensation Culture" Reviewed' (2005) 25 *Legal Studies* 499, 504–5.
[96] Except for the few previously heard in the small claims court: see *Williams, ibid*, 503, n 25.
[97] Eg, not distinguishing between claims lodged and those heard to judgment, as distinct from being withdrawn, struck out or settled out of court at some point along the way.
[98] R Lewis, 'Insurance and the Tort System' (2005) 25 *Legal Studies* 85, 88.
[99] Eg, in the year ending March 2003, the number of *accident* claims made to insurers had increased by only 0.2%. The very large overall increase in the figures for 2003–2005 reflects an exceptional number of vibration white finger and respiratory cases, 'entirely due to a surge in disease claims prior to closure of the Coal Health compensation schemes. In the same years, the number of accident claims actually fell': R Lewis, A Morris and K Oliphant, 'Tort Personal Injury Claims Statistics: Is there a compensation culture in the United Kingdom?' (2006) 14 *Torts Law Journal* 158, 174.
[100] *Ibid*.
[101] See Social Security (Recovery of Benefits) Act 1997, s 23 (1) and Social Security (Recovery of Benefits) Regulations 1997 SI No 2205, reg 6.

or settled.[102] If read in conjunction with other findings,[103] CRU's figures also provide a useful, broad brush picture of claims frequency over time. On the basis of such data, Lewis *et al* concluded that, overall, there is good reason to suppose that there has been a substantial increase in the number of personal injury claims since the 1970s and 1980s, approximately a threefold rise. Whereas the Pearson Commission had estimated that some 250,000 claims were pursued through the tort system in 1973, by 1997–1998, they exceeded 700,000 and for the period 2000–2005 seemed to have stabilised at around 700,000–750,000.[104] The equivalent CRU figures for 2006–8 were approximately 675,000, 711,000 and 733,000, respectively.

Various explanations have been proffered for the substantial increase since the early 1970s. Cane, for example, points to lawyers having been granted the right to advertise, the emergence and growth of firms specialising in personal injury, and the impact of the CMCs and the new CFA structure, as well as, more broadly, the burgeoning of a 'rights culture'.[105] All of these developments would have increased awareness of the right to sue and raised expectations of success; though, for reasons already outlined, we would be cautious about attributing too much influence to what intuitively might sound the most obvious explanation—the advent of 'no win, no fee' claims.[106]

Indeed, for present purposes, what is most significant about these figures is the relative stability of the claiming rates since 1997–8, and especially in the wake of the Access to Justice Act 1999, that signalled the end of legal aid for most personal injury claims. Of some 2,300 reports in the national press between 1993 and 2006 featuring the term 'compensation culture', virtually all appeared after 1998.[107] In other words, during the very period when claims advertising and no win no fee arrangements were becoming most prominent, when media 'revelations' of a 'compensation culture' were reaching new heights of intensity, claiming had levelled off:

> contrary to popular belief, the introduction of conditional fee agreements and the advent of widespread advertising by the claims industry have not increased the frequency of claims to any significant extent.[108]

In the period 2000–2005 there was, 'if anything, a downward trend,'[109] as further indicated by the CRU figures for 2006 and 2007. Overall, the figures point to a decade of relative stability, at odds with the assumption that the use by law firms

---

[102] Though CRU records the annual number of settlements, these figures are of limited use due to the degree of double-counting of interim and final compensation payments: Lewis *et al*, above n 99, 159, at n 8.
[103] Eg, those of the 'Pearson Report', above n 93; the ABI, and NHS clinical negligence statistics.
[104] Lewis *et al*, above n 99, 169.
[105] See Cane, above n 69, 193–4, and Lewis *et al*, above n 99, 170–1.
[106] See above, 153–5.
[107] See A Morris, above n 66, 353.
[108] Lewis, *et al*, above n 99, 171.
[109] Above n 99, 169.

of CFAs has resulted in excessive or irresponsible claiming. Lewis *et al* found no hard evidence of any significant increase in frivolous claims.[110]

The proclaimed existence, or imminence, of a litigation explosion is a recurrent theme with a long history.[111] Readily deployed, it is the kind of assertion that effortlessly achieves conventional wisdom status.[112] A major part of the problem is the disproportionate, often enduring, impact of vivid anecdotes, some fabricated, others misreported or exaggerated, as epitomised by the salience in England and elsewhere of the McDonald's Coffee case.[113] The spectre of countless frivolous claims arises from the assumption that the actual number is largely a function of the desire to sue. Yet the structural context of litigation, and the financial pressures that underpin it, suggest that knee-jerk assumptions about overhasty and inappropriate resort to law are misplaced. Only a minute proportion of personal injury victims actually choose to litigate, by comparison with those who seek a settlement, abandon their claim, or never pursue one at all. As we have seen, many decline to sue for diverse reasons, and even when legal advice is sought, it is the pragmatic stance of the law firms which largely determines whether or not litigation ensues.

The Incidence of Claims for Psychiatric Harm

It is instructive to note the sometimes counter-intuitive patterns in the level of tort claims within different categories of personal injury. In the period 2000–2005, the total number of *accident* claims notified to CRU declined by 5 per cent.[114] Claims

---

[110] '[A] mere rise in claims numbers is insufficient to establish the existence of a damaging compensation culture, as this insinuates that a significant proportion of claims are fraudulent, exaggerated or otherwise lacking in merit. We are not aware of any data that would support such a contention. The rise in the number of claims from the 1970s is equally consistent with there having been significant *under*-claiming at that time, with a subsequent increase in the proportion of those with genuine claims who chose to initiate legal action.' Lewis, *et al*, above n 99, 174–5.

[111] There is considerable agreement among legal historians that the real litigation explosion in England occurred between 1550 and 1750, during the transition from an agricultural to a commercial society: 'Round about the turn of the 16th into the 17th century, court usage per 100,000 of population was probably higher than it ever had been before or has been since.' C Brooks, 'The Longitudinal Study of Civil Litigation in England 1200–1996', in W Prest and S Anleu, *Litigation: Past and Present*, above n 67, ch 2, 28. See also C Brooks, *Lawyers, Litigation and English Society since 1450* (London, Hambledon Press, 1998) 70–1.

[112] For a classic example of widely-held, exaggerated assumptions about levels of claiming, see the Harvard Study findings on the gulf between perception and reality as to the incidence of medical malpractice claims in New York State: Harvard Medical Practice Study Group, *Patients, Doctors and Lawyers: Medical Injury, Malpractice Litigation and Patient Compensation in New York* (Cambridge, Mass, Harvard University, 1990).

[113] See above Ch 1, 19. See also, M Galanter, 'Real World Torts: An Antidote to Anecdotes' (1996) 55 *Maryland Law Review* 1093, 1161; W Haltom and M McCann, *Distorting the Law: Politics, Media and the Litigation Crisis* (Chicago, University of Chicago Press, 2004), and M Saks, 'Do We Really Know Anything About the Behaviour of the Tort Litigation System—And Why Not?' (1992) 140 *University of Pennsylvania Law Review* 1147, 1161.

[114] Lewis *et al*, above n 99, 160; as noted, the *overall* increase during this period (of 3%) was due to a substantial rise in the number of disease claims, 'hugely inflated in the period 1999–2004 by the Coal Health compensation schemes for vibration white finger and respiratory disease': 169.

for clinical negligence declined by 34 per cent, and for employers' liability by 21 per cent.[115] If asked to estimate any of these figures, most people would probably have guessed that there had been an increase, perhaps a substantial one. It is likely that they would have made the same assumption about claims for pure psychiatric harm. Yet these are claims for which there are no disaggregated figures in *Judicial Statistics*, and there is no source of statistically significant data covering the diverse range of circumstances in which they can arise. In the absence of empirical data on their incidence, are there any useful pointers to the likely effect on it of abandoning the existing special controls?

It should not be overlooked that even to approach the matter in this way puts critics of the current framework in a somewhat invidious position. The rules to which they object are largely arbitrary deviations from the general principles of negligence law, deviations now defended overwhelmingly by reference to an unsubstantiated fear of opening the floodgates. One might have thought that the burden of justification is rather on those who would uphold that departure from principle. On this view, granted that supporters of the status quo cannot provide conclusive proof that liberalisation would create a serious floodgates risk, they could at least be expected to supply arguments cogent enough to warrant special restrictions as a precautionary measure. In this balancing exercise, due weight would have to be given to the undesirable consequences of the restrictions and to the force of the counter-arguments. Mere repetition of dire warnings does not increase their credibility.

In fact, outside the sphere of pure economic loss, judicial scepticism about the floodgates argument is not uncommon. Thomas J's dissenting judgment in *van Soest* was particularly trenchant and dismissive. Stressing the 'dearth of empirical evidence', he said that:

> [m]any judges have tired of the point. Time and time again it has proved unfounded ... With centuries of development to its credit the law has not yielded one ascertained example of the Courts being inundated with the predicted flood of litigation.[116]

More specifically, he added:

> I do not doubt that the floodgates argument is also misplaced in the present [psychiatric harm] context ... It is apparent that, as several Judges have intimated, such empirical evidence as there is seems to confirm the intuitive perception that the disincentives to litigating in such cases are more effective regulators than particular liability rules.[117]

In the English case law, we might recall the general scepticism of the Law Lords in *McLoughlin v O'Brian*, most notably that of Lord Bridge: 'I believe that the "floodgates" argument ... is, as it always has been, greatly exaggerated.'[118]

---

[115] Above n 99, 160.
[116] *van Soest*, above n 12, *per* Thomas J (diss) 203.
[117] Above n 12, 203.
[118] *McLoughlin v O'Brian*, above n 2, 442. See above Ch 3, 60–61. In *White*, Lord Griffiths expressly dismissed the floodgates concern in respect of rescuers: above n 1, 464. Cf 'the familiar floodgates argument ... [is] not an argument to be automatically discounted. But nor is it, I think, an argument which

Obviously, such statements cannot currently be verified by empirical means, any more than those made by the prophets of doom. Lord Hoffmann, when considering whether removing the controls would entail a burden of claims too great for the insurance market or the public funds, said that:

> [t]hese are questions on which it is difficult to offer any concrete evidence and I am simply not in a position to form a view one way or the other.[119]

Yet if hard data are lacking, there are nonetheless grounds for doubting that there would be a significant floodgates effect.

A useful pointer would be the impact of leading cases that either did significantly extend the scope of liability or could plausibly be interpreted to have done so. The House of Lords decision in *McLoughlin v O'Brian* was such a case. As well as establishing the aftermath doctrine, as formulated by Lord Wilberforce, it was open to the interpretation that reasonable foreseeability sufficed for the duty of care and would later, for a brief period, be interpreted to this effect.[120] Lord Wilberforce himself envisaged that the extension of liability to include the immediate aftermath:

> may lead to a proliferation of claims, and possibly fraudulent claims, to the establishment of an industry of lawyers and psychiatrists who will formulate a claim for nervous shock damages . . . for all, or many, road accidents and industrial accidents.[121]

Yet an informal survey, conducted four years after *McLoughlin* was decided, indicated that none of the 10 major insurance companies questioned considered that there had been a dramatic increase in psychiatric injury claims,[122] a perception consistent with the generally sanguine approach in the case itself. There was a comparable finding, covering a longer time span, in the 'claimant-friendly' State of California, after its Supreme Court's path-breaking decision in *Dillon v Legg*, the first in the United States to abolish the restrictive 'zone of danger' rule.[123] As a result of inquiries made some 15 years later, Bell concluded that:

> the effect of expanded bystander recovery for psychic injury on California liability insurance rates is negligible. One major California liability insurance underwriter reported that it did not alter its actuarial tables to reflect psychic injury liability. The company has not even bothered to separate out data concerning liability claims for psychic injury because there have been only one or two such claims annually since *Dillon* was decided in 1968.[124]

can claim a very impressive record of success': *Attia v British Gas plc* [1988] QB 304, 320, *per* Bingham LJ. See also '[an argument] demolished by the majority in *McLoughlin*': *Hevican v Ruane* [1991] 3 All ER 65, 71, *per* Mantell J. Judicial readiness to 'flick on the floodgates switch' was criticised by Ipp J, in 'Policy and the swing of the negligence pendulum' (2003) 77 *Australian Law Journal* 732, 738.

[119] *White*, above n 1, 510.
[120] Ie in *Hevican*, above n 118, and, at first instance, *Ravenscroft v Rederiaktiebolaget Transatlantic* [1991] 3 All ER 73. See above Ch 3, 64, 67.
[121] *McLoughlin v O'Brian*, above n 2, 421.
[122] DS Greer, 'A Statutory Remedy for Nervous Shock?' (1986) 21 *Irish Jurist (NS)* 57, 77.
[123] Above Ch 3, 61.
[124] P Bell, 'The Bell Tolls: Towards Full Tort Recovery for Psychic Injury' (1984) 36 *University of Florida Law Review* 333, 366–7. Cf, 'more than a decade of experience with its broadened bystander recovery rule had shown that there would not be a "plethora of similar cases" nor would there be

Writing in 1994, Fleming observed that:

> the experience in the statutory Australian jurisdictions has not borne out fears of becoming swamped by unmeritorious claims in the wake of relaxing the requirements of actionability;[125] nor has the experience with such claims in the most liberal American jurisdictions figured in the complaints and conservative reform efforts of the defence interests. Perhaps the fears are after all largely imaginary, certainly exaggerated.[126]

The force of this conclusion is not substantially undermined by the recent introduction of restrictive statutory measures in Australia, which needs to be understood in the context of an 'insurance crisis' attributed, without hard supportive data, to rising litigation rates. In South Africa, too, there are indications that removing special controls has not produced a significant rise in the number of claims. In *Barnard v Santam*, the Constitutional Court commented on '[t]he very small number of claims' that had resulted from abandoning, some 30 years earlier, the requirement that claimants must fear for their personal safety.[127]

The Impact of Employees' Claims for Stress-Induced Psychiatric Illness

Any broadening of the bases for claiming naturally heightens floodgates fears and strengthens resistance to the removal or modification of prevailing controls. The recent extension of liability for psychiatric harm to diverse, non-accident-based situations[128] undoubtedly signals some potential for increased claiming, but its scope is inherently limited. This is because such situations mainly involve a prior relationship, often contractual in nature, and the relational element reduces the risk that a single event might generate a mass of claims.[129] Nonetheless, particularly as regards stress at work, fears persist of a substantial upsurge in individual actions. Among the public at large, the concern is not solely based on general

---

unlimited liability problems': *Campbell v Animal Quarantine Station* 632 P 2d 1066, 1071 (Haw 1981) (Supreme Ct of Hawaii, 1981), cited by Bell, 378, at n 180. Though Bell observed that this lack of claims might have reflected judicial reluctance to interpret *Dillon* as a move to unqualified reasonable foreseeability (439, n 8), it took the California Supreme Court some 10 years before it began to recharacterise *Dillon* 'proximity factors' as preconditions to liability, rather than aids to determining foreseeability: *Justus v Atchison* 565 P 2d 122 (Cal 1977). Cf *Thing v La Chusa* 771 P 2d 814 (Cal 1989). And see VE Nolan and E Ursin, 'Negligent Infliction of Emotional Distress: Coherence Emerging from Chaos' (1982) 33 *Hastings Law Journal* 583, 593.

[125] By making statutory remedies available to certain plaintiffs who did not see an accident or physical injuries: J Fleming (1994) 2 *Tort Law Review* 202, 204 (Review of Mullany and Handford, *Tort Liability for Psychiatric Damage*, 1st edn, 1993); see further, 2nd edn, above n 70 [16.30]–[16.180].

[126] *Ibid.* Interestingly, this is a rather more sanguine view than he had expressed some 25 years earlier: see JG Fleming, 'Distant Shock in Germany and (Elsewhere)' (1972) *American Journal of Comparative Law* 485, 491.

[127] *Barnard v Santam Bpk* 1999 (1) SA 202, referring to *Bester v Commercial Union Versekeringsmaatskappy van SA Bpk* 1973 (1) SA 769.

[128] See above Ch 4, and see P Handford, 'Psychiatric Injury in Breach of a Relationship' (2007) 27 *Legal Studies* 26.

[129] Cf Handford, *ibid*, 49, citing Dobbs' comment that, in such cases, '[t]here is no risk of unlimited liability to an unlimited number of people.' D Dobbs, *The Law of Torts* (St Paul: West Group, 2000) 849.

perceptions of a compensation culture. It also reflects the erroneous belief that work-related stress per se can ground a claim; whereas the law requires proof of psychiatric illness induced by stress and foreseeably caused by the employer's negligence.[130] The misconception is understandable, since media headlines frequently refer to awards for 'stress' or 'stress at work', as do some accounts of the claims themselves. That said, concern about proliferation also permeates the leading case law, partly because the special controls do not apply in the standard case of employees who are primary victims. The key decision of *Hatton v Sutherland*[131] endorsed the line of authority whereby claims for stress-induced psychiatric illness can be pursued in tort or contract, since they are governed by ordinary employers' liability principles, as '[c]ontractual claims by primary victims.'[132]

The absence of special controls helps to explain the somewhat narrow judicial interpretation of negligence in the employment sphere.[133] Crucially, despite elaborate requirements for risk assessment and preventive measures regarding the health and safety of the workforce,[134] and some largely commonsense expectations of employers,[135] a predominantly reactive role is all that is asked of them in respect of *individual* employees whose illness was induced by stress:

> [a]n employer is usually entitled to assume that his employee is up to the normal pressures of the job unless he knows of some particular problem or vulnerability.[136]

More especially where there is a large workforce, employers would not normally be expected to foresee the risk of psychiatric injury to particular employees without some kind of prior warning. At the same time, it is obviously inhibiting for a claimant to identify a specific mental health risk in terms that typically indicate an impending breakdown.[137] To admit or even hint at inability to cope is seldom a step to be taken lightly, as the Court in *Hatton* itself acknowledged: 'His very job,

---

[130] 'It is *foreseeable injury* flowing from the employer's breach of duty that gives rise to the liability. It does not follow that because a claimant suffers *stress* at work and that the employer is in some way in breach of duty in allowing that to occur that the claimant is able to establish a claim in negligence.' *Hartman v South Essex Mental Health and Community Care NHS Trust* [2005] ICR 782, 788 (CA), para 2, *per* Scott Baker LJ.

[131] *Hatton v Sutherland* [2002] EWCA Civ 76; affirmed by the House of Lords in *Barber v Somerset County Council* [2004] UKHL 13.

[132] *Hatton, ibid,* [21]. And '[t]here are, therefore, no special control mechanisms applying to claims for psychiatric ... injury or illness arising from the stress of doing the work which the employee is required to do.' [22].

[133] See, eg, P Case, 'Hues of Foreseeability: Employer liability for chronic stress and the impact of *Barber*' (2004) 20 *Professional Negligence* 192.

[134] Eg, Health and Safety at Work Act 1974; Management of Health and Safety at Work Regulations under the European Framework Dir 89/391/EEC. But see now Management of Health and Safety at Work (Amendment) Regulations 2003, esp reg 6. See further, K Wheat, 'Mental Health in the Workplace (1)—"Stress" Claims and Workplace Standards and the European Framework Directive on Health and Safety at Work' (2006) *Journal of Mental Health Law* 53.

[135] As outlined in *Barber,* above n 131, notably by Lord Walker [68].

[136] *Hatton,* above n 131 [43 (3)].

[137] Cf 'Unless ... there was a real risk of breakdown which the claimant's employers ... ought properly to have averted, there can be no liability': *Garrett v Camden London Borough Council* [2001] EWCA Civ 395 [63], *per* Simon Brown LJ.

let alone his credibility or hopes of promotion, may be at risk.'[138] Furthermore, the intimation, perhaps overstated, that an employer who offers a confidential advice and counselling service is unlikely to be found in breach of duty[139] may not prove reassuring. Though such provision can be of value, its therapeutic potential is liable to be outweighed by its perceived utility as a risk management device.

In practice, various difficulties surrounding causation act as another important constraint on the number of stress-induced claims. In *Barber*, Lord Rodger suggested that to prove causation, Mr Barber would have had to adduce 'expert psychiatric evidence' of the particular steps that his employer could have taken to have effectively safeguarded his health.[140] Stress-related illnesses commonly have several different causes, and many claimants will have been susceptible to mental illness. Even when they can show that the employer's breach of duty materially contributed to their condition, if there are multiple causes and the harm is divisible, the employer is only liable for 'that proportion of the harm suffered which is attributable to his wrongdoing'.[141] In a system where a high percentage of such claims is funded via CFAs, their low potential value relative to cost constitutes a significant disincentive to their being undertaken or pursued.[142] For example, a psychiatric report alone might well cost more than £500, and under the current Judicial Studies Board Guidelines,[143] the level of awards for minor psychiatric damage ranges from £850 to £3,450.[144]

It is also of interest to note the approach to work stress claims recently adopted by the High Court of Australia, in *Koehler v Cerebos (Australia) Ltd*,[145] not least because it drew on observations by Lord Rodger, in *Barber*, about potential conflict between tort and contract principles in such cases.[146] His concern was that a duty of care imposed on the employer in tort might be inconsistent with the terms of the employee's contract, thereby undermining freedom of contract in the sphere of employment.[147] In *Koehler*, by shifting the law's emphasis away from

---

[138] *Hatton*, above n 131 [15].

[139] Above n 138 [43 (11)], and applied in *Hartman*, above n 130, but not in the conjoined case of *Melville v Home Office*. And cf *Daw v Intel Corp (UK) Ltd* [2007] EWCA Civ 70.

[140] *Barber*, above n 131[27]. By the same token, it has been argued that, for primary claimants already in a contractual relationship with the defendant, proving foreseeability may be more onerous than for secondary claimants alleging shock-induced psychiatric harm from an incident where the parties are strangers. Ie where defendants may have reason to know how a particular claimant might react to their conduct, expert evidence of foreseeability has been seen as all the more desirable: see *McLoughlin v Jones* [2002] 2 WLR 1279 [38]–[44], *per* Brooke LJ. However, it would seem unlikely that Lord Bridge's 'judge-as-"educated-layman"' yardstick of reasonable foreseeability (above Ch 4, 112) was intended to discourage the use of expert evidence in standard psychiatric harm cases.

[141] *Hatton*, above n 131, para 43 (14)–(16).

[142] In *Hartman*, above n 130 [3], Scott Baker LJ observed that 'some of these cases are being fought over many days at great expense and . . . the time and cost are disproportionate to the real issues in the case and the true value of the claim.'

[143] See below Ch 6, 178–9.

[144] However, costs will sometimes be reduced by use of an agreed joint report by the treating consultant and, in practice, small claims are often settled on the basis of a report by a GP or psychologist.

[145] *Koehler v Cerebos (Australia) Ltd* (2005) 79 ALJR 845.

[146] *Barber*, above n 131. This issue was not pursued in the appeal itself.

[147] Above n 131, [2004] ICR 457, 465–9.

foreseeability in negligence and putting the terms of the contract centre stage, the Australian High Court has substantially reduced the scope for claims based on excessive workloads.[148] As yet, there has been little indication of English law adopting this approach,[149] and contractual terms can, of course, be broadly as well as narrowly construed.[150] They are also subject to such protection of employees as is afforded by health and safety legislation and the European Framework Directive.[151] Nonetheless, the leeway for restrictive construction highlights an unresolved tension in the employment sphere, between aspirations for healthy work environments, as reflected in contemporary legislative measures, and the old adage 'if you can't stand the heat stay out of the kitchen'. The latter sentiment has been voiced in several appellate judgments,[152] and is reinforced by English law's counter-intuitive stance that no occupations are intrinsically hazardous to mental health.[153]

The expectation that work stress claims would be closely scrutinised, implicit in the *Hatton* guidelines and endorsed by *Barber*, resurfaced in Scott-Baker's LJ's judgment in *Hartman*.[154] Mullany and Handford, while noting that '[e]mployer liability for the effects of work stress has been one of the fastest growth areas of psychiatric damage law over the past decade', also concludes that *Hatton*:

> had the desired effect in satisfactorily regulating work stress claims in the English courts. The employer's liability for causing psychiatric harm has been accepted but contained within appropriate limits.[155]

Such data as are available[156] would seem to bear out this conclusion. For example, though the Health and Safety Executive's findings indicate that illnesses related to stress, anxiety and depression constitute the second most common occupational health problem in the UK, after musculoskeletal disorder,[157] the ABI's figures show that:

---

[148] See P Handford, 'Work Stress: Retreat or Revolution?' (2005) 13 *Tort Law Review* 159.

[149] For an earlier, dissenting judgment based on it, see *Johnstone v Bloomsbury Health Authority* [1992] 1 QB 333 (Leggatt LJ).

[150] Especially by reference to the implied obligation of mutual trust and confidence: see above Ch 1, 000, and W Njoya, 'Employment, Implicit Contracts and the Duty of Care' (2005) 121 *LQR* 33.

[151] See Wheat above n 134.

[152] Literally so in *Johnstone*, above n 149, 348 *per* Leggatt LJ (dissenting). Cf '[T]hey are all adults. They choose their profession': *Barber*, above n 131 [14] *per* Lord Scott.

[153] See *Hatton*, above n 131[14] and [43 (4)], despite the indication, at [16], that stress is so common in some occupations that the employer is on notice that employees are at risk. Contrast the position in Australia: *New South Wales v Seedsman* (2000) 217 ALR 583 (police in child abuse cases).

[154] See above n 130.

[155] P Handford, *Mullany and Handford's Tort Liability for Psychiatric Damage*, above n 70, 571 [22.580] and 547 [22.140], respectively.

[156] Data on the actual incidence of work-related stress and related disorders are imprecise, relying mainly on surveys derived from self-reported information. See, eg, HSE, 'Stress-related and psychological disorders' (http://www.hse.gov.uk/statistics/causdis/stress.htm).

[157] Health and Safety Commission, *Health and Safety Statistics for 2005/2006 for Great Britain* (www.hse.gov.uk/statistics/overpic.htm).

stress has never made up more than 2 per cent of the common law occupational disease compensation claims in any year, and never more than half a per cent of all workplace compensation claims (accidents plus diseases).[158]

Nor are the awards or the directly associated costs as high as is often assumed:

> Six figure common law compensation payouts make the headlines, but are exceedingly rare. Common law [claims] ... generate about 60,000 cases a year, where a lot of people get a little. Most settlements are below £5,000 ... The Association of British Insurers puts the average cost of each settlement—the payment to the victim and the associated legal and admin costs—at just £10,000.[159]

At the same time, it should be borne in mind that the overall cost is appreciably higher when full account is taken of such factors as disrupted work schedules, expenditure of staff time, the impact on staff morale and on the reputation of the firms or institutions involved.

Conclusion on the Floodgates Fear as regards Psychiatric Harm

Analysing an Office of Fair Trading Report about the UK liability insurance market, in 2003, Parsons reached the following conclusions:

> Taken altogether, it cannot be said that there has been any dramatic expansion of tort liability [for personal injury], in recent years. Furthermore, possible and pending law reform, such as the Law Commission's proposals in relation to the law on psychiatric illness are unlikely to bring about any dramatic changes in the overall reach of tort law, even if they were to be implemented in full.[160]

The Law Commission had in fact sought an appraisal of how much its recommendations might cost, from the ABI. The ABI's bare estimate was that they might increase the number of personal injury claims overall by 10 per cent and require an increase in motor insurance premiums of 2–5 per cent.[161] Parsons observed that a 10 per cent increase in the *total* number seemed 'remarkably high', given the 'relatively small percentage of claims' for psychiatric illness and the fact that the Commission's recommendations would have a marked effect only on secondary victims.[162] Admittedly, the perceived risk of proliferation in pure psychiatric harm cases is predominantly associated with secondary claims. It is therefore reasonable to assume that they would increase to some extent, all the more so if, contrary to the Law Commission's proposals, the 'close ties' requirement were abandoned. Such pointers as we have, though, do not suggest that removing all the special controls would result in an unmanageable rise: the extra-legal barriers and disincentives to

---

[158] S Pickvance, 'A Little Compensation', *Hazards* 90, May 2005.
[159] Ibid.
[160] C Parsons, *An Analysis of Current Problems in the UK Liability Insurance Market*, Office of Fair Trading: Supplemental Report (2003) 37.
[161] Law Com Report, above n 2, paras 1.12–1.13.
[162] See Parsons, above n 160, 37, at n 36.

claiming would remain powerful constraints. Among non-accident-based cases, the potential for a significant rise has been most evident in work-related actions by primary claimants, but the scope for this has been limited by judicial interpretation. If, as we would argue, the liability threshold for 'purely' mental suffering should be less restrictive than 'recognisable psychiatric injury', there would no doubt be added concern about the potential increase in claims. However, before we explore what would be needed for such a shift to be feasible,[163] some consideration should be given to an aspect of the 'compensation culture' debate that has been gaining in prominence: the emergence, real or supposed, of an unhealthily risk-averse society.

Broader Policy Considerations

Whatever the reality, media accounts of an alarming rise in personal injury actions generally, and of a greater readiness to make false or trivial claims, are widely believed to be true.[164] A proposal to broaden the liability threshold for mental suffering, and to remove the other special controls, would doubtless be portrayed as a recipe for further clogging up the courts, imposing a disproportionate burden of cost and threatening the viability of the insurance system. However, a concern different in kind from those addressed so far has been voiced by some opponents of a less restrictive regime. It is that heightened fears of being sued would be an unwelcome addition to what they consider an increasingly corrosive climate of excessive risk aversion. Resort to defensive practices in the provision of services would, it is said, increase; beneficial activities would come under threat, and there would be added constraints on legitimate self-expression. Avoidance of beneficial risk-taking has already become a prominent social and political issue. In the legal context, it has reignited debate over the proper scope of liability in negligence, even prompting an inapt, if not redundant, statutory 'reminder' to the courts[165] that they may have regard to whether requiring a defendant to take particular precautions against a risk might prevent a 'desirable activity' from taking place.[166]

Chilling Effects: The 'Perils' of a Risk-Averse Society

The charge that we live in an excessively risk-averse society has several strands. There are claims that over-regulation is stifling commercial enterprise to the detriment of economic performance; that defensive strategies have hindered the proper

---

[163] See below Ch 6, 177–85.

[164] See eg, Morris, above n 66, 366; Millward Brown, above n 69; Better Regulation Task Force, *Better Routes to Redress* (London, Better Regulation Task Force, 2004). s 3, and R Mullender, 'Negligence Law and Blame Culture: a critical response to a possible problem' (2006) 22 *Professional Negligence* 2, 18.

[165] Significantly prefaced by the heading, 'deterrent effect of potential liability'.

[166] See Compensation Act 2006, s 1, below n 175 and Explanatory Notes to Compensation Act 2006, para. 17. See also House of Commons Constitutional Affairs Committee, *Compensation Culture: Third Report of Session 2005-06*, paras 53–68. And see below 168.

delivery of services by public and voluntary bodies, diverting scarce resources in the process, and that 'nanny stateism' prevails to such a degree that:

> our national resilience, self-reliance and spirit of adventure [are] being destroyed by a pervasive cultural demand for the elimination of all risk.[167]

The 'blame and claim' culture is seen as symptomatic of a general malaise, in which we are too quick to disclaim personal responsibility for our actions and too ready to assume the mantle of victim. Characteristic of many such assertions is their hyperbolic tone. Unrealistic expectations of a 'risk-free' environment have, it is said, nurtured a social climate in which 'safety has become the fundamental value of our times',[168] and:

> [t]he call to minimise risk is a call for a cowardly society ... If we are to have a courageous society rather than a cowardly society, we need to abandon the rhetoric of risk minimisation.[169]

We must renounce two 'fatal attitudes'—the 'reduction in personal responsibility' and a 'collective aversion to risk'.[170]

These libertarian concerns mirror the common law's traditional attachment to individual autonomy, strongly reasserted not long ago by the House of Lords in *Tomlinson v Congleton BC*.[171] In *Tomlinson*, Lord Hoffmann said that, for legal purposes:

> the balance between risk on the one hand and individual autonomy on the other is not a matter of expert opinion. It is a judgment which the courts must make and which in England reflects the individualist values of the common law.[172]

The case concerned a Council park with a lake in which swimming was prohibited, as indicated by prominent notices warning of the hazards. Because the notices were often ignored and a number of accidents had occurred, the Council had decided to alter the landscape to further minimise the risk of injury. Before this work began, the 18 year old claimant, who was aware of the notices, ran into the lake as he had done many times before and dived in, but the water was shallow and he suffered severe spinal injuries. The House of Lords found that the injuries had resulted from his own misjudgement of an obvious hazard. That there was an element of risk in the exuberant behaviour of the young, said Lord Scott, was 'no reason for imposing a grey and dull safety regime on everyone,'[173] a sentiment expanded upon, in particularly forthright terms, by Lord Hobhouse:

> In truth, the arguments for the claimant have involved an attack on the liberties of the citizen which should not be countenanced. They attack the liberty of the individual to

---

[167] L Rogers, 'The End of Risk', *New Statesman*, 30 Jul, 2007, 34, 35, commenting on L Berry, *et al*, *Risk, Responsibility and Regulation: Whose Risk Is It Anyway?* (London, Better Regulation Commission, 2006).
[168] F Furedi, *Culture of Fear* (London, Continuum, 2002) 1.
[169] O Letwin, *Nothing Ventured Nothing Gained*, speech to Centre for Policy Studies, 3 Nov, 2004.
[170] J Sunderland (President, CBI). Speech to Annual Conference, 8 Nov, 2004.
[171] *Tomlinson v Congleton BC* [2004] 1 AC 46.
[172] *Ibid* [47].
[173] Above n 171 [94].

engage in dangerous, but otherwise harmless, pastimes at his own risk and the liberty of citizens as a whole fully to enjoy the variety and quality of the landscape of this country. The pursuit of an unrestrained culture of blame and compensation has many evil consequences and one is certainly the interference with the liberty of the citizen.[174]

The tenor of the House of Lords judgment in *Tomlinson* amply demonstrates the common law's antipathy towards extensive regulation, and the decision was an important influence on the statutory provision concerning risk aversion in the Compensation Act 2006. Section 1 of the Act reinforces *Tomlinson*'s message, by proclaiming that the social value of desirable activities can help justify taking only limited precautions.[175] Since this provision adds nothing of substance to existing common law doctrine, it is best understood as a rather heavy-handed exercise in symbolic affirmation.

There is no way of determining with any precision the social impact of a phenomenon as value-laden as 'risk aversion'. Recent parliamentary inquiries into the matter have reached differing conclusions on whether or not it has become excessive.[176] Though respectable arguments can be made about bureaucratisation, regulatory overkill and undue resort to defensive strategies, much denigration of 'risk aversion' thrives on anecdotal accounts and nostalgic appeal to some former, mythic golden era. The force of the sentiments is often undermined by their ideological underpinnings and the sweeping nature of the rhetoric. In a study of recreational activities and the law published shortly after the decision in *Tomlinson*,[177] Fulbrook criticised the tone of some of the Law Lords' speeches[178]—a source of predictably sensationalised headlines[179]—for distracting attention from what might be better described as a 'fact-sensitive' judgment that entailed a difficult cost/benefit exercise. His conclusion about the cost/benefit balance as regards outdoor activities in general was that, even if 'zero risk' was unattainable, 'there have been very considerable gains made in safety at relatively low cost' and 'there are still plenty of inexpensive advances yet to be made.'[180]

---

[174] Above n 171 [81].
[175] 'A court considering a claim in negligence or breach of statutory duty may, in determining whether the defendant should have taken particular steps to meet the standard of care (whether by taking precautions against a risk or otherwise), have regard to whether a requirement to take those steps might (a) prevent a desirable activity from being undertaken at all, to a particular extent or in a particular way, or (b) discourage persons from undertaking functions in connection with a desirable activity.' Compensation Act, 2006, s 1.
[176] Eg, the House of Lords Select Committee on Economic Affairs (2006) 'could find no clear evidence to justify the widely-held view that the public are excessively averse or that Britain has become an excessively risk-averse society': *Government Policy on the Management of Risk*, Fifth Report, HL 183–1, June 2006, paras 97–100. On the other hand, another [recent] parliamentary inquiry reached the conclusion that there was 'plenty of evidence of excessive risk aversion': House of Commons Constitutional Affairs Committee, citing BRTF Report (2004), above n 164. See Morris, above n 66, 367.
[177] J Fulbrook, *Outdoor Activities, Negligence and the Law* (Aldershot, Ashgate, 2005).
[178] Including 'Lord Hoffmann's strident perspective in a sub-heading in that case, "*Free Will*"': ibid, 261. And see especially paras 44–7 of his speech.
[179] Eg, '[Law Lords] brand compensation culture as a "crippling evil"': *Daily Mail*, 4 Aug 2003.
[180] Fulbrook, above n 177, 262.

In this context, it is of interest to note the findings of a recent investigation into the perception and reality of risk, conducted by Zurich Municipal, a leading public services insurer and risk manager. After a six month internal risk assessment of the top 10 risks for four major services—education, charities, local government and housing[181]—it reached the following conclusion:

> Finally, it seems that the influence of the 'compensation culture' has been exaggerated. There has been a perception in parts of the media that many activities, from school trips to volunteering, have been choked by a fear of litigation. Although the risk of a growing compensation culture is recognised by different organisations, there is little evidence that this concern dictates behaviour. Our risk assessment put it bottom of the top ten risks, as did the public survey.[182]

Risk Aversion and Mental Harm

In the course of advocating broader recovery rules for psychic injuries, Bell observed that, '[g]ranting people an entitlement to psychic well-being simultaneously restricts their freedom to act in ways which risk [causing] psychic injury.'[183] From his perspective, the outcome would be positive; the law would be sending out the clear message that you cannot negligently inflict significant psychic injury with impunity. To those who see a society already mired in a compensation culture where misfortune is too easily transmuted into injustice, there is a more insidious message: that there would be an unhealthy general decline in frank and open communication, for fear of the legal repercussions of inadvertently causing mental or emotional harm.[184] This concern is already commonly voiced in settings such as health care delivery, welfare provision and education.[185] In much the same way, it is argued that explicit coverage of newsworthy events would be all the more vulnerable to censorship or self-censorship, and that self-expression in personal relations generally would become more constrained.

How high such fears rank in the risk-averse mind-set is hard to gauge. It is clear that there is a marked emphasis on risk avoidance and risk minimisation in the present-day managerial culture. It seems likely that there is a growing belief that relatively minor emotional distress can ground a legal action, and that an increasing number of people are prepared to 'have a go'.[186] There is also no reason to suppose that the obstacles to proving liability are widely appreciated, especially if

---

[181] Based on 'claims data, desk research and expert opinion', and an Ipsos MORI public attitude survey.
[182] Zurich Municipal, *Perception and Reality: The real risks for public service and charitable organisations* (2007) 31.
[183] Bell, above n 124, 346.
[184] Cf D Butler, 'An Assessment of Competing Policy Considerations in Cases of Psychiatric Injury Resulting from Negligence' (2002) 10 *Torts Law Journal* 13, 31–3, para 3.3.2.
[185] Cf '[S]chools, hospitals, Local Authorities are beginning to feel that they are more at risk from litigation than they really are . . . we can't afford to leave this impression unchecked' Lord Falconer, 'Compensation Culture'—Speech at Insurance Times Conference, 10 Nov, 2004.
[186] See Better Regulation Task Force, *Better Routes to Redress*, above n 164, 5-7.

the prevailing image is of an instant shock reaction to careless conduct or an insensitive comment. Nor does it help if exaggerated accounts of the propensity to sue continue to appear, even in publications not notorious for sensationalist copy.[187] There is no simple way of persuading people not to believe what, at some level, they may want to believe. In all the circumstances, a 'chilling effect' is not implausible.

On the specific issue of mental harm caused by negligent communication, we would only reiterate the built-in limits to liability: the relative rarity of serious psychic disorder ensuing, or being reasonably foreseeable, and, in particular, the difficulty of proving that any such disorder was attributable to the manner of communication.[188] More generally, we should not shy away from the position that in a mature and civilised society, risk aversion should primarily be seen as a virtue. Even its overstated linkage to a 'blame and claim' culture is not entirely negative. To the extent that heightened fears of being sued do reinforce a climate of risk minimisation, the resultant risk-averse behaviour would preclude at least some of the careless conduct that might otherwise occur. Above all, we should resist a return to the 'pull yourself together' mentality that typified much of the early case law and legal commentary on 'nervous shock', as epitomised in Magruder's observation that 'a certain toughening of the mental hide is a better protection than the law ever could be'.[189] Too often, appeals to self-reliance and to the need to accept personal responsibility are a convenient means of disguising a lack of personal responsibility by those whose negligence has caused the harm in issue.

A more rational legal framework is long overdue. It should be less constrained by psychiatric definitions and centre more directly on gravity of mental or emotional suffering. As well as having a more inclusive test for remediable harm, it should abandon the primary/secondary divide and dispense with artificial controls. Though there are grounds for believing that these steps would be unlikely to have the adverse consequences commonly predicted,[190] any such liberalisation is bound to be resisted, mainly because of the 'floodgates fear'. That fear will not be overcome without a quid pro quo. It will be argued that the most effective and appropriate means of overcoming it would be through limited adjustment to the compensation system.

---

[187] See eg, M Lawson, 'The baloney over Barney', *Guardian*, 15 Jun, 2007, and L Rogers, 'The End of Risk', above n 167.

[188] See above Ch 4, especially at 108–9.

[189] C Magruder, 'Mental and Emotional Disturbance in the Law of Torts' (1936) 49 *Harvard Law Review* 1033, 1035. And see above Ch 1, 12–18.

[190] See further, below Ch 6.

6

A Proposal for Reform

A New Test for Remediable Suffering

[I]n as much as damage is the gist of the action for negligence, the relevant question is where along the spectrum of possible reactions, ranging from unpleasant emotions to 'longer lasting reactions', the law places its marker as representing damage deserving of compensation.[1]

THE LAW DOES not have to confine redress for mental harm to conditions that constitute a 'recognisable psychiatric illness'. Nor does it do so when the suffering results from physical injury. Several possibilities merit consideration. The most radical solution would be to substitute an unqualified requirement, such as 'mental distress' or 'emotional harm'. Alternatively, a qualified test could be adopted, based on suffering that is serious or severe, as determined by criteria such as duration and degree of disablement or dysfunction.[2] Another option would be a liability threshold for *all* non-pecuniary loss, physical as well as 'non-physical', identified by a monetary yardstick of legally significant harm, to be determined by such criteria.[3] Though none of these approaches has found favour in the English courts, a number of judgments in other Commonwealth countries have indicated a marked preference for a less restrictive substantive test than psychiatric disorder and, in some jurisdictions, various statutory thresholds have been introduced.

The Substantive Basis of Liability

The case for an unqualified threshold for mental harm rests largely on the assumption that, as with physical injury, patently trivial claims would be discounted as de minimis and very few minor ones would be deemed worth pursuing. There is no suggestion that the countless daily instances of minor physical harm have led to an unsustainable flood of civil law claims, or that the absence of a liability threshold

---

[1] D Butler, 'Identifying the Compensable Damage in "Nervous Shock" Cases' (1997) 5 *Torts Law Journal* 67, 72.
[2] See below, 172.
[3] See below, 177–9.

for physical injury now poses a serious floodgates threat. As Cane notes in *Atiyah's Accidents, Compensation and the Law*:

> [I]n personal injury cases, the fact that (emergency) medical care is typically obtained free of charge under the NHS, that many employers will pay wages or salary for a reasonable period of absence due to sickness or injury, and that social security benefits are often available to injured persons, probably means that very many minor cases are never made the subject of a tort claim.[4]

Such considerations do not apply exclusively to minor harm of a physical nature. However, an unqualified test would be unlikely to find support among the judiciary and would be strongly opposed at the political level.[5] And, given finite resources, it is far from clear that compensation for minor, transient distress is a desirable, reformist goal.[6] In addition, though there would be little reason to expect a significant rise in fully litigated cases, there could be no guarantee that there would not be a sizeable increase in the number of questionable settlements.

A more compelling case can be made for a threshold that focusses directly on relative gravity of harm. As we will see, *within* the strict parameters of legally compensable psychiatric harm, judicial calculation of damages for non-pecuniary loss already lays great stress on how severely the claimant has been and is likely to be incapacitated.[7] However, though a psychiatrically recognised pathological condition may provide a 'convenient handle',[8] it neither exclusively nor invariably involves a high level of emotional disturbance or dysfunction. If the impact and relative seriousness of the harm is central to the social function of compensation, the law should provide redress for serious psychological harm that falls short of, or less tendentiously, does not entail a medically recognised psychiatric disorder.[9] Mindful that there can be substantial suffering, incapacity and dysfunction without all the hallmarks of a psychiatric disorder—and vice versa—a growing number of judges in Commonwealth jurisdictions have become more receptive to liability for substantial 'emotional pain', as distinct from ordinary distress or discomfort.

Some of the most outspoken judicial critiques, which include calls for an unqualified test, are to be found in the Canadian case law, notably Southin J's rhetorical question, in *McDermott v Ramadanovic Estate*:[10]

---

[4] P Cane, *Atiyah's Accidents, Compensation and the Law*, (Cambridge, Cambridge University Press, 7th edn, 2006) 209.

[5] See Department for Constitutional Affairs, *The Law on Damages*, Consultation Paper (CP 9) (London, Department for Constitutional Affairs, 2007), below 188–9.

[6] For criticism of tort-based damages for minor non-pecuniary loss generally, see below 179–83.

[7] See below 178–9.

[8] *van Soest v Residual Health Management Unit* [2000] 1 NZLR 179, 206 [105], per Thomas J.

[9] In fact, though neither pathological grief disorder (PGD) nor chronic fatigue syndrome (CFS) were included in DSM-1V, damages were awarded for PGD in *Vernon v Bosley* (No 1) [1997] 1 All ER 577. See Thorpe LJ, 610 (cf *Arrowsmith v Beeston*, unreported, CA 18 Jun 1998, 19, per Brooke LJ). CFS was accepted as a basis for liability in *Page v Smith* [1996] AC 155.

[10] *McDermott v Ramadanovic Estate* (1988) 27 BCLR (2d) 45.

> [W]hat is the logical difference between a scar on the flesh and a scar on the mind? If a scar on the flesh is compensable although it causes no pecuniary loss, why should a scar on the mind be any less compensable?

And again:

> [T]o the sufferer, what is the difference between physical pain and emotional pain? Indeed, the former may be easier to bear, especially with modern analgesics, than the latter. Therefore, with the greatest of respect, I reject Lord Denning's limitation (if he intended it as a limitation of law) of recovery to cases of 'recognisable psychiatric illness'.[11]

In *Mason v Westside Cemeteries Ltd*, Molloy J observed:

> I recognise the undesirability of lawsuits based on nothing more than fright or mild upset. However, in my view the more appropriate way to control these frivolous actions is by limiting recovery based on foreseeability (and perhaps proximity or directness) and by awarding limited damages and imposing cost sanctions in cases of a trivial nature.[12]

Of particular interest was the finding at appellate level in *Anderson v Wilson*, at a preliminary stage of a mass class action over fear of having contracted hepatitis B infection:

> It cannot be said in this case that it is plain and obvious that the claim for the tort of mental distress standing alone will fail.[13]

It is also noteworthy that, in 1999, the Supreme Court of Canada declared that the constitutional right to 'security of the person'[14] includes the right to 'psychological integrity of the individual.' It held that, for state action to be in breach of this right, it has to have a 'serious and profound effect on a person's psychological integrity', which:

> need not rise to the level of nervous shock or psychiatric illness, but must be greater than ordinary stress or anxiety.[15]

As is noted in *Mullany and Handford*:

> [i]t is not a large step from recognition of a constitutional entitlement to peace of mind to recognition of the case for common law protection from significant disturbance to mental and emotional harmony incapable of classification as psychiatric disorder.[16]

---

[11] *Ibid*, 53. And see above Ch 2, n 100. See also Southin J's later comments to like effect, at appellate level, in *Rhodes v Canadian National Railway* (1990) 75 DLR (4th) 248, 289. Cf *Cox v Fleming* (1993) 13 CCLT (2d) 305: damages for 'emotional scarring', *per* Ryan J (1995) 15 BCLR (3d) 201 (appeal dismissed), and '[i]t is difficult to rationalize awarding damages for physical scratches and bruises of a minor nature but refusing damages for deep emotional distress which falls short of a psychiatric condition': *Mason v Westside Cemeteries Ltd* (1996) 135 DLR (4th) 361, 379–80, *per* Molloy J.

[12] *Mason, ibid*, 380.

[13] *Anderson v Wilson* (1999) 175 DLR (4th) 409, 416 (Ontario Court of Appeal). Though the same Court subsequently reasserted, obiter, the accepted requirement of recognisable psychiatric illness: *Vanek v Great Atlantic & Pacific Co of Canada* (1999) 180 DLR (4th) 748. See below n 17.

[14] *Canadian Charter of Rights and Freedoms*, s 7.

[15] *New Brunswick (Minister of Health and Community Services) v G (J)* [1999] 3 SCR 46, 58–60.

[16] P Handford, *Mullany and Handford's Tort Liability for Psychiatric Damage*, (Sydney, Lawbook Co, 2nd edn, 2006) [2.170].

Though, in a subsequent decision, the Ontario Court of Appeal reaffirmed that recognisable psychiatric illness was required at common law,[17] its observations on the matter did not form part of the ratio of the case,[18] and it acknowledged that the test might merit reconsideration. In Canada, then, there are some signs of judicial disenchantment with the status quo.[19]

In other commonwealth jurisdictions, judicial calls for a more flexible common law threshold have been more sporadic. In Australia, they are mainly to be found in some of the earlier judgments of Kirby J,[20] but the sentiments expressed are unlikely to be heeded in the foreseeable future, due to the combined effect of *Tame* and *Annetts* and the post–Ipp statutory reforms.[21] The leading joint judgment of Gummow and Kirby JJ in *Tame and Annetts* acknowledged that:

> [i]n Australia, as in England, Canada and New Zealand, a plaintiff who is unable affirmatively to establish the existence of a recognisable psychiatric illness is not entitled to recover;[22]

and, within a year or so, virtually all Australian jurisdictions had implemented the Ipp Panel's recommendation that liability for pure mental harm requires a 'recognised psychiatric illness'. As regards New Zealand, we have already noted Thomas J's dissent in *van Soest*, challenging the exclusive hold of the orthodox test.[23] He envisaged a staged process of reformulation. Initially, the orthodox test would remain the normal requirement, whilst allowing compensation for comparable mental suffering that is plainly outside the range of normal human experience:

> [e]ventually, it may be enough for a mentally injured plaintiff to show that his or her grief and sorrow is more than the grief and sorrow which is part of the ordinary vicissitudes of life.[24]

In the United States, the extensive use of the term 'emotional distress' is apt to cause confusion, since both its meaning and the legal limitations on the right to

---

[17] *Vanek*, above n 13, 756–7 [25], [26] and [62]–[68]. Cf *Duwyn v Kaprielian* (1978) 94 DLR (3rd) 424, 438, per Morden J.

[18] The Court's decision was based on a finding that the claimants' reaction to a minor mishap was unforeseeable.

[19] See also *Graham v MacMillan* (2003) 10 BCLR (4th) 397. It is of interest that a very recent decision of the Supreme Court of Canada does not say in terms that a 'recognisable psychiatric illness' is the threshold for liability, but refers to the need for 'serious and prolonged' injury: *Mustapha v Culligan of Canada Ltd* 2008 SCC 27 [9], per McLachlin CJ, delivering the judgment of the Court.

[20] Eg, *Government Insurance Office v Best* (1993) Aust Torts Rep 81-210: 'The distinction drawn by law between compensation for grief... and compensation for depression is highly artificial': per Kirby J (diss), 62,092. Cf 'To adhere to stereotypes expressed in terms of abnormal grief derived from England, may work an injustice on Australian litigants for whom the norms are different and grief reaction more variable than was hitherto expressed to be the case': *Coates v Government Insurance Office of New South Wales* (1995) 36 NSWLR 1, 12, per Kirby P.

[21] See above Ch 4, 135–6.

[22] *Tame v New South Wales; Annetts v Australian Stations Pty Ltd* (2002) 211 CLR 317, 382 [193].

[23] See above Ch 1, n 43 and related text. See also Barker J's refusal to strike out a claim for 'mental anguish or emotional distress' resulting from fear of developing asbestos-related cancers: *Bryan v Phillips New Zealand Ltd* [1995] 1 NZLR 632.

[24] *van Soest*, above n 8, 206.

recover vary from one jurisdiction to another. In several States, recourse to qualifications such as 'serious' or 'severe', in order to weed out frivolous claims, also serves to produce a more flexible criterion than 'recognisable psychiatric illness'.[25] At the same time, however, especially in jurisdictions where 'peace of mind' is seen as one of the interests at stake, so that 'emotional distress' is construed broadly,[26] there has been correspondingly greater reluctance to abandon special limits on recovery such as the 'zone of danger' rule.[27] Setting the more expansive regimes in their wider social context, Partlett points to the 'remedial mission of American tort law'.[28] He highlights its commitment to deterrence, compensation and corrective justice, concluding that:

> [t]he category of liability in emotional distress, uncluttered by exact definition, allows the law sufficient 'wiggle room' to effectuate these remedial ends.[29]

On this view, technical psychiatric definitions, though valuable as indicators, can be subordinated to a more broadly conceived notion of harm measured by intensity, duration and functional incapacity. In *Molien v Kaiser Foundation Hospitals*, for example, a condition was said to be regarded as 'serious' if:

> a reasonable man, normally constituted, would be unable to adequately cope with the mental stress engendered by the circumstances of the case.[30]

Any such formula can, of course, be criticised as a recipe for uncertainty and invidious distinctions. However, these risks are by no means unknown under the prevailing English structure, and may well be outweighed by enhanced prospects of agreement between expert witnesses, thereby facilitating speedier resolution by settlement.[31]

In the English context, it is idle to suppose that the liability threshold will be extended without a significant, countervailing precautionary measure. In addition to the stumbling-block of the decision in *White*, the perceived risks of the floodgates opening and the cost of litigation rising would prompt wider concerns about

---

[25] Eg, 'The seriousness criterion adequately protects against fraud, trivial claims and unlimited liability by requiring severe and debilitating harm': *Molien v Kaiser Foundation Hospitals* 616 P 2d 813, 821 (Cal 1980). In some judgments the criterion seems tantamount to 'recognisable psychiatric illness'. Eg, 'The term "severe emotional distress" means any emotional or mental disorder, such as, for example, neurosis, psychosis, chronic depression, phobia or any other type of severe and disabling mental or emotional condition which may be generally recognized and diagnosed by professionals trained to do so.' *Johnson v Ruark Obstetrics and Gynecology Associates PA* 395 SE 2d 85, 97 (1990), per Mitchell J.

[26] Eg, *Thing v La Chusa* 771 P 2d 814, 816 (Cal 1989).

[27] See *Consolidated Rail Corporation v Gottshall* 512 US 532 (1994). And see *Tame* and *Annetts*, above n 22, [172]–[174] and [194], per Gummow and Kirby JJ. See further, *Mullany and Handford's Tort Liability for Psychiatric Damage*, above n 16, [1.250]–[1.280], [3.50]–[3.60] and [4.110]–[4.120].

[28] D Partlett, 'Tort Liability and the American Way: Reflections on Liability for Emotional Distress' (1997) 45 *American Journal of Comparative Law* 171, 184.

[29] Ibid, 192.

[30] *Molien v Kaiser Foundation Hospitals*, above n 25, 819–20.

[31] See Scottish Law Commission, *Discussion Paper on Damages for Psychiatric Injury* (Edinburgh, The Stationery Office, 2002) No 120, para 2.8. Cf 'Doctors can speak with a great deal of precision without needing to address the question whether the mental suffering is a recognisable psychiatric illness or not': *van Soest*, above n 8, 205, per Thomas J.

the affordability of the insurance that underpins the overall system.[32] Earlier, we focussed on the frequency of claims with little direct reference to their cost. Yet plainly frequency and cost are inextricably linked. Resistance to extending the scope of liability is driven, in part, by a belief that the ability and desire to sue 'at the drop of a hat', reinforced by irresponsible advertising, has already resulted in more claimants gaining unjustifiable or excessive awards and settlements, and in rising administrative costs. Such costs are notoriously high:

> The total costs of the system are nearly double the amounts paid out in compensation because the tort liability insurance system is so staggeringly expensive to operate.[33]

Our goal is a more rational liability structure for 'non-physical' personal harm that has a realistic prospect of being implemented. If precautionary measures are deemed essential, they need not take their current form of unprincipled *substantive* law restrictions. It would be preferable for them to operate, as far as possible, at a procedural level, through modification of the damages regime.[34] We would argue that the most appropriate practical response to fears that a broader test would threaten the viability of the overall system would be a threshold requirement for the award of non-pecuniary damages for *all* personal injury claims.

One way of allaying the fears that a broader test would arouse would be to introduce a threshold based on duration of the harm. Some 30 years ago, the Pearson Commission proposed excluding all personal injury claims for non-pecuniary loss experienced during the first 3 months after the injury. Primarily envisaged as a cost-saving device, and prompted in part by concern that minor injuries tend to be overcompensated in practice, this proposal was never implemented. Though it has the virtue of simplicity, as well as promising a considerable saving in costs, like any arbitrary threshold it has certain drawbacks. For example, the initial weeks after an accident are apt to be the most painful and disabling,[35] and excluding damages altogether would seem harsh where someone has endured intense pain or suffering for, say, 10 or 11 weeks.[36] In addition, a temporal threshold could give rise to undue, perhaps artificial and unseemly, dispute between experts over

---

[32] See generally, R Lewis, 'Insurance and the Tort System' (2005) 25 *Legal Studies* 85.

[33] Cane, *Atiyah's Accidents, Compensation and the Law*, above n 4, 396. The 'Pearson Commission' estimated these costs to be 85% of the value of tort payments to claimants: Royal Commission on Civil Liability and Compensation for Personal Injury (London, HMSO, 1978) (Cmnd 7054): vol 1, para 256. See also a more recent study finding that costs exceeded damages in 22% of successful cases: P Pleasance, *Report of the Case Profiling Study, Personal Injury Litigation in Practice*, Research Paper 3, Legal Aid Board Research Unit (1998) 40, fig 3.17. And see R Lewis, 'Increasing the Price of Pain: Damages, the Law Commission and *Heil v Rankin*' (2001) 64 *MLR* 100, 103.

[34] See, eg, S Ingber, 'Rethinking Intangible Injuries: A Focus on Remedy' (1985) 73 *California Law Review* 772.

[35] T Gill, 'Pearson: Implications for Victims of Industrial Accidents', in DK Allen, CJ Bourn and JH Holyoak, *Accident Compensation after Pearson* (London, Sweet & Maxwell, 1979) 153–4. The Pearson Commission found that about 95% of people injured in accidents recovered sufficiently to resume work within 3 months: see above n 33, vol 1, table 2.

[36] Eg high degree burns. See P Sherman, 'The Pearson Report and Insurance', in *Accident Compensation after Pearson*, ibid, n 35, 123–4. And see Law Commission, Consultation Paper No 140, *Damages for Personal Injury: Non-Pecuniary Loss* (London, HMSO, 1995) paras 4.23–4.26.

precisely how long the claimant's condition had or should have endured.[37] Some 20 years on, the Law Commission considered but also rejected this approach.[38]

The Case for a Monetary Threshold

Another option would be to introduce a monetary threshold. In his detailed American study of recovery for negligently inflicted 'psychic injury',[39] Bell advanced the notion of a fixed sum as the measure of legally significant injury for emotional distress.[40] His own ideal solution would have been to remove all the restrictive substantive controls and provide the same basis of recovery as applies to physical harm. However, were that unattainable, because of a perceived need to 'curb trivial claims with a legal restriction,'[41] he initially advocated deducting a fixed sum from any successful claimant's damages award.[42] As a result of a response to his article, he opted for a threshold approach that would enable claimants whose award exceeded the threshold figure to recover in full, and which would require claimants awarded less than the fixed figure to pay the amount awarded to the court.

The Pearson Commission had considered a monetary threshold for all personal injury claims, but dismissed it for several reasons. They thought that it would track severity of harm less closely than a time threshold; would need adjustment over time; might encourage exaggeration of the harm, and:

> would add to the uncertainties of litigation, since the plaintiff would have to attempt to evaluate his claim for non-pecuniary loss before deciding whether to bring an action.[43]

The force of these objections is open to question. A time threshold is not a particularly precise indicator of severity; adjustment is now an accepted feature of damages guidelines, and the courts have acknowledged that nowadays there are more refined means of assessment to expose exaggerated symptoms. There is also much to be said for claimants, or often in practice their advisers, notionally evaluating the claim. This effectively happens already, to the extent that the perceived merits and value of the claim are integral to a firm's readiness to pursue it on a conditional fee basis.

---

[37] D Hughes, 'Pearson: Implications in Road Accident Cases', in *Accident Compensation after Pearson*, above n 35, 142.

[38] As did 93% of its consultees who addressed the matter: Law Commission, No 257, *Damages for Personal Injury: Non-Pecuniary Loss* (London, HMSO, 1999) paras 2.25–2.28.

[39] Ie 'emotional distress' as applied in many US jurisdictions to cover all mental harm cases.

[40] P Bell, 'The Bell Tolls: Toward Full Tort Recovery for Psychic Injury' (1984) 36 *University of Florida Law Review* 333.

[41] *Ibid*, 389.

[42] See further, RN Pearson, 'Liability for Negligently Inflicted Psychic Harm: A Response to Professor Bell' (1984) 36 *University of Florida Law Review* 413, 429, at n 83.

[43] Royal Commission on Civil Liability and Compensation for Personal Injury, above n 33, vol 1, para 385.

As regards 'non-physical' harm, then, the courts would not have to determine whether there is a 'recognisable psychiatric injury'. This criterion should, it is suggested, be replaced by a new threshold of 'moderately severe mental or emotional harm'. The courts would assess the reality and value of the injury in terms of its relative severity, taking numerous relevant variables into account. Again, *in practice, this is what they already do*, when awarding damages for pain, suffering and disability associated with physical injury, and when assessing levels of compensable psychiatric harm. Expert evidence from psychiatrists would, of course, be admissible, and the proposed extension of the liability threshold would suggest a greater role, in certain cases, for other suitably qualified mental health professionals, such as clinical psychologists. Over time, aided by appropriately reformulated guidelines and, if need be, by counsel's advice on quantum, personal injury lawyers would acquire a general sense of the value of individual claims, in much the same way as happens now. By and large, if there were a monetary threshold, only claimants or advisers confident that the claim for non-pecuniary loss was worth more than the threshold amount would pursue it, effectively eliminating most trivial claims for personal injury and the majority of minor ones.

What the threshold figure should be could perhaps be determined by the Judicial Studies Board, as appropriately advised.[44] Under the prevailing system, damages for non-pecuniary loss are based on the court's assessment of what is fair and reasonable in the light of previous decisions, and for some 25 years now these assessments have been underpinned by the general guidance summarised in the Judicial Studies Board (JSB) *Guidelines for the Assessment of General Damages in Personal Injury Cases*.[45] In his foreword to the current edition, Mr Justice Owen states that:

> it is now only in rare cases that courts make awards outside the margins reproduced in the *Guidelines*. Anecdotal evidence suggests that this is also the case in negotiated settlements.[46]

The JSB's indicative figures include guidance on psychiatric damage under three broad headings: Psychiatric Damage Generally; Post-Traumatic Stress Disorder, and Chronic Pain.[47] In fact, the guidelines already contain a notional threshold figure for general psychiatric damage claims and PTSD, which are 'priced' according to four levels of severity: 'severe', 'moderately severe', 'moderate' and 'minor'. A variety of factors are used in evaluating the claims, notably ability to cope with work and day-to-day living; effect on relationships; treatment prospects; future vulnerability, and prognosis.[48] The current monetary range for minor psychiatric damage is £840–£3,450, the level of the award to:

---

[44] See below 183–4.
[45] Judicial Studies Board, *Guidelines for the Assessment of General Damages in Personal Injury Cases* (Oxford, Oxford University Press, 8th edn, 2006).
[46] *Ibid*, vii.
[47] Above n 45, 10–14.
[48] For a useful summary of how these variables can be fleshed out for forensic purposes, see WJ Koch *et al*, 'What's the Damage?' *Solicitors Journal Expert Witness Supplement* (Summer, 2004) 5. Cf Deakin, Johnston, and Markesinis, *Markesinis and Deakin's Tort Law*, (Oxford, Oxford University Press, 6th edn, 2008), 999–1000.

take into consideration the length of the period of disability and the extent to which daily activities and sleep were affected.[49]

For present purposes, the significance of the Guidelines does not lie with the particular figure or figures. Rather, the fact that they are routinely adhered to by the courts illustrates both the pragmatic approach already adopted for quantifying non-pecuniary loss[50] and the importance attached to relative severity of impact in those claims for which legal redress is currently available. Still more telling is the apparent salience of that impact in many of the estimated 99 per cent of cases that are settled out of court.[51] Already:

> [i]t may well be that in practice, much more will turn, in settled cases, on the effect of the symptoms on the claimant's lifestyle (e.g. are they confined to bed, unable to work, and so on), rather than on whether the symptoms amount to a recognised psychiatric illness.[52]

Is a Monetary Threshold a Step Too Far?

An explicit monetary threshold would, of course, signify a more overtly market-oriented than rights-based conception of claiming. However, in the age of the conditional fee, one should be slow to impugn it as an unthinkable reduction of the legal process to a form of gambling. Moreover, encouraging claimant evaluation by imposing financial penalties for trivial or undue litigation long predated the introduction of conditional fees. For example, it has long been the case that, after proceedings have commenced, a claimant who rejects a formal offer by way of 'payment into court' and proceeds to trial, only to be awarded no more than the amount paid in, bears the costs of both parties from the latest date on which the offer could have been accepted. Since 2000, either party can make a formal offer of settlement.[53]

If it be granted that a more defensible framework for mental and emotional harm is a desirable aim, it might still be objected that as a means towards achieving it, a monetary threshold for non-pecuniary loss, especially if applied to *all* personal injury cases, would be an unprincipled overreaction—a sledgehammer to crack a nut. To address this objection, we need to explore further the nature of damages for non-pecuniary loss, to appreciate the 'disproportionate importance' they have acquired,[54] especially in small claims, and their problematic status in the

---

[49] Judicial Studies Board, *Guidelines*, above n 45, 12, where it is also stated that '[a]wards have been made below this bracket in cases of temporary "anxiety"'. This reflects the fact that the guidelines cover pain and suffering resulting from physical injury as well as 'pure' psychiatric harm. The range for minor PTSD is £2,300–£4,825.

[50] Cf '[A]lways a practical exercise in approximation': *Harriton v Stephens* (2006) 226 CLR 52, 79 [82], per Kirby J.

[51] Cf Lewis, 'Insurance and the Tort System', above n 32, 88.

[52] Cane, *Atiyah's Accidents, Compensation and the Law*, above n 4, 85–6.

[53] Where a claimant's offer of settlement is not accepted but is exceeded as a result of the trial, the court may order additional interest on damages: Civil Procedure Rules 1998, 36.21 (1), (2).

[54] Lewis, above n 33, 101.

broader social and economic context of compensation, as 'a major cause of the excessive cost, inefficiency and injustice of the tort system.'[55] It will be argued that, as a matter of social priorities, there are cogent independent reasons for dispensing with such damages for all minor claims.

Orthodox theory dictates that common law damages for personal injury are intended, as far as possible, to *restore* claimants to the position that they would have been in but for the injury[56](emphasis added). They are available for pecuniary loss, including medical and care expenses as well as loss of actual and prospective earnings, and for 'non-pecuniary' loss, being essentially the effects of the injury by way of pain, suffering and loss of amenity (or disability). Traditionally, the common law requirement of restoring claimants to their pre-tort position has been expressed as a principle of 'full compensation', applicable 'to pecuniary and non-pecuniary damages alike.'[57] As regards non-pecuniary loss, the consequences are striking. The Pearson Commission's data indicated that, in 1973, pain and suffering accounted for some two thirds of all damages, and that, for claims of up to £5,000 (at 1977 prices), non-pecuniary loss accounted for proportions ranging from 63 per cent to 78 per cent of the total payment,[58] proportions which are unlikely to have declined dramatically since.[59] The Commission also found that only 1 per cent of claims reached the courts; that, at 1977 prices, about 60 per cent of tort settlements amounted to £500 or less, and only about 1 per cent exceeded £10,000. [60] The very high proportion, and therefore high overall cost, of small claims is apt to be obscured by the media's inevitable focus on 'mega-claims'. As Atiyah has observed, 'a very large part of the cost of the whole system is actually devoted to funding these small claims.'[61]

To appreciate more fully why the predominance of 'full' compensation for non-pecuniary loss is seen as problematic, it is necessary to consider how perceptions of its purpose have changed over time. In its pure form, the compensation system is described as one based on corrective justice.[62] However, as damages for *non-pecuniary* loss cannot, by definition, 'restore' claimants to their previous position, they cannot literally correct the wrong done, and for many years there has been a tendency to assert that they should be 'fair' or 'reasonable' rather than 'full'.[63] It

---

[55] Lewis, above n 33, 101.

[56] *Livingstone v Rawyards* (1880) 5 App Cas 25, 39.

[57] *Heil v Rankin* [2001] QB 272, para 23, *per* Lord Woolf MR. For a valuable overview of sources of compensation, and of how the tort system in practice treats people with minor injuries relatively more generously than those with serious injuries, see Cane, *Atiyah's Accidents, Compensation and the Law*, above n 4, 18–29.

[58] Even in larger claims (over £25,000) it accounted for 48%. See 'Pearson Commission', above n 33, Vol 2, tables 107 and 108. Cf Law Commission, *Damages for Personal Injury: Non-Pecuniary Loss* (1999), above n 38, para 3.38.

[59] Lewis, above n 33, 102–3 and n 18.

[60] *Pearson Report*, above n 33, Vol 1, paras 78–9 and table 6. In 1995, the DSS estimated that half of the cases reported to it under CRU were being settled for £2,500 or less: DSS *Memorandum of Evidence to the Social Security Select Committee* (1995) HC 196, para 40.

[61] PS Atiyah, *The Damages Lottery* (Oxford, Hart Publishing, 1997) 16–17.

[62] See EJ Weinrib, *The Idea of Private Law* (Cambridge, Mass, Harvard University Press, 1995).

[63] See, eg, *Warren v King* [1964] 1 WLR 1.

has been argued that they can nonetheless contribute to 'corrective justice' if the concept is construed more broadly, as requiring 'redress' rather than restoration. So construed, this element of compensation may be seen as having a significant declaratory and symbolic role, asserting both the reality of the non-pecuniary loss and the defendant's fault in causing it.[64]

That tort law has its roots in the responsibility of the individual wrongdoer to right the wrong done is undeniable. Yet there has long been an air of unreality about attempts to insist on the conceptual purity of the corrective justice model, and even when recast in a more plausible form it can only partially correspond with the way the compensation system operates. Today, a more forward-looking, instrumental view is commonly taken. Where money is not commensurate with the adverse effects of injury, it cannot eliminate them; yet it can serve as a source of solace and therapeutic benefit—a practical contribution towards rehabilitation and improved emotional stability—to alleviate such diminished wellbeing as results from the injury but is not remediable by damages for pecuniary loss. The coherence and moral force of the corrective justice rationale largely depends on the wrongdoer's obligation to right the wrong. Its central tenet is seriously undermined once it is acknowledged that, overwhelmingly, tort damages are, in the first instance, paid by insurers[65] and, ultimately, largely funded by consumers or the public at large; not by the individual wrongdoer.[66]

It follows that damages for non-pecuniary loss are more realistically portrayed as a means of fulfilling social policy aims within a welfare model of distributive justice.[67] This characterisation is especially apt for the numerous cases where an employer or public body is held vicariously liable for the wrongdoer's negligence. It is noticeable that in *Heil v Rankin*, a major appellate decision that reviewed the levels of damages for non-pecuniary loss,[68] the Court of Appeal took into account the impact on insurance premiums, and on an NHS under financial pressure, of increasing them.[69] Although it opted for a tapered increase for non-pecuniary loss

---

[64] MJ Radin, 'Compensation and Commensurability' (1993) 43 *Duke Law Journal* 56. And see B Chapman, 'Wrongdoing, Welfare, and Damages Recovery for Non-Pecuniary Loss in Corrective Justice', in DG Owen (ed), *Philosophical Foundations of Tort Law* (Oxford, Oxford University Press, 1995) ch 18.

[65] '[I]t is insurers who run the tort system': Lewis, above n 33, 110. For a defence of the judicial obligation to adhere to the principles of individual responsibility and corrective justice, see J Morgan, 'Tort, Insurance and Incoherence' (2004) 67 *MLR* 384.

[66] Ie through the pricing of goods and services, marginal increases in insurance premiums, and, in the case of public bodies, via taxation. Cf Law Commission, Consultation Paper No 137, *Liability for Psychiatric Illness*, (London, HMSO,1995), para 4 (2).

[67] Cf the sentiment that the police at Hillsborough should not 'have the right to compensation for psychiatric injury out of public funds while the bereaved relatives are sent away with nothing': *White v Chief Constable of South Yorkshire Police* [1999] 2 AC 455, 510, *per* Lord Hoffmann; and Lord Steyn's subsequent description of *White*: 'a hard case. But reasons of distributive justice were decisive.' Steyn, Lord, *Perspectives of Corrective and Distributive Justice in Tort Law*, John Maurice Kelly Memorial Lecture (Dublin, University College Dublin, 2002) 7.

[68] *Heil v Rankin* [2001] QB 272. Unusually, a five-judge Court of Appeal was convened.

[69] Reasons for recent increases in damages include the cost implications for treatment and long term care of advances in medical technology and life-prolonging techniques; and of reduction in the discount rate applied to future pecuniary losses and the rising cost of providing for such losses when

over £10,000, up to a maximum one third increase for the 'most serious' cases, it rejected any increase where the award was assessed at below £10,000.[70] Yet, given scarce public resources, as a matter of social priorities it would have been reasonable to introduce a threshold that excluded the numerous claims for non-pecuniary loss that fall far below £10,000. Not only do such thresholds feature in other jurisdictions,[71] but provision for non-pecuniary loss rarely features in sources of compensation other than tort law. For example, cover for it is not normally sought by people who take out private insurance, perhaps suggesting that compensation under this head of damages is neither a general expectation nor seen as a high priority. Nor is it a general feature of social security provision.[72]

In certain respects at least, an instructive comparison can be made between negligence-based compensation for personal injury and the state-funded Criminal Injuries Compensation Scheme. Set up for the victims of violent crime that has been *intentionally* or *recklessly* caused, it covers both physical and mental injury, the latter defined as 'temporary medical anxiety, medically verified, or a disabling mental illness confirmed by psychiatric diagnosis.'[73] Under the scheme in place since 2001, the right to compensation has been based on a detailed tariff that excludes redress for non-pecuniary loss from 'minor injuries', the threshold figure being £1,000. No doubt the introduction of a threshold reflected stock concerns about a proliferation of trivial or suspect claims. Yet the contrast with the approach to damages in negligence remains striking. Here we have two compensatory systems, both in broad terms funded by society at large, yet a threshold has been imposed only for the victims of the more heinous conduct, who typically attract *more* public sympathy. Under present dispensations, as Cane has noted, it is difficult to see 'why there should not be a lower limit on tort damages of £1,000, as there is on compensation under the Criminal Injuries Compensation Scheme.'[74] In part, then, it is a matter of perception. Where awards are readily identifiable as publicly funded, there is a correspondingly marked focus on social priorities in the allocation of scarce resources. The imposition of a threshold is felt to be less objectionable than in the context of damages for negligence, where there

---

income levels were rising well above price inflation. See R Lewis, A Morris and K Oliphant, 'Tort personal injury claims statistics: Is there a compensation culture in the United Kingdom?' (2006) *Torts Law Journal* 158, 172–4.

[70] The Law Commission Report on non-pecuniary loss (1999), above n 38, saw £2,000 as the base for 'serious injury'. It, too, did not advocate any increase for 'non-serious' injury.

[71] They now exist in almost all Australian jurisdictions, expressed either in monetary terms, or as a level of impairment, or as a percentage of 'a most extreme case'. See, eg, Personal Injuries (Liability and Damages) Act 2003 (Northern Territories); Wrongs Act 1958 (Victoria) as amended by the Wrongs and Other Acts (Public Liability Insurance Reform) Act 2002 (Victoria), and Civil Liability Act 2002 (NSW), respectively.

[72] 'Disablement benefit' for long-term incapacity under the Industrial Injuries Scheme is an exception.

[73] Criminal Injuries Compensation Scheme, 2001, para 9, pursuant to the Criminal Injuries Compensation Act 1995. The scheme provides a practical alternative to what would almost invariably be a fruitless tort action against an insolvent defendant.

[74] Cane, *Atiyah's Accidents, Compensation and the Law*, above n 4, 157.

is a lingering belief that the wrongdoer pays, and where the ways in which the 'public' ultimately foots the bill are less transparent.

More generally, it is always salutary to recall that, as the Pearson Commission established, tort-based awards and settlements for personal injury serve only a minute proportion of accident victims. Is it appropriate that the benefits of a 'system' paid for by the bulk of the population should be reserved for the approximately 6.5 per cent of the public whose accidental injuries are due to the careless conduct of other individuals, which they were fortunate enough to be able to prove? Over the years, the marked contrast between the elaborate provision for successful tort claimants and the plight of most other accident victims[75] has prompted numerous proposals for reform, in England and elsewhere. The most radical solutions involve abolishing the common law negligence action, and either replacing it by comprehensive 'no fault' liability or leaving it by and large to individuals to take out first party insurance against accidents.[76] It is beyond the scope of this work to explore the respective merits and shortcomings of these approaches,[77] neither of which is remotely on the political agenda in Britain.[78] It is however worth noting that, though conceptually almost polar opposites, they are at one in demonstrating how dysfunctional 'the wrongdoer must pay' rationale is as a model for accident compensation in the modern world.

Conclusion

There are sound theoretical and practical reasons for modifying the rules on damages for non-pecuniary loss across the board. It is proposed that there should be a uniform monetary threshold that excludes minor, transient harm, whether physical, psychiatric or emotional; that tapered awards should be available for

---

[75] Cf the 'enormous disparity': *Hodgson v Trapp* [1989] AC 807, 823, per Lord Bridge. And note the view that, because tort claimants already have preferential treatment among accident victims, and because compensation for intangible losses can have an inappropriately punitive aspect, '[i]t is perhaps only in the most serious cases of long-term pain and loss of faculty resulting from major physical injuries that there is a good case for damages for non-pecuniary loss.' Cane, above n 4, 173.

[76] Under the New Zealand comprehensive no-fault accident scheme, introduced in 1974, the limited provision for non-pecuniary loss—for permanent loss or impairment of bodily function—was abolished in 1992 and replaced by a modest 'independence allowance' for permanent disability of 10% or more. For analysis of the first party insurance insurance approach, see, eg, Atiyah, *The Damages Lottery*, above n 61, 185–93.

[77] For detailed accounts see Cane, *Atiyah's Accidents, Compensation and the Law*, above n 4, especially ch 18; Atiyah, *The Damages Lottery*, above n 61, Atiyah, 'Personal Injuries in the Twenty First Century: Thinking the Unthinkable', in P Birks (ed), *Wrongs and Remedies in the Twenty-First Century* (Oxford, Oxford University Press, 1996) ch 1 and D Harris, D Campbell and R Halson, *Remedies in Contract and Tort* (London, Butterworths, 2nd edn, 2002). See also J Conaghan and W Mansell, 'From the Permissive to the Dismissive Society: Patrick Atiyah's Accidents, Compensation and the Market' (1988) 25 *Journal of Law and Society* 284.

[78] '[P]ressure to replace the tort system is now all but non-existent': Cane, *Atiyah's Accidents, Compensation and the Law*, above n 4, 462–3. And again, '[a]t the beginning of the twenty-first century it seems clear not only that the tort system is here to stay, but that it will become an increasingly important part of society's provision for the disabled': 266–7.

moderately severe harm and more substantial awards for the most serious. In broad terms, the approach would be very similar to that adopted by the JSB, but with a suggested threshold in the region of £2,000 (some 55 per cent to 65 per cent lower than the thresholds introduced in Australian jurisdictions). Such a provision should put to rest any concerns about an overload of minor claims and, as regards mental harm, would in practice exclude the majority of claims currently within the JSB Minor Psychiatric Damage band.[79] The kind of adjustment argued for is the more readily achievable because it is relatively modest in scale and the method of judicial calculation would remain essentially the same. The JSB, by virtue of its experience and current role, would be the natural body to oversee the implementation of such proposals. Yet its experience has inevitably been shaped, and constrained, by the need to 'distil the conventional wisdom contained in the reported cases.'[80] In faithfully reflecting that conventional wisdom, it has attributed to mental harm monetary values which have always been low by comparison with those for physical injury, more conspicuously so now that the former's relative gravity is openly asserted by the courts themselves. In addition, the current guidance on mental harm is too skeletal. It would be highly desirable to establish a more broadly-based committee to advise the Board on the monetary threshold; the respective bands, and the levels within them for moderately severe and severe injury, and on appropriate realignment of the indicative amounts, as between physical and 'non-physical' harm.[81]

The choice of a monetary threshold as a key component of the proposed reforms would admittedly introduce a new element of arbitrariness into the existing legal framework for mental harm. Yet one of its express aims would be to convince sceptics that the law can safely relinquish the many other arbitrary elements which have made that framework so unsatisfactory. Wherever a threshold is set, there will always be hard cases at the margins. It is not a step to be taken lightly, since, albeit as regards relatively minor harm, the effect would tend to be greater on people of limited means. However, it is preferable that hard cases should arise at the lower end of the pain and suffering scale, where general health care and welfare provision can, for the most part, adequately address needs; where reasonable expectations are correspondingly lower, and where disproportionately high administration costs are the more likely to result in over-compensation. Currently, too many hard cases arise where suffering and disability are more severe

---

[79] £840 to £3,450. As noted earlier, it is anticipated that claims would rarely be made unless claimants or their lawyers could be reasonably confident that the threshold would be exceeded. Though claims for personal injuries of up to £1,000 can be brought under the County Court 'small claims' procedure, they are relatively rare, in part due to the potential cost of legal assistance and expert evidence.

[80] Judicial Studies Board, *Guidelines for the Assessment of General Damages in Personal Injury Cases* (Oxford, Oxford University Press, 1st edn, 1992) Foreword by Lord Donaldson of Lymington, ix.

[81] In Australia, the Negligence Review Panel ('Ipp Review') recommended the establishment of an advisory body to produce an equivalent to the JSB *Guidelines*: see Department of the Treasury, *Review of the Law of Negligence: Final Report* (Canberra, Department of the Treasury, 2002), rec 46 (c), and a panel of experts to develop guidelines for assessing whether a person has suffered a recognised psychiatric illness: rec 33.

and longer-lasting. There is no obvious reason to suppose that a broader liability test tempered by a monetary threshold would result in a flood of claims. Any negative consequences of such increased claiming as might ensue should be more than compensated for—financially, by savings from an across the board threshold and, as a matter of justice, through more principled decision-making in the more severe cases.

The Proposed Framework in Outline

In *van Soest*, Thomas J exhorted courts to 'abandon inhibitions born of a past era and revert to fundamental principle.'[82] In the English context, the prospects of such a court-led reversion seem remote, given the prevailing view in the House of Lords that the search for principle on psychiatric harm 'was called off in *Alcock*'.[83] If a more coherent structure is to emerge, an Act of Parliament is almost certainly needed. Its imprimatur would, in any event, be highly desirable to minimise attempts to resuscitate earlier precedent, and to ensure that the new compensatory structure operated prospectively. The legislative process would also be a more effective means of drawing attention to the social justice considerations involved, and of asserting a commitment to enhanced emotional wellbeing as a social value. It is suggested that the following changes should be introduced:

—Abolition of the primary/secondary divide;
—A new liability threshold, for all claimants, of 'moderately severe mental or emotional harm';
—Standard negligence principles of reasonable care, reasonable foreseeability and causation for all cases;
—A monetary liability threshold for non-pecuniary loss,[84] and
—two categories of damages for non-pecuniary loss: 'severe' and 'moderately severe'.

If implemented, these proposals would alter the existing law in a number of respects. The preconditions for duty of care that presently apply to secondary claimants would lose their mandatory status. Where appropriate, proximity as to time, space and relationship, direct perception, and shock-induced injury would still feature as possible indicators of whether a given risk of harm was predictable; but they would do so as aspects of a more open-ended determination of duty of care as a function of reasonable foreseeability, 'sufficient proximity' and that

---

[82] *van Soest*, above n 8, 209.
[83] *White*, above n 67, 511, *per* Lord Hoffmann.
[84] To be applied to *all* personal injury cases. It is not envisaged that the threshold figure should be deductible where the claimant has succeeded, since this would unduly inhibit claiming at the lower end of the scale. By the same token, a claimant who would notionally have been awarded a sum below the threshold should not incur any financial penalty on that account.

which is 'just and reasonable' in the circumstances. For example, in some circumstances, assumption of responsibility by the defendant would be a very significant consideration.

In the light of previous doctrinal developments and controversies, certain aspects of how 'reasonable foreseeability' is best determined need further clarification. It is proposed that, in respect of *all* claimants, it should be necessary to prove that at least moderately severe mental or emotional harm was reasonably foreseeable, so that blame attaches only to conduct for which it is fair, just and reasonable to adjudge defendants culpable.[85] As regards causation, for reasons previously advanced, it is suggested that Lord Bridge's 'educated layman' test should be retained as the measure of 'reasonable foreseeability'.[86] As regards *who* is foreseeable, the artificial test of 'normal fortitude'[87] should not be a precondition of liability for any claimants. At most, it should be seen as one aspect of the determination of '*reasonable* foreseeability' in the circumstances, an aspect which might carry little or no weight where the defendant had prior knowledge of a claimant's unusual susceptibility.

In short, there would be a duty to take reasonable care not to cause someone to suffer at least moderately severe mental or emotional harm either directly or as a result of the death, injury or imperilment of another, where such a consequence was a reasonably foreseeable risk. It follows that rescuers, other helpers and involuntary participants would have their claims determined on the basis of reasonable care in all the circumstances. So, too, would bystanders, who, though not categorically condemned to fail,[88] would very rarely recover in reality. The monetary threshold would be a strong disincentive to pursuing spurious or trivial claims and should also discourage most minor ones, sufficiently so to dispel concerns about an undue rise in claims resulting from removal of the special controls and extending the liability threshold.

Remaining Barriers to Reform

A Legally Undervalued Core Value

The more deep-seated explanations for the present state of the law are rarely addressed. Imagine, for the sake of argument, that by the time our ancestors had acknowledged a need to compensate for the effects of physical injuries, they had

---

[85] This would also apply to severe mental or emotional harm that follows physical injury. And see above Ch 3, especially n 130 and related text.

[86] See *McLoughlin v O'Brian* [1983] 1 AC 410, 432. And see above Ch 4, 112.

[87] *Bourhill v Young* [1943] AC 92, 110. See also *Tame v New South Wales* (2002) 211 CLR 317, 35 [201], *per* Gummow and Kirby JJ. Cp *Mustapha v Culligan of Canada Ltd* [2008] SCC 27.

[88] *Alcock v Chief Constable of South Yorkshire Police* [1992] 1 AC 310. And see McBride, NG, and Bagshaw, R, *Tort Law* (Harlow, Pearson Education, 2nd edn 2005) 100–2.

acquired an informed understanding of harm to the psyche, instead of one grounded in myth, fear and superstition. It is reasonable to assume that the long-lasting reluctance to provide an adequate remedy for it would not have been so marked. In part because that understanding proved so elusive, it has never been easy for mental well-being to acquire the resonance of bodily integrity, despite the fact that it is universally sought and highly valued. At least until comparatively recent times, it would have been asking a lot of the judiciary to have freed themselves from the widespread mistrust of intangible harm. Yet, even today, this core value remains legally undervalued by comparison with its physical counterpart, with a renewed fear of proliferating claims superimposed on ingrained wariness. The case for viewing the negligent disruption of mental well-being as equally worthy of redress has become vulnerable to arguments about 'adding to' already extensive and costly remedial regimes.

In her seminal article on the mythology of injury and the devaluation of 'ethereal' torts,[89] Levit observed that:

> [t]he initial division of deserving and undeserving plaintiffs is the separation of those suffering physical injuries from those suffering mental injuries. Those incurring physical harms are readily compensated. Those incurring psychic harms face scepticism, heightened burdens of proof, and a history of precedents that treat the interest in emotional equilibrium as unworthy. In infliction of emotional distress cases, the injuries complained of are often presumptively treated as pre-existing flaws in the individual's psychological make-up.[90]

'The history of ethereal torts,' said Levit, 'displays a consistent and repeated pattern: the devaluation, diminishment, and dismissal of injuries to the psyche,' despite the wealth of evidence that 'it is precisely those sorts of injuries that harm people profoundly—injuries that matter the most.'[91] 'Many of the decisions rejecting recoveries for injuries to emotional equilibrium', she argues, 'seem to be statements regarding social conformity',[92] the differential treatment signalling a measure of distrust that effectively questions the authenticity of intangible injuries. Inauthenticity, though not always to be equated with fraud, easily shades into it. Clearly suspicion of fraud is one of the main strands of the 'compensation culture' as often depicted in the media. Yet, as Thomas J has observed, previous perceptions of a danger that false claims might succeed 'are today difficult to sustain in the light of developments in medical knowledge.'[93] A similar conclusion is implicit in the Government's official stance that the 'compensation culture' is a problem of perception rather than reality.[94] Granted that Levit's focus was on

---

[89] N Levit, 'Ethereal Torts' (1992) 61 *George Washington Law Review* 136.
[90] *Ibid*, 175.
[91] Above n 89, 191. Cf 'The loss of our mental health is a more fundamental violation of our sense of self than the loss of a finger.' R Stevens, *Tort Law* (Oxford, Oxford University Press, 2007) 55.
[92] Levit, above n 89, 176.
[93] *Van Soest*, above n 8, 205.
[94] 'The Government is committed to tackling perceptions of a compensation culture': Department for Constitutional Affairs, *The Law on Damages*, Consultation Paper (CP 9) (London, Department for Constitutional Affairs, 2007), 8.

intangible harm in United States jurisdictions, her account could be seen as equally, if not more, apt when applied to the more restrictive English law. The reality is that we have not sufficiently freed ourselves from the psychological and cultural attitudes of earlier times. Unfortunately, in the light of the Government's very recent review of the area, there seems to be little prospect of statutory reform in the near future.

Lingering Doubts Specific to the English Law Context

In May 2007, nearly a decade after the Law Commission's Report on *Liability for Psychiatric Illness*, there was a Governmental response from the then Department for Constitutional Affairs,[95] in the form of a Consultation Paper.[96] In an eight page chapter, the Commission's proposals for legislation were cursorily rejected.[97] The general tone was somewhat complacent about current deficiencies in the common law. We are told, for example, that because the Commission's Report was published before the House of Lords had overruled the Court of Appeal in *White*:

> the climate in which the Commission made its recommendations has to some extent changed, although it is recognised that *perceived* difficulties still exist.[98] (emphasis added)

In similar vein, we are reassured that:

> [i]t appears from subsequent case law that the courts are interpreting the requirements established in *Alcock* in a flexible and sensitive way.[99]

Most significantly, the Paper asserts that:

> [i]t is difficult at this stage to see how legislation could successfully assimilate the differing perspectives and arguments in this complex area into a simple and coherent system which would improve upon the current principles established by the courts, without running the risk of imposing rigid requirements which are not readily able to accommodate developments in medical knowledge and jurisprudence, and without opening the way to speculative and inappropriate claims.[100]

It is a curious defence of the existing framework that statutory removal of largely arbitrary, mandatory restrictions runs the risk of imposing 'rigid requirements . . . not readily able to accommodate developments in medical knowledge'. A gross mismatch of law and medicine is, after all, a major source of the prevail-

---

[95] Now the Ministry of Justice.
[96] Department for Constitutional Affairs, *The Law on Damages*, Consultation Paper, above n 94.
[97] Though consultees were invited to comment on the chapter, it was the only area on which no specific questions were put to them.
[98] See Consultation Paper, above n 94, para 83. Cf 'what [the Commission] *perceived* as the confusing and often arbitrary requirements of the current common law.' *Annex B—Psychiatric illness partial Regulatory Impact Assessment*, under Benefits, Option 1 (emphasis added).
[99] Above n 94, para 89. Cf 'Although the current need to prove a tie of love and affection could be viewed as potentially distressing and intrusive': para 88.
[100] Above n 94, para 89.

ing incoherence and inflexibility. In the very next paragraph, the Paper seeks to defend the shock requirement—a prime example of the mismatch—as having 'a practical use in that it ensures that the causation test is met', adding that '[w]ithout shock the evidential complexities of the case increase and investigating it becomes more costly.'[101] There is not a little irony in the unwillingness to countenance legislation, tersely expressed in the Paper's overall summary:

> No changes to the law are proposed in this chapter, as the Government considers it preferable to allow the courts to continue to develop the law in this area.[102]

This conclusion sits oddly with the almost universal denigration of the 'current principles' by the judiciary, the English and Scottish Law Commissions and academic commentators. It is diametrically opposed to Lord Steyn's perception of the special controls as a 'patchwork quilt of distinctions which are difficult to justify' and his view, shared by Lord Hoffmann, that reform is now only achievable by Parliament. It is dispiriting that the Department of Constitutional Affairs was content to leave development of the law on psychiatric harm to the courts, in the knowledge that the House of Lords had already declared it beyond judicial repair. The reliance on judicial development in this sphere also jars somewhat with the none too subtle general 'guidance' to judges in Part One of the Compensation Act, 2006, to rein in the scope of the standard of care. At all events, the upshot is that yet another opportunity for rationalising the legal framework seems to have been thwarted, in large measure by considerations extrinsic to legal principle.

It is unfortunate that the scope of the substantive law on liability for psychiatric illness featured in a Consultation Paper on damages which opens with the words, '[t]he Government is committed to tackling perceptions of a compensation culture . . .' *Any* loosening of the special controls would hardly be seen as a positive contribution to that overall aim. It is also noticeable that no independent or claimant organisations seem to have been directly consulted in connection with the DCA's Regulatory Impact Assessment. The National Health Service Litigation Authority (NHSLA) and the Association of British Insurers (ABI), who were consulted on the potential impact of implementing the Law Commission's proposals, provided estimates of increased costs, but no explanation is provided of how they were arrived at.[103]

Concluding Remarks

Undeniably, there are only finite resources for legal dispute resolution. However, it does not follow that assertion of a floodgates risk should, without more, determine the limits to recovery in one particular area of tort liability. Such a rigid stance begs

---

[101] Above n 94, para 90. See also paras 91–3.
[102] Above n 94, para 97.
[103] See Association of Personal Injury Lawyers, *The Law on Damages: A Response by the Association of Personal Injury Lawyers*, Jul 2007, paras 74–5.

a number of questions. It conveniently sidesteps the issue of what constitutes an acceptable or appropriate incidence of litigation, both overall and in any given sphere. Once the law itself has acknowledged the importance of a given sphere, it has to give due weight to the implications for social and individual justice of excluding meritorious claims within it. Failure to do so is an abdication of responsibility which strikes at the heart of the law's aspiration to provide justice, undermining its potential as an educative and humanising force. In the context of mental suffering, it also argues an abdication of its potential to act as an empowering and therapeutic agent.

In a political climate of railing against trivial claims and a perceived compensation culture, the immediate prospects for a more principled approach appear bleak. Yet it is too defeatist to insist that reform along the lines proposed could never find official support. For such reform to be implemented, the Government would need to be convinced that any risks, real or perceived, would be outweighed by the benefits of a fairer and more coherent liability regime. In response to the DCA's concern about legislation 'opening the way to speculative and inappropriate claims,'[104] the Association of Personal Injury Lawyers (APIL) said that:

> [i]t would ... be inequitable for people who have suffered a recognised psychiatric illness to be denied the damages to which they are entitled due to an erroneous public policy aiming to prevent a mythical eventuality.[105]

'Mythical' is perhaps too strong. Yet one can still deplore the eagerness to allay fears which have not been substantiated. And though the suggested monetary threshold for non-pecuniary loss could be interpreted in the same light, it seems likely that, as regards the disposition to sue, it would mainly reflect what already happens in practice.

In any event, we should not lose sight of the fact that a level of 'speculative and inappropriate' claiming occurs across the whole legal spectrum. It is not such an exceptional feature of claims for pure mental harm as to warrant the untenable rule structure that currently obtains. The argument that a regime rooted in 'reasonableness' would be a recipe for uncertainty would be more persuasive had the special rules provided, if not certainty, at least clear guidance. In fact their very unreasonableness is itself a source of uncertainty, as judges increasingly face an unenviable choice between reluctantly applying, reinterpreting and subverting them. The current controls cause serious harm when they deny redress to severely injured victims of negligent conduct:

> The elimination of harm which we *know* is occurring is preferable when such elimination merely creates a possibility other harm will occur.[106]

The Consultation Paper may be right to conclude that the politics of the matter dictate a precautionary approach, but that still leaves scope for reshaping the boundaries of liability in a more coherent fashion.

---

[104] DCA, above n 94, para 89.
[105] APIL, above n 103, para 71.
[106] P Bell, 'Reply to a Generous Critic' (1984) *University of Florida Law Review* 437, 445.

BIBLIOGRAPHY

Adams, G, 'The Greed behind our Compensation Culture', *The Independent*, 14 March, 2005.
American Psychiatric Association, *Diagnostic and Statistical Manual of Mental Disorders* (Washington DC, American Psychiatric Association, 4th edn, TR 2000).
Appleyard, B, 'Living Dangerously in our Dreams', *The Independent*, 26 July, 1995.
Ashworth, A, 'Victim's Rights, Defendant's Rights and Criminal Procedure', in A Crawford and J Goodey (eds), *Integrating a Victim Perspective within Criminal Justice* (Aldershot, Ashgate, 2000) ch 9.
Association of Personal Injury Lawyers, *The Law on Damages: A Response by the Association of Personal Injury Lawyers*, July, 2007.
Atiyah, PS, 'Personal Injuries in the Twenty First Century: Thinking the Unthinkable', in P Birks (ed), *Wrongs and Remedies in the Twenty First Century* (Oxford, Clarendon Press, 1996).
—— *The Damages Lottery* (Oxford, Hart Publishing, 1997).
Baker, MG, and Menken, M, 'Time to abandon the term mental illness' (2001) *British Medical Journal*; 322: 937.
Bell, P, 'The Bell Tolls: Towards Full Tort Recovery for Psychic Injury' (1984) 36 *University of Florida Law Review* 333.
Bell, P, 'Reply to a Generous Critic' (1984) 36 *University of Florida Law Review* 437.
Berry, L, et al, *Risk, Responsibility and Regulation: Whose risk is it anyway?* (London, Better Regulation Commission, 2006).
Better Regulation Task Force, *Better Routes to Redress* (London, Better Regulation Task Force, 2004).
Birks, P, *Harassment and Hubris: The Right to an Equality of Respect* (John Maurice Kelly Memorial Lecture, University College Dublin, 1996).
—— (ed), *Wrongs and Remedies in the Twenty-First Century* (Oxford, Oxford University Press, 1996).
Block, N, and Doherty, B, 'Personal Injury: a cultural myth' (youclaim.co.uk).
Bohlen, FH, *Studies in the Law of Torts* (Indianapolis, Ind, Bobbs-Merrill, 1926) 254 (reprinted in (1902) 41 *American Law Register (NS)* 141).
Bracken, P, *Trauma: Culture, Meaning and Philosophy* (London, Whurr, 2002).
Brooks, C, *Lawyers, Litigation and English Society since 1450* (London, Hambledon Press, 1998).
—— 'The Longitudinal Study of Civil Litigation in England 1200–1996', in W Prest and S Anleu, *Litigation: Past and Present* (Sydney, University of New South Wales Press, 2004).
Bryant, B, Mayou, R, and Lloyd-Bostock, S, 'Compensation Claims following Road Accidents: a six-year follow-up study', (1997) 37 *Medicine, Science and the Law* 326.
Butler, D, 'Proximity as a Determinant of Duty: The Nervous Shock Litmus Test' (1995) 21 *Monash University Law Review* 159.

Butler, D, 'Identifying the Compensable Damage in "Nervous Shock" Cases' (1997) 5 *Torts Law Journal* 67.
—— 'An Assessment of Competing Policy Considerations in Cases of Psychiatric Injury Resulting from Negligence' (2002) 10 *Torts Law Journal* 13.
—— *Damages for Psychiatric Injuries* (Sydney, The Federation Press, 2004).
Byrne, P, 'Psychiatric Stigma: Past, Passing and to Come', *Journal of the Royal Society of Medicine* 1997; 90: 618.
Cane, P, *Responsibility in Law and Morality* (Oxford, Hart Publishing, 2002).
—— *Atiyah's Accidents, Compensation and the Law* (London, Butterworths, 6th edn, 1999).
—— *Atiyah's Accidents, Compensation and the Law* (Cambridge, Cambridge University Press, 7th edn, 2006).
Capper, D, 'Damages for Distress and Disappointment—The Limits of *Watts v Morrow*' (2000) 116 *LQR* 553.
—— 'Damages for Distress and Disappointment—Problem Solved?' (2002) 118 *LQR* 193.
Case, P, 'Curiouser and Curiouser: Psychiatric damage caused by negligent misinformation' (2002) 18 *Professional Negligence* 248.
—— 'The Scottish Law Commission's *Discussion Paper on Damages for Psychiatric Injury*' (2003) 19 *Professional Negligence* 395.
—— 'Hues of Foreseeability: Employer liability for chronic stress and the impact of *Barber*' (2004) 20 *Professional Negligence* 192.
Catala, P, and Weir, JA, 'Delict and Torts: A Study in Parallel (Part III)' (1964) 38 *Tulane Law Review* 663.
Chapman, B, 'Wrongdoing, Welfare, and Damages Recovery for Non-Pecuniary Loss in Corrective Justice', in DG Owen (ed), *Philosophical Foundations of Tort Law* (Oxford, Oxford University Press, 1995).
Clevenger, SV, *Spinal Concussion* (Philadelphia & London, FA Davis, 1889).
Cohen RI, and Pfeffer, JM, 'Accident Neurosis Revisited' (1987) 27 *Medicine, Science and the Law* 177.
Conaghan, J, and Mansell, W, 'From the Permissive to the Dismissive Society: Patrick Atiyah's Accidents, Compensation and the Market' (1988) 25 *Journal of Law and Society* 284.
Cooke, R, Sir, 'Tort Illusions', in PD Finn (ed), *Essays on Torts* (Sydney, Law Book Co, 1989) ch 4.
Crisp, A, 'The tendency to stigmatise', *British Journal of Psychiatry* 2001; 178: 197
Crisp, A, *et al*, 'Stigmatisation of people with mental illnesses', *British Journal of Psychiatry* 2000; 177: 4.
Croner's *Employment Briefing*, issue 82, 30 May, 1995.
Davies, M, 'The End of the Affair: Duty of Care and Liability Insurance' (1989) 9 *Legal Studies* 67.
Deakin, S, Johnston, A, and Markesinis, B, *Markesinis and Deakin's Tort Law* (Oxford, Oxford University Press, 6th edn, 2008).
Department for Constitutional Affairs, *The Report of the Lord Chancellor's Committee to Investigate the Activities of Non-Legally Qualified Claims Assessors and Employment Advisers* (London, Department of Constitutional Affairs, 2000).
—— *The Law on Damages*, Consultation Paper (CP 9) (London, Department for Constitutional Affairs, 2007).
Department of Health, *General Public Attitudes to Mental Health/Illness* (London, Department of Health, 1999).

Department of Social Security, *Memorandum of Evidence to the Social Security Select Committee* (1995) HC 196.
Department of the Treasury, *Review of the Law of Negligence: Final Report* (Canberra, Department of the Treasury, 2002) ('Ipp Report').
Descartes, R, *Discourse on Method and the Meditations* (FE Sutcliffe, ed) (London, Penguin Books, 1968).
Doak, J, 'The Victim and the Criminal Process: an analysis of recent trends in regional and international tribunals' (2003) 23 *Legal Studies* 1, 31.
Dobbs, D, *The Law of Torts* (St Paul, West Group, 2000).
Dolding, L, and Mullender, R, 'Law, Labour and Mental Health' (1996) 59 *MLR* 296.
Dwyer, JL, 'The Vernon Saga' (1998) 6 *Tort Law Review* 91.
Earengey, WG, 'The Legal Consequences of Shock', reprinted in (1992) 60 *Medico-Legal Journal* 83 (first appeared in vol of the *Medico-Legal and Criminological Review* (1933)).
Eastman, N, 'Case Study: Psychiatric Injury', *Medical Negligence Update*, Conference Paper (London, IBC Legal Studies and Services Ltd, 1996).
Erez, E, 'Who's Afraid of the Big Bad Victim? Victim Impact Statements as Victim Empowerment and Enhancement of Justice' (1999) *Crim LR* 545.
Erichsen, JE, *On Railway and Other Injuries of the Nervous System* (Philadelphia, Henry C Lea, 1866).
—— *On the Concussion of the Spine, Nervous Shock and Other Obscure Injuries of the Nervous System* (New York, William Wood and Co, 1875).
Evans, RW, 'The Effects of Litigation on Treatment Outcome with Personal Injury Patients' (1994) *American Journal of Forensic Psychology* 12; 4: 19.
Fairgrieve, D, 'Pushing back the Boundaries of Public Authority Liability: Tort Law Enters the Classroom' (2002) *PL* 288.
Falconer, Lord, 'Compensation Culture': Speech at the Insurance Times Conference, 10 November, 2004.
Feinberg, J, *Harm to Others* (New York, Oxford University Press, 1984).
Fenn, P, *et al*, *The Funding of Personal Injury Litigation: comparisons over time and across jurisdictions* (Department for Constitutional Affairs Research Series, Feb 2006).
Fleming, JG, 'Remoteness and Duty: The Control Devices in Liability for Negligence' (1953) 31 *Canadian Bar Review* 471.
—— *Introduction to the Law of Torts* (Oxford, Clarendon Press, 1967).
—— 'Distant Shock in Germany and Elsewhere' (1972) *American Journal of Comparative Law* 485.
—— (1994) 2 *Tort Law Review* 202 (Review of Mullany and Handford, *Tort Liability for Psychiatric Damage*, 1st edn, 1993).
—— *The Law of Torts* (Sydney, LBC Information Services, 9th edn, 1998).
Freckleton, I, 'New Directions in Compensability for Psychiatric Injuries', *Psychiatry, Psychology and Law*, vol 9; 2002, 271.
Fulbrook, J, *Outdoor Activities, Negligence and the Law* (Aldershot, Ashgate, 2005).
Fulcher, G, 'Litigation-induced Trauma Sensitisation (LITS)—A Potential Negative Outcome of the Process of Litigation', (2004) *Psychiatry, Psychology and Law* vol 11, 79.
Furedi, F, *Courting Mistrust: The hidden growth of a culture of litigation in Britain* (London, Centre for Policy Studies, 1999).
—— *Culture of Fear* (London, Continuum, 2002).
Galanter, M, 'Real World Torts: An Antidote to Anecdotes' (1996) 55 *Maryland Law Review* 1093.

Gardner, J, 'Stalking' (1998) 114 *LQR* 33.
Geffin, M, 'Practice trends: personal injury', *Solicitors' Journal*, 13 April, 2007, 448.
Gelder, M, *et al*, *Oxford Textbook of Psychiatry* (Oxford, Oxford University Press, 3rd edn, 1996).
Genn, H, *Paths to Justice* (Oxford, Hart Publishing, 1999).
Gilbert, E, 'The ATE Legal Expenses Insurance Marketplace: An Overview' (2004) *Journal of Personal Injury Law* 99.
Giliker, P, 'A "New" Head of Damages: Damages for Mental Distress in the English Law of Torts' (2000) 20 *Legal Studies* 19.
Gill, T, 'Pearson: Implications for Victims of Industrial Accidents', in DK Allen, CJ Bourn, and JH Holyoak, *Accident Compensation after Pearson* (London, Sweet & Maxwell, 1979).
Glassner, B, *The Culture of Fear*, Washington Center for Consumer Law (New York, Basic Books, 1999).
Godefroi, H, 'On Compensation for Railway Injuries', *Papers Read before the Juridical Society: 1863–70*, vol 3, 689.
Goffman, E, *Stigma: Notes on the Management of Spoiled Identity* (New York, Prentice, 1963).
Goodhart, AL, 'The Shock Cases and Area of Risk' (1953) 16 *MLR* 14.
—— 'Emotional Shock and the Unimaginative Taxicab Driver' (1953) 69 *LQR* 347.
Greer, DS, 'A Statutory Remedy for Nervous Shock?' (1986) 21 *Irish Jurist (NS)* 57.
Gross, R, *Psychology: The Science of Mind and Behaviour* (London, Hodder & Stoughton, 3rd edn, 1996).
Halligan, PW, Bass, C, and Oakley, DA, (eds), *Malingering and Illness Deception* (New York, Oxford University Press, 2003).
Haltom, W, and McCann, M, *Distorting the Law: Politics, Media and the Litigation Crisis* (Chicago, University of Chicago Press, 2004).
Handford, P, 'Psychiatric Injury in the Workplace' (1999) 7 *Tort Law Review* 126.
—— 'Work Stress: Retreat or Revolution?' (2005) 13 *Tort Law Review* 159.
—— *Mullany and Handford's Tort Liability for Psychiatric Damage* (Sydney, Lawbook Co, 2nd edn, 2006).
—— 'Psychiatric Injury in Breach of a Relationship' (2007) 27 *Legal Studies* 26.
Harris, D, *et al*, *Compensation and Support for Illness and Injury* (Oxford, Clarendon Press, 1984).
Harris, D, Campbell D, and Halson, R, *Remedies in Contract and Tort* (London, Butterworths, 2nd edn, 2002).
Harvard Medical Practice Study Group, *Patients, Doctors and Lawyers: Medical Injury, Malpractice Litigation and Patient Compensation in New York* (Cambridge, Mass, Harvard University, 1990).
Haslum, MN, 'Dyslexia' in RL Gregory, (ed), *The Oxford Companion to the Mind* (Oxford, Oxford University Press, 2nd edn, 2004).
Havard, J, 'Reasonable Foresight of Shock' (1956) 19 *MLR* 478.
Hayward, P, and Bright, J, 'Stigma and mental illness: a review and critique', *Journal of Mental Health* 1997; 6: 345.
Health and Safety Commission, 'Health and Safety Statistics for 2005/2006 for Great Britain' (www.hse.gov.uk/statistics/overpic.htm).
Health and Safety Executive, *Stress at Work: A Guide for Employees* (London, HMSO, 1995).
—— 'Stress-related and Psychological Disorders' (http://www.hse.gov.uk/statistics/causdis/stress.htm).

Heffey, P, 'The Negligent Infliction of Nervous Shock in Road and Industrial Accidents (Part II)' (1974) 48 *Australian Law Journal* 240.

Hilson, C, 'Liability for Psychiatric Injury: primary and secondary victims revisited' (2002) 18 *Professional Negligence* 167.

Hirst, M, 'Assault, Battery and Indirect Violence' (1999) *Crim LR* 557.

Home Office, *Violence: Reforming the Offences Against the Person Act 1861* (London, Home Office, 1998).

Horder, J, 'Rethinking Non-Fatal Offences against the Person' (1994) 14 *OJLS* 335.

House of Commons, Constitutional Affairs Committee, *Compensation Culture: Third Report of Session 2005-06*.

House of Lords Select Committee on Economic Affairs (2006), *Government Policy on the Management of Risk*, Fifth Report, HL 183–1, June 2006.

Howarth, D, *Textbook on Tort* (London, Butterworths, 1995).

—— in K, Oliphant, (ed), *The Law of Tort* (London, LexisNexis Butterworths, 2nd edn, 2007) ch 12.

Howarth, D, and O'Sullivan, JA, *Hepple, Howarth and Matthews' Tort: Cases and Materials* (London, Butterworths, 5th edn, 2000).

Hughes, D, 'Pearson: Implications in Road Accident Cases', in DK Allen, CJ Bourn, and JH Holyoak, (eds) *Accident Compensation after Pearson* (London, Sweet & Maxwell, 1979).

Humphrey, N, *Soul Searching: Human Nature and Supernatural Belief* (London, Chatto & Windus, 1995).

Ibbetson, D, *A Historical Introduction to the Law of Obligations* (Oxford, Oxford University Press, 1999).

Ingber, S, 'Rethinking Intangible Injuries: A Focus on Remedy' (1985) 73 *California Law Review* 772.

Ipp, D, 'Policy and the swing of the negligence pendulum' (2003) 77 *Australian Law Journal* 732.

Jones, M, 'Liability for Psychiatric Illness—More Principle, Less Subtlety?' (1995) 4 *Web Journal of Current Legal Issues*.

—— *Medical Negligence* (London, Sweet & Maxwell, 3rd edn, 2003).

—— 'Liability for Psychiatric Damage: Searching for a Path between Pragmatism and Principle', in J Neyers, E Chamberlain and S Pitel (eds), *Emerging Issues in Tort Law* (Oxford, Hart Publishing, 2007).

Judicial Studies Board, *Guidelines for the Assessment of General Damages in Personal Injury Cases* (London, Blackstone Press, 1st edn, 1992)

—— *Guidelines for the Assessment of General Damages in Personal Injury Cases* (Oxford, Oxford University Press, 8th edn, 2006).

Kendell, RE, 'The distinction between mental and physical illness' (2001) *British Journal of Psychiatry* 2001; 178: 490.

Kerr, T, 'The Broadening Notion of Psychological Injury in Tort Subsequent to the *Phelps* Litigation' (2004): http://www.kbw.com.

Koch, WJ, *et al*, 'What's the Damage?' *Solicitors Journal Expert Witness Supplement* (Summer 2004) 5.

Kostal, RW, *Law and English Railway Capitalism 1825–1875* (Oxford, Oxford University Press, 1994).

Law Commission, No 218, *Legislating the Criminal Code: Offences against the Person and General Principles* (London, HMSO, 1993).

Law Commission, Consultation Paper No 137, *Liability for Psychiatric Illness* (London, HMSO, 1995).
—— Consultation Paper No 140, *Damages for Personal Injury: Non-Pecuniary Loss* (London, HMSO, 1995).
—— No 247, *Aggravated, Exemplary and Restitutionary Damages* (London, HMSO, 1997).
—— No 249, *Liability for Psychiatric Illness* (London, HMSO, 1998).
—— No 257, *Damages for Personal Injury: Non-Pecuniary Loss* (London, HMSO, 1999).
—— No 263, *Claims for Wrongful Death* (London, HMSO, 1999).
Lawson, M, 'The baloney over Barney', *The Guardian*, 15 June, 2007.
Lawton, F, Sir, 'A Judicial View of Traumatic Neurosis' (1979) 47 *Medico-Legal Journal* 6.
Legge, D, *An Introduction to Psychological Science* (London, Methuen, 1975).
Leibson, DJ, 'Recovery of Damages for Emotional Distress Caused by Physical Injury to Another' (1976–77) 15 *Journal of Family Law* 163.
Letwin, O, 'Nothing Ventured Nothing Gained', speech to Centre for Policy Studies, 3 Nov, 2004.
Levit, N, 'Ethereal Torts' (1992) 61 *George Washington Law Review* 136.
Lewis, R, 'Increasing the Price of Pain: Damages, the Law Commission and *Heil v Rankin*' (2001) 64 *MLR* 100.
—— 'Insurance and the Tort System' (2005) 25 *Legal Studies* 85.
Lewis, R, Morris, A, and Oliphant, K, 'Tort Personal Injury Claims Statistics: Is there a Compensation Culture in the United Kingdom?' (2006) 14 *Torts Law Journal* 158.
Lunney, M, and Oliphant, K, *Tort Law: Test and Materials* (Oxford, Oxford University Press, 3rd edn, 2007).
Magruder, C, 'Mental and Emotional Disturbance in the Law of Torts' (1936) 49 *Harvard Law Review* 1033.
Maguire, M, and Bennett, T, *Burglary in a Dwelling* (London, Heinemann, 1982).
Mahendra, B, 'Mind and Body: Medicine and Law', in MDA Freeman and A Lewis (eds), *Law and Medicine: Current Legal Issues vol 3* (Oxford, Oxford University Press, 2000) 559.
Matthews, E, 'Mental and Physical Illness—An Unsustainable Separation?', in N Eastman and J Peay, *Law Without Enforcement: Integrating Mental Health and Justice* (Oxford, Hart Publishing, 1999).
Mayou, R, Tyndel, S, and Bryant, B, 'Long-term outcome of motor vehicle accident injury' (1997) *Psychosomatic Medicine* 59(6), 578.
McBride, NJ, and Bagshaw, R, *Tort Law* (Harlow, Longman, 2nd edn, 2005).
McCormick, CT, *Handbook on the Law of Damages* (St Paul, Minn, West Publishing Co, 1935).
McHugh, Justice, 'Neighbourhood, Proximity and Reliance', in PD Finn (ed), *Essays on Torts* (Sydney, Law Book Co, 1989) ch 2.
McIvor, C, 'Liability for Psychiatric Harm' (2007) 23 *Professional Negligence* 249.
Mendelson, D, *The Interfaces of Medicine and Law* (Aldershot, Dartmouth Publishing Co, 1998).
—— 'English Medical Experts and the Claims for Shock Occasioned by Railway Collisions in the 1860s—Issues of Law, Ethics, and Medicine', (2002) 25 *International Journal of Law and Psychiatry*, 303.
Mendelson, G, 'Outcome-related compensation: in search of a new paradigm', in PW Halligan, C Bass and DA Oakley (eds), *Malingering and Illness Deception* (New York, Oxford University Press, 2003) ch 17.
Miller, H, 'Accident Neurosis', *British Medical Journal* 1, 919, 992 (1961).

—— 'Mental After-effects of Head Injury', *Proceedings of the Royal Society of Medicine* (1966) 59, 257.

Millward Brown, *Effects of Advertising in respect of Compensation Claims for Personal Injuries* (London, Department for Constitutional Affairs, 2006).

Ministry of Justice, *Pleural Plaques*, Consultation Paper (CP 14) (London, Ministry of Justice, 2008).

Moorhead, R, 'Conditional Fee Agreements, Legal Aid and Access to Justice' (2000) 33(2) *University of British Columbia Law Review* 471.

Morgan, J, 'Tort, Insurance and Incoherence' (2004) 67 *MLR* 384.

Morris, A, 'Spiralling or Stabilising? The Compensation Culture and Our Propensity to Claim Damages for Personal Injury' (2007) 70 *MLR* 349.

Mullany, NJ, 'Psychiatric damage in the House of Lords—Fourth time unlucky: *Page v Smith*' (1995) 3 *Journal of Law and Medicine* 112.

—— 'Fear for the Future: Liability for Infliction of Psychiatric Disorder' in Mullany (ed), *Torts in the Nineties* (Sydney, LBC Information Services, 1997).

—— 'Negligently Inflicted Psychiatric Injury and the Means of Communication of Trauma—Should it Matter?', in NJ Mullany and AM Linden (eds), *Torts Tomorrow— A Tribute to John Fleming* (Sydney, LBC Information Services, 1998).

Mullany, NJ, and Handford, P, *Tort Liability for Psychiatric Damage* (Sydney, Lawbook Co, 1st edn, 1993).

—— 'Hillsborough Replayed' (1997) 113 *LQR* 410.

—— 'Moving the Boundary Stone by Statute—the Law Commission on Psychiatric Illness' (1999) 22 *University of New South Wales Law Journal* 350.

Mullender, R, 'Negligence Law and Blame Culture: a critical response to a possible problem' (2006) 22 *Professional Negligence* 2.

Mullender, R, and Speirs, A, 'Negligence, Psychiatric Injury, and the Altruism Principle' (2000) 20 *OJLS* 645.

Njoya, W, 'Employment, Implicit Contracts and the Duty of Care' (2005) 121 *LQR* 33.

Nolan, D, 'Recovering Damages for Psychiatric Injury at Work' (1995) 24 *Industrial Law Journal* 280.

—— 'Reforming Liability for Psychiatric Injury in Scotland: A Recipe for Uncertainty?' (2005) *MLR* 983.

—— 'New Forms of Damage in Negligence' (2007) 70 *MLR* 59.

Nolan, VE, and Ursin, E, 'Negligent Infliction of Emotional Distress: Coherence Emerging from Chaos' (1982) 33 *Hastings Law Journal* 583.

O'Sullivan, J, 'Liability for fear of the onset of future medical conditions' (1999) 15 *Professional Negligence* 96.

Page, HW, *Injuries of the Spine and Spinal Cord Without Apparent Mechanical Lesion and Nervous Shock in their Surgical and Medical Aspects* (London, J and A Churchill, 1883).

Parsons, C, *An Analysis of Current Problems in the UK Liability Insurance Market* (Office of Fair Trading: Supplemental Report, 2003).

Partlett, D, 'Tort Liability and the American Way: Reflections on Liability for Emotional Distress' (1997) 45 *American Journal of Comparative Law* 171.

Pearson, RN, 'Liability for Negligently Inflicted Psychic Harm: A Response to Professor Bell' (1984) 36 *University of Florida Law Review* 413.

Peysner, J, 'Compensation Crazy: Do We Blame and Claim Too Much?' in E Lee *et al*, *Compensation Crazy: Do We Blame and Claim Too Much?* (London, Hodder & Stoughton, 2002).

Phillips, Lord, 'Liability for Psychiatric Injury', Personal Injuries Bar Association Annual Lecture (2004).
Pickvance, S, 'A Little Compensation', *Hazards* 90, May 2005.
Pleasance, P, *Report of the Case Profiling Study, Personal Injury Litigation in Practice, Research Paper 3*, Legal Aid Board Research Unit (1998).
Pleasance, P, et al, *Causes of Action: Civil Law and Social Justice* (London, Legal Services Commission, 2004).
Pollard, C, 'Victims and the Criminal Justice System: A new Vision' (2000) *Crim LR* 5.
Radin, MJ, 'Compensation and Commensurability' (1993) 43 *Duke Law Journal* 56.
Rodger, Lord, 'Law and Medicine: an Odd Couple?' Personal Injuries Bar Association, *Newsline* (2006) 3.
Rogers, L, 'The End of Risk', *New Statesman*, 30 July, 2007, 34.
Rogers, T, 'Diagnostic validity and psychiatric expert testimony' *International Journal of Law and Psychiatry* (2004) 27, 281.
Rogers, WVH, *Winfield and Jolowicz on Tort* (London, Sweet & Maxwell, 17th edn, 2006).
Royal Commission on Civil Liability and Compensation for Personal Injury ('Pearson Report') (London, HMSO, 1978) Cmnd 7054 ('Pearson Commission').
Ryle, G, *The Concept of Mind* (London, Hutchinson, 1949).
Saks, M, 'Do We Really Know Anything About the Behaviour of the Tort Litigation System—And Why Not?' (1992) 140 *University of Pennsylvania Law Review* 1147.
Sanders, A, et al, 'Victim Impact Statements: Don't Work, Can't Work' (2001) Crim LR 447.
Sartorius, T, et al, 'Progress towards Achieving a Common Language in Psychiatry' *American Journal of Psychiatry* (1995) 152, 1427.
Scottish Law Commission, *Discussion Paper on Damages for Psychiatric Injury* (Edinburgh, The Stationery Office, 2002) No 120.
—— *Report on Damages for Psychiatric Injury* (Edinburgh, The Stationery Office, 2004) No 196.
Sherman, P, 'The Pearson Report and Insurance', in DK Allen, CJ Bourn and JH Holyoak, *Accident Compensation after Pearson* (London, Sweet & Maxwell, 1979).
Skene, L, and Luntz, H, 'Effects of Tort Law Reform on Medical Liability' (2005) 79 *Australian Law Journal* 345.
Simister, AP, and Sullivan, GR, *Criminal Law: Theory and Doctrine* (Oxford, Hart Publishing, 3rd edn, 2007).
Smith, H, 'Relation of Emotions to Injury and Disease: Legal Liability for Psychic Stimuli' (1944) 30 *Virginia Law Review* 193.
Spigelman AC, Chief Justice of New South Wales, 'Negligence: The Last Outpost of the Welfare State' (2002) 76 *Australian Law Journal* 432.
—— 'Negligence and Insurance Premiums: Recent Changes in Australian Law' (2003) 11 *Torts Law Journal* 91.
—— 'Tort Law Reform: An Overview' (2006) 14 *Tort Law Review* 5.
Spinoza, B, *Ethics* (1677) (Oxford, Oxford University Press, 4th edn,1937, tr W Hale, revised edn, A Hutchinson Stirling).
Sprince, A, '*Page* v *Smith*—being "primary" colours House of Lords' Judgment' (1995) 11 *Professional Negligence* 124.
—— 'Negligently Inflicted Psychiatric Damage: A Medical Diagnosis and Prognosis' (1998) 18 *Legal Studies* 59.
—— 'Malingering and the Law: a third way?', in PW Halligan, C Bass, and DA Oakley (eds), *Malingering and Illness Deception* (New York, Oxford University Press, 2003) ch 18.

Stapleton, J, *Disease and the Compensation Debate* (Oxford, Clarendon Press, 1987).
—— 'The Gist of Negligence', (1988) *LQR* 213.
—— 'In Restraint of Tort', in P Birks (ed), *The Frontiers of Liability*, vol 2 (Oxford, Oxford University Press, 1994) ch 7.
Steele, J, 'Scepticism and the Law of Negligence' (1993) 52 *CLJ* 437.
—— ' "Breach of Duty Causing Harm?" Recent Encounters between Negligence and Risk', in *Current Legal Problems 2007* (Oxford, Oxford University Press, 2007) Vol 60.
—— *Tort Law: Text, Cases, and Materials* (Oxford, Oxford University Press, 2007).
Stevens, R, *Tort Law* (Oxford, Oxford University Press, 2007).
Steyn, Lord, *Perspectives of Corrective and Distributive Justice in Tort Law*: John Maurice Kelly Memorial Lecture (University College Dublin, Faculty of Law, 2002).
Summerfield, D, 'Does Psychiatry Stigmatize?', *Journal of the Royal Society of Medicine*, 2001; 94: 148.
—— 'The invention of post-traumatic stress disorder and the social usefulness of a psychiatric category', *British Medical Journal* 2001; 322: 95.
Tarsh, MJ, and Royston, C, 'A Follow-up Study of Accident Neurosis', *British Journal of Psychiatry*, 1985; 146: 18.
Taylor, Lord Justice, *Interim Report on the Hillsborough Stadium Disaster* (London, HMSO, 1989) Cmnd 3878.
Teff, H, 'Liability for Negligently Inflicted Nervous Shock' (1983) 99 *LQR* 100.
—— 'Liability for Psychiatric Illness after Hillsborough' (1992) 12 *OJLS* 440.
—— 'The Requirement of "Sudden Shock" in Liability for Negligently Inflicted Psychiatric Damage' (1996) 4 *Tort Law Review* 44.
—— 'Liability for Negligently Inflicted Psychiatric Harm: Justifications and Boundaries' (1998) 57 *CLJ* 91.
—— 'No More "Shock, Horror"? The Declining Significance of "Sudden Shock" and the "Horrifying Event", in Psychiatric Injury Claims' in S McLean (ed), *First Do No Harm: Law, Ethics and Healthcare* (Aldershot, Ashgate, 2006).
Tennant, C, 'Liability for Psychiatric Injury: an Evidence-based Approach' (2002) 76 *Australian Law Journal* 73.
The Times, Editorial, 29 November, 1991
—— Editorial, 24 April, 1999.
Trindade, F, 'The Principles Governing the Recovery of Damages for Negligently Caused Nervous Shock' (1986) 45 *CLJ* 476.
—— 'Nervous Shock and Negligent Conduct' (1996) 112 *LQR* 22.
Toynbee, P, 'A Culture of Compensation Makes Victims of us All', *The Guardian*, 21 April, 1999.
Ursano, RJ, Lang, BG, and Fullerton, CS, 'The Structure of Human Chaos', in Ursano, Lang and Fullerton (eds), *Individual and Community Responses to Trauma and Disaster: The Structure of Human Chaos* (Cambridge, Cambridge University Press, 1994).
Vincent, C, and Robertson, IH, 'Recovering from a Medical Accident: the Consequences for Patients and their Families', in C Vincent, M Ennis and RJ Audley, *Medical Accidents* (Oxford, Oxford University Press,1993).
von Hirsch, A, et al, (eds), *Restorative Justice and Criminal Justice: Competing or Reconcilable Paradigms* (Oxford, Hart Publishing, 2003).
Wainwright, D, and Calnan, M, *Work Stress: The making of a modern epidemic* (Buckingham, Open University Press, 2002).
Weinrib, EJ, *The Idea of Private Law* (Cambridge, Mass, Harvard University Press, 1995).

Weir, T, *A Casebook on Tort* (London, Sweet & Maxwell, 7th edn, 1992).
—— [1993] *CLJ* 520 (Review of Mullany and Handford, *Tort Liability for Psychiatric Damage*, 1st edn, 1993).
—— 'Errare Humanum Est', in P Birks (ed), *The Frontiers of Liability*, vol 2 (Oxford, Oxford University Press, 1994).
Wessely, S, 'Liability for Psychiatric Illness' (1995) 39 *Journal of Psychosomatic Research* 659.
Weston, C, 'Suing in Tort for Loss of Computer Data' (1999) 58 CLJ 67.
Wheat, K, *Napier and Wheat's Recovering Damages for Psychiatric Injury* (Oxford, Oxford University Press, 2nd edn, 2002).
—— 'Mental Health in the Workplace (1)—"Stress" Claims and Workplace Standards and the European Framework Directive on Health and Safety at Work' (2006) *Journal of Mental Health Law* 53.
White, RCA, and Atkinson, R, 'Personal Injury Litigation, Conditional Fees and After-the-Event Insurance' (2000) *Civil Justice Quarterly* 118.
White, T, and Melville, A, 'Hey, but who's counting?: the metrics and politics of trends in civil litigation' in W Prest and SR Anleu (eds), *Litigation: Past and Present* (Sydney, University of New South Wales Press, 2004) ch 6.
Wightman, J, 'The Limits of the Rules on Recovery for Psychiatric Damage in the United Kingdom' (2000) 8 *Tort Law Review* 169.
Williams, K, 'State of Fear: Britain's "Compensation Culture" Reviewed' (2005) 25 *Legal Studies* 499.
Witting, C, 'Physical Damage in Negligence' (2002) 61 *CLJ* 189.
—— *Liability for Negligent Misstatements* (Oxford, Oxford University Press, 2004).
—— 'Duty of Care: An Analytical Approach' (2005) 25 *OJLS* 33.
World Health Organisation, *International Classification of Diseases and Related Health Problems* (Geneva, World Health Organisation, 10th Revision, vol 1, 1993).
Wright, EW, *National Trends in Personal Injury Litigation: Before and After 'Ipp'* (Canberra, Australia, 2006).
Yarrow, S, *The Price of Success: Lawyers, Clients and Conditional Fees* (London: Policy Studies Institute, 1997).
Zurich Municipal, *Perception and Reality: The real risks for public service and charitable organisations* (Zurich Insurance Company, 2007).

INDEX

Accident-based psychiatric illness
  aftermath 69
  Alcock 66–72, 74
  Anns test 65–66
  distributive justice 91–96
  immediate aftermath 69
  McLoughlin v O'Brian 59–64
  mode of communication 69–70
  nervous shock 7–8, 60
  Page v Smith 74–75, 77–83
  policy considerations 65–66
  primary victims 75–83
  proximity of relationship 68–69
  rescuers 83–92
  secondary victims 75–83
  sudden and gradual assaults on the nervous system 70–74
  White v Chief Constable of South Yorkshire 74–75, 86–96
After-the-event insurance
  compensation culture 153–55
Aftermath
  accident-based psychiatric illness 69
  Australia 131
  Hillsborough football ground disaster 3, 69
  nervous shock 60
Aggravated damages
  negligence 29
  tort 29
Adjustment disorders
  classification 6
American Psychiatric Association (DSM-IV) 6, 7
Anns test
  accident-based psychiatric illness 65–66
Anxiety disorders
  classification 6
Australia
  abnormal sensitivity 132
  aftermath 131
  bars to recovery 133–35
  insurance crisis 135
  Ipp Report 135, 136
  legislative developments 135–37
  lessons to be learnt from 137–38
  limiting devices, use of 131–32
  negligence 133
  non-standard cases 132
  personal injury litigation trends 137
  psychiatric harm 130–139
  reasonable forseeability 131, 132, 133
  recognisable psychiatric illness 130–31
  reform proposals 174
  secondary victims 136
  sudden shock 133

Bereavement awards
  fatal accidents 21
Blame and claim culture 18–20
Breach of contract
  common law 26–28
  mental harm 26–28

Canada
  reform proposals 172–74
Claims management companies
  compensation culture 20, 153
Common law
  breach of contract 26–28
  harm
    development of liability 43–54
    early legal views 40–41
    historical development 37–39
    minimum actionable harm 37–39
    nervous shock, development of liability for 43–54
    overview of nervous shock cases 54–56
    'railway spine' 41–43
    recognised psychiatric illness 52–54
    Victorian era 41–43
  historical development 37–39
  mental harm 26–31
  tort, damages in 28–31
Communication of bad news
  fear for the future 109–13
  negligence 103–109
Compensation culture
  addressing perception 33–34
  after-the-event insurance 153–55
  blame and claim culture 18–20
  claims handling 153–55
  claims management companies 20, 153
  conditional fees 20, 153–54
  development 2
  frequency of claims 155–66
  insurance companies 154

Compensation culture (*cont.*):
  Legal Aid 20, 153
  personal injury 20
  reform proposals 176
  use of expression 20
Conditional fees
  compensation culture 20, 153–54
Criminal law
  adversarial process 32–33
  comparisons 31–33
  mind-body distinction in 32
  offences against the person 31–32
  protection from harassment 32
  restorative justice 33
  victims' rights 33

Damages
  assessment of 178–79
  compensation 30–31
  non-pecuniary loss 179–83
Depressive illness
  classification 6
Diagnosis
  mental harm 4
  physical injury 4
  policy considerations 143–45
  recognisable psychiatric illness 144–45
  uncertainty 143–45
Direct perception
  Hillsborough football ground disaster 3, 4
Discrimination cases
  emotional harm 21
  injury to feelings 21
  structure of law 21
DSM-IV 6, 7
Dualism 11
Duration of harm
  reform proposals 176–77
Duty of care
  nervous shock 47

Emotional distress
  United States 5, 174–75
Emotional harm
  approach of law to 2
  discrimination cases 21
  embracing liability for 20–31, 173–75
  fatal accidents 21
  legal overreach 33–34
  meaning 5
  minor harm
    mental and emotional harm 4–5
    recovery of damages for 2
  modern statutory developments 20–22
  pure emotional harm 2
  recognised psychiatric illness 5
  stigmatisation of 12–18

False imprisonment 28
Fatal accidents
  bereavement awards 21
  emotional harm 21
Floodgates argument
  policy issues 149–51
  psychiatric harm 165–66
  tort 29–30
Frequency of claims
  employees' claims 161–65
  personal injury claims 155–58
  psychiatric harm 158–61

Harm
  categorisation
    generally 1–4
    ICD–10 6, 7
    legal problems 7–10
    medical problems 5–7
    mental and emotional harm 4–5
    problems 5–10
  common law
    development of liability 43–54
    early legal views 40–41
    historical development 37–39
    minimum actionable harm 37–39
    nervous shock, development of liability for 43–54
    overview of nervous shock cases 54–56
    'railway spine' 41–43
    recognised psychiatric illness 52–54
    Victorian era 41–43
  DSM-IV 6, 7
Hillsborough football ground disaster
  aftermath 3, 69
  Alcock 66–69
  direct perception 3, 4
  distributive justice 91–96
  immediate aftermath 3, 69
  mode of communication 69–70
  police officers 83–91
  primary victims 3
  proximity 3–4, 68–69
  psychiatric harm 3
  rescuers 83–91
  revisited 83–91
  secondary victims 3
  standard negligence test 3
  sudden and gradual assaults on the nervous system 70–74

ICD–10 6, 7
Immediate aftermath
  Hillsborough football ground disaster 3, 69
Injury to feelings
  discrimination cases 21
Insurance companies
  compensation culture 154

Index

Intangible harm
  disparagement of 10–20
  mind and body connection 10–12
  resistance to compensation for 18–20

Legal Aid
  compensation culture 20, 153

McLoughlin v O'Brian 59–64
Medical negligence
  claims resulting from 117–21
  decline of 'sudden shock' requirement 113–14, 119–21
  duration of distress reaction 114
  event 115–16
  horrifying events 121
  horror violently agitating the mind 117
  post traumatic stress disorder (PTSD) 121
  psychiatric harm 113–21
  shock, conception of 115–17
  sudden shock cases 113–14
  suddenness 116–17
Mental harm
  approach of law to 2
  breach of contract 26–28
  common law 26–31
  diagnosis 4, 143–45
  embracing liability for 20–31
  forms 2
  meaning 4–5
  modern statutory developments 20–22
  stigmatisation of 12–18
  terminology 4–5
  tort, damages in 28–31
Mental illness
  stigmatisation of 12–18
Mind
  dualism 11
  nature of 11
  philosophical issues 11
  terminology 11–12
Monetary threshold
  reform proposals 177–83

Negligence
  aggravated damages 29
  Australia 133
  communication of bad news 103–109
  psychological detriment, negligently causing 122–24
Nervous shock
  See also Psychiatric harm
  accident-based psychiatric illness 59–64
  aftermath 60
  altruism, rewarding 51
  conclusions 56–57
  development of liability for 43–54
  Dillon factors 61

  direct consequences of conduct 46–47, 52
  direct and natural effect of shock 45
  duty of care 47
  evidential issues 44
  fear for oneself limitation 46–47
  floodgates argument 60, 61
  history of term 7–9, 13
  immediate aftermath cases 60
  McLoughlin v O'Brian 59–64
  mind-body connection 45–46
  overview of nervous shock cases 54–56
  proximity 62–63
  reasonable forseeability 48–52, 62–63
  recognisable psychiatric illness 52–54
  remoteness of damage 50–51
  secondary victims 64
  unforeseeable plaintiff 48–49
News, communication of bad 103–13

Pain and suffering
  tort 28
Personal harm
  categorisation
    DSM-IV 6, 7
    generally 1–4
    ICD-10 6, 7
    legal problems 7–10
    medical problems 5–7
    mental and emotional harm 4–5
  legal overreach 33–34
  legal problems of classification 7–10
  meaning 4–5
  medical problems of classification 5–7
  pain and suffering 21–22
  primary reactions 6
  secondary reactions 6
Physical injury
  approach of law to 1–2
  diagnosis 4
  minor emotional harm caused by recovery of damages 2
  preoccupation of law with 4
Police officers
  Hillsborough football ground disaster 83–91
Policy
  accident neurosis 146–47
  administration of justice 142
  broader considerations 166–70
  claims-handling process 153–55
  common justifications for special controls 141–70
  compensation neurosis 145–46, 147
  diagnostic uncertainty 142, 143–45
  disincentives to claiming 151–52
  disproportionate liability 142, 148–49
  floodgates argument 149–51, 165–66

Policy (*cont.*):
  frequency of claims
    employees' claims 161–65
    personal injury claims 155–58
    psychiatric harm 158–61
  generally 141
  paternalism 145
  proliferation of claims 149–55
  public perception of law 141–42
  rehabilitation 142, 145–48
  risk-averse society 166–70
Post traumatic stress disorder (PTSD)
  classification 6
  distinctiveness 6
  medical negligence 121
Primary victims
  accident-based psychiatric illness 75–83
  Hillsborough football ground disaster 3
  proximity 2
Protection from harassment
  criminal law 32
  legal developments 9–10
  meaning of harassment 10
Proximity
  generally 2
  Hillsborough football ground disaster 3–4, 68–69
  nervous shock 62–63
  primary victims 2
  shock-induced illness 2–3
Psychiatric harm
  accident-based illness. *See* Accident-based psychiatric illness
  Australia 130–139
  communication of bad news
    fear for the future 109–13
    negligence 103–109
  emotional harm distinguished 5
  exceptions to the special rule structure 125–30
  floodgates argument 149–51, 165–66
  frequency of claims 158–61
  Hillsborough football ground disaster 3
  induced over time 97
  medical negligence 113–21
  negligence causing psychological detriment 122–24
  negligent communication of information 103–109
  non-accident-based 97–130
  primary/secondary divide 75–82, 97–98
  prior link between claimant and defendant 98–99
  prolonged exposure to harm 97
  psychological detriment, negligently causing 122–24
  recognisable psychiatric illness 6–7, 52–54
  secondary victims 2

services, negligent provision of 99–103
  stress at work 22–26
  work-related illness 22–26
Psychological detriment, negligently causing 122–24

Reasonable foreseeability
  Australia 131, 132, 133
  psychiatric harm 47–52, 62–64
Recognisable psychiatric illness
  Australia 130–31
  diagnosis 143–45
  nervous shock redefined 52–54
Reform proposals
  Australia 174
  barriers to reform 186–89
  Canada 172–174
  compensation culture 176
  duration of harm 176–77
  emotional pain 172
  framework, outline of 185–86
  generally 171
  measure of harm 175
  monetary threshold 177–83
  physical injury 171–72
  precautionary measures 175–76
  qualified test 171
  rational liability structure as goal 176
  rationale 183–185
  relative gravity of harm 172
  substantive basis of liability 171–77
  United States 174–75
  unqualified test 171, 172–73
Rehabilitation
  policy 142, 145–48
Remoteness of damage
  nervous shock 50–51
Rescuers
  accident-based psychiatric illness 83–91
  Hillsborough football ground disaster 83–91
Restorative justice 33
Risk-averse society 33
  mental harm 169–170
  perils of 166–169
  policy 166–170

Secondary victims
  accident-based psychiatric illness 75–83
  arbitrary distinctions 4
  Australia 136
  Hillsborough football ground disaster 3
  nervous shock 64
  psychiatric harm 2
Services, negligent provision of
  psychiatric harm 99–103
Shock-induced illness
  proximity 2–3

sudden assault on nervous system 3, 113–15
Stress at work
  frequency of claims 161–65
  psychiatric harm 22–26
Sudden assault on nervous system
  shock-induced illness 3, 113–15
Sudden and gradual assaults on the nervous system
  accident-based psychiatric illness 70–74

Tort
  aggravated damages 29
  damages in 28–31
  false imprisonment 28
  floodgates argument 29–30

pain and suffering 28
purpose of damages 30–31

Unforeseeable plaintiff
  nervous shock 48–49
United States
  Dillon factors 61
  emotional distress 5, 174–75
  reform proposals 174–75
  zone of danger rule 61

Work-related illness
  frequency of claims 161–65
  psychiatric harm 22–26
World Health Organisation
  ICD–10 6, 7